Contents

Chapter 1 Recognition and Tribute 11
Chapter 2 The Southside 27
Chapter 3 The First Ward neighborhood, ... 43
Chapter 4 A few Notable Persons 55
Chapter 5 South Buffalo (South) 61
Chapter 6 The Hopkins Street/Hickory Woods area, ... 65
Chapter 7 South Park Avenue (south) 81
Chapter 8 Bars 99
Chapter 9 A few Individuals' 105
Chapter 10 The Valley - Little Hollywood 115
Chapter 11 Seneca Street North (Route 16) 127
Chapter 12 Seneca/Babcock Area: 133
Chapter 13 Seneca Street (South) 145
Chapter 14 Life in the Abbott Road Area 175
Chapter 15 Abbott Road Folks 187
Chapter 16 McKinley Parkway 195
Chapter 17 The Roman Catholic 201
Chapter 18 Common Life 205
Chapter 19 Education for Baby Boomers 211
Chapter 20 Downtown Shopping 225
Chapter 21 Baby Boomer 235
Chapter 22 People around the Neighborhood 241
Chapter 23 Several Well-Known 245
Chapter 24 Baby Boomer 255
Chapter 25 Life and Times of Baby Boomers 263
Chapter 26 Watching TV 271
Chapter 27 Watching Buffalo Sports on TV 279
Chapter 28 Baby Boomer Influences 283
Chapter 29 Changes in the mid 60's and 70's 287
Chapter 30 Baby Boomers and Cars 293
Acknowledgements 303

SOUTH BUFFALO

The way it was

2nd Expanded Edition

By: Roger Roberge Rainville

Printed in The U.S.
Second Edition
ISBN: 978-1-945423-18-5
(c) 2020 All Rights Reserved
All rights reserved. No part of this publication may be reproduced, distributed, or transmitted in any form or by any means, including photocopying, recording, or other electronic or mechanical methods, without the prior written permission of the publisher, except in the case of brief quotations embodied in critical reviews and certain other noncommercial uses permitted by copyright law. For permission requests, write to the publisher, addressed "Attention: Permissions Coordinator," at the address below.

For Permissions and Contact: randyjohnson@ilncenter.com
International Localization Network ILN
Home of: Five Stones Publishing

SECOND EDITION of SOUTH BUFFALO

The Way It Was

Life of the Baby Boomers in the 40's, 50's, 60's, 70's

By: Roger Roberge Rainville

Old First Ward

GATEWAY TO SOUTH BUFFALO

photo by R.R.Rainville

Featuring:

Old First Ward - South Park Avenue

Hopkins Street/Hickory Woods

The Valley - Seneca/Babcock - Seneca Street -

Abbott Road - McKinley Parkway

Tim Bohen

In writing my book, "SOUTH BUFFALO –The Way It Was," I was inspired by Tim Bohen who wrote a book about Buffalo's Old First Ward called, "AGAINST THE GRAIN – The History of Buffalo's First Ward." Anyone interested in Buffalo history or anyone who lived in the Ward, and has read this impressive work, can appreciate the great contribution it is historically and his goal for writing it; to keep alive the many stories and facts of that great area of Buffalo. The tremendous time of research and effort it took him to make it the acclaimed literary work that it is, is commendable! To one of the most notable promoters of the First Ward of the "Gateway to South Buffalo," - thank you.

Work Dedicated To

I'd like to dedicate this project to all of the folks who built the South Side/South Buffalo. To the living and deceased; first and foremost, the folks from the "Old First Ward," and the areas of; the Valley, Seneca/Babcock, Elk Street, Hopkins Street, Abbott Road, McKinley Parkway, South Park and Seneca Street. They are the reason the South Side/South Buffalo was the special place it was from the 1940's - 1970's. Also, very fitting and most importantly, I dedicate this to the Great and Greatest Generation; those who lived through World War I, the Depression, World War II, and the Korean War.

A special section is dedicated to them, our war heroes. They raised families and created strong communities in the South Side of Buffalo. Special kudos goes to all the grandmas, grandpas, moms and dads who raised the Baby Boomers. They were the backbone of our families and communities.

My own grandmother Laura (Saint-Pierre) Rainville was born in 1896 and lived up to 1984. She lived before, and though, the 40s, 50s' 60s' 70s and beyond. She, along with so many other grandmothers and grandfathers, played a part in the lives of Baby Boom generation. It is said that a generation is twenty years. This work will feature two generations, from the 1940's-1970's.

Wikipedia states that the start of the Baby Boomers was 1946, the year after World War II ended and lasted until around 1964. I was born right at the start, November 1946. It's probably a good idea to include people born a bit earlier than 1946 and those born a bit later than 1964. My oldest brother, Gilles, was born in 1942 and considers himself a Baby Boomer. For that matter, I had three siblings born before 1946 and five siblings born after me. We're all Baby Boomers.

FOREWORD

A Baby Boomer wrote… "As of 2020 – people born in the 40's have lived in eight decades, in two centuries and in two millenniums. They had the best music, the fastest cars, root beer floats, drive-in theatres, and happy days. And, they aren't even that old yet!"

A statement spoken by many South Buffalo folks: "You can take the boy or girl out of South Buffalo, but you can't take South Buffalo out of the boy or girl." One of the things some South Buffalo guys were noted for was using of the term,"Yous." Example: "How yous doin'?" or "How yous guys doin'?"

Comments from Contributors

As you read, you'll bump into the following comments made by some of my interviewees about South Buffalo on the subject of life in the 40's, 50's, 60's, 70's and the present.

George Tutuska - "What makes South Buffalo great? "It's not events, places or buildings, it's the people."

Jim Anthony -"The 50s and 60's were magical, possibly the best times of my life"

Tim Fitzgerald -"I'm proud as the Lord to have been born in the Old First Ward. It still means a lot to me."

Bert Guise Hyde - "South Park Avenue (OFW) was once a booming area with all kinds of businesses. It was great!"

Joe Lucenti (Valley) -"Even after leaving this area, a lot of people I know come back to visit. It's still their home! Even me! I like coming back here now and then. My heart is definitively still here." Dan Neaverth (Seneca/Babcock) - "I think if you talked to any of the members from the 50's and 60's, they would all agree that some of the best times of their lives were spent at The Club (Boys Club)." Pete Hermann - "Growing up in South Buffalo was a great experience! It was a blast growing up on Olcott and Choate Ave."

Iva Miller - "I wouldn't want to have lived anywhere else. So sad Seneca Street isn't what it was. "It's really sad to see so much of what we had is gone. It was great growing up there." Mr. Ed Miller (Seneca area) - "It was great living here! I have many fond memories of this area." Gerry Regan - "There was always something going on in that park." (Caz Park) Ralph Batchelor - "Seneca Street will always be special to me, lots of great times and many good memories."

Roger Pasquarella (South Buffalo) - "It was one of the best neighborhoods because of friends, locally, and from other neighborhoods and other schools. There was a strong camaraderie." James "Butch" Wilson - "I never regretted being from South Buffalo. There's no other place like it and never will be. Oh, the memories!"

Tom Best - "If I could, I'd go back and live in the Abbott Road area in a heartbeat. I loved the camaraderie we had."

Steve Banko II - "The role of George Hermann in the lives of many young men in the South Buffalo area can't be overstated. Men like George (at Mulroy Playground) and Paul Head (at Hillary Playground on Mineral Springs), went way beyond the call of their profession and really impacted our lives." Ed and Lori Cudney (McKinley Parkway) - "There's no other place we would rather live than right here in South Buffalo. It's a wonderful place, close to theatres, green space, and our awesome waterfront. We even like the winters."

Jack Heitzhaus (McKinley Parkway) - "It's the most wonderful place you can live in. The people here are magnificent."

James Mahoney - "It's really sad to see how much of what we had, is now gone. It was great growing up in the Abbott Road area."

Dan Shea - "I was always proud to say I was born and raised in South Buffalo. We had deep roots and a sense of pride in the neighborhood. Good old South Buffalo! It was sacred!" Kevin Caffery (Abbott Road area) - "It was a great life. I established long friendships. It was a time and place of close knit families and safe neighborhoods to grow up in." Dave Caruso (Triangle area) - "South Buffalo was a strong community with strong family values and family ties. It was a place where everyone had numerous friends from diverse nationalities." Pat Nightengale - "Lifelong friendships were developed with real community spirit, and pride in being able to say 'I'm from South Buffalo'. It was a place, and a time that is hard to explain. It had to be experienced."

Bobby Greene - "South Buffalo was one of a kind in the 50's, 60's and 70's. There was no place like it back then. It was very special. As I get older and talk to other guys from that time, the feeling is, we wish the old neighborhoods could be the way they were. Younger people today have no idea how great it was. It can't be put into words. It was something that had to be lived to understand. It was awesome!" "Digger" Kennedy - "What I love about South Buffalo are the close friends I have and the fun I have with them. To me, this is God's country, where people are ready to help people at any given time." Bill Holihan – "Seneca Street is a special place. The closeness and interaction the people have makes it what it is. The great times I've had here with family and friend keeps me here. Another thing I like about the area is that people police their own neighborhood."

My own statement - "It was great living in South Buffalo. It wasn't a perfect place, but all the different aspects of it made it special. A lot of the memories of people, places and events have not faded with time."

Introduction

The reasons I undertook the task of writing a SECOND EDITION of documenting people, places and events of the Old First Ward, the Valley, the Seneca/Babcock area, and other South Buffalo areas, is the same as was presented in my first book. In this edition, I also needed to make a few corrections and very importantly, I needed to APOLOGIZE to the folks of the Hopkins/Hickory Woods area for having left them out of the first edition. A thousand pardons!

First Edition and Second Edition

Still keeping in mind the extreme changes the neighborhoods have experienced from their glory days, I kept a lot of the original material from the First Edition. Besides tweaking a few things, I needed to add a lot more in the way of; individuals and certainly, our "Lady Boomers" of the neighborhoods where they lived back in South Buffalo's hay days, and give the Hopkins/Hickory Woods area its due recognition.

As with the first, this book was written not only for the South Buffalo Baby Boomers, but for their children, grandchildren and great grandchildren to remember and/or learn about the "the way it was" for the folks who lived there during the 40's, 50's, 60's, and 70's.

In the first edition I stated, "It's important to preserve in print, the history of that generation." I still feel the same about the subject. We shouldn't forget the past. There are a lot of good and cherished families, friends and neighborhood memories that are connected to them.

"When all the Baby Boomers are gone, so will all the memories of that time be gone."

The First Edition

"SOUTH BUFFALO – The Way It Was," took at least ten years to finish; between working a full time and part time job and being hit with prostate cancer. It was a mix of my own memories, hundreds of hours of research, interviews with nearly two hundred individuals, dozens of trips through the neighborhoods, taking hundreds of photos, thousands of hours of writing, editing, re-writing and more editing and writing. Through this journey, I was able to gather and compile many neat facts, comments and stories about the life and times of the Baby Boomers.

Second Edition

This "SECOND EDITION" was also very time-consuming. The process took pretty much the same course as the first book with research, gathering information, doing interviews, taking photos, and the long process of writing and editing.

Hope you enjoy it. And thanks for making the first edition a success. It wound up in the hands of Buffalo and former South Buffalo folks scattered all over the United States; New York City and many areas throughout New York, several places in Florida, Texas, Kentucky, California, North Carolina and other states.

Special Feelings about the South Side

There was something special about being part of the South Side neighborhoods back in its hay days, and in many ways, it's still special being part of; the First Ward, the Valley/Little Hollywood, the Hopkins/Hickory Woods area, Seneca/Babcock, and areas connected to Elk Street, Abbott Road, Seneca Street, McKinley Parkway or South Park Avenue; whether one still lives there or not.

Those areas, except McKinley Parkway, were much, much different than they are today. When folks who used to live in the old neighborhoods drive through or visit there, they readily see what and how much things have changed. Their hearts are genuinely saddened.

"A lot of that 'special something' is now gone and will never, can never return."

In order to understand, you would have to have lived there during the years that are presented in this book. Pat Nightengale, a former South Buffalonian, put it perfectly…
"It was a place, and a time that is hard to explain. It had to be experienced."

This project is a documentation of people who shared an immense array of unforgettable experiences while living on the south side of Buffalo during the Baby Boomer decades. This book is my way of keeping alive the memories of a unique time, places, people and events.

When folks who lived there meet on occasion after a time of not seeing each other, the tendency is to shoot back in time to have a few laughs and relive some of those memories. One or more of the following questions might pop up…

"Wow Skippy, how long has it been since the last time we saw each other?"

"Yo Paddy, how long ago did you move from Stephenson to Manhasset?"

"Hey Wagner, whatever happened to Scrooge? Is he still around?"

"Do you remember Crystal Beach when Mickey nearly fell out of the Comet ride?"

"Do you remember hopping garages and watching Bobby falling through the roof?"

"Do you remember Sister Mary Augustine and how she controlled her class?"

"Do you remember going to the Fazio - or Timon dances where Father Tim supervised?"

"Ronnie, remember shooting pigeons under the Tifft Street Bridge with our BB guns?"

"Remember Pops, the old guy who use to live under the Tifft Street Bridge?"

"Do you remember Caz pool, Joey Keane, and guys belly-floppin' off the high board?"

"Do you remember when we had our first drink at Mischler'sBar?"

"Eddy, how many years did you put in at Bethlehem Steel?"

"Hey Masullo, what's the fastest car your brother Joe had back in '66?"

"Hey Beak, what was the best band you ever heard at the Astro-Lite?"

"Remember when Sudzy drove to Florida with a bunch of guys in his hearse?

"Do you remember the Rocks and Squeaks, and the way they looked?"

"Remember when Ernie and Art did a double-man dive at Caz pool?

"Hey Butch, do you remember who had the fastest car in South Buffalo?"

"Is that bar on the corner of Germania and South Park still open? It used to be Talty's"

"Remember when McGir did a 'flying eagle' on his motorcycle down South Park?"

"Did you go to the Woodstock concert back in '69?" It was far out, man."

"Did you ever get that job at the Chevy or Ford plant, Franky?"

"Where were you when the Blizzard of "77 hit us?"

For those of you who lived through those years, put on your mental walking shoes and reminisce. For those of you who didn't, you might find it interesting, amusing and informative. As my buddy George Rodriguez might say, Vámonos. (Let's go, y'all.)

About the book

SOUTH BUFFALO -The Way It Was - Life of the Baby Boomers will take you from the World War I, to the 40's through the 70's and a bit beyond in some cases. It also includes some current information about people, places and events.

The individuals presented in the book make up a good cross section of people throughout all sections of the South Side from many families and extended families.

You will find the book is historical, educational, interesting and fun to read. It is filled with personal accounts of people's lives from all walks of life, about their neighborhoods, families and friends.

Although quite impossible to include every southsider's name in this project, I'm sure most of you will know a ton of folks as you read and will be able to relate to the numerous stories and anecdotes. Enjoy!

Chapter 1 Recognition and Tribute

to Our Service People

I found it right and proper to start our trip down memory lane giving honor to the grand-parents, parents, and the Baby Boomers themselves who experienced a lot of hardships and great losses because of wars; WWI, WWII, Korea, and Vietnam. So many members of the "Great Generation," the "Greatest Generation" and "Baby Boomer Generation" lost their lives or lost loved ones in those wars. It's only right to remember those who sacrificed their lives as well as the survivors who fought for our freedoms. Because of these great men and women, we can enjoy a strong, safe, and free America.

Thank you!

The *"Great Generation" And World War 1 (The Great War)

This will be one of several apologies I will make as you read this SECOND EDITION. An apology is due to the Baby Boomers' grandparents for not being mentioned in the first addition. That would be the moms and dads that came before the "Greatest Generation" – the ones whose fathers and husbands lived and fought in World War I, also called the *"Great War," whose "foot soldiers" were dubbed, "the Doughboys."

DOUGHBOYS

Although a bit removed from the "Baby Boomer" era (1946-1964) they raise the "Greatest Generation" children and many played a very important role in the lives of the Baby Boomers; some even raising them. My hat's off to them!

In hindsight, I realized that I needed to begin with them in this edition and then move on to ... the Boomer generation's parents - the "Greatest Generation." If I may, I'd like to refer to the WWI era folks as the "Great Generation." Many of them came to America as immigrants looking to start a new life in the "New World." So many came with barely any possessions and made a life for themselves. They learned English, assimilated, worked hard, and contributed greatly to building America.

A Tribute to the Doughboys of World War I

Men from the great generation were called on to fight overseas in the First World War. It was overwhelming. There had always been wars between nations all over the world, but never one that encompassed - all the nations of the world. It was a staggering campaign!

For those of you who may be curious about the use of the term, "doughboys," Wikipedia offers the following possibilities; some seem a bit far-fetched. I'll leave it up to you to pick one you like.

First possibility: During the Mexican War of 1846-48, when American infantrymen made long treks over dusty terrain, giving them the appearance of being covered in flour, or dough; unbaked dough or the mud bricks of the area known as adobe.; with "adobe" transformed into "doughboy."

Second possibility: America's men in the Army and Marine Corps (foot soldiers) under General Pershing were dubbed "Doughboys." One of the explanations for this name was that the "buttons on the soldiers' uniforms looked like "flour dumplings" or "dough cakes" - called "doughboys."

Third possibility: Another explanation was that in World War I, female Salvation Army volunteers went to France to cook millions of doughnuts and brought them to the troops on the front line.

One of the running jokes for the term's origin was, *"The doughboys were* **"kneaded"** *in 1914 but did not rise until 1917."* Moving on...

The Doughboys joined European forces and help take down the enemy. It was a brutal war with many injured and many dead. The war began on July 28, 1914 and ended November 28, 1918. In all, more than 70 million souls lost their life.

By the end of May 1918, 4,355,000 US men ended up fighting there. After the fighting was done, about 126,000 United States soldiers were killed, 204,000 wounded. The combined number of all US soldiers killed or wounded came to 8% of all men sent into battle. Great Britain sent 8,905,000 of their own troops. By the end of that war, this includes all nations, 8,538,315 soldiers died.

World War I was a conflict that included all the major nations of the world. Those nations that formed an allied force against Germany, Austria-Hungary, and Turkey were mainly; France, Great Britain, Russia, Italy, Japan, the United States, and Middle Eastern countries.

Now then, the total number of military and civilian casualties, were around 40 million with an estimated 15 to 19 million deaths and 23 million wounded military personnel from all nations; making it the deadliest war in human history. Of those numbers, 9 to 11 million were military personnel, 8 million were civilians. Of the total count, around 6 million died due to war-related famine and disease. About two-thirds of military deaths in were in battle.

What a waste of lives and cities that were devastated. Recalling the lyrics from one the Baby Boomers' favorite songs from 1970 that says it all… "War, what is it good for? Absolutely nothing!" All nations involved lost…no one won!

Here are a few names I was able to obtain from South Side folks of their grandads that served in WWI, and the persons who submitted them:

- Morgan O'Connell from the Ward (Bill Kimmitt's grandpa),
- Harry J. Noonan (Kristine Noonan's grandpa)
- William Shields (Debbie Shields' grandpa)
- Howard Cleveland Thompson from the Valley, Fulton Street (Sheila Thompson's grandpa)
- Harry Lindner – shared WWI era stories with James Shine from Alamo Street.

Last of the Doughboys
Frank Woodruff Buckles,
February 1, 1901 – February 27, 2011

Special honors were given to the last U.S. World War I soldier, Army corporal Frank Woodruff Buckles, (aka) Wood Buckles, service number 15577 after his death in 2011. He died at the age of 110 and 26 days on February 27, 2011 in Charles Town, Virginia and was laid in Arlington Cemetary. Buckles also served in the Army during WWII.

He came out of Fort Riley in Kansas and served as an ambulance and motorcycle driver for his unit on the front lines in Europe. He was awarded the WWI Victory medal.

Interestingly, for me and a few South Buffalo boys; myself from the South Park area, Jimmy Miller from Pries Street, John Eustace from the Seneca Street area, and Eddy Feneziani, Marty Breel, and Steve Bokan from other parts of South Buffalo, were all stationed at Fort Riley, Kansas in 1966.

A South Buffalo man (Michael Malley) shared the following about his paternal grandfather. "He fought in the battle of the Argonne Forest, France and suffered from the effects of a poison gas attack for the rest of his rather foreshortened life."

No name given, but Mike said that his maternal grandfather also fought in WWI and was stationed in Paris. His grandddad, being that he was German-American, Mike said, "I often wondered why he went and what his role was behind the lines."

A salute to our World War I soldiers!

World War II - 1939 - 1945

Iwo Jima flag hoisting

From September 1, 1939 through Sept 2, 1945, the United States was involved in World War II. It was fought by what came to be known as the "Greatest Generation". Those were the men and women who came through the "Great Depression" of the 30's. I salute those who gave their all on the battle fields. One out of every four married women entered the work force in factories and provided materials needed for our military men. Representing the female workers in a government campaign ad to draw women into the work force for munition factories and shipyards was the iconic **Rosie the Riveter.** Rosie was represented by a young lady that displayed our country's colors by wearing a red and white bandana on her head, blue overalls and flexing her bicep proclaiming: **"We Can Do It!"** It was a good thing for America and our fighting men, but not so much for the ladies, because they rarely earned more than 50% of what men did. Never-the-less, those Patriotic gals pressed on - for America. A salute to those grand ladies!

Rosie the Riveter

Franklin D. Roosevelt was our president during that war which was the deadliest conflict in history. It is said that worldwide, over 60 million people died from direct combat, collateral casualties, sickness, diseases or famine. The United States with a population of 131,021,000 at the time lost nearly 420,000 brave souls. Most of our American WWII veterans have now gone to their eternal rest. America salutes you!

U.S. soldiers were needed in several parts of the world where major warfare was going on. On the Atlantic side of the globe, European battles where fierce where Hitler and Mussolini wreaked havoc. On the Pacific side, Japanese planes from an aircraft carrier bombed Pearl Harbor in Hawaii in 1942. Six months later, Japan's navy planned on attacking the island of Midway to destroy the base where America had ships docked and planes on its airfield. The "Battle of Midway" is where a South Buffalo man was credited with upsetting Japan's plot to dominate the Pacific and spoil their goal of attacking America's west coast next. C.W. McCluskey of South Buffalo, a huge war hero!

Rear Admiral Clarence Wade McClusky

News Paper Headlines 1942...

"South Buffalo pilot's mettle turned the tide in Battle of Midway"

C.W.McClusky belongs in this section of the book, but I decided to feature him later in order to place him in the South Buffalo neighborhood of his youth – the Hopkins Street/Hickory Woods area. His actions really did "turn the tide" of the war in the "Battle of Midway."

Buffalo Connection With
The WWII's "Sullivan Brothers"

Although not from the south side of Buffalo, the five well-known Sullivan brothers from World War II have a warm place in the hearts of ALL the Sullivan's in the First Ward and other Sullivans scattered throughout South Buffalo and elsewhere. Hey, there may be a Sullivan family in South Buffalo that is a distant relative of the five lads. You never know. If you go to Doc Sullivan's Bar on Abbott Road, for sure, the name of the "famous five" brothers has come up numerous times. It is an honored name with that "Irish pride" connection.

Sullivan brothers

The Sullivan

The connection with Buffalo and the Sullivan brothers comes in the way of the monument that sits in **Buffalo's Naval & Military Park** in the Buffalo River, off Lake Erie. The USS *The Sullivans* (DD-537) is a *Fletcher*-class destroyer ship named in honor of the Sullivan brothers who lost their lives when their ship, USS Juneau was sunk by a Japanese submarine during the **Naval Battle of Guadalcanal** on November 13, 1942. The devastation over the news that all five perished had to be unimaginable to their parents. America salutes the parents and the boys.

In 1977, "The Sullivans DD-537" ship and the USS Little Rock were donated to the **Buffalo and Erie County Naval & Military Park** in **Buffalo, New York.** The ship now serves as a memorial and is open for public tours.

The Sullivan brothers were sailors who served in the Navy during World War II. Although two of the oldest had already served, all five decided to enlist at the same time in the Navy as a way to avenge the death of a friend who was killed in the Pearl Harbor air strike perpetrated by the **Imperial Japanese Navy Air Service** on December 7, 1941.

The five brothers were the sons of Thomas (1883–1965) and Alleta Sullivan (1895–1972) of **Waterloo, Iowa**. In order of their age, they were; George Thomas Sullivan, 27 (born December 14, 1914), Francis Henry "Frank" Sullivan, 26 (born February 18, 1916), Joseph Eugene "Joe" Sullivan, 24 (born August 28, 1918), Madison Abel "Matt" Sullivan, 23 (born November 8, 1919), and Albert Leo "Al" Sullivan, 20 (born July 8, 1922).

They enlisted on January 3, 1942, with the stipulation that they serve together. The Navy had a policy of separating siblings, but this was not strictly enforced. George and Frank had served in the Navy before, but not the others. Their moto was; *"We stick together."* So, all five were assigned to the **light cruiser USS Juneau.**

SPECIAL NOTE: The Navy dedicated two destroyers named "The Sullivans" to honor the brothers: The Sullivans (DDG-68) and The Sullivans (DD-537). These were the first American navy ships ever to be named after more than one person. The motto inscribed on both ships was the very motto of the Sullivan brothers held to, *"We stick together."*

A salute to the Sullivan brothers!

Korean War

Korean monument

Only 5 years after WWII the United States became embroiled in another war on June 25, 1950. In 1951 US News & World Report called it the *"Korean conflict."* It was sometimes referred to as *"The Forgotten War,"* due in part to the fact it was never a declared war and ended in an *"unsatisfactory stalemate."* America sent 1.8 million soldiers into combat. It isn't forgotten. America lost 37,000 of its brave soldiers who never got to see their families again. Over 100,000 were wounded, both physically and emotionally. War is war, no matter the length, reason or location. No one really wins and the losses are immense.

You've seen those still living from both WWII and Korea march proudly in parades or meet up at the many VFW posts throughout the United States. If there is a veteran in your family, take time to sit with him or her and thank them and see if they'll talk about their combat experiences. Once they're gone, all that they could have shared with you will also be gone. It would be good to write down anything that can be passed on to their children, grandchildren, great grandchildren and beyond; just something to think about.

Jean Aures, (my father-in-law) a World War II and Korean War veteran shared how he made an unbelievable 52 trips back and forth across the Atlantic during WWII on the U.S. Smart, a destroyer escort ship. During one attack on the ship, he shot down a German plane that came so close that he was able to clearly see the pilot's face.

America salutes all the Korean veterans!

Vietnam War

VIET NAM Memorial

Not too long after Korea, the United States joined the Viet Nam War. This war was fought by Baby Boomers, as well as men who fought during WWII and the Korean War. Of these three wars, this one proved to be our lengthiest at the time. To many folks, it was our most unpopular and misunderstood war. American soldiers were involved in it for sixteen years, from March 1959 through April 30, 1975. The United States lost more than 58,267 brave men and over 304,000 wounded. The country of Viet Nam between 1954 and 1975 lost 3.8 million of its own. It was the first televised war reported on the news every night with recent footage; much of it, very graphic.

An apology needs to go out to the 5,000 ladies who served in Vietnam in the Army Nurse Corps for not being mentioned in the first edition. These ladies did not go into battle but were extremely crucial to the war effort there. Honors were given to Lieutenant Sharon Lane who was killed when a Soviet-built rocket fired by the Vietnamese Army hit the hospital she was working in, in 1969. Seven other American women died in Nam from accidents and illness.

The breakdown of the deaths among those who went to Nam courtesy of the "Veteran Post," are; 39,996 that were 22 years of age or younger ~ 8,283 who were 19 ~ 33,103 who were 18 ~ 12 who were 17 ~ 5 who were 16 ~ 3 sets of fathers and sons ~ 31 sets of parents who lost 2 sons ~ 997 killed on their first day in battle ~ 1,448 killed on their last day ~ 8 women (nurses) ~ 244 soldiers were awarded the Medal of Honor. 153 of them are on the Wall in Washington, D.C.

Huye copter gunner

If you've ever seen actor Mel Gibson's movie, **"We Were Soldiers,"** with **Mel and Sam Elliott** in lead roles, you have some idea as to how fierce the fighting was in Vietnam for many. I was stationed at "Marshal Field" Kansas (a helicopter base) in 1966 and met a man that was on R&R (rest and recuperation) who was wounded in that "La Drang Valley" (The Valley of Death) battle in 1965. He was a helicopter Door-Gunner fighting off attackers as his helicopter made an approach to take on the wounded. He told me, "I saw the guy that shot me." He was wounded in the shoulder.

The Wall Says It All

To the men who lost their lives on the battlefields of Vietnam, here's a poem I wrote sometime after having escorted the Vietnam Movable Wall in a nearly 2,000 strong motorcycle procession that ended in East Aurora, New York, in thee summer of 2000, America salutes you!

We are a country who says - in God we trust!
With men who went to serve and died for US
Our nation stands because we dare to take a stand
Standing against enemies from any foreign land .... The Wall says it all

We all love this country - land of the free
But you know the cost of freedom isn't free
It's been paid by all who went and stood tall
So our nation and others would not fall ……………….The Wall says it all

Look at the names of sons written in stone
Brave and valiant souls who are now gone
It's the wall of those who fell, courageous men
Who laid down their lives like faithful friends………The Wall says it all

They left their loved ones and their beloved land
Many never returned, they fought to the very end
Folks come to see the names of those heroes gone above
The sons of mothers and fathers, who were so loved …The Wall says it all

Those who returned told stories and remembered well
How they and so many others went through hell
Serving their country with honor and great pride
Honoring especially the thousands of men who died …The Wall says it all

We are a country who says - in God we trust!
With men who went to serve and died for US
Our nation stands because we dare to take a stand
Standing against enemies from any foreign land ...... The Wall says it all
RRRainville (10/31/2012)

So many families from the Buffalo area had to say good-bye to someone who served our country during Nam and previous wars. **We salute you all.**

Near War and the Kennedys
John F. Kennedy

J.F. Kennedy

Backing up just a bit to 1962, during Kennedy's presidency, it must be noted that a war between the United States and Russia nearly erupted during what was called, the "Cuban Missile Crisis". It began on October 15 and ended October 28, 1962. That stretch of time was dubbed the "13 Day Crisis." Russia's leader, Nikita Khrushchev had entered into an agreement with Fidel Castro to place nuclear arms on Cuban soil and positioned submarines armed with missiles aimed at the United States. Key West was only 80 miles away and the mainland, 90 miles away.

The reason for the offensive had to do with the "Bay of Pigs" attack on Cuba with CIA-financed and trained Cuban refugees who wanted to overthrow the Castro regime. It was a failure. Castro then welcomed Khrushchev to bring in armaments.

This was the first time in our modern era that the United States mainland was directly threatened with war. The Baby Boomers had never experienced war. It was extremely scary for them. The threat of war was at their doorstep with the very real possibility they could see America devastated.

With Russia threatening nuclear war, the government recommended that people build bomb shelters in their backyards. I remember a South Buffalo family took in some of their young relatives from Florida so they would be safer in the event Russia launched missiles. It wouldn't have taken long for missiles to cover the 90 mile distance. It wasn't only Florida that was in danger; Russia had several other major United States cities targeted as well.

Thank God it never escalated to the point of nuclear war. Had it happened, one can't imagine the immense devastation our country would have suffered. We would have been involved in a war that would have resulted in unimaginable destruction.

President John F. Kennedy Assassinated

May 29th 1917 – November 22, 1963

The year following the Cuban Missile Crisis America received a terrible blow at the hands of an assassin or assassins.

John F. Kennedy was a World War II hero who became our 35th president. News that he was assassinated came as I was sitting in my Social Studies class at South Park High School. Our president was in Dallas, Texas on November 22, 1963 at 12:30 PM when he was shot while sitting in an open-top convertible. Dr. Hayes, our school principal, came over the loud-speaker to announce the sad news. He asked that everyone quietly gather their books and leave the school. The students were in shock. Many girls and some guys wept, while others just walked out in a daze as the reality of it sunk into their heads. The United States had lost its leader. It was a terrible day for our country.

The debate as to whether or not there were one or more shooters is still active today. Personally, as do a great number of people, I believe others besides Lee Harvey Oswald were involved. Those in power who maintain that Oswald was the sole gunman will never admit that it is more believable that there were at least two shooters, possibly three. It would be very interesting to finally find out what actually happened on November 22, 1963.

Bobby Kennedy Assassinated

November 25, 1925 - June 6, 1968

Bobby pix

President Kennedy's younger brother Robert "Bobby" Kennedy served in the Navy and followed in his older brother's footsteps by campaigning for the presidency. Bobby had served his brother in the White House as Attorney General. On June 5, 1968, he was shot and killed by 24 year old Palestinian immigrant, Sirhan Sirhan, at the Ambassador Hotel in Los Angeles California, using a .22 caliber pistol. After a three hour surgery at the Good Samaritan Hospital in Los Angeles, Bobby lay in intensive care but never recovered. He died at 1:44 AM on June 6, 1968.

Police Logo

Policemen/Police women and Firefighters

Precincts

Precinct #7

Before I move ahead, I want to give our men and women in blue, a big salute for putting their lives on the line for all the folks on the South Side.

Back the old days, each Buffalo borough had its own police station (precinct). Former law enforcement officers; Ken Bienko, Dennis Adams and Bart Adams, provided me with the following names of officers that served the First Ward's precinct 7 at 355 Louisiana Street in the 60's and 70's. My apologies for any names missed or misspelled…

Capt. Harlan Schlesshinger, Lt. Robert Carey, Floyd Duke, Sal Pelonaro, Ken Maida, Simon Manka, Leroy Thomas, Harry Tschampl, Earl "Porky" Adams, John Geary, Jerry Stover, Norm Gill, Tim Gill, Sal Carbone, Tom (TC) Smith, Mike Brady, Murray Wright, Mike Gasper, Randy Joseph, Bingo Callahan, Danny Redmond, Joe Ransford, Bill Cooly. Thank you for your service!

Officer Bienko

Ken Bienko was born and raised in the First Ward. Like so many of the Ward lads, he too was tagged with a nickname; his was "Bertha" - a takeoff from the word "birth."

As Ken tells it, "I used to play basketball at "Pets" (Our Lady of Perpetual Help) and was never good." He laughed and said, "My average was .5. After playing for a while, I finally scored and one of the guys yelled, 'Birth of the born!" (like born again). From that, I was dubbed 'Burtha."

I asked Ken if there was an incident when he was on duty that really stuck in his mind. He said, "Yeah! We got a call that a house on Catherine Street was burning. As we got close, I could see smoke and flames. Out of that smoke, I saw this big guy walking down the street with no shirt on, covered in blood. I didn't want to put him in the squad car with him that way but had no choice. We checked the property and found his girlfriend/wife had been bound with duct tape. We found out the two had been in a very bad argument and the guy had pulled off the gas line from the kitchen stove and threatened to blow up the place. According to the woman, he lit up a match to light a cigarette and that set off an explosion from all the gas that got built up in the kitchen. Both were blown through the wall and into the attached garage."

Ken worked out of the South District at # 7 station in the Ward, # 5 station on Delevan Avenue, and station #15 on South Park Avenue with the rank of Lieutenant. His last two posts were as Lieutenant, Commander of Homicide in "C" District, and lastly, at 911 dispatch. Thank you for your service!

Precinct #9

The South East part of South Buffalo (Seneca Street area) had Precinct 9 to watch over the good people there in the 60's and 70's. Again, as in the Wards former Officers; Ken Bienko, Dennis Adams and Bart Adams, provided me with the following names of officers that served at the Ninth Precinct at Seneca and South Side.
They were:

Captains: Eugene Corcoran and Kevin Harmon

Lieutenants: Daniel Redmond, George Bennett, John Zloty, Norb Kupinski, Jim Schmigel, Charles Schweinlein, Ed Doobe, and John Kujawa,

Police Officers: Bob Williams (from Potter Road), Phil Susic, Charley Manley, Mike McPartlin, Kevin Kelly, Russ Riemen, Tom Neil, Bob Neil, Mike Harrington, Kevin Keane, Claudia Childs, Patti (Bowers) Pierce, Dick Lane, Rodney Pelein, Ron Wayneright, Tom McCarthy, Ken Bienko, Terry (T-Man) McLaughlin, Norm Appleford, Aloysius Skierczynski, Alvin Pustulka, William Mullin, Thomas McCarthy, Phil Secek, John McNearney. **Thank you for your service!**

Forgive any misspellings...if not exactly right, it's like playing horse shoe, I get a point for being close.

More names from Precincts 9 and 15

Again, according to Ken Bienko, Dennis Adams and Bart Adams, I was provided with names of officers from these two stations from the Boomer generation era; lawmen and women they served with or were acquainted with: Capt. Fran O'Donnell, Lt. John Kelly, Lt. Russ Mona, Lt. Billy Shore, Lt. Tom Krug, Lt. Mike McCarthy, Al Pustulka, Al Dee, Gerry Wright, George Smith, John O'Rourke, Al Kazpernak, LaRue Hopper, Marion Przybyla, Bob Meegan Sr., Bob Meegan Jr., Paul O'Brien, Mark Morgan, Vinnie Cala, Larry Best, Mart Gasper, Leo Kennedy, Rich Courtney, Anthony LeBron, Monica Reh, Brenda Callahan, Dennis M. Adams, Ed Witaszek, Mitchell Krieger, Michelle Chmurk, Mike Kaska, Richie Courtney, Jack O'Keefe, Officer Dempsey, and Mike Judge. Mike's brother Pat Judge, worked out the downtown narcotics office. Other names of law enforcement men I was given that worked out of downtown or Southside precincts; Mario Pratts, Tim Lopez, Dean Jackson, John Joskowitz, Paul Kane and Eddy Standish. Thank you for your service!

Firehouses and Firefighters

Firefighter Logo

In the Ward

Our hats are off to smoke-eaters that fought fires and saved lives and properties and to those that continue that very important service. The Ward has or had… Hook and Ladder No. 8 at 174 Chicago Street - Engine 10 at 30 Ganson Street (Company disbanded in 2003) - Engine 29 at 315 Ganson Street, and Engine 20 at 155 Ohio Street.

At South Park and Whitfield once was a police station and fire house – Precinct 15 and Engine #30. It was built around 1908, later moved to Seneca and Southside as Ladder 10, Squad 2 and shared a complex with Precinct 9. Our hats are off to former and present firefighters and the police officers that occupied those facilities. Thank you for your service!

In the Valley

The Valley had Hook and Ladder 5 and Engine 6 located at Seneca and Larkin until the 30's. It was then relocated to Smith and Fulton and eventually moved to Hook and Ladder 10 at Southside and Mesmer. The latter station closed in the mid 60's and the firefighting chores fell on Hook and Ladder 15, Engine 6 at Clinton and Bailey. Thank you for your service!

On Abbott Road

Thank you to former and present smoke-eaters of Hook and Ladder 16, Engine 4 at 939 Abbott and Hollywood. The fire house at this site has been a part big part of South Buffalo since 1966. Before that, Lieutenant Pat J. Coghlin said that Engine 4 was located on Fuhrman Boulevard prior to the 60's in the old Ford Plant. Thank you for your service!

On Southside Parkway

Hook and Ladder 10, (Squad 6) was at 131 Southside and Mesmer, right across South Park High School. It was built in the early 1900's. In the 1950's, a new station was built at Southside and Seneca Street, housing Engine 25, Hook and Ladder 10, and Rescue Squad 30.

Thank you to former Ladder 10 smoke-eaters for all you did in saving lives and properties and for being a part of South Buffalo. Thank you for your service!

Fireman, Lieutenant Pat J. Coghlin

I'd like to feature Lieutenant Pat J. Coghlin, a retired firefighter who I had the pleasure to speak with at the "Buffalo Fire Historical Society," 1850 Williams Street near East Lovejoy. It is a museum with a huge quantity of Buffalo's history and firefighting memorabilia. Lieutenant Coghlin was in charge of the museum when I spoke to him.

Pat J. Coghlin grew up in North Buffalo. His dad was Pat V. Coghlin. His mother Helen (Walsh) was a South Buffalo lady. She came from Durstein Avenue off Seneca Street.

Before becoming a fireman, Pat served in the Navy in Little Creek, Virginia from 1959 until 1962. He started as a fireman in 1965 at Hook and Ladder 3 on Spring Street. From there, he went on to Colvin and Linden as 7Th Battalion Chief's Aide. His next assignment found him at Fillmore and Paderewski Drive. After that, he was at Engine 21 at Jefferson near Best. Making the rank of Lieutenant, he was stationed at Engine 24 at Leroy and Albert, then, on to Engine 33 at Kehr and Winslow. Lastly, he went to Broadway and Monroe at Rescue 1.

Thank you for your service!

Chapter 2   The Southside

– Intro

South Buffalo has families that have connections with a lot of people that come from the Old First Ward, the Valley and Seneca Babcock. Many stayed right where their families originated from, but many moved. With the migrations away from OFW, the Valley or the Seneca-Babcock areas, a lot of folks ended up in the areas of Hopkins Street/Hickory Woods, Seneca Street, Abbott Road, McKinley Parkway and South Park. But there's always that connection to the old neighborhoods. On my own street, there were at least a dozen families that had direct ties to the Old First Ward, the Valley, or the Seneca-Babcock area.

Many families from Seneca Street had relatives who lived on, or off, Abbott, Hopkins, McKinley or South Park. Case in point: The Colern family from the South Park area has relatives in the Seneca Street area. The South Buffalo Buckleys are relatives of the Old First Ward Guise and O'Shei families. There are numerous such cases.

South Park, Timon and Baker Victory are high schools where many students from all of the South Buffalo areas met and started friendships. This also includes students from Kaisertown and East Lovejoy. Joe Liberti from Tifft and Greg Vaughn from the Seneca-Babcock area, both South Park High students, have been close friends since high school.

Outside of school, students usually didn't venture into other sections of Buffalo unless they were invited there. Typically, a South Park guy would not go hang around Abbott, Seneca, Seneca/Babcock, Valley or Old First Ward areas unless he knew someone there. But keep in mind, because of family ties between all of the South Buffalo areas, friends and relatives would end up visiting different neighborhoods for family gatherings and special occasions.

Areas where South Buffalo guys would not usually go to were: the West Side, East Side, Kaisertown and East Lovejoy. It wasn't their turf. Baby Boomers had all they needed right in their own neighborhoods and their lives pretty much revolved around it. I remember that going to downtown Buffalo gave me a feeling of being a bit out of place. It wasn't my turf. It wasn't home. It wasn't South Park Avenue. I am sure people from other neighborhoods like, Hopkins/Hickory Woods, Abbott, McKinley or Seneca Street, had the same feelings. What we all enjoyed and felt comfortable with as Baby Boomers was our own neighborhood, neighbors, family, and lots of local friends. That's… the way it was.

Avenues, Roads, Streets, and Parkways

I found it interesting that when speaking of roadways, you'll find the terms: street, avenue, road and parkway in Buffalo and elsewhere. According to my research, "avenues" are main thoroughfares and "side streets" are supposed to be called… streets.

Examples of main thoroughfares; you have South Park Avenue …but Abbott Road … Hopkins and Seneca Street …and McKinley Parkway. In the City of Buffalo, although they are main roadways, we have Main Street and Delaware Avenue. Folks, I have no idea why it's broken down that way. My old street was, and still is, Altruria Street; while the next street over, (a side street), is called Lockwood Avenue. I'll just leave it there.

South Park/Route 62

Every southsider knows that South Park Avenue (part of US 62) starts at Main Street, goes through the center of the Old First Ward, by the Valley and into South Buffalo-south. But, what most folks don't know is just how unique U.S. 62 is …because of its length.

It begins north of us in Niagara Falls, New York, continues through Wheatfield and is part of Niagara Falls Boulevard and Bailey Avenue. After that, it makes a left at Bailey and South Park and goes through Lackawanna, Blasdell, Hamburg, Eden, Collins Center and Gowanda. It continues through Amish country near Randolph and then on to Jamestown, New York. You will need to travel much further south before you run out of route 62, through such cities as Oil City, PA, – Columbus, Ohio, Buffalo, Ohio, Bradstown, Kentucky, New Madrid, Missouri, Corning, Arkansas and then pass through Matador, Texas, through Hobbs, New MX and finally El Paso, Texas at the Mexican border of Juarez, Mexico. With that bit of information, let's get back to the streets.

From the foot of Main Street and South Park to the former Lackawanna bus turn-around across from the old Coffee Pot at South Park and Nason Parkway where you can see a mural of Jackie Gleason (aka) Ralph Kramden on a bus, there are eighty-two side streets.

To help you navigate as you read along and head south, here is a list of the streets that cross South Park from the foot of Main Street.

OLD FIRST WARD	Harvey Place	Josie	Ridgewood
Main	Bolton Place	Pries	Okell
Washington	Euclid	Coronada	Marilla
Illinois	St. Stephens Place	Como	Ashton/Eden
Mississippi	Smith St.	Olcott	Dallas
Baltimore	**ALL THE REST**	Columbia	Cantwell
Columbia	Owahn's Pl	Tifft	Downing
Michigan	Lee St.	Richfield	Leland
Moore	Bertha	Crystal	Aldrich
Marvin	Abby	Bloomfield	Dorrance
Chicago	Germania	Amber	Parkview
Louisiana	Boone	Choate	McKinley Pkwy
Hayward	Hopkins	Lockwood	
Alabama	Payson	Whitefield	
Hamburg	Lilac	Altruria	
Sidway	Buffalo	Sheffield	
Illinois	Bailey	West Woodside	
Red Jacket	Verona	Woodside	
Katherine	Good	Ladner	
Fitzgerald	Alamo	Mariemont	
THE VALLEY	Remolino	Reading	
Van Rensselaer	Macamley	Harding	
Elk	Keoster	Colgate	
Leddy	Trowbridge	Culver	

Nason Pkwy (Lackawanna) where "The Coffee Pot Restaurant" once operated near to Botanical Gardens. As of 2020, you could still see a mural with bus driver Jackie Gleason (aka) Ralph Kramden on the side of the building.

Bus driver Ralph Kramden was the main character in the hit TV sitcom, "The Honeymooners." The show only ran from 1955 until 1956 for 39 episodes and became known as the "Classic 39."

The Old First Ward
Cradle and Gateway to South Buffalo
The borders, some history, businesses and its people

To speak or write about the South Side/South Buffalo and not start with the Old First Ward would be - unpardonable. It is the cradle of the South Buffalo region. That's where the spirit of Buffalo was born. The other neighborhoods all branched off from there. The importance of its location is that it is close to downtown Buffalo and the waterfront. Buffalo was first settled in 1789 and the city itself was founded in 1801.

The Old First Ward (OFW) covers about one square mile. It has Fuhrman Blvd and Lake Erie to the west, Michigan Street to the north (actually, Main Street), South Park Avenue is at its center, the I-190 Thruway to the east, and next to the tracks where Fitzgerald Street is located, is its southern boundary.

In my research about the Ward in 2020, I dug up the following statistics. The average age there was between 40 and 50. Sixty percent of residents owned their own home in a population of about 1,645 people and growing. Double homes averaged between, $120,000 to $130,000. Back in the 50's and 60's, according to Joan Graham at the museum, the OFW had between 5,000 and 6,000 residents. The demise of the grain mills and other industries has caused the population to significantly decrease. I remember in the '60's when there were residential buildings as well as bars and restaurants on the lower part of Washington Street - which is on the fringe of the First Ward.

Old First Ward Community Center

To begin my research, I went to the Old First Ward Community Center and met Laura Kelly, the center's director. She guided me to the 1st Ward's museum on Hamburg Street so I could gather material for this project. That proved to be a very good start. There, I met Bertha "Bert" Guise-Hyde, Peggy May-Szczygiel and Joan Graham Scahill who run Waterfront Memories and More. They told me that the first settlers in the area were called "Beachers" because they lived along the beaches of Lake Erie which included the Small Boat Harbor area along with Times Beach and the Marine Drive area. Two beacher families were the Lattimers and the Freitas.

Bert Guise-Hyde said:

"As time went on and the city grew larger and larger. Catholic Churches were set up throughout Buffalo and the different communities were referred to as 'parishes.' People were connected to specific Catholic churches that revealed what part of the city they were from."

The waterfront was where ships came and went and a great number of Irish people settled there around 1842. They came to work the grain elevators, emptying ships of their grain. They worked the docks, rail lines, and other industries. By 1850, Buffalo had a population of around 80,000 people with many, residing in the Old First Ward. The grain elevators were a major industry and grain was shipped out via the Erie Canal (built 1817-1825) and by rail to many parts of New York and other eastern states. By 1850, the city of Buffalo was ranked 10th in the United States for population growth and commerce.

Grain Elevators

The first steam-powered storage grain elevator was built in Buffalo in 1842 at the foot of Commercial Street and named "Dart's Elevator" after its inventor Joseph Dart. The elevator had a capacity of 55,000 bushels of grain. Dart's elevator had leather conveyors with buckets [scoops] attached to them. Ships were now able to unload grain at a rate of 2,000 bushels per hour instead of 2,000 per day when it was all done manually.

By 1863 Buffalo had 27 grain elevators. You may think your job doesn't pay much, but in 1895 a scooper worked long, hard hours and only made around $300 a year; about a dollar a day based on a five-day week. The elevators are still there today as a reminder of Buffalo's glory days. Take a ride through the Old First Ward by the Buffalo Creek and Buffalo River areas to get a glimpse of those massive structures. They are awesome!

scoopers

That Old First Ward area became known as "Elevator Alley." A great number of the First Warders worked the grain mills and elevators. It was arduous work with dangerous conditions for the scoopers. A scoop was a large four foot wide, metal shovel hooked to pulleys by ropes and chains to conveyer contraptions used to empty ships of their grain cargo. A "Grain Shoveler" or "Scooper" was the man responsible for filling the scoops. The grain dust was explosive and suffocating. In early times, the men wore make-shift paper masks to filter the air they breathed.

In an article written in January of 1996 by Louise Continelli (News Fashion and Lifestyle writer), she featured the end of an era highlighting the hardworking "grain scoopers" on Buffalo's First Ward docks and railcars.

One of those workers was nicknamed, "Jim Boy" Smith. She said, "He scooped grain along with "Bummy," "Brownie Hairs," "Weepers" and "Diapers." How about those nicknames, folks?

She quoted "Jim Boy" talking about nicknames. He said, "The Irish love nicknames. If you didn't like it, they kept it up worse."

Louise stated, "When Buffalo was still the gateway from the Midwest to the East Coast, nearly 3,000 of these laborers with hearts and guts of steel worked up to 20 hours a day."

Jim Boy Smith, who lasted four decades said, "To be honest with ya, there were many men who went down there (in the hold) and didn't last one day.

Jimmy Griffin (Buffalo's former mayor) and his brother both worked as scoopers. Jimmy dropped out of high school to scoop grain for the railroad and recalled how tough the job was. He said, "It was pretty rough work. The first couple weeks your arms and back would be sore - throwing the shovel. You'd have to wear a filter over your mouth because of the grain dust. Sometimes you didn't wear it because it was uncomfortable. The upside was that you'd wash the dust down with a couple of beers at noontime."

Jim Boy said, "Buffalo was queen of the lake, and there was a lot of work unloading grain from the ships and boxcars. When I had 20 years on the job, they still called me a baby, 'cause some of those old *'harps' stayed till they were 80 years old. Doing that work felt good! The crews did the job, and stuck together. It was hot and tiresome, but we were paid well. It was enough to raise a family of seven children in the First Ward." At the time of the interview, Jim Boy still lived there. *("Harp" - term used to refer to a person of Irish descent. Celtic Harps can be seen on Irish coins)*

A couple of other men took on the job of unloading grain. One man was Jack Suto, a second generation scooper. His father was a former president of Local 109 Scoopers Union.

The other man was, Jack Driscoll from Vincennes Street. He told me, "I spent 40 years as a scooper, from 1962 to 1994. Four generations in my family did that work going back to 1918 when my grandfather Pat Driscoll did scooping. Then, my own father Dennis, me, and my two sons, Pat and Tim joined the Scooper crews."

I stopped into the Swanne House in January of 2020 and spoke to owner Tim Wiles about scoopers he knew. Here's a list of some of those hearty men. Forgive any misspellings. Tim did the best he could to provide me with the names. Here we go; Rick Carr, Jackie Conway, Steve Barrett, "Hump" O'Leary, Ricky Light, Dennis Smith, Dennis "Bunky Boy" Evoy, Ricky Canazie, Dennis Schollar, Dan and Eddy Cunningham, and John Carney from Vincennes Street.

Buffalo's Scoopers' Run for the Last Time

Writer Carolyn Thompson featured the scoopers in an article published February 11, 2003. She wrote, "A century ago, Buffalo boomed as ships from the Great Lakes transferred cargo to canal boats for passage through the Erie Canal. More than 1,000 shovelers were needed to keep up."

She continued, "Buffalo's grain scoopers, hardworking holders-on from a bygone era, went to work for a final time this week to finish manually unloading more than 600,000 bushels of wheat from an aging cargo ship. Fred Brill, president of the Grain Shovelers Local 109 said, 'All the scoopers wanted to be there at the end - for "the last hurrah."'"

She added, "At 68, Robert Matevia was the oldest scooper, and the most experienced with 48 years in the holds. Like many scoopers, Matevia also worked in construction, a job that allowed the flexibility needed for the grain shoveling that diminished into part-time work over the decades."

At the end of his career, he was quoted as saying, "This is it! This is the last. It's going to be weird after 48 years not having to come in here. It's been good."

To honor our Scoopers, here's a statement made by Lorraine Pierro of the city's Industrial Heritage Commission.

"In the early afternoon with the ships' holds empty, the scoopers gathered in a tavern named McCarthy's, a bar proud of its Irish heritage. A trait shared by the scoopers who have always been almost exclusively Irish is they were boisterous behind bottles of beer and their memories. They drank to the end of an era."

A big salute to the First Ward grain scoopers!

Old First Ward Businesses on South Park Avenue

"You don't know what you've got till it's gone!"

I asked Bert Hyde at the Ward Museum what the South Park strip of the First Ward was like with regards to businesses, stores and other tenants in the 40's, 50's, 60's and 70's. She said, "South Park Avenue was once a booming area with all kinds of businesses. Not anymore."

She gave me a chart with a host of stores and businesses. Here are several that existed on South Park Avenue in the years above. Bert made sure I noted the 19th century tavern known as the "Swannie House" at 170 Ohio and Michigan. As of 2020, it is a 120 plus year old establishment that is run by Tim Wiles.

Swannie House

I spoke to Tim in January of 2020. At the time, he'd owned the bar since 1983. It was a part time job as he worked for National Fuel. He said he bought the place from the Swanerski family and the name was changed to the Swannie House. He said, "This is one of the most valuable corners in the city."

He was proud to mention that former Mayor Jimmy Griffin and his brother Tom brought their father who was suffering from dementia, to his establishment every Sunday to spend time with their aging dad. At the time, Wiles was around 26 years old.

Tim said, "It felt good seeing the Griffin boys bring their dad in every Sunday."

He pointed to the same seats they occupied every time and said, "Jimmy would sit on his right and Tom on his left."

He told me, "Seeing the Griffin boys take time to spend with their dad that way gave me a good feeling."

Tim went on, "Mayor Griffin used me as an example to a group of businessmen about starting businesses in Buffalo. He told them, "Tim Wiles took all the money he had to buy the bar and made it successful."

Continuing with Businesses on South Park, (most are gone)

- -Along South Park Avenue was Louie's Masque Theatre owned by Louie Sanelli. It was nicknamed "The Rat Hole Theatre."
- -142-150 South Park and Chicago was the Karle Saw Company. Phone number was TL 3-8043
- -211 South Park - The Malamute Bar - Tim and Morgan Stevens purchased it and renamed it "Ballyhoo Links & Drinks" Sept. 28, 2014.
- -321-27 South Park there was the Harris Lumber Yard
- -357   Previty Groceries.
- -384   Lanigan's Park
- -   Loblaw's near Louisiana Street
- -397   McGrath's Restaurant
- -399   Desiderio's Restaurant.
- -400   Dublin Restaurant
- -402   A gas station at Louisiana
- -403   Liberty Wine and Liquor
- -405   Market
- -408   Marine Trust Bank,
- -418   Speakman's Hardware Store
- -410   Starr Credit Jewelers
- -423   Turk Max Variety Store.
- -430   Pantera's Cut Rate Drugs Store
- -475   Arriy's Leader Drug Store
- -528   Saint Valentine's School and Church
- -543   Mazurek's Bakery (formerly South Park Bakery) It became Mazurek's Bakery in 1933 under Frank and Jean Mazurek, then son Jack and his wife Carol, and finally, Ty Reynolds and Nick Smith. It has been in business for 87 years as of 2020. They sell a variety of pastries and the very popular "Paczki" (ponch–kees) before Lent. In case you're not familiar with Paczkis, they are delicious doughnuts typically filled with strawberry or raspberry jelly. At the time of my interview with employee Angie, she had been worked at the bakery for over 30 years and still lived in the Old First Ward. Mazurek's was one of the most sought out stores at Easter time.

Joe Lucenti from the Valley said: "People from all over would come to Mazurek's Bakery. One of the most desired items was their rye bread. There used to be a line out the door all the way to Hamburg Street."

Another special food item for Easter was sausage. Joe told me: "For that, people would go to Kurzanski's Meats on Fulton Street. What could be better than kielbasa from Kurzanski's and rye bread from Mazurek's Bakery?"

- - 555 South Park, across from Saint Valentine's and near Mazurek's is the Adolf's Old First Ward Tavern.

Adolf's Old First Ward Tavern   Mazurek's Bakery

- -559 South Park was Mary's Restaurant - ran by Mary (Mohnach) Simonick operated from 1962 to 1993. Mary's son Robert "Rip" Simonick was the Sabres longest employee as equipment manager. Her oldest son Joseph pitched for the Saint Louis Cardinals. Mary lived on the same 1st Ward street from 1942 to 2003. She passed away December 15, 2003.

- -586 South Park South Buffalo TV Service

More Old First Ward businesses that were, or are still operating...

- -222 Mackinaw Neth's Delicatessen
- -The Swannie House at 170 Michigan at Ohio is over 120 years old and was originally called the
- -"Swanerski House." It is the oldest tavern in the city. It was established by Gibson Williams and John Swanerski in 1886.
- - Flood's Tavern on Louisiana Street
- -Milt's Tavern/Carmen's Tavern, now gone was on the corner of Ohio and Louisiana
- -General Mills - foot of Michigan Street
- -The Bison City Rod and Gun Club on Ohio
- -Advantage Trim & Lumber on Ohio
- -The defunct grain elevators that made Buffalo world known
- -Great Lakes Fibers Corporation on Ohio
- -Lafarge North American concrete company on Ohio and Ganson Streets.
- -Rigidize Metals Corp on Ohio Street.
- -Gerdeau Ameristeel on Ohio Street.
- - A bit removed from the Old First Ward but very close neighbor is the old Freezer Queen Foods Company on Fuhrman Blvd. It was started by businessman Paul Snyder in 1958. Snyder also started Darien Lake Amusement Park in 1964. I worked at Freezer Queen as a forklift driver in '68 and '69.
- -The Small Boat Harbor - 1111 Fuhrman Blvd
- -Dug's Dive – 1111 Fuhrman Blvd. at the Small Boat Harbor (now "Charley's")
- -Another grain silo at the Gallagher Beach site Fuhrman Blvd near the foot of Tifft Street.
  -Tifft Street Nature Preserve which covers 264 acres 1200 Fuhrman Blvd

There are two bridges that cross the Buffalo River in the Ward. One is the *"Ohio Street Bridge"* that has Louisiana and Ohio Streets forming a "V" split as you cross it, and then, there's the *"Michigan Street Bridge"* that connects Ganson Street and Michigan Avenue near General Mills.

- -Saint Mary's Cement Co. on Ganson Street.

Bridges
The Skyway

Skyway and lift bridge

The Skyway that goes over a part of the First Ward was a much needed highway (high, in the literal sense). Once upon a time, there were only lift or swing bridges to allow ships to move inland through the Buffalo River to unload cargoes and to allow people access to the Fuhrman Boulevard, west of South Park. To expedite the flow of traffic, a high thoroughfare was needed to provide a quicker route in and out of downtown and south on the I-190 to Fuhrman and the southern towns along and near Lake Erie. The solution was, our present day "Skyway." Before that, vehicle traffic came to a halt when the bridges were raised to allow ship to move into the Buffalo River to get their business done.

In 1950 construction began on our 100 foot high Skyway and can certainly be considered part of OFW territory. It was completed in 1955. If the wind is blowing just right when I drive over the Skyway on my motorcycle, I get filled up on the smell of Cheerios cereal when I crest the top near General Mills. The I-90 Thruway was built in the 50's and completed in 1964. It was a tremendous improvement to get northbound traffic flowing from the I-190 to downtown Buffalo and from the south towns and Route 5 travelers coming from the towns near, and along the Lake Erie shore.

First Ward Bridge Disaster

Tying in with the grain elevators and shipping, if you went toward Lake Erie on Michigan from South Park Avenue to get to Fuhrman Boulevard, Baby Boomers around in January of 1959 remember the disaster of the Michigan Street lift bridge near Ganson Street that was right next to General Mills and connected directly to Fuhrman Boulevard. It was called the South Michigan Street Bridge. An article on the removal of that bridge stated: "It was rendered inoperable and was removed by the City of Buffalo in 1964."

What Happened?

For more information on the topic, I was directed by Peg Overdorf to check out some of the articles written about it or to contact her brother Gene; that he could tell me all I wanted to know about the tragedy.

Here's what I dug up. On January 21, 1959, the South Michigan Street lift-bridge was hit by a cargo ship anchored in the Buffalo River called the "Michael K. Tewksbury." The disaster was actually caused by two ships. As the story goes, the other ship, the MacGilvray Shiras, broke away from its post in the Buffalo River at the Central Grain Elevator owned by the Continental grain company. When its mooring lines snapped, the Shiras drifted downriver, ramming the Tewksbury, which was tied up across from Silo City at the Standard Elevator near the foot of St. Clair Street. Both ships moved together down the "serpentine" Buffalo River, but by the grace of God, managed to avoid the Ohio Street Bridge. It was raised for winter.

First Ward Historian - Gene Overdorf

If you want to know anything about the Old First Ward, the grain mills/silos, Buffalo Creek and the Buffalo River areas, Gene Overdorf is the man you'd want to speak with. He's the local OFW Historian. He was born in the Ward and lived at 72 Mackinaw Street, attended Our Lady of Perpetual Help School, Bishop Timon High School, and SUNY at Brockport. For the past forty years, Gene has researched and documented the history of the Old First Ward and the Buffalo Irish community. He's interviewed many of the Ward's folks through several years, gathering information and stories about the area and its people.

He's given numerous talks about the Ward. On Saturday January 18, 2020, I had the opportunity to hear him do a talk about the infamous "Tewksbury" ship and Michigan Street bridge incident of January 21, 1959. This took place at the Tewksbury Lodge (restaurant) that is located on Ohio Street on the banks of the Buffalo River.

Gene said, "The Michigan Street Bridge was a manned lift bridge at the time, but at the moment of the crash, the crew wasn't around. They were taking a break at the nearby Swannie House." He said, "In their defense, there was no reason to believe that any ship would be coming down the river in January."

To add to the intrigue of the whole incident, Gene stated, "The Buffalo River is the most serpentine river in North America; for those ships to have made all those turns without doing more damage, is simply amazing!"

He said, "The Tewksbury smashed into the bridge at 11:17 pm and wedged itself across the river, causing an ice dam. The ice backed up the water's flow and caused a spill into the First Ward neighborhood, flooding an 18-block area. Crews worked feverishly for ten days to clear the river."

Besides the devastation in the First Ward, he said, "The backup also flooded the Republic Steel Plant area on South Park Avenue and the Maritime Milling Co. on Hopkins Street and surrounding homes."

The News reported that, "People fled in their night clothes as ice chunks as big as 35 feet by 25 feet and 3 feet thick caved in cellar walls, slammed autos around like chips, uprooted trees and knocked down utility poles,"

The South Michigan Street Bridge was done, but the Tewksbury ship's damage was minimal. After repairs were made, it continued services until its retirement in 1975.

Tewksbury Restaurant

In memory of the Tewksbury, Peg Overdorf, Director of the Valley Community Center, opened an excellent restaurant on the Buffalo River right across from the Labatt's Beer six-pack grain elevators at 249 Ohio Street. She named it, the Tewksbury Lodge.

Blizzard of '77

    Before moving on, I pause to remember another devastating Buffalo event that effected everyone nearest Lake Erie - the Blizzards of '77.

    The biggest news item for 1977 was the "blizzard." It started on January 28 and lasted into February. Buffalo was hit with a very severe blizzard that made news around the world. All Buffalo areas were shut down tight. There was a strict driving ban. No one was allowed on the streets; not that anyone really wanted to be outside in the bitter cold. The city and outlying areas were complete disasters. Over twenty people died. Some were literally buried in their cars under massive snowdrifts caused by 70 mile per hour winds that came off the wide open expanse of Lake Erie. Some snow drifts were as high as 30 feet. Many individuals were rescued in time, but unfortunately, some were not. A few froze to death or were asphyxiated from carbon monoxide after having to stop because of the zero visibility and leaving their cars running for warmth. They were trapped, with little hope of being found. It was horrendous. Buffalo was declared a State of Emergency. Besides being known as the Queen City, Buffalo also became known as "The Blizzard City." Knowing Buffalo winters, we all knew there would other huge winter storms coming down the road. Remember the infamous blizzard of January 18, 1985 hit Buffalo, dropping over 33 inches of snow with winds gusting over 50 miles an hour. How about the back to back years of 2013 and 2014 blizzards? Both happened in November; 2013 on November 16, and the following year, November 17, 2014 with seven feet of snow or more.

Chapter 3 - The First Ward neighborhood,

Irish pride, nicknames and individuals

The First Ward Community

As I went through some of the streets in the Old First Ward on the west side of South Park I could sense the pride of the community. Bert from the Hamburg Street museum stated that the Old First Ward was once, "very family oriented." Although it is a very old neighborhood with aging houses, I did not get the sense that it was rundown. I noticed quite the opposite. A great many houses were refurbished with new siding, new porches and steps.

I thought to myself, "These folks are keeping up their houses. They take pride in the way the neighborhood looks."

On average today, many of the houses that are doubles in the OFW are worth between, $120,000 to $140,000. Not bad for an old neighborhood, eh? Many of them have been handed down to family members as parents passed away. A lot of folks have lived there all their life. The people living there value the neighborhood of their fathers, family ties, and the Irish culture. They have great community pride.

As I turned from South Park onto Hamburg Street, I noticed how many American flags were flying from porches or flag poles. The pride they demonstrate is not only for their neighborhood and their Irish heritage, but also, for their country, the United States of America. I salute you Old First Ward

The OFW, as previously mentioned, had a lot more people several decades back. It has shrunk greatly in number, and most of the businesses are gone. As far as schools go, PS #4 at South Park and Louisiana is still active. There was another elementary school operating back in the 70s, PS #34 elementary at 108 Hamburg Street. It was demolished around 1976.

There were three Catholic schools in the OFW; the mainly Polish-rooted Saint Valentine Church and school that was founded by Father Brejski and located at 522 South Park. It was around from 1925 to 1963. Another elementary school in the Ward that closed was Saint Brigid's at the corner of Fulton and Louisiana streets.

The only Catholic Church still active is Our Lady of Perpetual Help on the corners of O'Connell and Alabama streets. Its elementary school closed years ago. That particular area with the church and the houses all around it reminded me of the 1944 movie "Going My Way" with Bing Crosby as Father O'Malley, Ingrid Bergman as Sister Mary and Barry Fitzgerald, the elder priest with the thick Irish brogue, as Father Fitzgibbon. If I were to tie a prayer to that great neighborhood back in its hay day when the Irish dominated it - it would be this well-known Irish prayer…

May the road rise up to meet you,
May the wind always be at your back,
May the sun shine warm upon your face,
The rain fall softly upon your fields,
And until we meet again,
May God hold you in the palm of His hand.

Driving through there, I could imagine what it was like in the Ward with all the families, docks, rail lines, grain mill activities and businesses up and down South Park. So much of it is now gone. Like other areas throughout Buffalo, the Old First Ward can never be what it once was. A good portion of the east side of South Park's First Ward is where the Commodore Perry Projects are located as well as quite a few homes. The OFW had a concentration of Irish that occupied the homes there. But the east side of the Ward in the projects has had a mix of nationalities for many years now. I was told by the folks at the museum that the Commodore Perry Housing Project was "the first of its kind in the United States."

Two former "project" residents I came to know are Bill Nicholson and Danny Jordan. Bill was raised in the Ward's projects from the late forties till 1961 when his family moved further south to Lockwood Avenue. While on Lockwood, he attended Holy Family, graduated from South Park High, did his stint in Nam in the 60s, got married, worked for the US Postal Service, and retired in Hamburg, New York.

Danny Jordan lived in the projects before the family got bigger and had to move to larger quarters. He came from a family of nine children, born to William Jordan and Anna (Stoehr). His siblings are Bill Jr., Robert, Richard, Lawrence, Joanne, Mary-Ellen, John, Danny (himself), and Kathleen.

He recalls having lived in the Ward for only a short time as a child. The family relocated to 105 Elk Street near the Valley's South Park/Elk split for a time. His clan moved several more times. After Elk Street, the Jordans found themselves on Keppel Street in the Seneca-Babcock area, and subsequently, to Ashton Street off of South Park, then, one more move to Marilla Street.

This moving around was fairly common for a lot of Baby Boomers. For Danny and company, it was four moves. I put myself in that category – with six moves. As a kid, our family lived in three different houses in Québec, one place in Welland, Ontario, onto America in Orchard Park, and finally, South Buffalo. It was never a "feel-good" experience. Think of it...new neighborhoods, new sets of friends, schools, churches; and for some who came from other countries, like Nino and Adele Petrili from Italy who only spoke Italian, George Rodriguez from Puerto Rico, speaking Spanish, or my clan from an all French-speaking culture, it wasn't easy. But, we all adapted to our new English-speaking country and ...ASSIMILATED!

From his time in the Valley, Dan remembered an area known as the "Rainbow District" there. As he put it, "It was named that because of the variety of nationalities between Fillmore, Van Rensselaer and Hydraulic Street." His own wife Joanne came from neighboring Kaisertown and enjoys living in South Buffalo.

The Shamrock Run
Old First Ward/Valley Irish Pride

Shamrock

There are two big events that need to be mentioned: the Shamrock Run and the Saint Patrick's Day Parade. The Shamrock 8K Run has been a springtime event in the Old First Ward for 38 years as of 2016. According to Kenny Castillo (an OFW resident) Jimmy Griffin was part of starting this event. It draws over 5,000 runners which includes people from the Ward for sure, but also from many other parts of the city and beyond. A young lady named Pam Greene, originally from Florida and living in West Seneca, took part in 2015 and 2016, and a family from East Aurora made it a yearly event. At the end of the run it's party time with Irish gusto. One of the sayings about those who partake in the event is: "No matter what your heritage is, everyone is Irish at the Shamrock Run."

There's that Irish pride. Érin go Brágh. (actually, Éirinn go Brách), "Ireland Forever."

The Saint Patrick's Day Parade is an event where you see Irish pride in full bloom.

The City of Buffalo had Saint Patrick's Day Parades starting mid-March 1848 which continued for 19 years. It was put on by the "Friendly Sons of the Saint Patrick Society." The largest parade in the city was held in 1876. There were other parades but the trend didn't last. There were breaks from 1917 to 1935, and more breaks during the World War II years of 1942 –1945.

Saint Patrick's Day Parade Revived

In 1969, the Valley Community Association was formed. The community center building at the corner of South Park and Liddy Street was completed in 1971 and named the Fr. Carmichael Center.

Peg Overdorf is Executive Director of the Valley Community Association. She founded the "Old Neighborhood Saint Patrick's Day Parade" in 1994 as a way of bringing back that much missed event the folks of that area loved. The parade makes its way through the Valley and Old First Ward neighborhoods.

Peg was quoted to say, "I grew up in a household where my parents put a lot of emphasis on our Irish heritage. It was always a huge part of our lives. St. Patrick's Day was special. It brought everyone in the family and everyone in the neighborhood, together. That's what I wanted to recreate with the parade."

In 2016 the Ward and Valley celebrated its 23rd parade. It started at the Valley Community Center on Leddy Street. From the Center it went down Harvey Place, Saint Stephens Place, over to Elk Street, then to South Park and over the bridge until it got to Hamburg Street. It took a left and went to South Street. It used to turn down O'Connell, but was rerouted to South Street which is wider and a better fit for the parade. There was no parade in 2020 because of the Corona Virus (COVID19) aka "The China Virus."

Friend of the Valley
Richard Leonard

Richard Leonard, a man who has a heart for the Valley and fully appreciates the Saint Patrick Day celebration that the people there share, wrote the following poem. He came to the Buffalo area from Massachusetts in 1962 and first settled in East Aurora. He also lived in West Seneca and finally at 83 when I spoke to him, made his home in Orchard Park.

He was invited to a birthday party in the Valley by the Ward's - Bill "Chip" Butler several years ago. Rich said, "It reminded me of home (Massachusetts.). I fell in love with the area right away."

Richard was Chip's supervisor at the Army Corps of Engineer and got to be good friends him and his family.

Although a bit lengthy, for those who share his appreciation for that area of Buffalo, you'll truly enjoy this. Many of you will recognize a lot of the names mentioned, if not all of them.

"HOOLEY IN THE VALLEY"
A poem Written May 31, 2003
By: Richard Leonard

(A Hooley is an Irish get together with traditional music and dancing – and for sure, food and beer)

They had a parade and Hooley in the Valley
A small neighborhood tucked away down in South Buffalo
The sun shone bright and warm ...sure was okay
Good Saint Patrick blessed the Valley today

Sure, it was a bit smaller than our Delaware Avenue way
Though it was much better, the Valley people say
For this is an enclave of Irish legend and lore
Genuine yesterday, genuine today, and forever more

Apparitions of First Ward history on the scene, quite alive
Tall Michael Quinn with his tall top hat astride
Green "Ireland Forever" banners raised to the sky
First, during the First Great War, to be unfurled again in thirty-five

Up from the Buffalo River mist, they come about
Erie Canal builders, scoopers, tugboat and rail men
With brogues as thick as warm Guinness Stout
Heavy tools are put aside for this great day

Quick now, the parade has started at old Smith Street
Grand Marshall Mike Overdorf has all on their feet
Sons and daughters of the Ward now pick up the green banners
Firemen, policemen, politicians, laborers, and children ...all Gaelic demeanor

The Police Emerald Society steps forth proudly
Followed by "Fir Doi Tean" firefighters cheered so proudly
The shiny red bumper and long ladder truck
Many a young lad with lasting visions of such

Old friends of the Valley step out together again
Their hearts in the Ward there with their large clans
There were the Leahys, the Sumbrums, Bouquards, Overdorfs,
Buttlers, Higgins, Gallivans, Hassets, Burkes, McCarthys and Smiths
And far too many to go on with this list

Tommy Michael's Clydesdale horses and Sherriff Gallivan's mounted police
Equestrian pomp advancing up Elk Street and south on South Park towards O'Connell Street
And here comes Jim Boy's navy boat with no battle to fight
Except to chase winding green serpent in flight

A red bearded leprechaun was seen carrying a pot of gold
Perhaps a pied piper with tartan dancers in tow
The bag pipers with their high pitched mystical sounds
As if the mist from the river wafted faeries and clowns

In these blue-collar workers, the great tradition of Buffalo seen
The neighborhood has sent forth journalists, generals, Bishops, priests and nuns
Bright and leaned women and men
Clan fathers and mothers gave all for them

The parade is over; the Hooley now begins
Parade watchers and late comers quickly settle in
Peg, Mike, and their good workers greet you with cheer
You're as welcome as the shamrock here

The tables fill quickly, the Ward's loyal draw close together
The Stout is flowing as it has in Ireland forever
The smell of corn beef and cabbage drifts into the hall
The kitchen is ready to satisfy all

Old men regale on the Ward's heroes with pride and acclaim
General "Will Bill" Donovan of World War Two fame
Jimmy Slattery, the dapper and dandy boxing champ
Jimmy Griffin, the tough grain scooper turned mayor, not to recant

Laughing toddlers dance about like wayward elves
While mothers and fathers enjoy themselves
Old neighbors exchange greeting and fond memories of
School thirty-three, Timon, Mount Mercy, Canisius, and South Park camaraderie

College age students with smiles and beer all around
Young keen eyes searching coolly, yet seriously, abound
Perhaps to find the shy Colleen with the beguiling eyes
Or that clumsy boy, now a quite charming guy

The band has been playing Irish ballads all the while
Sad or glad as befitting the moods of the Emerald Isle
A bit noisy to hear and sing all the words clearly
But surely the feeling comes through quite dearly

Not just the Irish celebrate this glorious day
The changing neighborhood is here on display
Hispanics join in to honor Saint Patrick today
Tis no wonder since the children join in school and in play

Dancers with Shannon flowing curls mingle about
Skirts and vests, a collage of color that brings true Irish out
Green, blue, white, orange, and black colors swirl and shout
So enchanting, you keep looking back no doubt

The floor is cleared to give the young dancers more room
Out they come like Kerry dancers in bloom
Backs so straight, legs and curls a flying o'er the room
Spellbound, Celtic drums and their hearts in tune

Proud parents with their parents stand close by
These enthralling sons and daughters before their eyes
Mother and daughters keep this dance alive
An ancient Hibernian tradition never to die

The Hooley is over is seems too soon
A soft night, a touch o' green o'er the moon
God and Saint Patrick brought us this day
The ghosts of the Valley grudgingly return to their graves

Back to the Ward...
McCarthy's Bar

As you travel down Hamburg Street, you come across the well-known McCarthy's Bar and Tavern at 73 Hamburg Street. Gene McCarthy opened it in 1963 and around 2012 new owners Bill Metzger and Matt Conran took over. It has the cozy feel of Cheers (popular 1980's sitcom) restaurant and pub with its regulars - retired folks and workers from the General Mills plant, business people who come to have lunch or dinner and drinks, and to hear good live music. McCarthy's owners also operate the Old First Ward Brewery that is right next door to the bar.

While visiting McCarthy's in 2017, I asked bartender Hannah Lowman if there was anyone around who I could speak to about the area. She pointed to 81 year old John "Jackie" Donnelly from the Tennessee-O'Connell area who was sitting by the window having a brew.

"I'm here every day," he told me.

When I asked Jackie what was special to him about the Old First Ward, his response was:

"I just love it here. I'll never move out. I'm staying in the neighborhood and will never move away. I've been in the same house here in the Ward for 81 years. When parents pass away, a lot of the kids keep the houses instead of selling them off and moving elsewhere."

I asked him what differences he's seen in the Ward that he wasn't pleased with. He said, "In the old days, being Irish was very strong. People back then used to practice being Irish and you knew who was Irish in the neighborhood and who wasn't. People used Irish terms and even spoke it. Today, it's hard to tell who's Irish. But, there are still a lot of us here. It's still a great place to live."

Jackie mentioned a few of the guys he knew back in the day: Jim "Boy" Smith and his brothers, Pete and Joe. Also, Mike Miller.

He said, "Most of the guys I hung with are gone." Someone said that Jackie passed away in 2018.

The Other Side of the Tracks and Names of some of the OFW Residents

When you get to McCarthy's Tavern and Restaurant, you'll see a set of railroad tracks a stone's throw from there. The other side of the tracks takes you into another portion of the Old First Ward. It's still the OFW, but those tracks once made a distinction between its residents.

It seems that at one time, the tracks were a line of demarcation. Pre-Baby Boomer Joan Graham Scahill told me that the folks residing on the side of the tracks nearest the Buffalo Creek were referred to as "Creek Rats" back in the day. Joan was one of them. Although it sounded negative, she clarified by saying:

"The term wasn't necessarily a derogatory one. It was just meant to give a location for those who lived closest to the creek. All the folks, whichever side of the tracks they were from, were all Old First Ward people. No one was above the other. We were all equal."

I don't know which side of the tracks he was from, but Tim Fitzgerald who was born in the OFW in the early 50's and later lived on Whitfield told me, "I'm proud as the Lord to have been born in the Old First Ward. It still means a lot to me."

I've yet to meet a person who was born or lived in that area, ever say that he or she regretted having lived there. There's that pride; of being part of a people and place. It's something that imbeds itself in the soul of a person or group of people and stays with them all of their life.

Some of the people Tim and wife Ann Kenefick came to know or were acquainted with in the OFW are: Scud and Vi Mann, Marty Mann, Danny Bodkin, Jim Flood (owner of Floody's Tavern), Corky Connors, Tim and Mike Connors, Jack and Mary Fitzgerald, Jack Montando, the Kenefícks, Francis, Bob and Joe; also, the Hofstetters, Travis', Catanzaros, Mullens, Horrigans, and the Simoniks.

Bert Guise-Hyde and Dan Concheiro Names and Nicknames

Bert from the museum and OFW, a Baby Boomer herself, recalled others. Some of the people I also knew are noted by an asterisk: John Cummings, *William "Whitey" Guise, Pete May, *Mike Flood, Pat Stilt, Beau Korek, Duke Holland, *Mike "Cats" Catanzaro, Gene Dunbar, Betty Stack, Sue Griffin, Tom Szczygiel, Richy Hoar, Cindy Morris, Sue Eynow, Moe Hassett, Shela Hassett, Kenny Zabawa, Ace Hassett, Val Galanti, *Tommy, Jack and Jimmy Shine), and *Jimmy O'Connor.

I spoke to Dan Concheiro at Tully's Bar in the Valley who had the following acquaintances in the Ward back in the day: Frank and Beth Badaszewski, Tom, Joe, Maryann, and Paul Heidinger, Doug Beltram, Jim and Angelo Bouquard, Bob Rodgik, Ray and Ellen Conchiero, Tom and Peg Wahl, Ted, Gene and Peg Overdorf.

One can't help but notice how many "nicknames" pop up when you start mentioning people from anywhere on the South Side. Buffalo News writer Ray Hill, in an article back in October of 1988 about the Ward couldn't help but list several fine First Warders; some with unique appellations.

Example: **Tug** Wilson, **Turkey** Quirk, **Goosey** Evans, **Coo Coo** Flannigan, **O.O.** Leary, **Moon** Mullins, **Ace** Bonner, **Happy** Hooligan, **Potatoes** McGowan, **Harp** Eagan, **Scooper** Dempsey, **Bum** Lawless, **Honey** Lampshire, **Pickles** Robinson, **Duke** Crotty, **Spit** Dray, **Clerk** Mahoney, **Dusty** Flood and **Hi Lo** Caven.

The above are all guys. The ladies didn't normally play that game like the guys did ...of giving their friends' nicknames, but one lady did get tagged. That'd be Bert Guise-Hyde of the OFW Memories and More Museum. And, it wasn't from friends.

She said, "The local boys gave me the name **"Bert-Alert,"** because if I caught them drinking or smoking in the neighborhood, I'd chase them down, bring them to their house and tell on them. So, if they were up to their wayward ways and saw me coming after them, one kid would yell, 'BERT-ALERT!' to warn their friends I was coming. It was part of me being a mother of three, keeping my own kids in line and trying my best to help other moms in the neighborhood; keeping their boys from doing what they shouldn't be doing."

Going back to the men's nicknames, how do you go into a job interview and be taken seriously if you're introduced to a prospective boss as ...**Coo, Coo** Flannigan, **Potatoes** McGowan or **Pickles** Robinson? I'd love to be a fly on the wall to see how something like that would go, wouldn't you? Imagine the initial introduction by a secretary...

"Ahem! Excuse me, Mr. O'Connell. There are two gentlemen here to see you for job interviews; a Mr. 'Coo Coo' Flannigan and a Mr. 'Pickles' Robinson. Oh, and tomorrow, a Mr. 'Potatoes' McGowan and Mr. 'Spit' Dray will be in at 9 am for interviews as well."

Back in the day, just about every guy had a nickname, at least for a while. Mine was "Ramjet." I could add that to my pen name...Roger Roberge **"Ramjet"** Rainville. All "R's" - NAW! I don't think so. In a later chapter about TV shows, I've included a funny "true" story about that nickname.

Other guys with nicknames that I knew were; Digger, Stanley Stingray, Duke of Earl, Pops, Otis, a couple of guys named Skip, Frenchie, Beak, Tank, Spook, Hick, Lilley, Monk, Jet, Mack, Pudgy, Smokey, Jack-O-Lantern, Shy, Sonny, Buckwheat, and a ton of others. It's just the way it was.

The 1st Ward's Szuder Clan's Record Births!

Carolanne (Szuder) Kerl

In this book, I mention large families. In Carolanne Szuder's case, her father Bruno's family had a couple of very unique stats that I have never heard of. As you read about her folks, you'll see what I mean.

Carolanne and her grandparents Joseph Kotrys and Mary (Bok) were from the First Ward. Grandpa Joe and Grandma Mary lived at 145 Vincennes with their six children. Sally (married Nick Marinelli), Helen (married Stanley Szalkowski), Bertha (married Leonard Laskowski), Teddy (married Casey Dominiak), Emily (married Bruno Szuder), and Joseph (married Mildred Skinner).

Her father Bruno's lineage comes from Anthony Szuder (1884-1954) who lived at 366 Perry Street and mom Agnes Mroczek (1887-1966), came from 146 Fulton. Anthony and Agnes certainly set some sort of WORLD RECORD by having; for one, three sets of twins, and second, all of them were boy/girl sets!

Here's the run down on the Szuder clan, [1] Jenny (Filipowitz), [2] Esther (Wicka), [3] Twins Helen (Weislo) and unnamed male still-born, [4] Twins Bruno and Bertha - (Bertha passed away at age 5 from a train accident) [5] Twins Charlotte (aka) Bertha and Walter (aka) Eddy, [6] Julius, [7] Joseph, [8] Mary (Montalbano), [9] Frank, and [10] John.

Carolanne's parents, *Bruno Szuder and mom Emily (Kotrys), were married August 11, 1945. They lived at 515 South Park Avenue in the Ward and had three children; Anthony, Dennis, Carolanne. In the 50's and

60's, her and her siblings attended School 34 on Hamburg Street where the principal was Mrs. Marafino. Two of her favorite teachers there were Miss Edith and Mrs. Gomez.

Her close friends were; Marcy Mazurek (of Mazurek's Bakery) and Nancy Giambroni whose family owned the local penny candy store.

Some of her leisure time was spent listening to music on a transistor radio- WKBW. (Baby Boomer moms and dads, explain transistor radios to your kids and grandkids.) Another activity that was common among Carolanne's friends was roller skating and building what they called back then, a "gig."

She explained it this way; "They "gigs" were homemade scooters. We pulled apart roller skates wheels and nailed them to both ends of a board, then took a wooded pop crate and nailed it to the one end of the roller board, (that's the part we would hold on to when using the scooter. We would decorate the pop crate with different bottle caps."

Besides the above, she enjoyed just hanging out with friends at their house or in back of their parents' businesses.

Speaking of businesses, Carolanne remembers certain businesses between Alabama and Hamburg streets; her friends' parents' businesses for sure like Mazurek's Bakery, but also, the Friendly Inn, Dr. Tumiel's Office, and Adolf's Old First Ward Grill. Her family once owned and operated Szuder's Cleaners at 515 South Park from 1946 until 1963. What was very convenient, the family lived in the upstairs flat.

She has fond memories of riding bikes near the grain mills, taking short bus rides to Main Street to shop with her mom and eating lunch at the Neisner counter where her mom's sister, Aunt Sally, worked.

I asked her how she felt about her old neighborhood, the Ward. She said, "I remember how the Ward had so many friendly people and everybody knew each other. It was a safe place to live. But now, it's sad. When I go down there and see that our store is gone, only a vacant lot remains. I get a sad feeling when I ride by; I have a lot of memories connected to it. "

Like so many Boomers, Carolanne no longer lives in the Ward. She married and moved out of the neighborhood but has never forgotten the First Ward and all the people, places, and good times there.

Career wise, she spent 38 years (1977-2016) as a 911 police dispatcher for the Lancaster Police Department.

A few Individuals – Their thoughts about the OFW

As I was driving down South Street in the OFW, I saw four teenage girls walking and thought I would get their views of the Ward. Two were Ward girls and two others were guests from streets off South Park (south of Tifft Street). I asked the two who lived in the Ward. "How do you like living in the Old First Ward?"

One responded: "I love it. Love living here." The other added: "There are no conflicts here."

I asked the other two girls if they liked where they live in South Buffalo. One said "There's too much drama where I live; too many fights and drugs."

The other said: "I like it here better. It feels friendlier than in the South Park area where I live."

I asked mailman Chris Mulvaney on his route on South Street his feelings about the Ward. He said: "It's friendly here. I like the 'old school' effect, the people, houses, neighborhoods, and the vintage look and feel."

I encountered Tim Dickman at the Master Market at Louisiana and South streets. He'd been an Old First Ward resident for years. I asked about a bar I used to go to in the late 60s that was located at Ohio and Louisiana streets. He said:

"Oh yeah, that was Milt's Tavern. It became Carmen's Tavern. Around the 4th of July in1998 it caught fire. People near the place were setting off fireworks and something lit up the place. It was destroyed. When the police investigated, it was funny; a whole bunch of guys turned themselves in at Precinct 7 at Louisiana and Miami. There was no way of knowing who did it, so the cops let 'em all go."

Tim added: "All of those guys I knew are no longer around."

I personally remember that Milt's had great hamburgers back in the 60s, where me and a lot of the guys who worked at Freezer Queen used to go to cash our paychecks at noon on Fridays, order a hamburger, down a couple of beers, then rush back to work.

A First Ward Barber Shop

Many of the First Ward's side streets once had delis, bars and barber shops. There aren't as many around that cater to men only like there used to be. Today, there are a lot of "unisex" shops that do both, men and women's hair. Well, right near McCarthy's Pub, I came across "Rock Boyz Barber Shop" at the corner of Hamburg Street and O'Conner Avenue owned by Ron Rocklin. He once worked for Dan Callahan at Bob's Barber Shop on Seneca Street that began in the 50s.

At the time of my visit (January 2020) with Ron, his shop had been opened a year and a half. Ron has lived in the Ward all his life as well as other family members. It used to be Tricia's Corner Deli about forty years ago, from the late 70's to around 1995.

Ron said, "The building had been vacant since about 1995. I gutted it and remodeled the entire inside. I'm a First Ward guy. This is where I feel at home."

Chapter 4 A few Notable Persons

from the Old First Ward and South Buffalo

William "Wild Bill" J. Donovan

The Old First Ward had several people who were born there or had a connection to it and made a name for themselves. The most illustrious was William "Wild Bill" J. Donovan. He was born in January of 1883 and lived on Michigan Street. He attended Saint Bridget's on Louisiana and Fulton streets then transferred to Nardin Academy and finally, attended Columbia University Law School. He died in February of 1959. The university erected a bronze statue in his honor in 1979.

Writer Richard Dunlop said of him, *"He was the most renowned person to come out of the Old First Ward"*

Dunlop wrote about Donovan's part in World War II as the director of what was called, the OSS (Office of Strategic Services). That office was the precursor of the CIA and he is regarded as being the *"Father of the CIA."* Dunlop said this concerning Donovan: *"Hitler feared and hated him more than any other American."*

Many of you remember the building across from the old War Memorial Auditorium on lower Main Street (The Aud, as we called it). Right across the street stood the General William J. Donovan Building, built in 1962 and used for 45 years.

"Wild Bill" J. Donovan was a highly decorated U.S. soldier, a lawyer, intelligence director, and diplomat. By the time he finished his service duties, he amassed an incredible number of service medals:

Congress Medal of Honor - American Campaign Medal - The Distinguish Service Medal - Asiatic-Pacific Campaign Medal - 2 Oak Leaf clusters - European-African/Mid-Eastern - Distinguished Security Medal - Campaign Medal - Silver Star - WWII Victory Medal - Purple Heart with 2 Oak Leaf clusters - American Occupation Medal - Security Medal - Germany Clasp -Mexican Border Service Medal - Armed Forces Reserve Medal - WWI Victory Medal with 5 Campaign Bars - Army of Occupation of Germany Medal.

Jimmy "Six Pack" Griffin (June 1929 - May 2008)

Hizzoner Jimmy Griffin, one of our "older" sons came from the Old First Ward then moved to Dorrance Avenue near Abbott Road. He worked as a scooper in the grain mills, a railroad engineer and bar owner. His greatest achievement was becoming the 56th mayor of Buffalo January 1, 1978, serving 16 years as mayor. Everyone who knew him remembers the slogan "Gimme Jimmy" as a political campaign slogan.

During his office as mayor, he was instrumental in erasing the city's $19 million deficit and was part of the resurgence of Buffalo with new development and construction. The downtown baseball stadium known as Pilot Field was one of his pet projects. I remember when I worked for International Cable and Mayor Griffin was a guest on Paul McGuire's "Sportsline Show." He brought a model of the stadium to the TV studio and spoke excitedly about building it right in the middle of downtown Buffalo. Built in 1979, this was big news. Besides the stadium, many other improvements took place in the city under Griffin's leadership.

He was also known for a statement he made on radio and TV when the infamous blizzard of January 18, 1985 hit Buffalo, dropping over 33 inches of snow with winds gusting over 50 miles an hour. His suggestion to get through the foul weather was, "Stay inside. Grab a six-pack and watch a good football game." Hence the nick-name, "Jimmy Six-Pack."

Feisty Jimmy Griffin was a different kind of candidate and mayor. There is no denying that he ruffled more than a few feathers. He never minced words. He shot straight-from-the-hip when it came to certain issues and publicly spoke his mind on more than one occasion. Sometimes things got pretty heated. I believe he even got into a bit of fisticuff with someone who pushed his button by using foul language in front of his wife. That opponent lost the match.

He got himself kicked off Channel 7's AM Buffalo show with host Brian Kahle in 1987 over a discussion about allegations that federal money was mishandled by his brother Tommy. Some subjects were better left alone while in the company of the Mayor. If you wanted to get into a verbal battle with him, he wasn't shy about telling you off or getting his point across. I call it, "Going South Buffalo on someone." A lot of folks loved to hate him while many truly loved him. Whatever side you were on, you must admit that he was an unforgettable character.

First Ward Giant, "Big Red" Carroll

John Francis "Big Red" Carroll of the Old First Ward was one of the tallest men in the world at 8 feet 7.75 inches. Born in 1932 at 9 pounds 5 ounces, he was five and a half feet tall by the time he reached age 12. At the age of sixteen, he shot up to six foot, two inches and wore size 16EEEE shoes. He attended Bishop Timon High School where he was a definite asset to the basketball team. By the age of twenty, he was over seven and a half feet tall. In his younger days, he was able to pick up one end of a car; the back end I'm sure.

As an adult he served as a local park supervisor, superintendent of Isle View Park in the Town of Tonawanda and county parks. John served as Republican committeeman and ran unsuccessfully for county supervisor in 1955 and 1957. He died in 1969 at the age of thirty-seven.

The Tutuskas and Conways

While researching my book, I stopped at the Old Triangle Tavern at South Park and Germania. I spoke to bartender George Tutuska II and learned he had ties with the Old First Ward. I also found out the tavern had several names before becoming the Old Triangle Tavern. It once was Talty's, the 19th Hole and Burke's Tavern.

George began talking to me about his background and who he was connected to. His Hungarian grandfather, Dave Tutuska (wife Irene) had a barbershop on Catherine Street and great uncle, B. John Tutuska, a First Warder, held the offices of Erie County Sherriff and Erie County Executive.

George II's grandfather, Dave Tutuska and four of his brothers served during World War II. They were; B. John Tutuska, Andy, Pete, and George. His own dad, George and his brother Dave didn't serve during the Vietnam War, but brother Donny actually fought in Nam. George's dad's clan include; George Sr. and siblings, Dave, Donny, Gloria, Linda, Beverly, Cathy, and Mary Beth.

His mother was Marjorie (Conway – Irish heritage). Her dad was William "Bill" Conway (wife Alice O'Connor). Grandpa Bill got into the Guinness World Record Book for having been the youngest man to obtain a ship's Master Pilot license to handle ships on the Great Lakes at age 22. He came in first on the list of those who took the intense test for the license.

Before achieving the "master pilot" status, Conway actually began working on ships when he was 16 years old as a "deckhand" at the Great Lakes Dredge & Dock Company. After obtaining the master's license, he became the Captain on the fireboat "Edward M. Cotter" for over 30 years.

Cotter Fireboat]

In the early 50's, the Skipper was instrumental in fighting a fire on an oil barge and a ship called the Penobscot that collided in the harbor. He pulled out bodies from the pilothouse and piloted the burning Penobscot out of the harbor. He was awarded the "Butler Medal" for heroism. It was the highest medal awarded by the Buffalo Evening News.

Conway was also involved in tackling a couple of other notable fires. One was at the Pillsbury plant where he used the turrets to pump water on flames and pulling out some of the mill workers to safety. The other fire was that of the "Semet Solvay Company,". A year out of retirement, he came to assist the Buffalo Fire Department. Semet Solvay was part of Allied Chemical and was sold to Tonawanda Coke in 1978.

Bill Conway owned Conway's Pub on O'Connell and later sold it to Sammy McCarthy – Gene's brother.

George Jr. himself has a claim to fame. In 1986 he formed the Buffalo based group the "Goo Goo Dolls", along with John Joseph Theodore "Johnny" Rzeznik and Robby Takac. George was the drummer for the band and played on the group's triple platinum album, "Dizzy UpThe Girl." He was with the band until 1996.

After the Goo Goo Doll stint, around the years 2000, he started another group called "Jack Daw." Around the same time he started the band, he also organized the "Irish Festival" at Caz Park that as of 2020, has had a 20 year run. The festival also owes its success to backers/supporters; Jim Neenan, Ray McGurn, T. Caufielf and Ron Sokolawski, as well as a host of other proud South Buffalonians that made it all happen.

While talking with George about South Buffalo, he wanted to stress what made South Buffalo great. He said, "It's not events, places or buildings, it's the people."

Notable Boxers Tied to the Old First Ward

Boxer Jimmy Slattery

Jimmy Edward "Shamus" "Slats" Slattery was an Old First Ward and Valley idol. He was born on Fulton Street and bought a house for his mom on Bolton Street in the Valley with his first boxing winnings. Slats was born in 1904 and died in 1960. He was one of former Mayor Griffin's four top heroes.

As the story goes, Slats' start in boxing stemmed from a fight he had with a 210 pound thug who snatched a box of chocolates out of his hands that he bought for his mother on Valentine's Day. He didn't let the matter slide.

According to details given by writer Timothy Bohen, author of "Against the Grain," the story went like this, "There were about two hundred people watching the match where young Slats beat the bully in about 30 minutes. His father saw his son's potential as a fighter and brought him to the First Ward Athletic Club. Jimmy's boxing career started when he was 16 years old."

He turned pro in 1923 at age 17. At 175 pounds, Slats fought as a light-heavy weight. He had 129 fights and was inducted into the Buffalo Sports Hall of Fame in 1992 and the International Boxing Hall of fame in 2006. He had 114 wins, 51 knockouts, 13 losses and 0 draws. One of his best weapons was his left punch. He retired in 1931.

One story about this OFW son was that he'd throw money out of his car window as he drove through the Ward streets to help poor children buy shoes for school. He was honored in 2006 by having a sign placed with the Bolton Street sign of his childhood residence that reads "Jimmy's Place." Going north on South Park, Bolton is a couple of streets on your left just before the curve leading to the bridge going toward the Old First Ward.

I found out that I am connected to Slats through marriage. Kathy Byrnes Aures is my sister-in-law, married to my wife's brother, Gary Aures. "Shamus" Slats is her distant cousin. She explained the lineage this way; "My dad was Patrick Byrnes. His mom was Agnes (Byrnes) Hickey who was my grandmother. Her father was Michael Hickey (my great grandfather.) Her father's sister was Mary Hickey. Mary (Hickey) Slattery was Jimmy Slattery's mom. That makes his mom, my dad's great aunt ...and my great, great aunt; making Jimmy my distant cousin."

Richard "Rocky" Fumerelle "The Blond Bomber"

South Buffalo-born Rocky Fumerelle, "The Blond Bomber" who attended South Park High fought as a middleweight from 1955 to 1963. In 1955, he won the Buffalo Golden Glove novice middleweight title and repeated that title the following year. He went undefeated in 19 amateur bouts. He was taken to San Francisco along with Bobby Scanlon by manager Mike Scanlon. He retired in 1963 because, "It wasn't fun anymore."

Rocky settled down and studied communications and property management at Canisius College for a few years. He married Rita Cafarella.

Bobby Scanlon

Another boxer from the OFW was Bobby Scanlon. He was born in 1936. He spent part of his life at the Father Baker Orphanage. He started off in Golden Gloves and went on to fight as a pro light-weight at 5 foot 6 inches.

In writings by Art Benjamin, Nick Kobseff and Lou Sabella, one statement about Bobby went like this:

"Because of his choirboy looks, he was frequently a target of bigger and tougher kids. He turned to boxing and became the orphanage's champion."

He turned pro in 1954 and fought, primarily, in Buffalo, Rochester, New York, Syracuse and Erie PA. Part of his record was that he was undefeated in 22 fights. Eventually, that number rose to 32 fights ending in wins. Between 1958 and 1960, his career had run its course. By the end of his fighting days, his record stood at: 42-12-1. During his career, he fought 412 rounds in 55 fights. He retired in 1966. After his boxing days were over, his life went downhill. Bobby's buddy Rocky Fumerelle said this:

"Bobby Scanlon was his own worst enemy. Had he taken better care of himself, I have little doubt that he would have been the Lightweight Champion of the world."

One source stated that Bobby struggled to find meaning to his life after his career. His life was boxing. After a while, his health started to diminish. Sadly, he died in a fire in the Lackawanna Hotel on June 23, 1975 at the young age of 39.

Jimmy Ralston

Although not a Ward guy, Jimmy Ralston, born in Riverside, was another Buffalo-born boxer that had ties with pro fighters from the Ward. He knew Bobby Scanlon and most of the other Buffalo boxers in the 60s.

He told me, "I liked Bobby a lot. He was a good guy. He wasn't flashy and never played the role. He was a quiet, nice guy. I was very sad when he passed away."

Ralston was rated 6th in the world. Like Bobby, he too fought in the Aud in Buffalo. His career record was 19-1-1. I spoke to Jimmy in November of 2015 at Talty's. He told me about a match in he had in 1969 where he knocked out a guy in 7 seconds of the first round. WOW!

Chapter 5 South Buffalo (South)

South Buffalo Baby Boomers

Samples of who did what careers wise

As you read, you'll find that some of the characters were not top of the class types nor did they mind their moms and dads all the time. A few people ended up making very bad choices with some even doing a bit of jail time. Most guys and girls were better focused and more or less knew where they might be heading in the future. Take Kevin Caffery for instance. He said, "I knew at the age of five what I wanted to be."

Here are names and careers of a few of the Baby Boomers who came from South Buffalo.

Clergy

Fred Betti, James Higgins and Jack Mattimore became priests. Joe Di Sarno became a missionary to the Fillipines.

Federal Law Enforcement

John and Tom Thurston from Crystal - FBI agents

Buffalo law officers

Five Nigrellis: Dad Joe, and sons; (Stephen, Michael, Peter, and Joe Jr.) - Jim "Jet" Jackson - Bart Adams, Joe O'Shei - Dan Redmond and Lissa Marie Redmond - Jim Shea (Buffalo PD) - Joe Denecke - George Amplement - Joe and Tony Prendergast - Joe and Lenny Weber - David Caruso (from police officer to inspector) - Kevin Caffery from Milford Street (ace helicopter pilot) Sheriff's Department - Ernest P. Masullo (became Evans Town Chief of Police) - Tom Best and Dan Shea (promoted from police officer to detective in Hamburg) - Officer George Battaglia became the first active member on Buffalo's Swat Team in 1966 serving around thirty years.

Firefighters

Neil Keane, Jim Anthony, *Mike Catanzaro, Alan Forcucci, John Tevington and Carl Villalobos.

*Mike Catanzaro, From the Old First Ward lost his life in an immense propane blast December 27, 1983 at 191 N. Division & Grosvenor streets.

Lawyers

Billy Bond (same family as Mary Bond's Deli at the corner of Harding) - Tom and Kevin Brinkworth, Will Curtin - John McGee - Mike Caffery

Teachers/School ties

Terri Schuta – principal at South Park High

Joe Lucenti - became a principal at Albion High

Adele Petrilli - became a Spanish language teacher

Larry Murtha

Medical Field

Joe Morganti – (*Pharmacist*) - Margie Morrison - Karen Lobuglio - Marcia Miniri

Businessmen

Roger Pasquarella - Dennis Dargavel - Billy Held - Billy West - John Mugas

Politics

Jimmy "Six-Pack" Griffin - mayor of Buffalo 1978 to 1993 - Richard and James Keane - Brian Higgins

Tony Orsini - Mickey Kearns - Tim Kennedy - Mark Schroeder - Carl Paladino

If you listened to WKBW AM Radio in the 60s and beyond, DJ Dan "Smiling Dan" Neaverth from the Seneca/Babcock area was one of the most well-known radio and TV personalities in Buffalo and beyond.

Most of the guys and gals we came to know got decent paying jobs in offices, large companies or manufacturing plants in the Buffalo area. Remember the steel plants and all other companies Buffalo once had? Here are some that employed hundreds and even thousands of people.

All of the Grain Elevators, Old First Ward area (aka) "Elevator Alley"

General Mills/Gold Medal Flour on Michigan and Ganson streets

Bethlehem Steel, Lackawanna all along Route #5

Buffalo Tank Division, Lake Avenue in Blasdell

Republic Steel, South Park near Buffalo Creek

Buffalo Forge, 490 Broadway

Donner Hanner Coke off South Park Avenue - Abby and Mystic area

Tons of jobs in the secretarial field

Nursing

Hairdressing

Barbers

Buffalo Train Terminal - Central Terminal, Paderewski Dr. 1929-1979

Courier Express Newspaper, Main Street

Westinghouse Electric, Genesee Street, Cheektowaga

Worthington Pump, Kaisertown area, off Clinton near Bailey

Buffalo China, Seneca Street near Bailey

Trico Plant #1, 817 Washington St.

Trico Plant #2, 2495 Main Street

Trico Plant #3, 500 Elk Street - between Goham and Babcock was the first of the three to close.

It operated from 1917 until closing on the '80's.

Mobile Refinery 625 Elk Street

National Aniline Chemical Company/Dye Plant, South Park and Lee Streets

Nabisco Bakery Company - 243 Urban Street (East Side)

Numerous trucking companies – city and long-haul drivers

Bus drivers – NFT, long distance lines, and school buses

Trico Plants - History

The Trico plants came about when Trico's founder, Buffalo born (1886) J.R. Oishei hit a bicyclist on a rainy day while driving his car – no wiper blades back then. In 1916, he was driving down Delaware Avenue in a rain storm and a cyclist ran into the National Roadster he was driving. The cyclist wasn't seriously hurt, but still, it bothered Oishei and he vowed that, "that was not going to happen again." In 1917, he founded the Trico Products Company to make the first wiper blades. Back then, one had to manually operate the rubber squeegee wipers. It was through the efforts of Buffalo engineer, John Jepson that the Trico windshield wipers were produced. Initially, the Packard, Lincoln, Cadillac and, Buffalo's Piece Arrow car makers bought Trico's products. For well over 60 years, the Trico company provided good-paying jobs for many Buffalo area workers.

Women's Careers

Some typical jobs or careers for women in the 40's to 70's

Margie Weber put a list together for me of what types of jobs most of the ladies got into back in the day. She said, "A lot of women in 1940s worked in factories when WWII was going on. We all heard of Rosy the Riveter. In the 1940's, 1950's and 1960's, there were many stay-at-home moms with 'latchkey kids' before that phrase came into our language. Some moms joined PTAs, led Girl Scout and Camp Fire Girls and most families had only one car. For shopping, a lot of women took busses downtown or walked to get groceries for the family.

When families needed two incomes to afford buying homes or to send kids college, women returned to the workforce. We always had women working in banks, grocery and drugstores, as teachers, and nurses from way back. I think mid in the '60s was when career choices for women, for economic reasons, began. As independence soared in our so-called modern society, so did divorces and legal separations.

More women found themselves taking college courses and began filling evening classes; returning to the books, to become professionals. Many lost husbands in Vietnam and this created a need for women to find employment and for many, a need for Day Care centers that took a chuck out of their paycheck and brought on additional financial stress. This brings in the grandparents who were often absolutely needed to help care for school-age grandchildren until they got older and able to more or less 'fend for themselves.' This gave the working baby boomers much needed peace of mind as they went off to work."

Chapter 6 The Hopkins Street/Hickory Woods

its people and businesses

Before we head further down South Park to check out the businesses and its people, we need to note that there was another very vibrant section of South Buffalo... the Hopkins Street/Hickory Woods and Triangle area.

First, my most sincere apologies to the folks who live or lived on Hopkins Street and its surrounding areas for being left out in the first "SOUTH BUFFALO – THE WAY IT WAS" book. Thanks to all who provided me with information of this section of South Buffalo for the SECOND EDITION.

This part of the south side has some very interesting facts that South Buffalo people either never knew about or forgot. You'll see what I mean as you read on.

According to the ladies at the First Ward Museum, Bert Guise-Hyde, Peggy May-Szczygiel and Joan Graham-Scahill, the section known as "Hickory Woods" is comprised of only the streets that are to the west of Hopkins Street. The section to the east where Bailey, Abbott and South Park meet is known as the "Triangle," and the streets to the east along Hopkins are simply part of South Buffalo proper.

As I did with the other seven areas of the South Side, here are the streets that intersect Hopkins Street. Starting at South Park and Hopkins, going toward Tifft, they are:

Pembina St.	Osage St.
Baraga St.	Koester St.
Good Ave.	Trowbridge St
Mystic Ave.	Pries St.
Sirret Ave.	Payne Ave.
Beacon Ave.	Providence Ave.
Spaulding St.	Garvey Ave.
Houston	Tifft St.

Before Hopkins and off of South Park, there is a street called, "New Abby" that runs into Abby Street. There's a park that is tucked between Germania and Boone Streets near Bell Street called "Boone Park." All the while I lived in South Buffalo, I never heard of that park.

Other streets and a park connected to Tifft from Hopkins toward South Park are; Folger, Allegany St., and "Mulroy Park" also known as "George Hermann Park". The renaming of the park came about through Bob Domzalski's effort to honor Mr. Hermann's great contribution to managing the park back in the 50s, 60s and 70s, and being part of the lives of so many of the young people back then. Bob passed away in January of 2020 after a long battle with cancer. Thank you, Mr. Hermann and Bobby.

Hopkins Street Origin
Where did the Name come from?

Hopkins Street is part of the City of Buffalo in an area in South Buffalo known as the "Brownfield Opportunity/Hickory Woods/Triangle area." The street was named for Brigadier General Timothy S. Hopkins, a War of 1812 general. There is also Hopkins Road (Amherst) that was named after the General. The South Buffalo Hopkins is a north-south road opened in 1855 that leads from South Park Avenue towards South Park Lake in Lackawanna (the lake is 1.44 miles around). Historically, the entire Hopkins neighborhood was a mix of commercial and industrial enterprises.

General Hopkins

Although Hopkins Street may be seen as a name of just another South Buffalo street, it might interest the folks from that area to know that General Timothy Hopkins was a descendent of Stephen Hopkins who came over on the Mayflower. It's also interesting to note is that there was a second Stephen Hopkins who was one of the signers of the Declaration of Independence AND... another Hopkins, Ichabod Hopkins, was a signer of the Constitution in Philadelphia on behalf of Massachusetts. That's cool! Hopkins Street-area folks have famous men they can boast about that are connected to their turf.

Ichabod Hopkins had a son, Timothy S. Hopkins. He was born in Massachusetts in 1776. Unbelievably, at the age of 22, he came on foot from there to settle in Clarence. He purchased land in 1804 from the Holland Land Company. He was the first to grow wheat on that Holland Purchase farmland in Clarence Hollow. When it was ready to be processed into flour, he had to travel to Street's Mill at Chippewa, Ontario; a village that became a part of the City of Niagara Falls, Ontario. This was a distance of 40 miles! The trip took four days and included a ferry ride from Black Rock, where only one family resided – the family of the ferry owner!

During the War of 1812, Timothy Sorvil Hopkins rose through the rank to Brigadier General. He was an important part of the Battle of Buffalo (also known as the Battle of Black Rock), where he was stationed. Following the war, he resigned from his post.

In 1819, he became the first Supervisor of the Town of Amherst and later served as Justice of the Peace. His reputation spread through the area and later became Sheriff of Erie County. He followed that post by being elected to the New York State Assembly.

Timothy S. Hopkins married a lady named Nancy Ann Kerr in Williamsville. Their marriage was the first recorded marriage in Erie County. They settled on Main Street on a farm in Snyder, near where Amherst Central High School is currently located. They had a son named Nelson Kerr Hopkins who ended up serving as President of the Buffalo Common Council in 1865.

Nelson bought a great parcel of land in the South Buffalo area, near the same place, George Washington Tifft (for which Tifft Street was name) settled in as a dairy farmer around 1826 till 1842. Hard to imagine today that …that section of South Buffalo was farmland. Moving on….

Historically, in 1904, the "Sisters of Mercy" opened a 30 bed hospital in a home on Tifft Street that started at South Park and Tifft and was eventually moved across from where Folger Street and Mulroy playground are located.

Lilac Street War Hero

Before visiting the Hopkins/Hickory Woods area, I needed to honor a "super war hero" from that part of South Buffalo…

WWII Hero
Rear Admiral Clarence Wade McClusky
News Paper Headlines 1942...

"South Buffalo pilot's mettle turned the tide in Battle of Midway"

C.W.McClusky

As I did research for the Hickory Woods area, I came upon a very special and important man that came from there. His name is Clarence Wade McClusky - born in Buffalo June 1, 1902. He lived in South Buffalo's Hopkins/Hickory Woods area and was a South Park High School graduate. He was one of five children. His father, Clarence Wade McClusky Sr., was of Scottish ancestry and worked as a bookkeeper and accountant for a Buffalo company. He died in an auto accident in 1928. His mother, Mary, known as May, was Irish Catholic and lived until 1953.

In McClusky's early years, the family lived on Lilac Street in South Buffalo, but later moved to Tuscarora Road. One of his brothers was Robert. He became a Buffalo firefighter. Another brother named Frank, lived in Lackawanna.

Clarence McClusky was intrigued by airplanes when flight was still in its infancy when he was a young boy. During his years living at 54 Lilac, and a student at elementary School 28, he decided to see if he could "fly."

Phillip M. McClusky, his only surviving son was quoted in an article, saying, "His first flight experience was jumping off a roof with an umbrella; he broke his arm!"

According to records, he went to South Park High School in 1918. He was bright, especially in math, and graduated at 16. He also played on the school's football team as quarterback.

His Navy Career

He became a Navy pilot, graduating from the **United States Naval Academy** in 1926, and served on the USS Enterprise Carrier. In 1940, he was assigned to Fighting Squadron Six (**VF-6**), based on **USS Enterprise**. At the rank of Lieutenant Commander, he became the Enterprise's **air group** commander in April 1942. That squadron fought in the "Battle of Midway" in the Pacific during World War II in June of 1942, six months after the Japanese attack on Pearl Harbor. Japan's navy was headed by naval officer, Marshal Admiral Isoroku Yamamoto. He was the one that master minded the attack on Pearl Harbor.

During the **Midway battle**, while leading his air group's scout bombers on 4 June 1942, forty year old Commander McClusky's decisions and actions led to delivering Japan's navy one of its worst defeats. There were two U.S. squadrons out that day in the search of the enemy; McClusky led one, and **Lieutenant Richard "Dick" Best** commanded the other.

Seventeen of McClusky's dive bombers were either shot down or ran out of fuel and crashed into the ocean. Many pilots and crew members were later rescued. Also, an entire squadron of 15 torpedo planes from the USS Hornet never returned and only one pilot was later rescued. McClusky was shot in the shoulder but staued in the fight. By the time he landed back on the carrier, he was running on fumes and had over 50 bullet holes in his plane.

For his actions in this pivotal battle, which turned the tide in the war, McClusky was awarded both, the **Navy Cross** and the "Bronze Star." The Navy Cross is the highest non-combat decoration award given for heroism, and the Bronze Star, for heroic achievements in combat.

In his honor, on the 74th anniversary of the "Battle of Midway," there was a special ceremony held on the **USS Little Rock at the Buffalo** & Erie County Naval and Military Park at Canalside on June 4, 2017.

South Park High School Honors McClusky

Terri Schuta came from the Hopkins Street area and lived on Lilac Street, just a few houses from where our war hero once lived – at 54 Lilac. She attended South Park High and graduated in 1978. At this writing (2020), she was South Park High's principal.

In an interview, she said, "I grew up at 67 Lilac and had no idea that someone of such historic significance was from my little street in my little neighborhood. What are the chances?"

She held a special ceremony to install a plaque on the wall at the school for the 75th anniversary of the Midway battle to honor McClusky. She stated, "It is a great honor for us to honor him and the plaque will be a permanent tribute for future generations to take pride in his accomplishments. We want the students to be part of the research and make it a meaningful project for South Park High School and most importantly, give our former alumnus the distinction he deserves."

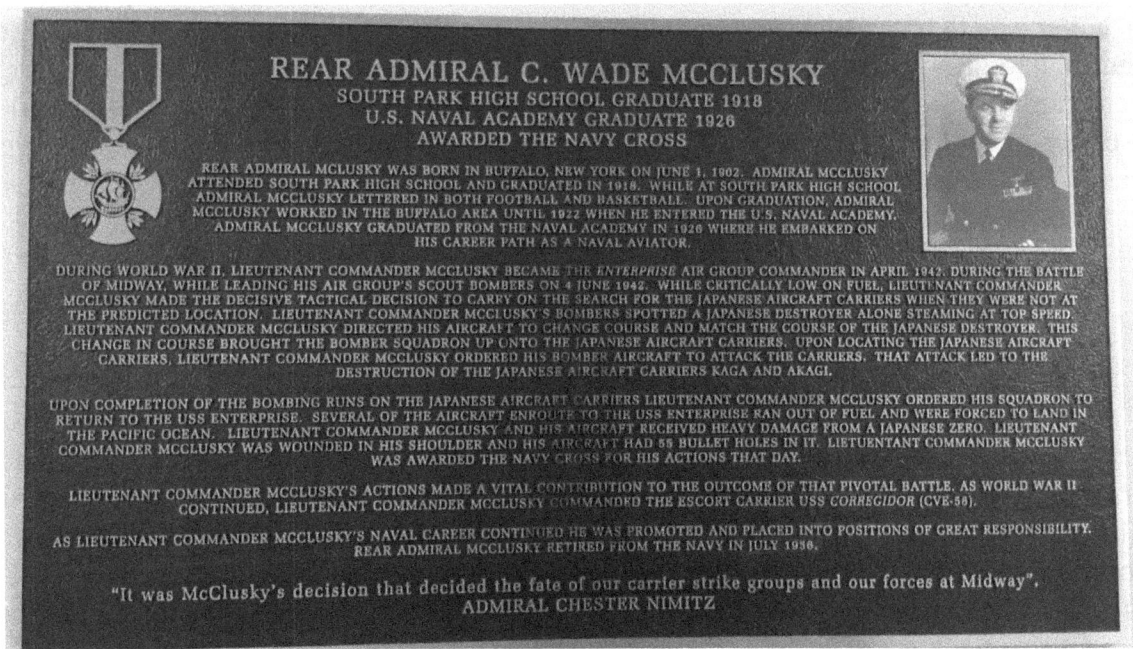

One last note about our South Park High/Hopkins area hero; as I was writing about C.W. McClusky's World War II heroic actions in this edition, Hollywood released the movie – **"Midway"** around November 8, 2019. His role was played by actor Luke Evans, and the second squadron leader, Lieutenant Best was played by actor Patrick Wilson. Well-known actors in the film that played major roles were; Dennis Quade, Woody Harrelson and Nick Jonas. I went to see the film by myself and was very moved by the graphic scenes of the Pearl Harbor bombing and the ensuing Midway battle scenes. A must see for any WWII veteran – especially, Navy pilots and sailors of U.S. carriers.

A salute to those who fought in that battle ...and thank you!

Life in the Hopkins/Hickory Woods area

Hopkins Street and its neighborhoods, as with all the other South Buffalo neighborhoods, was once a unique place in its own right with close-knit families, many businesses such as; delicatessens, barber shops, trucking companies, service stations, bars, diners, hotels, restaurants and more.

A man by the name of Joe Morganti who once lived at 584 Hopkins broke down the area for me. He said. "This neighborhood, like other parts of South Buffalo has its own unique sections. One of them is the Hickory Woods area. It's about 1 square mile. It includes our family's house on Hopkins. Other streets tied to that area are; Abby, Boone, Bell, Germania, Mystic and O'Connor street. My brother John used to attend Hickory Woods picnics over 20 years ago."

Oh, and as for how the Hickory Woods area got that name, I asked several people and four responders pretty much said the same thing, "hickory trees."

Tony Orsini, who lived near the area stated, "The reason it's called Hickory Woods is because they planted hickory trees between the sidewalks and the streets in that section of the Hopkins area."

Like the other South Side areas, the Hopkins neighborhood was once as diversified as the rest with Irish folks for sure, but also, with other ethnic groups. My Sicilian/French/German wife Donna lived at the corner of Good Avenue and Hopkins with parents, Jean-Frank Aures (French/German) and Connie Durso-Aures (Sicilian), older sister Diane and younger brother Gary. Diane and Donna attended P.S. 28 at South Park and Verona Place before moving to West Seneca. Her Italian grandparents (Durso) on her mother's side lived at 564 Hopkins. In the Durso clan, there was dad Frank, and mom Mary, with son Nunsio, daughters Jennie Durso Caruso, and Connie Durso Aures.

A Tribute to a Special Lady"- Aunt Rosie"

"Mother Cabrini"of Hickory Woods

In this part of South Buffalo lived a grand lady. Dennis Starr and Ronnie Wentland are Hickory Woods men that were part of the Taylor Park crew and are related to a dear lady called Rosie Di Sarno, (aka) Aunt Rosie, to family and friends alike. She was Dennis' grandma and Ronnie's aunt. She lived at 309 Germania in Hickory Woods. Dennis from O'Connor Street and Ron from Germania said that her house was, "The hub for activities in our neighborhood with tons of kids gathering there all the time and affectionately called her, Aunt Rosie."

Dennis said, "I remember me and a lot of my friends would sit on her front porch playing chess and talking away for hours. It was the place to be."

Both Dennis and Ron raved about her cooking and generosity and went back and forth talking about how she would feed and care for anyone in the neighborhood. Each adding to the story, they said, "Every Sunday was pasta day. Saturday night, Aunt Rosie would make a big, and we mean, a BIG - pot of sauce, and prepared meatballs, sausage, and braciole. The next day (Sunday), she'd heat all that up and put out a huge rigatoni meal for the whole family and friends. Her meatballs were the best!"

Ron laughed and said, "I once told her, "Hey Aunt Rosie, your meatballs are better than s*x!' All she said was marone." (literally... Madone or Madonna... generally used to express surprise or shock. It's also used to mean "damn!)

One of the men said, "She used to make a bowl full of fried meatballs and bring it out on the porch. If any of the kids outside were hungry, she'd invite 'em up and fed them. She had a great heart."

Both Dennis and Ron said, "If she saw children needing coats, sweaters, gloves or anything else, she'd do what she could for them. She took care of anybody, regardless of their ethnicity; she helped them all. And since she wasn't able to get to the store, the neighborhood boys would stop in and ask her if she needed anything from the corner deli or Park Edge."

Ron stated, "I remember her parish priests coming from St. Agatha to bring her communion two or three Sundays a month. And, I remember Aunt Rosie always having a rosary in her hands." Dennis concurred.

That's "the way it was" for the neighborhood with the benevolent Aunt Rosie Di Sarno; "Mother Cabrini" of Hickory Woods, as I call her.

Mother Cabrini (Frances Xavier Cabrini) was the youngest of thirteen children and born pre-mature. She was born in 1850 in Lombardy, Italy and passed away in 1917. She opened an orphanage in New York City and took care of children. She also started the "Missionary Sisters of the Sacred Heart" in 1880 to serve orphans. She was the first US citizen to be canonized a saint. This happened July 7, 1946. Her feast day is celebrated November 13 and she's the "Patron Saint of immigrants."

Linda (Di Sarno) Holtz

Connected to Aunt Rosie, aside from Dennis and Ronnie, there is also Linda (Di Sarno) Holtz. She has a third cousin named Joe Di Sarno. He's been doing missionary work in the Philippines for at least 30 years. At the time of this writing, 2020, Aunt Rosie's son *Tony Di Sarno Jr. is alive at 94 years old and Linda's father, Richie Di Sarno - 90, also alive.

Linda's cousin, Ronnie Wentland said, "During World War II, Tony Jr. saw action in Italy. And, while he was fighting there, he was able to go to the town where his father was born - the town of Sarno, Italy.

Linda said, "Ronnie is a cousin to my cousin Dennis Starr. Dennis, his brother Gary and sister, Gail, grew up in the Hickory Woods area. Their mother, Mary, was Aunt Rosie's daughter.

Going back to missionary Joe Di Sarno, Dennis Starr said that Joe had an incident while working at Republic Steel that changed his life. Dennis said, "Joe was doing some maintenance high up on the rail of a crane, and for some reason, the operator moved the crane forward and caused Joe to fall. By the grace of God only! ...his leg was snagged by a cable. He hung upside down until people were able to get to him."

Here are some of Linda's memories of "the way it was." She said, "My father's mom owned a store on Hopkins Street when they were younger. I grew up on Allegany Street off Tifft and remember that at one point, there were over 90 kids on the block. Most of them had siblings who were friends with me and my siblings. Everyone played together. I remember the many times we played kickball and dodgeball in the street. Although Mulroy playground was right behind us, we all played right in the middle of Allegany Street, close to home.

For school, we all went to Holy Family around the corner and when I went to high school, my friends and sister and her friends all walked together to Mount Mercy. What's neat is that I still hang out with my Mount Mercy friends. We graduated in 1969."

Joe Morganti, family and friends
More about Hopkins Street

I was very pleased to be put in touch with a former resident, Joe Morganti through David Caruso (former resident) of Lilac Street. His father's name was John and mom, Lucy. Lucy was from the Forcucci clan. Joe's siblings were; his brother John-(spouse Judy Keller), sister Sharon (spouse-Bob Kimaid), and brother, Ron (spouse-Annette Barone).

Joe told me, "My family lived in a two story house at 584 Hopkins. It was my grandma, Elvira's home when I was growing up. My dad, John Morganti, married Lucy Forcucci who came from a family of 10 children. Most of her siblings later settled in South Buffalo on Payne Ave, Portland St, Abbott Rd, Houston St., and Koester St." One of her siblings was Tony Forcucci, who married a lady called, Celia. Their sons were; Anthony, David, Alan and Peter.

As for the type of neighborhood he grew up in, Joe said, "It was very blue collar and diverse with good hardworking people, working in steel plants and car factories. The ethnic diversity in the Hopkins neighborhoods was rich. In the 50's and 60's when I lived there, we had; Polish, Irish, German, Italian, Mexicans. Some of the family names that marked the nationalities living there then were; Krafts, Sardinas, McCooeys, Maliks, Doctors, Dillsworths, D'Angelos, Gasperowskis, Potobinskis, Cunninghams, Raimondos, Morgantis, Forcuccis, Di Sarnos, Faillas, Lockwoods, Campos, Dursos, Wecks, and Ciavarellas."

School – Education

For Joe's education and most of the boys and girls in his neighborhood, he remembers P.S. 28's with principal, Miller and some of his teachers; Miss LaMay, Miss Brennan, Miss Kleinfelder, Mrs. O'Brien, and Miss Bowheiss, Mr.Sprague, Mr. Bassett, and Mrs. Saab. For their high school education, the choices for the guys was; South Park High on Southside Parkway, Timon on McKinley Parkway or one of the trade schools like Emerson on the East Side, Hutch Tech on Elmwood or Burgard High on North Elmwood near Buffalo State College. For the girls, it was South Park and Mount Mercy.

Leisure Activities & Memories

As with most boys living in that area, Joe had memories of how and where he spent some of his leisure time. He said, "I remember going to the south side of the Tifft Street Bridge to explore but was careful to avoid the pools of water there. The water was polluted with chemicals. There was no EPA testing for contaminants back then. The giveaway was that the water in the ponds was tinted multiple colors."

The land and ponds to the north side of the bridge were somewhat cleaner but some were multi-colored. We explored the fields in the summer and often played cowboys and Indians, or army, or did target practice with our BB guns. In the winter, we ice skated and played hockey on the frozen ponds. Dave Caruso recalls that some of the tinted ponds never froze in winter due to the heavy concentration of chemicals in them.

Other memories Joe had; his repeated visits to Pete Failla's deli to buy lunch meats and Hostess cupcakes for school lunches at P.S.28. He said, "I remember annoying old Pete in his Deli by taking forever to decide on which penny candy to spend my dime on. I also loved buying a bottle of "Tru-Ade" and sitting on the store window-sill leafing through comic books trying to decide on which comic book to spend my 10 cents on."

More of Joe's memories of the 50s and 60s - he fondly remembers playing sports till dusk on Lilac Street with friends. In the 50's, it was the Forcucci family picnics at Buffalo Beach. In his younger years, he spent a fair amount of time watching sports - NFL, NHL and going to the Seneca Theater. In the 60s, he loved staying at summer cottages with friends at Crystal Beach. As for hangouts while in High School, that was the Villa Pizzeria on South Park, dances at Timon High School on McKinley and Fazio's Capitol Hall on South Park. Later, as he came to legal drinking age, (18 years old) he put down a few pints at the Dash Inn on Abbott Road, and Lerczak's Log Cabin out at the lake in the town of Evans.

His close circle of friends back then were; Dave and Jim Caruso , Greg Collins, Johnny Iannuzzelli, Pete Bartolotta, Barry Russell, Paul Malik, Sammy D'Amico, Bill McCooey, Dan Podgorny, Ray Berta, Jack White, Gary Sadowski, Jerry Kowal, Doug Grant, Buddy Casheba, Dick Malizioso and Rick Jones.

Some of the young ladies Joe associated with in the Hopkins neighborhood in elementary school were; Patti Burns, Carol Held, Lucy Naworta, Carol Gentile, Lynn Rice, and Eileen Kois,

In high school, there was; Mary Siska, Kathy English, Jeanne Grossjean, Marge Robillard, Marge Tomasello, Bonnie Eich, Karen Maroone, Chuck Steinman from Amber - is still a good friend, and another classmate was, Eugene Nawotniak from Sheffield.

For his traveling to and fro ...his first car was 1965 Ford Mustang, stick shift that cost him $750. He also had a 250cc Suzuki motorcycle.

His favorite singers or bands were the British invaders - the Beatles and Rolling Stones. Favorite songs for him were the Beatles' "In My Life," (from the "Rubber Soul" album 1965) and the Rolling Stones' "Satisfaction." (from the "Out of Our Heads" album 1965)

In the early 70s, he was all grown and attended on to UB (SUNYAB) to study pharmacy, graduated, got married to Lynn Ranger in 1971, and worked at the VA, ECMC, then, Kenmore Mercy Hospital. The cherry on top of all that was the birth of his two daughters, Heather in 1976, and Danielle in 1980.

Businesses along Hopkins

Like all the other neighborhoods I studied, I wanted to know what kinds of businesses and industries were around back in the "hay days." Joe said, "On Hopkins and Good Street, there was Sardinia's Deli, at Houston St., Pete Failla's Deli, and another at Koester called Malik's Deli. There was also Raimondo's Meat Market. There were at least of three them on Hopkins. There was also Norm's Bait Shop at Houston St., a barber shop with Dan the Barber at Good and Hopkins, Nap's Baber shop on Sirret, and several gas stations from South Park to Tifft. On the west side of Hopkins between Tifft and the railroad bridge, there was a large factory called Bliss and Laughlin Steel and a grain mill. There also were a few trucking companies."

Other businesses in the Hickory Wood area named by Dennis Starr, Joe Avolio, Ron Wentland, and Tony Szymkowiak were; Ross's Deli, Tutuska's Deli, Ely's Bar on O'Connor Street, Di Sarno's Groceries, Bergman's Groceries. And on South Park, Bruckman's Car Repair that also moved entire houses, Garage Strom's Bakery, Vinny Amigone Groceries, Koch's Clothing, a Dry Cleaner, at Good and South Park, Tri Abbott Hardware and Koch's Clothing near Good St., and a Five and Ten Store at Remolino. Oh, and for the Italians, the "South Buffalo Italian Social Club" at Macamly.

In the fifties major roadwork had to be done on Hopkins. Joe said, "Trucking Companies on Hopkins Street received a boost in the late 50's after the city dug the street down about 6 feet and rebuilt it in order to accommodate heavy trucks. Some of those outfits along that strip were; Interstate Trucking and Mid-States. Near the trucking outfits, behind the back yards of some of the houses on the west side of Hopkins, there were open fields in the 50's where, once, people planted *"victory gardens," or "Vegetable gardens." They eventually disappeared as the trucking companies needed more and more parking areas to accommodate the rigs."

"Victory gardens" Patriotic Americans during WWII and the Korean War planted fruit and vegetable gardens in fields near their homes (for their own use) in order to allow the fruits and vegetables produced by farmers to go to the men and women in our armed forces.

More Friends and Businesses

Joe spoke to former residents Paul and Butch Malik at a party in September of 2019 and asked them about their parents' delicatessen (Edward and Mary). They said, "Our deli had the largest penny candy counter in the area, and kids going through the process of picking out what they wanted, was absolutely tortuous! When they came in to buy candy, our parents would send one of us to wait on them. Our mom ran the fireworks business at the store." She told Paul that the sale of fireworks paid for the outdoor swing in their yard." At the time of Joe's interview 2019, Paul was 73 and Butch, 70.

Paul was part of the war effort in Vietnam. He was an Air Force pilot and his assignment was doing air to air refueling of fighter jets. Unlike many South Buffalo guys who never pursued college, Paul was motivated to seek higher education; he earned a chemistry degree at UB in 1967 and MBA in 1976.

Moving ahead again... during that same discussion at the party about the old neighborhood, Joe was able to obtain the names of a couple of bars in the neighborhood from back in the day. According to Paul and Butch, at Hopkins and Sirret was, "Gay Haven," and another near Koester that was called "Bar L."

Joe contacted another old friend from the past; a Hutch Tech High School classmate by the name of Dave Kozak (Dellwardt). Dave lived at 40 Amber St., a few doors down from Hopkins. As with the Malik brothers, Joe asked him about the old days in the neighborhood.

Dave said, "I remember playing street football/baseball in empty lots that were at the end of Amber, near Hopkins. The games were interrupted by cars that came by. One of the downsides of playing in that area was that there was a derelict grain mill that was the source of many rats running around in the neighborhood. In those empty fields, we'd play "guns," and when we got older we'd go fishing at South Park Lake and the Small Boat Harbor. We actually ate some of the fish we caught in the lake."

Dave Kozak Dellward- Vietnam Top Gun Pilot

Joe gave me some very impressive details about Dave Kozak Dellwardt's military career. He said that Dave went to the U.S. Air Force Academy, graduating in 1968. After training in the F-4 Phantom jet, he ended up in the Danang, Republic of Vietnam in Nov 1971. He completed an amazing 188 combat missions in the Phantom, including some of the most hazardous duties of the Nam era. He came home with two "Distinguished Flying Crosses", fifteen "Air Medals", and numerous other decorations. The remainder of his thirty year career included; attending Fighter Weapons School (USAF version of Top Gun) where he set a couple of records. He later became an instructor at the prestigious flight school.

Dave used his piloting experience as an airline captain with Continental Airlines which began in 1979 after he transferred from active duty to the reserves. He moved back to South Buffalo in 1989 and, at this writing (2019), he lives on McKinley Parkway.

The worst part of his airline career came on September 11, 2001 when he was trying to land in Newark and witnessed the attack on the World Trade Center.

In retirement, Dave is not bored. His hobbies include; gardening, golf, travel, Spartan Obstacle Course races, and Ninja Warrior competitions. He competed on American Ninja Warrior at age 69 and as of 2019, continued training to compete. That IS ...impressive!

A salute to you, Dave!

Theresa Schuta

Theresa (Terri) Schuta is another product of the Hopkins Street area. Her dad, John Drilling and mom, Catherine (Corica), along with siblings; Francine, Mary Magdeline, Patricia and John, once lived at 67 Lilac Street.

Her, and siblings attended P.S. 28 – Principal, Miss Gentile. Terri said, "As a young child on Lilac St., it was not unusual for our mom and other moms to send us to School 28 through narrow Buffalo Street that was connected to our backyard. We'd walk down Buffalo Street and go through the playground lot and into the back entrance of the school. And, we'd use the same route to go cash our dad's check at the Marine Midland Bank on the corner of South Park and Abbott."

From P.S. 28, Terri went to Saint Agatha's elementary school. The principal was Sister Kateri. After that, she went to Southside Jr. High - Principal Rocco Lamparelli. Her high school years were at South Park High - Principal John Mattimore, where she graduated from in 1978.

She recalls a time when things were simpler with few frills? How many of you can say your family didn't have a car back in the 50s and 60s? Such was the case for the Drilling family.

Terri said, "My family never had a car. My parents did all of their food shopping at Amicone's Market on South Park. Every Saturday Jimmy Housekencht would deliver our groceries. It was such a simple and wonderful life being raised in that time period."

You might think that one of Terri's favorite pastimes might have been just hanging out with the gals in the neighborhood and chatting, but actually, her favorite thing to do was playing baseball for her CYO club. But, besides baseball, other things that occupied her time were; hanging out at Boone Park as a child, going to friends' houses in her teens, and attending events at her church - Saint Agatha's.

Her close circle of friends in neighborhood and school were; Joanne Kearns, Allison Behm, Althea Duringer, Dee Dee Devole, Martha Heoflich and Michele Roberts and the Blake family of eleven. The Blake clans' names are: Jack, Sharon, Peggy, Teresa, Linda, Debbie, Mary, Jean, Patrick, Michael, David.

Those of you who were familiar with the Hopkins area Terri lived in, you might recall the stores she remembers in or near her neighborhood; Vince Amigone's Market where her mom had worked, Koch's Dry Goods and Hardware, and Campbell's Drugs Store. Herkie's Deli, Nap Robitaille's Barber Shop, Okah's Catering on the corner of Alamo, Sally Tutuska's deli on Germania and Pambina, Finka's bar near Talty's at Germania and South Park.

One of the memories of the 70s that has really stuck with her is the famous, or infamous, "Blizzard of "77." Anyone who experienced that incredible storm can never forget how bad it was.

Like many young ladies in their late teens, back in the day, Terri didn't own a car. It was the "norm" for Baby Boomers to walk wherever they had to go; unless they went to downtown Buffalo on the South Park bus number 16. Even going from the Hopkins area to the Seneca Theatre, they'd walk… as the guys would say back then, they'd "Hoof it."

Like all teens, back in the 60s and 70s, Terri enjoyed music. Her favorite artists were; John Denver, James Taylor, and Chicago. She didn't have any particular favorite songs from among that list of singers, she loved all of their songs.

Reflecting on what her old neighborhood was like, she said, "It was great having neighbors that were like family, even today, many are still close. The downside is that you can see how much it has aged, and that is has changed a lot demographically from the old days."

Career wise, the Hopkins area folks can be proud of her. As of 2019, she was South Park High's principal and getting ready for her well-deserved retirement in 2020.

Terri, thank you for being part of one of the most important things we can do for our young people - educating them!

Mary (Gugliuzza) Brucz & Co.

In January of 2020, I had the pleasure of sitting down with the Peter Gugliuzza, Mary Agatha Gugliuzza Brucz (Pete's cousin), neighbor, Dolores Antonelli Guadagno and family friend, Patty Gilmour. The first three are products of Hickory Woods, and Patty, now residing in Hickory Woods, came from Culver Street.

Just to verify once more, I asked Pete why the Hickory Woods area was called that. He said, "It was because a lot hickory trees were planted in this part of South Buffalo when they developed the area." Dolores and Mary agreed with Pete.

When I asked what the percentage of Italians made up the neighborhood, it was agreed by all that in its hay day, it was probably 75% Italians, maybe more. They all spoke about their neighborhood with nostalgic pride and the connection they had to the people there. It's still a very special place to them.

Mary Agatha Gugliuzza Brucz: Interestingly, Mary's middle name is "Agatha." As she said, "I got that name due to the generational connection to Saint Agatha's Church that was once in this neighborhood." She lives in the same house her grandfather moved in, in 1923. She said, "I have so many wonderful memories of gatherings in this house. It was the place to be for a lot of our family celebrations, holidays, and parties. It was great!"

Mary was an only child. Her father was Louis Gugliuzza and her mom, Josephine Ockibine. She attended P.S. 28 and Nardine Academy. Some of her close friends are; the McCooeys, the Webers and the Balesteris. A favorite place to socialize was Boone Park and a few stores she remembers frequenting were; Ross' Delicatessen, Talty's Tavern (South Park and Germania), and Green's Tavern. Career wise, she worked as Director of Food Service for the Cheektowaga/Sloan USFD.

Dolores Antonelli Guadagno: Before meeting Dolores, Mary had told me, "Dolores is a lifelong resident of the Hickory Woods area and in her eighties she's one of the last remaining ladies in the area from its glory days."

Reflecting back on the good old days of life in the neighborhood, Dolores said, "I've lived here all my life and am one of the last remaining seniors here. It's the best; there's no better place. There's nothing like it in the world. I feel blessed having lived in this neighborhood with all the great people I came to know. We were one big family, and I'm still very close to many of my neighbors."

She spoke about her life on Germania Street and how she lived upstairs from her parents when she got married. She said, "This (Hickory Woods) is home. Where else would I go? I just love it here."

Patty Gilmour who joined in the talk also expressed her fondness for the neighborhood. Culver Street was home base growing up, but Hickory Woods is where she feels very much at home, now.

She said, "My family lived on Culver Street, off of Hopkins. I'm one of twelve children."

Her dad was Harold Gilmour and her mom, Marie (Sullivan). The children in order of birth were/are: John, Susan, Michael, James, Kathleen, Paul, Thomas, Mary-Jane, Janice, David, Patricia and Robert.

That's quite a crowd at the supper table and even more crowded with mom and dad. People who didn't grow up with at least eight, ten children or more kids in the house have no idea what that is like. I know (one of ten) … and Patty certainly knows what social dynamics makes it all work.

Peter Gugliuazza is Mary's cousin. He grew up near his grandparent's home, not far from Hickory Woods. He said, "Although I came from Altruria, I was always here at my grandparents' house for dinners and family gatherings. As a matter of fact, when I was five or six years old and the older guys played craps at the corner of Germania and Pembina, they had me be a "lookout" to let them know if the cops were coming." He laughed and added, "When they did show up, all the guys would scatter; the cops would scoop up the money and leave." All in all, it was a friendly and very close-family community."

Pete remembered a lot about this old place. He said, "At Germania and Pembina, there was a building owned by Phillip (Butch) Tumminelo, his son Tony and grandson Luciane Mascellino. Way back, there was a tavern in the front part and a butcher shop in the back. Later, it became the well-known Garbo's Seafood Tavern that featured seafood cooked in the Chesapeake Bay style. It was run by Phillip's daughter Catherine and son-in-law, Joseph Garbo. There also was another hotel in the area. It was located at the corners where South Park, Abby and Germania come together. It was called the Oriole Hotel."

Since South Buffalo was well-known for having "a few pubs," (wink, wink), I asked Pete if he could guess how many gin mills there were in the neighborhood back in the day. He said, "Hickory Woods probably had at least 8 or 9 bars."

It was very interesting speaking to this group of Hickory Woods present and former residents. As I mentioned names like the Schipanis (Dominic & Lucy), the Dursos, the Carusos, the Forcuccis, the Di Sarnos, Dennis Starr, Ronnie Wentland, "Aunt Rosie," the Millers, and Morgantis; they knew them all. They mentioned that Aunt Rosie and Lollie were famous for their meatballs and gnocchis.

Mary said, "During the elections, I remember going with my dad to one those green voting booths, they use to place in all the neighborhoods. Later, I worked as an "election inspector" with Jenny Durso from Lilac Street, and Mrs. Marie Siska from Pembina Street."

Wondering what other places of business that were around and are now gone, the group mentioned; Charlie's Frontier Trucking on Mystic where there were cabin-like motel units and a diner for the truckers. They talked about three businesses in a row on O'Connor Street; a tavern, a butcher shop, and Elsie's Deli; three different product items, but no competition. The bar took care of providing "beer" and other alcoholic beverages while the butcher shop did "meats only" and the delicatessen offered "foodstuff" – no beer or meats. It was understood that the businesses would not compete by duplicating the items the others sold. This was community life at its best!

As Mary (Gugliuzza) Brucz said, "The neighborhood was like one big family. Everyone took care of each other. Oh, and our Catholic church at Mystic and Germania was also part of what kept the neighborhood together. It was first called "All Souls Church" and later, "Saint Agatha's," which relocated on Abbott Road."

Other Hickory Woods Residents

Making my way around through the streets of the west side of Hopkins Street, I came upon a house at Germania near Mystic that just stood out as one of the very best kept properties. Frank Schneider and Annette Daluisio reside in that two family house. Annette's dad is Mike Deluisio from Sheffield Ave.

Frank gave me names of some of the businesses that used to operate near his house. He mentioned several businesses such as; Sally's, a community store that used to sell penny candy, pop, beer, cigarette and a few foodstuff items. Two more such stores were; Joudie's, and Rosie's. At one section toward the brownfields, Frank remembers that there was a hotel for the truckers, and "Talty Pubs" located at the corner of Germania and South Park.

The Hop Inn/Can You Diggit, Rejuvenation

The Hop Inn Tavern at 317 Hopkins was once owned by a man whose last name was Swieck as of 1966. According to new owner, James Kennedy, way back it was called, Maverick, then, the Hop Inn. It was closed for over a year. In a Buffalo newspaper article in July of 2017, reporter James Fink wrote about remodeling the old establishment by its new owners.

He wrote; "James Kennedy has the former Hop Inn at 317 Hopkins Street near Tifft Street under contract and plans to reopen the tavern as a 'more adult-friendly' restaurant and bar."

Jim "Digger" Kennedy

While gathering information about the Hopkins area, I stopped in the bar/restaurant and spoke to employee Linda Cassaci who said the owners were; Jim "Digger" Kennedy and Tim Lopez from Altruria. In the same article mentioned above, Kennedy stated that the renovation plans included a small outdoor patio, a good size dining area inside and that they would offer "traditional pub menu items like chicken wings, beef on weck and other sandwiches." The revamped restaurant reopened under the name "Can You Diggit," in the summer of 2019.

While speaking to Digger, I looked around the place and saw that they had installed eight flat-screen TVs, and keeping part of the décor "the way it was," the bar had hooks just below the edge of it for people to hang their hats, coats or a more practical use, for ladies to hang their purses there. One more item that caught my eye was the brass tubular footrest that fits in with the old-style look. Nice touch!

More about "Digger"

A lot of South Buffalo guys got nicknames as they got into the various groups that hung together. Well … James Kennedy's nickname didn't come for his peers. His dad gave it to him. It had to do with when James was "Little Jimmy Kennedy."

The way he told it was, "When I was a little kid, I had this thing about going in the back yard and digging holes in the grass and dirt. This would drive my mom crazy and she'd get after me to stop! After a while, my dad said, 'Jimmy, with all that digging you're doing, you're going to dig your mother into a grave!' He said, "The name stuck to this day." And now, you now the rest of the story!

"Digger" Kennedy from Lockwood Avenue is the son of Leo and Marion (Rooth). His siblings are; Leo, Anne, Tim, Sean, Maggie-Marion.

He's a retired Buffalo Police officer who did duties at old Precinct 5 and then at the "A" District station on South Park Avenue. Some of his colleagues and friends are, Mario Pratts, Tim Lopez, Dean Jackson, John Joskowitz, Paul Kane and Eddy Standish.

Ron and George Miller
Remember Hickory Woods

Ron Miller is another Baby Boomer, along with his parents and nine siblings that hailed from the First Ward initially and ended up in South Buffalo's Hickory Woods section, on Boone Street. Like so many other folks in his area, he remembers well what it was like being part of a very large family.

The list of this fine Miller clan goes as follows. The heads of the household were Milford (Bill) or (Doggie) Miller, and mom, Eleanore (Hess). Their son Ron was the oldest, and after him were, Donna, Cheryl (Dixon), Billy, Kathy, Robbie, Paula (Kantowski), George, Suzie (Weber), and David. That's ten Millers, folks - twelve with mom and dad.

As per Ron's account of his family, his brothers and sisters went to Our Lady of Perpetual Help in the First Ward, and after moving to Hickory Woods, everyone went to Elementary P.S. 28 on South Park and Bailey. For Ron at least, it was South Park for his high school education.

Ron remembers a large family that lived right next door. The McCooey parents had eight, making this clan an even ten sharing the living space. The parents were Dutch and Loretta. The children were; Frank, June, Kenny, Sharon, Sandy, Lizzy, Kevin, and Jack.

Growing up, Ron got to know a lot of people. Here's the list he gave me of some of his acquaintances or those that were his close friends; Patti Gaskill, Steve "Skip" Gombos, Nicki Salono, Paul Furseka, Artie Eisensmith, Bobby Deitral, Bobby Panful, Bernie Kuhn, Tom & Genie Schubbe, Bill Craver, Jr. Harrie, Bobby Di'Sarno, Vinny Antonelli, Paulie Dombrowski, Jim Helding, Norm and Tom Isch, Fred Langdon, Jim Montroy, Bill O'Donnell, Bob Straines, Dave Skinner, George Setlock, Joe and Tony Szymkowiak, Gary Starr, and Tommy Di'saziac.

Answering the question, "where did you hang out...

Ron said, "I hung with the Taylor Park crew near South Park High School. Other places where we got together were; Georges Restaurant with Mrs. Mudd and Momma "K", or at Seba Bissetti's Atlantic Gas Station, the Villa Pizzeria, or at Mr. Donuts across from Park Edge. Four of us worked at Park Edge; Joe Avolio, Nino Petrilli, Tom Scubbe and me. I have great memories of our "du-wop" sessions out front of Mr. Donuts, racing on Ohio Street in my four-speed '69 Camaro. My first car was another classic, a 64' mustang (stick)."

Businesses Ron remembered

I wanted to know what businesses Ron remembered from his old neighborhood. He listed the following: Howard & Mildred Bergmans Hopkins Deli, Katie Ross' Germania Deli, Sally Tutuskas' Germania Deli, Herky's South Park Deli, Sardinia's Hopkins Market, Jack Young's Hopkins/Mystic garage that later became Norm & Ernie's Garage, Farrel's Tavern on Germainia Street, Elias' Tavern on Abbey Street, my uncle Gibby Green's Tavern on Baraga Street, Price Trucking at Bell and Germania Street, Interstate Trucking on Hopkins that experienced a lot of neighborhood vandalism!"

As for his impression of what he feels his old neighborhood is like today, he had this to say. "Too bad this neck of the woods has changed so much. It was a lot better back when I was young."

Having driven through the Hickory Woods and the rest of the Hopkins area, I agree with Ron's statement. To me, Hopkins Street seemed to have a lot of tenants that have not taken care of the properties; that would be homes and houses that are rented. Homes that are owned by the people living in them are better kept, as a whole. On some streets, one can see the pride they take in taking care of the houses and yards – good "curb-appeal."

Back to Ron and his time in his "hood," he flashed back in time to what his favorite singers, musical groups and songs were. "One of my favorite groups was Dion and the Belmonts. (actual name, Dion Di Mucci) singing "A Teenager in Love" (1959), "I Wonder Why" (1958) "The Wanderer" (1961 and "Teen Angel" (1958). I really liked Roy Orbison songs like; "In Dreams" (1963), and "Only the Lonely" (1960). Conway Twitty's 1958 song "Only Make Believe" was and still is an all-time classic. Elvis Presley's "Heartbreak Hotel" (1958) and "Hound Dog," released in 1956 were a couple of my favorites sung by the King of Rock 'N Roll. Ricky Nelson also had some great hits that I liked a lot. Songs like, "Poor Little Fool" (1958), "Lonesome Town" (1959), "Hello Mary Lou" and "Traveling Man" released in 1961. One artist that was different was, Dwayne Eddie. He put out great guitar instrumentals or was the main sound on songs like; "Rebel Rouser" (1958), "Forty Miles of Bad Road" (1959), and "The Ballad of Paladin." (1962)."

As a settled down adult, from 1965 to 1976, Ron worked construction as a pile driver for local 1976 and retired as a millwright from the GM Harrison Radiator Plant in Lockport.

Chapter 7 South Park Avenue (south)

Its people and Commerce

The South Buffalo neighborhoods were so different from what we see of them now with regards to the commerce that once existed. People with their heart still there are saddened as they ride through the area because of what they see or don't see. Gone are the many specialty shops and stores. It would be safe to say that from the good old days of my time there, at least 90% to 95% of the establishments and businesses that existed on South Park are now gone. That's how much it has changed. As you read the lists, you'll easily see what we once had.

Bob Regan who moved from Scranton PA to 149 Ladner Street in November of 1955 was a fountain of information concerning what once existed all along the southern part of South Park Avenue. You'll read more about him as you make your way through this trip. The list starts at Abbott and South Park and makes its way to Dorrance Avenue at the Buffalo/Lackawanna railroad trestle. There may be a few places missing, but most will be listed.

Although the following list of stores and businesses may be a bit boring, I felt it was very important to make it as complete as possible as a keepsake and to remember just how many businesses were there. I've weaved in personal memories, statements and stories from individuals. There were a few other businesses a bit north of South Park and Abbott Road, but, I'll start the list at that location. Some of the locations of the businesses as I head south may not be in order, but they existed in that general area. Forgive me if I missed or misspelled the names of any person or stores.

Businesses and people

At South Park and Abbott was: The South Buffalo Cab service, a Marine Midland branch that became an M&T bank and across the street was PS #28. Then, there was Hal Casey dealer, Dick Kratz Chevrolet which eventually moved to South Park and Okell Street. Russo's Trophy Room Lounge, Ray Lak's Chevrolet, Campbell's Drug Store, Strohm's Bakery, S & P, Sirett, Koch's Department Store and Dry Goods Store, McPartlan's Bar, the Red Brick Inn, the Villa Pizzeria which is now the Bread of Life Church, Sheehan Ford dealer at the corner of Koester and Holfinger's Delicatessen. Across from that is Taylor Park next to South Park High School where one of the crews that hung out there included:

Nino Petrilli, Bob Rabitore, the Bunch brothers (Dave and Chuck), George Carroll, Owen, John and Jim Bugman, [Owen died of cancer at 21], (continuing the list) …Ron Wentland, Sam Giritano, Joe Nappo, Joe Avolio, John Faliero, Vito Bovo, John (Camel Jockey) Adimey, Tony Szymkowiak, Nick Ciavarello, Larry Jones, Tom White, Rich Fuller, Jim "Fats" Billings, Mark Schmidt, Bill Craver, Paul Fraicca, Skippy Gombos, Dennis (Froggy) Starr and his brother Gary, Ed Berger, and Mike Mazur. Part of this group of guys made up what was known back in their youth as, "The Jets."

Where some of the "Taylor Park" boys above came from

And stories about them…

Dennis (aka) "Froggy" Starr lived in Hickory Woods at 280 O'Connor in his youth with his mom, Mary (née Di Sarno) and siblings, Gary and Gail. In more recent years, some of the Taylor Park guys set up a Friday noon lunch at Dennis Starr's "Side by Side Antiques" shop at 26 Abbott Road across from St. Agatha's. I stopped there on October 16, 2019 to gather information for this project. The guys provided me with great info that became a part of this book of "the way it was." Thank you, lads!

He has a love for felines and canines. He has five rescued cats in his "Side by Side Antique Shop" on Abbott, four more at home, and... 2 dogs!

He said to me, "When I bought this shop (Side by Side Antiques), and was sitting at my desk one day, I heard noises coming from the back of the store. A cat had a litter of five kittens up in the ceiling area and as the kittens were able to move, they made their way to an opening that dropped down in the wall between the drywall. I heard this meowing, so I made a large enough hole in the drywall to get the little guys out."

To his nickname, "Froggy", I'm inclined to add, (aka) "The Cat Man" or "Zoo Keeper." Dennis loves his pets. If you go in his store, you can't miss the five cats that keep him company.

Joe Avolio is also from the HickoryWoods area. His father was Gurieno Avolio and his mother, Anna D'Amore. His siblings are, Pat, Gino or (Cino), and Louise (Plizka). He loved living in Hickory Woods and meeting with friends at Taylor Park to pass the time.

Is rabbit good eatin'?

Joe recounted a story about when he as a kid and had a rabbit for a pet. He said, "I'd get discarded lettuce from the Park Edge Market and fed it to my rabbit. It got pretty fat. My grandma Rafaela D'Amore who came from the old country and was used to killing chickens in the morning back home and serve them for supper, took a hammer, hit my rabbit in the head, skinned it, gutted it and cooked it. She served it up that same night for supper but, I just couldn't eat much of it." That's "the way it was" for Joey growing up with Granny D'Amore.

Mike Mazur came from Trowbridge Street. His father Ted and mom Gertrude raised three children, Mike, Christine and Fred. His dad worked at Bethlehem Steel Plant 46 years.

A couple of Mike's good memories from his youth are his 8 years at P.S 28 and learning to play the drums. As a young adult, he formed the "Mike Mazur Band" and played in many of the local clubs.

In his 30's, he put out a 7 inch 33 1/3 EP (extended play) record with four songs on it called, "Blue Collar City," with lyrics that reflected Buffalo life. Instead of having an "A" and "B" side markings, the record reads, "East Side and West Side." The songs on the east side are, "Blue Collar City (4:18) and "2nd Shift Shuffle" (2:45). The other side had, "Queen City Bound" (2:51) and OTB Blues (4:16).

Most local Buffalo artists and bands didn't and still don't get air time on the local radio stations, but Mike Mazur's record did. It got played on two local stations; WZIR-FM and WBFO-FM. That's the way it was for Mike. At this writing, in his sixties, he still sings and plays.

John Faliero was a resident of Hopkins Street with his dad, Marino and mom, (maiden Martello). Besides John; Marion, Sam and Shirley made up the rest of that clan. To John, South Buffalo is – "home", and his special memories about living there, "The guys I hung with."

Tony Szymkowiak's father was John and his mother's maiden name - Kuras. Tony came from a family of nine children. His family lived on Baraga Street across from Gunner Greene's Bar. He loved living in South Buffalo and when asked about special memories of his youth, he simply said, "friends."

John Adimey is the son of George Adimey and Marion (Beck). He comes from Payne Avenue where he shared the house with siblings Maryann, Regina and Monica. His feelings about South Buffalo, he said, "It was the best place to live back in the day."

A younger guest from the tail end of the Baby Boomers that came around to gather at the "Side by Side Antiques" site for the Friday feasts was, **Edwin "Spaghetti" Borrero**. He used to have a "food truck" stand at the corner of Hopkins and Tifft.

Funny Story

To protect the "guilty," I'll not mention names... While speaking to Dennis during an interview with him, he recounted a story about a couple of guys he knew that got lost going around South Park Lake. Folks! It ONLY goes in a circle and there's NO WAY one can get lost! But you see, the two lads had ingested some kind of "medicine," - THC. They were wasted, and although there were at least FIVE entrances/exits in and out of there in the 60's, the effect of the meds they took numbed their ability to navigate their way out. Those of you that knew the layout of the park back in the day can relate. According to Dennis, they went round and round and round for about a HALF HOUR or so. That's scary! The moral of the story – DON'T DO DRUGS! But... they were good boys and later did well; getting married, having children and working steady jobs.

Southside Parkway
And South Park High School

So.Pk High

Southside Parkway, although very short compared to the other main Southside roads, needs to be mentioned because of one particular site; that being, South Park High School at 150 Southside Parkway. Southside Parkway starts at South Park and Como and ends at Seneca Street.

At the time of my research, South Park High was headed by Principal Theresa Schuta, with assistant principals; Molly Forero, Joshua Miller, Michael Moris and Kathleen Thomas.

Plans to build the school began in 1914 and completed in 1916. The school's moto is; Vires acquirit eundo" (meaning) "We gather strength as we go." Their mascot is the "Bear" and the yearbook is called, "The Dial."

Speaking with Principal Schuta, I found out that during the peak Baby Boomer days of the 50's, 60's, and 70's, the school had between 1,800 and 2,400 students enrolled. She said, "In 1978 when I graduated, the junior class had about 600 students and the senior class, 652. Presently, the enrollment stands at 850 with a junior class of 180 and seniors, 220. Comparing the numbers, it's a huge decline from the former years when the average family had 5, 6 to 10, even up to 16 children. In my own family, with our parents, we were 7."

When I went to South Park in the early 60s, I met people from different parts of Buffalo's south side, as well as Kaisertown and East Lovejoy. Here's list of some of the people I came to know: Alceo Aguzzi, George Amplement, Anita Branchini, Bill Cashion, Mike "Cats" Catanzaro, John J. Carney, Melanie and Judy Choyne, Angelo "Sonny" Ferrari, Dan Clouden, Joe Daleo, Will Durolek, Will Emerson, Bonnie Eich, Eddy Feneziani, Dianne Greasart, Joan and Jeanne Hartman, Noreen Isch, James Kless, Clyde Leto, Joe and Pat Liberti, Linda Marchinko, Dan and Tom Mattingly, Don McCutcheon, Denny McDonald, Marie McGavis, John Maxim, Karen Mutton, Tony Pacella, Ray Philips, Egidio Pezzuti, Jack Pugh, Harvey "Skip" Reed, Linda Rice, Nivian Rodriquez, Barry Russell, Marlene Schafer, Earl "Duke" Thompson, Greg Vaughn, Paul Whelan, Tom Willard, Joe Williams and Don Wright.

My favorite teacher was Ms. Sheila Maloney. She inspired me to write.

I knew many more, but too many to list. Reading these names, I'm sure those of you who went to South Park High in the early 60's, know most of them.

Besides South Park High, this strip of South Buffalo did not have much in the way of businesses or establishments. At 187 Southside Pkwy near Heacock Park, there was a Baptist church for a very long time and is now the "Good Shephard Community of Faith Church." There was one business that went as far back as the 50's into the 60's – Niles Delicatessen near the corner of Josie Place and Southside.

Moving along…

Going further down South Park near Taylor Park, there was a soda shop, the Capital Theater which became Fazio's Hall, and for a short time, Fazio's Peppermint Lounge. Then there was Crehan's Club Como, The Phone Booth Lounge run by James "Hobie" Lafferty, the OK Inn, Shea's Triangle Bar, Como Deli, Coster's Transmission, a liquor store, the old Post Office, an A&P Super Market, Phone Company, Sterlace Bar/Blarney Castle, Hector's Hardware, Nightengale Funeral Home, and at the corner of Tifft Street and South Park, Holy Family Church with the kindergarten through eighth grade school behind the church.

History of Holy Family Church Site

from Steve Cichon

Buffalo historian/writer, Steve Cichon provided the following about buildings at the corner of South Parks and Tifft Street.

He stated, "The home of William J. "Figgy" Connors stood at the corner of Tifft and South Park - the current site of Holy Family Church. When the church was built, the Conners' mansion was moved across Tifft Street and served as Mercy Hospital. When my grandmother was a little girl, she lived at 814 Tifft directly across from Folger Street. There were no buildings between her house and the hospital, which stood across Tifft from where the former Holy Family grammar school and Mulroy Park are today."

South Buffalo Tommy Nelson McNaughton stated, "My father-in-law's grandfather, Jacob Adrian, moved the Connors' house that stood at Tifft and South Park that became Mercy Hospital. His construction company built the church and the rectory in 1902. Photos can be seen at the present Mercy Hospital hallway near the emergency room."

Holy Family School was built in 1915 and grew to 1,500 students at one point.

Mercy Hospital as you may well know is located on Abbott Road and Lorraine Avenue. How many of you Baby Boomers were born there?

Holy Family Church is now called, Our Lady of Charity Parish at Holy Family, with their office on Okell Street at Saint Ambrose Church.

Sacristan Audrey Kunz and Holy Family Church

Audrey is the "Sacristan" for Holy Family. Her function is, taking care of all preparations for the various events; baptisms, marriages, funerals, lawn fetes and any other special event connected to the church.

She lives on Tifft Street and did so most of her life with a short stay on Kenefick Street. Her dad was Arthur Nelson Kunz who came from Strathmore Street and her mom, Jane (Panek), was a First Ward lady. Jane's dad, Anthony Panek, was a shoemaker in the First Ward. Audrey is the oldest of seven children. Her siblings are, Arthur Jr., Deborah, David, Patricia, Mary-Jane, and Karen.

As I was leaving, I stopped Audrey and pointed to the hand bell on the step of the altar. I told her, "I believed that is the same one I used to ring when I was an altar boy here in the early 60's." I couldn't help myself. I picked it up and rang it. That sound reached way back into my memory as soon as I did it. I immediately connected with the way it sounded. It was a trip going back to something like that.

Tony Orsini

Tony and Johnny Orsini were well-known by all the guys in the Hopkins, Tifft Street and South Park areas, especially as barbers for many of the Boomers. Here's what he had to say about the "good old days."

"I started out in the hickory woods area at 5, then, we moved to 23 Allegany with Mulroy playground just over the fence of my backyard. That's where I learned to pitch pennies. I graduated to higher stakes at an early age when I joined the older men in dice games every Sunday.

The funny thing about those dice games was that when we knew the cops were going to storm in to break it up, there'd be 15 or more men with suits playing basketball on the court adjacent to the where we were shooting dice; making it look like nothing 'illegal' was going on, just men having a nice Sunday basketball game before mass. The church was just a short distance from the playground. As the cops rushed in, a lot of the younger fellas hopped over the six foot fence and ended up in our cellar."

Family

Tony continued, "Like a lot of other families in South Buffalo, I had cousins that lived quite a few blocks away from me; Frank, Jesse, Pat (aka Luke), and Joe Orsini. They lived on Whitehall Street. It lines up with Cantwell off South Park and continues between McKinley and Abbott Road; about a mile away.

Living close to Holy Family, that's where I went for my elementary education. My cousins went to P.S. 67 and Saint Martin's. Two other cousins of mine lived off Seneca at 82 Armine; Lou and Rocky Fumerelle. Rocky was one of the most notable boxers in the city of Buffalo. He was known as "The Blond Bomber" and fought as a middleweight from 1955 to 1963. (You've already read up on Rocky in the Ward section)

Turf Rules

I remember going back over seventy years that we learned unwritten rules about boundaries or "turf." Some people couldn't or wouldn't go from South Park to Abbott Road or Seneca and the same for those people coming from Seneca or Abbott to South Park. Because of our diversified family roots (Italian), we were accepted in certain areas, but not other areas. That's just the way it was. South Buffalo was made up of mostly, Irish, German, Polish and Italians.

Some of the Italian families in our area were; Orsini, Morganti, Fredo, Pacella, Liberti, Forcucci, Durso, Caruso, Parisi, Petrilli, Marini, Masullo, Lobuglio, Rizzo, Miniri, Collura, Battaglia, Pasquarella, Morabito, Mariano, and several more. As you can see, there were a lot whose families originally came from "the Boot" (Italy mainland) or the "football," the island of Sicily."

The Esquires' Club

Some of the youths formed clubs. The one Tony belonged to was the "Esquires." He said, "While growing up as teens in that Tifft Street/Hopkins area, we organized a special group of friends and called ourselves, the "Esquires"." My brother Johnny, who was loved by many, especially me, with my father's help, put a stairway on the side of the garage in the back yard of Allegany so we could get to the upper section where our club would meet. I have more great memories of that time than I can count. It was special living in that part of South Buffalo."

Moving on Down South Park again…

Across from Holy Family on the same side of the South Park was Joe Corto's Barber Shop and across the street from Joe's there was Sinclair's gas station. There were a couple more businesses on both sides of South Park before Crystal. There was Biday's Delicatessen near Tifft, a hobby shop and auto parts store.

From Tifft Street to Choate my contributors remembered places like, Morrison's Delicatessen, the NU-WAY Supermarket at Richfield and Hempling's Pharmacy on the corner of Crystal. Then, there was Paul Wiles Texaco station - still there at this writing now Dick O'Neill's Auto Service. Next to the gas station was Murray's Delicatessen and next to that, the Chat and Nibble's Soda Bar. Across the street on the corner of Bloomfield was a little diner called Laddy Boys and on the other side of Bloomfield was Mueller's Tavern which first became Ann's Inn and later, the Nine-Eleven Inn.

Crossing the street, on one corner of Amber, was Gene Wahl's Tavern which became Pal Tony's Bar. It caught fire, was demolished in the late 60's. The other corner, as of 2020, it still has Mr. Submarine. It's been there since the mid-sixties. Next door was Jerry Barrett's Cycle and Machine Shop and next to that, the Liberty Bank. Crossing again, there was the Star Liquor store and next to that Louie's Hat, Shoe Repair and Shine Shop. Later, I will tell you a bit more about Louie's Shop.

A few steps from Louie's was, our beloved poolroom run by Harry Aldridge where representatives from every generation came in to shoot pool.

Harry (aka Monk) Aldridge's Pool Hall

Everybody who hung out somewhere on the strips (South Park Abbott Road, Hopkins, McKinley and Seneca Street) had special places they liked to go. For me and many others, it was Harry's Poolroom, two doors down from Nick's Texas Red Hots near Choate. We played such games as; eight ball, straight pool, oddball, five/nine, pea-pool and so on. The pool hall brought in people from all the neighborhoods. We had guys from Lackawanna, Blasdell, Seneca Street, Abbott Road, Hopkins, McKinley, the First Ward, the Valley and other areas.

From time to time, someone would get yelled at by Harry "Monk" Aldridge. Even 'Sis,' Harry's wife, who was there almost as much as Harry was, would sometimes light into some young buck who got out of hand and would chastise him like a mom would. All the boys respected her. If anyone dared go over the line against Sis, it was the wrong thing to do. All the regulars had her back and they made sure she was safe. She was like a mom or better yet, a grandma. Disrespect was not an option at Harry's pool hall.

No one can forget the way Monk would sit in his comfortable stuffed chair near the little office area with the cash register behind him. He smoked quite a bit. Both he and Sis used a cigarette holder when they smoked. We thought it was unique. It was "Harry and Sis unique". You know what I mean. Sometimes, he didn't get to enjoy his smoke very long. It's interesting that even with all the noise in the pool room he'd often fall asleep after he lit up. Watching to see how long the ash at the end of his cigarette would get before it fell right into the ten inch round, two inch high can, became a thing for us to do as we played pool. It was right below the arm rest. He'd sleep and the cigarette would burn out completely. When he woke up he'd look at his cigarette holder, take out the burned butt and simply insert a fresh one. I believe his cigarette brand was Raleigh.

Pool Room Story

One night Angelo "Sonny" Ferrari was ready to sink a ball in the corner pocket. It was a "berry" as we called them - an easy shot. Mike Smith was at the end of the table, face level with the table and urging Sonny to nail it! He hit the ball really hard. I mean hard! He sank the target ball but the cue ball kept going and knocked out two of Mike's front teeth. Ouch! I saw Mike in the spring of 2016. We talked about that incident and had a good laugh.

Harry had eleven tables in his pool hall. They were the old types from the twenties or thirties maybe. They were neat. His best table, number 4, was right near the cash register and his soft chair. From time to time he'd show the guys in the place a few trick shots. He always used that pool table, fourth from the door as you walked in. There was also one upstairs at the end of the hall. From there, we could look down at most of the other tables and catch the action.

Speaking of catching the action, the pool hall had elevated seats against the left side that were on platforms like downtown at the Hippodrome Pool Hall. They were good seats to watch some of the money games and the really good players who would take on any comers. There were some very good shooters who came by. Harry had known many of the greats like William Joseph "Willie" Mosconi (1913-1993) from Pennsylvania, world champ in the 40s and 50s; and Rudolph Walter Wanderrone Jr. "Minnesota Fats" (1913-1996) from New York, NY. Some of Buffalo's top players graced his tables. It was truly a classic pool hall in the grandest sense. At the time, we didn't fully appreciate what we had there. This is one of the things you needed to have experienced to get a true sense of what the place was like and what it offered. Those of you who played there know what I'm talking about.

One of the top players was Joe McGir from Lockwood Avenue. I remember playing eight ball with him one time for $1 a game in 1964. In the first game, he destroyed me. For the second game, he spotted me three balls. Lost that one too! Joe, knowing how good he was, gave me a fighting chance that would give me hope for winning at least one game. In the next game he spotted me five balls. Nobody ever spots anyone five balls in an eight ball game. That's ridiculous! I wasn't a bad pool player, but five balls!

"I said; "Okay, let's do it." All I had to do was sink two balls and the eight ball. No problem. He even let me break. I thought, "That's good. I get to break. Alright, I gotta win this one." Do I even have to tell you what happened? Yep. I missed my first shot. He ran that table and just laughed. I didn't. I smiled, but I was totally demoralized. Do you think I ever played any more money games with Joe? I may be dumb at times, but I'm not stupid.

Bob Regan was also one of the top shooters there. I didn't play pool too often with him. He could run a table and pull off shots I couldn't dream of pulling off. I remember one day when John Harmon from Crystal Avenue was home on leave from the Navy and Regan was on leave from the Army. Both had been regulars at the pool hall. With his usual wit, Bob said:

"Hey John, how about you and me have an Army-Navy game?"

It got a good laugh out of everyone. We knew Bob was better than most of the guys he hung out with but we didn't know how well John would do against him. Anyway, John laughed and took on the challenge. Bob won.

Classic "Monk" Whit

Dan Mattingly, another one of the Baby Boomer poolroom boys had a little run-in one day with Harry. He told me how Harry had chastised him for doing something that had upset him. He said that he lashed out at him with a tongue twister that went something like this:

"You don't know how little you know of how much you know, and that's all you know of how little you know of what you know - that's how much you know of how little you know of all you know."

I would have loved to have been there for that one. That is pure Monk classic stuff.

By the way, in the 1965 South Park High senior yearbook, the quote that accompanied Dan's name was; "Born Comedian." He was very amicable and ~ funny.

The pool room under Harry's command lasted until a bit beyond the mid-sixties. Bernie Blanchard took it over for a while and then Larry Martinez from Blasdell ran it in the late sixties. I even took a shot at running it in 1971. I think it only lasted from August till December.

Onward we go....

Next to the poolroom was Schere's Market which became Alexander's Lounge and next to that was Nick's Texas Hots. Right next to that at Choate was Ralph's Delicatessen. On the same side of South Park was, Donovan's 5 and 10 Store which later became Jack Bonner's Lounge. Liberty Bank (as already mentioned) was across the street. It is a Key Bank, now.

Nick's Texas Hots

Nick's was really unique. For starters, it was so small that maybe ten or twelve people could fit in there at one time semi-comfortably. On their limited menu were basic, breakfasts, cheeseburgers, a few different types of sandwiches and of course, their specialty, hot dogs. The price back then was 25 cents each. I'm told that in the late fifties, you could get five for a dollar. Let me repeat that, five for a dollar! The thing that made them special was the sauce. You know... that spicy brown gravy meat sauce.

It made the hot dog very different from hot dogs one ate at a back yard Bar-B-Q. It wasn't only the sauce but also the wieners and the buns. Nick's used one of the top wiener brands in the city. I don't know if they were Wardynski's or Sahlen's, but they were always good. I'm thinking, Sahlens. The buns were kept in a little container where they were slightly steamed which gave them a fresh taste. That, combined with the sauce, made for a treat anytime. Abbott Road and Seneca Street had their own hot dog restaurants too. They were all great places to enjoy "Texas Red Hots."

On your left as you walked in to Nick's was the grill by the front window and the "take-out counter with cash register. There were three men that worked there, brothers Louie and John with partner Johnny Povlakis who eventually went his own way and took over the Wayside Restaurant in the 60's. The Wayside is now owned by Dennis Spinelli from Crystal Avenue. Like me, you probably wondered who the heck Nick, was? None of the men working there was named "Nick," ...so who was it? It was part owner, Louie's son.

The place was a gold mine. One man worked the grill and the other two worked the French fry pit, made sandwiches, served the coffee, tea, milkshakes, soft drinks, and cashed out customers. There was a counter with four or five stools, and I think, three two-person tables against the right side wall. That was it. They were busy from opening until closing. You would walk in and give your order to the counterman who would repeat it with strong a Greek accent so that everyone would do his part in preparing the food and drinks. It would go something like this...

"Order to go. I need one chi-burger, one fry and one Pepsi"

OR "For counter, I need chocolate shake, two up, one fry." (Two up meant hot dogs with everything on them)

OR "Order for table 2. Two up, one chi-burger, one Pepsi, one tuna sandwich and a coffee."

The orders kept getting filled like that all day. Everything would only take a few minutes to make. A lot of the food was for take-out. When Saturday Night Live did a skit on a Greek short-order restaurant back in the 70s, anyone who went to Nick's immediately related to it. It was almost as if the skit writers of SNL had eaten there and got their idea from them. The way the comedians on that show went through their material was a lot like being - at Nick's.

Those of you who were younger can also remember that if you lingered too long at the counter or at a table, one of the owners would urge you to hurry up to make room for other patrons. Older people usually hate and left as soon as they were done. But, some of the younger folks tended to stretch their stay. Louie, John or Johnny weren't shy to tell you, "Okay, you boys are done! You here long enough! We got more people who need a seat. Let's go!"

And...that's the way it was at Nick's Texas Hot. They've been closed for years. No more Greek grill and countermen. What great memories.

More businesses

After Nick's, just around the corner from South Park, was an important part of the community; "Spoonley the Train Man," at 37 Choate. Everybody knew Chester Spoonley, and many went there to get their first train set or purchase items to add on to their existing set.

A slight aside here; I was told that Jim Morgan of the famed 1957 Ford Fairlane 500 with a 427 engine that laid rubber on South Park a few times, lived above Mr. Spoonley back in the 60s.

Across from Choate was the Liberty Bank and next door, Koch's Shoe, Spark's Bakery and Horrigan's Meat Market, then, Daisey's Deli and a Coal Company. At Lockwood was Parson's & Judd's Pharmacy with a classic soda fountain. Who can forget that? About everyone on the strip went there and enjoyed a soda, a sundae or an ice cream cone. Crossing the street at Whitfield was Bob Mallon's Men's Store and the Dudley Library. Crossing again, there's the Black Dog Saloon -still active, then there was Bell's Market which I believe was an IGA Market at one time, next was the Woodside Furniture store on the corner of Altruria Street. I could never understand why it was called "Woodside Furniture" when it wasn't on Woodside.

Marge Weber stated that before it became Mike Scrip's Woodside Furniture, it was the original South Park Presbyterian Church. A new church was built on McKinley between Lorraine and Alsace.

Next to Precinct 15 was Belvedere Cleaners where I got my sharkskin pants cleaned and pressed and next to that, there used to be a motorcycle sales and services business where I bought my first motorcycle, a 1965 Suzuki 250cc. On the other side of Altruria Street from Woodside Furniture was Lou Bielli's Dodge dealer. Along with the car dealership, there was a tavern named Agaro's Italian Restaurant which became Sperduti's, then Bill's Manor, and lastly, before it burned down, the Barber Shop, owned by Tony Orsini. Back across the street there was a shoemaker, a barber shop and another delicatessen. Next to that was Felong's Tavern. Across from Felong's at the corner of Sheffield on the same side of South Park was the Sheffield Inn which later became O'Conner's and is currently Talty's Bar owned by Dennis Talty. A few feet next from there, we had trampolines during the summer of 1963. The next two businesses were Ullenbruck's Delicatessen. According to Sam Fassari, across from Ullenbruck's, stood Broker Motors, a Studebaker/Packard dealership. At the corner of Woodside was a Cadet dry-cleaner.

On the other corner of West Woodside was La Hacienda Pizzeria. It was initially owned by Sam Coro. I seem to remember two men working the place in the sixties; I believe one was Ralph and the other Sonny. I also remember Mary Marcucci and her mother were waitresses.

In the 70's, Gary Schintzius and Doug Alessandra took it over and added submarine sandwiches to the menu. Next to that was a Helpee-Selfee coin laundromat where I and a lot of other guys remember ducking in during some cold winter days to get a little relief from the cold before continuing on to wherever we were going. Next to the laundromat was Gannon's Delicatessen. I went to Holy Family with Paul F. Gannon, one of Mr. Gannon's ten kids.

The head of the house was Joe Sr. who came from PA when the Bethlehem Steel Plant opened. Him and his wife Kathryn (Starkey) lived on Woodside Avenue along with their children; Joe Jr., Mary Pat, Jean, Robert, Irene, *Paul, Thomas, Kathryn (aka) Kathy, David, and Nelson.

By the way, *Paul invented the "Pegxco Spotter Club." It's a modified golf club for disabled golfers to sink their "T" and spot their golf ball. He passed away in 2017 from cancer and is now golfing on God's green acres.

Across from the Gannon delicatessen at Woodside was a Texaco service station. Across the street from the station, you would find Tony and Johnny Orsini's Barber Shop. Next to that was Drapper's Jewelers and Power's Drug Store. At Mariemont, there was a muffler shop. Across the street was Fachko's, which later became the South Park Grill, owned by Ron Delano. The owners and name changed again to the "Avenue Pub," or "The Pub." Next to that are Buffalo Builder's and Aberdine Glass. Behind the last two, there was a beer distributing company that lost a few cases of beer at the hands of some unscrupulous young men from the area.

On the same side of the street was Bob Senco's Gulf station. He was well-liked and respected. He would allow some of the boys who frequented the Deco Restaurant across the street to put a few dollars of gas on a tab. I can remember him spotting a few delinquent patrons hanging around the restaurant. He'd go over and threaten to send "Vinnie from Jersey with a baseball bat to collect" - if they didn't pay up. Only kidding! He was a great man. He would simply walk over to remind them it was time to settle their tab. Most of the guys did the right thing. Bob heard a lot of stories from delinquent debtors. It was like a cop stopping them for a traffic violation. Bob heard a lot of reasons for not paying in a timely manner. Anyway, they'd eventually take care of what they owed. As of 2020, Bob was still with us - in his 90s.

Deco Restaurants

Deco's founder was Gregory Deck who was born around 1900 and died in 1969. He started his business at the age of 18 with a hot dog stand back in 1918. He went to Canisius College but dropped out to expand his business. His first enclosed restaurant was situated on Eagle and Pearl Street in 1921 and the last one was locate at 389 Washington Street which stayed open until 1979. For those of you who remember and frequented the Deco restaurants way back then, you can read about Gregory Deck's amazing success story online.

In my lifetime, I've made a lot of connections, and would you believe I have one with the Deck family. I taught French to Gregory Deck's grandson, Paul Deck, at Canisius School in the early 1990s. Several years after Paul was done with school and began working, he remembered me and sent me a Christmas card, which I still have.

The Deco restaurant in our neighborhood was known as Deco 22 in the Buffalo area. Along South Park there were three and Seneca Street had five. Few people may know this, but there were 50 Decos in the Buffalo area at one time that were open 24 hours a day. Below is a list of which street and number they were located.

Where Deco Restaurants Were Located	
Bailey Ave. at 856, 1834, 2855 & 3144	Jefferson Ave. at 1316
Best St. at 393	Main St. at 248, 1001, 1390, 1528(offices), 1578, 1857, 1955, 2948 & 3292
Broadway Ave. at 171, 901 & 1650	Michigan Ave. at 403
West Chippewa St. at 29 & 142	Military Road at 340
Clinton St. at 1437	Niagara St. at 219, 1116, 1159, 1615 & 2801
Delaware Ave. at 2320 & 2944	Seneca St. at 60, 741, 1670, 2222, 2447
East Delavan Ave. at 1040	South Park Ave. at 48, 309 & 2132 (DECO #22)
West eagle St. at 24	Washington St. at 389 (last in Buffalo at 609 behind Ellicott Square Bldg.)
Ellicott St. at 169	Williams St. 426 & 771 (This last one was right near the site for road tests
Elmwood Ave. at 516	
West Ferry St. (Commissary) at 935	
Fillmore Ave. at 385, 1387 & 2385	
Genesee St. at 599 & 808	
Hertel Ave. at 1338	

An awful lot of the South Park young adults and adults spent time there. It had a lot of regulars, day and night. Harry's pool room owner would often take a walk down South Park to have his supper there.

Bombing at Deco 22

There were numerous incidents that occurred in and around Deco 22. One of our fine young men miscalculated as he backed up his car toward the side of the restaurant and ran into it with sufficient force that it knocked over the large milk machine and numerous other items off the wall.

Another time Dennis McDonald and I were sitting in a booth by the window on the Harding Street side when we saw an individual come by, open the sliding window and then walk away. Moments later, in came this canister which landed on the floor and began spewing out bright, thick orange smoke. At first, we thought it would only let out a little smoke and stop. Nope! It poured out bright orange smoke until the entire restaurant was completely filled with it. Elsie, one of the waitresses freaked out and screamed,

"It's a bomb, it's a bomb. Get out... Get out..."

Denny and I realized it was only a smoke bomb. We got out anyway - just in case. Shucks! We didn't get to finish our coffee. True to their claim, Deco did serve the best cup of coffee in Buffalo.

Boxer Bobby Aldridge at the Deco

I'd like to slip in a story about a Lackawanna/South Buffalo Golden Glove New York State Champ who was involved in an incident outside South Buffalo's South Park Deco 22. First of all, you have to know from what I knew of Bobby, he seemed nice; not a wise guy or menacing in any way. Every time I saw him he was joking and laughing with his friends or engaged in some conversation. I never saw him being aggressive or unruly. If I'd say "hi" to him, a pleasant "hi" came right back.

A friend of his, Ray Colpoys, reinforced that: "I always saw Bobby as a guy who was mild mannered and humble. He never looked for trouble or instigated bad situations. But, if trouble came along, he'd take care of business. Not once did I ever hear him boast to people in bars or anywhere else that he was a boxer. He pretty much kept that under his hat."

One night, some guy came by the Deco and hassled Bobby. He began taunting him a little with something like, "So, I hear you're a pretty good boxer. I hear you're bad. Come on, show me something. Let's see what you can do."

Bobby could have let it go, but you have to understand that for some people, a challenge is a challenge. He felt that backing down was not an option. After all, his buddies were watching and he just couldn't let it go. There was pride and reputation at stake - New York State Champ and all.

According to one of the guys that saw it, the story I got was, "the men danced around a bit and throwing a few punches trying to score. After a bit of time, Bobby threw a series of explosive punches and put the guy down."

End of story. Now, everyone knew what he could do. No real damage done to challenger beyond a few bruises to both his body and his ego.

Years later, Bobby lost his life from a gunshot to the stomach. I never got the details as to what happened exactly; only that he was shot and drove himself to the hospital. The police were called and when they asked him, "Who shot you?" ...he wouldn't give up the shooter's name; he simply said, "John Wayne."

Deco Patrons and new businesses after it closed

After I did an online post about the old restaurant, the following people let me know that they remember Deco 22 very well; how they or someone they knew, made it a regular stop. Some of the respondents were; Doreen Dirge, Alvin Pustular, Donald Watson, and Mike Farrell.

Peggy Morrell said, "My mom used to meet up there to eat with family and friends."

After it closed in the early 70's, it reopened as an "Arthur Treacher's Fish & Chips." The present owner of "Pete ~N~ Paul's Pockets" believes it was also a pet store for a short time. Pete ~N~ Paul's Pockets, was originally opened by brothers Pete and Paul Stumpt in 1982. It's been in business for nearly forty years under the same name and has been in good hands since 1994 under new owner, Gary Gerber.

Moving along...

On the other corner from the Deco was Mary Bond's delicatessen at Harding Street with its own crew of guys who would gather there to pass time. Across the street was Vanott Machine Corp. owned by Jimmy Mungovan's father and across from that was the Poplar Inn. Then there was Murphy's Insurance and Dr. Sullivan's Office. At Culver and South Park was a gas station, and across from that, still going south on South Park was Loblaw's Food Market where you got S &H Green Stamps with your purchases.

Green Stamps and More Businesses

S & H Green Stamps were popular from 1930's till the 1980's started by a couple of guys by the name of Sperry and Hutchinson.

Customers would receive stamps at the checkout counter of supermarkets, department stores, gasoline stations and other retailers, which could be redeemed for products in the S & H catalog. Businesses supplied booklets in which to paste your stamps. The downside of that process was that you had to lick all the stamps unless you did it the smart way by using a sponge. The glue tasted terrible. The amount of stamps given for each purchase was up to the business owners. Customers got one stamp for each 10 cents spent. The books contained 24 pages and filling a page required 50. Each book contained 1,200 points.

After Loblaw's closed, it became the NU-Way Market. At the edge of the parking lot going south was the second location of Tony Orsini's Barber Shop.

Tony had a door at the back of his shop that led to who knows where. While waiting to get my haircut one day I saw guys come in and disappear into that room. I asked "What are those guys doing back there?

Johnny and Tony replied: "Oh, they're just playing cards - Pinochle. They love Pinochle"   Hmmm, I'm not sure about that.

Delicatessens and Prices

In the 40's, 50's and 60's, there were between thirteen to fifteen delicatessens along the strip from the Triangle at South Park to Dorrance. Getting bread, milk, coffee, cigarettes and beer was never a problem. For many households, the corner deli was the place for most moms to get bare necessities.

A mom would pick out one of her kids, perhaps Clancy, and say, "Hey Clancy, go to the corner store and get me a quart of milk, a loaf of bread and pack of Luckys (cigarettes). Oh, and if you'd like, you can get yourself a chocolate bar. Here's a DOLLAR. Now, make SURE you bring me back the change! I need every dime I can get to make it till your father gets paid on Friday."

Non-Baby-Boomers might think… "The writer must have made a BIG mistake with the prices! You couldn't possibly have bought all those things for only a buck back then; especially when cigarettes are almost $10 a pack today!"

NOTE: 1960 – a quart of milk 20 cents, bread 20 cents, cigarettes 23 cent, and a candy bar 5cents, for a grand total of …68 cents! The extra 32 cents could buy you the Courier Express morning paper for almost a week. There you go! Today, that bill would run you over $15.00 and that 7 cent newspaper is now $2.00 each when you buy them daily.

Today (2020), a dime can't even come close to buying you a cup of coffee. Back in the 40's, 50's and part of the 60's, a dime would buy you a cup of java ~ also referred to as "cup of Joe," or a cup of "Jamoke." So, if you know the phrase, "Hey brother, can you spare a dime?" …it was generally linked to someone down on his luck looking for money to buy himself a cup of "Joe." Another phrasing was, "Hey buddy, can you spare a dime?"

Continuing with South Park businesses…

At South Park and Ridgewood was Cuthbert's delicatessen. This was the place where some of the guys would get three quarts of Topper Beer for a dollar according to one of my sources. Folks, these are quarts, not regular size bottles.

Across from the deli was PS #29 where many from that area hung out playing handball, shot dice and past time away just hanging out chatting.

Next, depending on who I spoke to, I got varying lists of the names of car dealers that occupied the following site: Across from school #29 at 2600 South Park and Okell was Schwartz Buick a car dealership that covered both corners. This is where Jimmy (Crystal Avenue) Miller bought his first car after he came out of the service in the late 60s.

At the corner of Marilla and South Park was another site for hanging out. On the corner was South Park Electric and across the street was DePottey's Pharmacy which later became McNearney's Pharmacy. Across the street, McLaughlin's Delicatessen, owned by Vic McLaughlin's dad. Marilla and South Park was full of Baby Boomers. Some of the people in the crew that hung out in that area were:

John Ranne, Billy Held, Mike Knezevic, Bob Fulmer (one of the first on the strip to ride a motorcycle), Louie Clouden with a couple of his brothers, Vinny Catanzaro and several more.

The next group was primarily from the area of Eden and Aldrich streets. Some of the names that come up in that crew were:

Doug Kroll, Doug Kelly, Jack and Dennis Sixt, Mike and Shawn Smith, Ted and Mike Pasiecznik, Dan Riordan and several others.

On the same side of the street was Murphy's Funeral Home. There were two or three more small businesses after the funeral home.

Across from Murphy's, South Park United Methodist Church, the Wayside Restaurant, Dave's Service Station and then Sorrento Lactalis Milk Products followed in line.

Wayside Restaurant

Back to the Wayside Restaurant, Johnny Povlakis from Nick's Texas Hots took over the business in the 60s. Dennis Spinelli from Crystal Avenue worked for Povlakis and eventually bought it when Johnny retired in 1979. It's a well-known eatery among South Buffalo folks with off-road parking. Great place to eat.

Not only for South Buffalo folks. Very few people know that the Wayside was a stop-over for Hillary Rodham Clinton when she ran for a seat in the New York Senate in 2000. According to Dennis' recollection, she, along with over a dozen secret servicemen and a whole bunch of her aides, about 40 in all, took over the entire restaurant. You're probably dying to know what Ms. Clinton ordered, aren't you? Well, it's TOP SECRET! Actually, she had a simple "cheese omelet" for breakfast. The stop lasted about two hours. She won the State Senate seat and served from January 3, 2001 until January 21, 2006.

The Rest of the Businesses

The next businesses were a Mobile Station on one corner of Aldrich and Cutinelli's Delicatessen on the other corner. Next to Cutinelli's was the Mr. Softy Ice Cream trucks' home base. Between Aldrich and Dorrance (city line) were; the City Line Hotel and Recckio's Bowling Alleys at 2422 South Park built in 1920.

There weren't many of us who were interested in bowling. It was for the older crowd, married couples and fans of bowling who were into leagues. I don't recall any one in any of the groups ever saying; "Let's go bowling Friday night." It wasn't our thing, although, some of the young people did bowl now and then. The Alleys were owned by Alfred Castricone

Across from Recckio's, before the railroad trestle/bridge was, Mangano's Bakery where you could actually see all the baked goods being prepared as you looked through huge windows. You could get a dozen doughnuts for 75 cents back then. Today at Wegmans they're over $1.00 each (2020). And, the last business before the bridge was/is a scrap yard called Metalico.

On South Park Avenue, there used to be over 100 businesses and establishments from Abbott and South Park to the city line. Today, you'd be lucky to find a handful of the original places. This gives you an idea of what South Park had. Sorry for any I missed. Some of the people I asked to furnish the names of businesses couldn't recall every single one. Remember this covers a span of over 60 years. I hope it brought back some neat and interesting memories.

South Park/Lackawanna Border

The Astro-Light night club and Drinking

The next point of reference was the railroad bridge/trestle beyond Dorrance - the South Buffalo-Lackawanna border. We had little interest in going beyond that point. The only attraction was South Park Lake and the Botanical Gardens. Sometimes, we would go into Lackawanna to attend Friday night dances at OLV High School or go to a carnival on Ridge Road. As we got older, there was the "Astro-Light Night Club" on Ridge Road where we'd go to hear some of the best bands in the area and hang out with friends.

One of our guys, Ray Colpoys, tended bar there. Again, eighteen was the legal drinking age then. It was pretty cool getting your Sheriff's Card as a picture ID to get into bars. Our driver's license in those days didn't have our picture and was only a thin card with basic information. It stated ones name, address, birth date, height, weight and eye and hair color. To get into bars a lot of underage guys and girls, usually 16 and 17 year olds) would simply get someone's license that had matching height, color of eyes and hair and a birth date making them eighteen. I still have my Sheriff's Card.

Here's a quick anecdote about ingesting too much alcohol as a beginner drinker. It was pretty cool as you started downing a few bottles. But when the "alcohol snake" bit you, you'd either get; falling down drunk, pass out, or become really sick and find yourself "bowing down" to a toilet bowl or the ground to purge out the "evil brew."

The room is spinning

If none of those things happened, perhaps you remember lying down on your bed and feeling just "one click" away from vomiting when the room started spinning and you ended up yielding to the porcelain bowl or on the floor. The funny thing about laying there and the room starting to spin; how many of you remember putting one foot down on the floor hoping to stop the wild spin? That never worked! Glad to say I didn't repeat over drinking after a couple of those extremely, nauseating room-spinning episodes. I haven't drunk since the 70's.

Chapter 8 - Bars

Our Social Network System

One thing about bars everywhere in the neighborhoods is that people from various groups came to socialize. Some bars were frequented by mostly older people in the neighborhoods while other bars were mostly for the younger crowd.

Inside these gin mills, there would also be different crews who hung and drank together. From time to time guys from one crew would walk over to another group and talk about any number of subjects from up-coming get-togethers, who died, who was getting married to who, for ball games, parties or sometimes, someone had a question that needed an answer from guys of another crew. Someone might have heard that so and so did this or that, and there was the curiosity to find out exactly what happened and get as many details as possible concerning the "hero" or "culprit."

Examples: When did Bob and Marie get married?" Or "Who started the fight during the football game between South Park and the guys from Abbott Road or Seneca Street?" Or "What caused Teddy to crash his car out there on McKinley?" Or "What started the fire at Pal Tony's at the corner of Amber?" Or "Who cut down the tall pine tree at the McKinley-Red Jacket circle?"

On the last item, somebody knew. Some laughed at the downed tree incident on McKinley (McClelland Circle), but a lot of folks took it very personal; feeling as though someone messed with their neighborhood and they - didn't like it!

Not all, but some of those familiar social networking bars on the south side of Buffalo were or are: the First Ward's Swannie House on Ohio and Michigan Streets, McCarthy's at 73 Hamburg Street, Adolf's Old First Ward Tavern at 555 South Park, and neighbor to the Ward, Tilly's on Smith Street in the Valley.

In the First Ward, lots and lots of history and memories were made at the Swannie House on Ohio Street and the Malamute at South Park and Michigan, now the Ballyhoo.

Further down on South Park and Germania, near the Republic Steel plant was a Hickory Woods inn called the Triangle Saloon (now closed - once was one of four Talty bars.) Next bar, the Trojan Room located next to the bank near the corner of South Park and Abbott. Here's one where people wanted to know who took a pet pony some kid in the Ward had, loaded it into a convertible, took it to the Trojan Lounge and had some girl ride through the bar a la "Lady Godiva." Who were those fine upstanding young men? Most of the people who witnessed the episode …knew.

Moving further down South Park, there was Jimmy Russo's Trophy Room where they had great bands playing there and then, McPartland's a bit further south. Next, the Nine-Eleven Inn at 11 Bloomfield and the Black Dog Saloon across from old Precinct 15.The Hop Inn on Hopkins, renamed - Can You Digg It - with owners James "Digger" Kennedy and Tim Lopez. Back to South Park, and Talty's at South Park and Sheffield.

Going to Abbott Road, there were many more bars such as Griffin's Irish Pub, the Buffalo Irish Center, Smitty's/Doc Sullivan's and Molly McGuire's.

Seneca Street has and had a ton of watering holes. Starting with the longest standing "inn" at 2423 Seneca, you have Daly's Tavern. Going north and past the Seneca Theatre, we have/had Shanahan's, the Blackthorn, and the Rush Inn.

These are just a few, and I mean just a few, of the gin mills the South Side once had. More will be said about some of the bars already mentioned.

Paul Roorda and his crew at "Park Avenue Imprints" in Lackawanna have produced a T-shirt and hoody with the names of all of the past and present South Side gin mills he could find. It's very impressive.

The Reunion at Talty's - Baby Boomers Reminiscing

It was at a reunion at Talty's Tavern in 1999 that inspired me to write this book. I heard many of the guys talking about what South Buffalo used to be like, all the guys they knew, the stores and businesses that were there, and what the neighborhoods were like. They talked a lot about what they remembered and missed. I thought it would be great to have a book that would feature a lot of what we Baby Boomers once shared back in the 40s, 50s, 60s and 70s.

The idea of a South Buffalo reunion was sparked by Lockwood Avenue Kevin McCarthy's death in January 1999. Joe McGir (deceased 2007, Lockwood boy) was in town from Florida. Dennis Talty, Danny Jordan from Marilla, Joe Nappo (deceased 2006 - from the Taylor Park crew) and several others from the South Park area were at a concert at the Buffalo Marina in August of 1999. I asked those who were there to spread the word that we'd do an impromptu reunion of the South Buffalo crews at Talty's Bar at Sheffield and South Park. I asked a few of the guys to call anyone they knew and tell them to meet there August 27, 1999.

Besides some of the guys mentioned above, me, Bob Regan and Butch Wilson were very instrumental in spreading the word about the reunion. The night arrived and at least thirty-five to forty people showed up. It was mostly guys who came from several crews of different neighborhoods and age groups. It was certainly, a guys' night. It wasn't a large number considering the couple of hundred guys or more everybody knew up and down the strips of South Park Avenue, McKinley, Abbott and Seneca Street. But it wasn't disappointing at all.

At that first get-together, the people that attended loved it and ask if we planned on doing it again. We did, and in December of '99, it happened. This time, about seventy-five or more guys and some ladies showed up. What a gathering it was. Dennis Talty held at least two a year for several years from then on; one in the summer, and one between Thanksgiving and Christmas. As of 2019, Dennis still put out the invitation for the South Buffalo "old timers" to gather at Sheffield and South Park.

Every time we got together since 1999, we'd see someone new popping in. One of the guys who finally made an appearance was Bob Domzalski from Amber Street. I remember coming in to Talty's and Roger Pasquaralla asked me, "Hey Rog, do you remember this guy?"

I took a good look but I didn't recognize him. He looked like one of the guys from ZZ-Top with long grayish hair and a long grey beard, but that smile... it was the same one I remembered from when he walked the neighborhood as a young man. It took me a little while and then it hit me. "Bob Domzalski!"

It was great seeing him and chatting a bit. Some guys hadn't seen each other in over 40 years. It was fun going over events, memories, and stories about our lives there. At our first reunion, some of us sat down and started counting guys who had passed on. We came up with nearly 40 names. From that first reunion until 2016 we lost between 15 to 20 or more people. That brings the total to more than 50 of our Baby Boomers, gone.

Dennis Talty

Dennis Talty from Lockwood Avenue has been a great promoter of South Buffalo and Irish Pride. He is a Holy Family and Timon High grad and studied at Bryant & Stratton School of Business. His dad's name is James and mom, Helen (Shannon) born in Buffalo. Dad came from County Clare, Ireland and his grandmother on his mom's side was from County Roscommon, Ireland.

Although he has lived in other houses as an adult, after his parents passed away, he came back to live in the same Lockwood Avenue house where he was raised. Not many of South Buffalo's sons or daughters can claim that. I was told that his family has been in the "pub business" for over 100 years...all named "Talty's." It all started with his Uncle Tony and Uncle Joe. Both Taltys opened bars back in the 30's. Joe opened what is now the Black Dog Saloon on South Park and Tony opened one on Bloomfield near South Park where tavern Nine-Eleven is located. Lastly, we come to Dennis and friend Bob McConnell who took over O'Connor's Pub in 1984 at 2056 South Park and Sheffield and named it, Talty's Tavern/Night Club. It provides its patrons with great atmosphere and top shelf music by some of Buffalo's best musicians. Dennis said, "Between O'Connor's and Talty's, this bar has been in business for over seventy years."

Bedsides the great mix of people, the drinks and music, Talty's has a pool table and one of the very few shuffle boards around. You'll also find an old style wooden phone booth with the seat and coin telephone still intact. It's NOT a rotary dial type, and as with the few existing mounted phones you find in area businesses, the service has been disconnected.

I believe the phone companies should still have a few phone booths around for older people that don't have cell phones, or to be able to have a place in noisy facilities where people could have a quiet, private conversation. Also, in case someone's CELL becomes inoperable, it'd be a good stand-by asset. Just saying!

It's worth mentioning that Dennis lived in Ireland in the 70's after a stint in the Army. He ran his aunt's pub for a couple of years that was left to his father after she passed away. As he tended the pub, the locals came up with a nick name for the six foot plus young man from the States; they gave him the name, "Big Yank."

Back in the States, from his bar on South Park, Dennis established the "Shortest Saint Patrick's Day Parade." It goes ONE BLOCK ...from Woodside to Sheffield. And, of course, he is the parade's "Grand Marshall." Once the short parade is over, everyone goes in to celebrate with food, music and a few pints of a mixture of; barley, water, hops and yeast ...called BEER!

Billy McEwen,   Joe Head,   Jim Brucato

Bob McConnell from Lockwood was partners with Dennis Talty for sixteen years. Jimmy (Crystal Ave) Miller bartends on occasion, and for years, Bobby Hartman from Lockwood was in charge of scheduling bands that came in to play four to five nights a week. Billy McEwen was elected to the "Buffalo Music Hall of Fame" in 1989," Joe Head in 1992 and Jim Brucato, around 2011.

Classic story

While we have Billy McEwen in sight, I have to share a story about Billy's son, Maxwell (Max), who passed away in December of 2016. As part of Max's eulogy, this is how family friend Joe Head told the story,

"Being of Scottish blood and keeping with South Buffalo traditions of promoting his heritage, Max and some other South Buffalo Scottish-blooded lads wanted to honor Scotland's patron saint, Saint Andrew, on or about November 30th 1990. They put on Scotsman's kilts and paraded themselves in their fine-looking attire at one of their favorite pubs.

When their friends saw them, someone said, 'Hey, those are great-looking kilts, man! Didn't know you guys owned any. Where the heck did you get 'em?

Max answered, 'Oh, they're not ours. One of my friends has a sister with friends who go to Mount Mercy; we borrowed the girls' skirts to take the place of the kilts."

Here's a fitting Scottish saying for the lads' daring spoof, "Yerr aff yerr heid!" (You're off your head!/ You're crazy!) Crazy maybe ...but sure is funny as heck! Tis a grrreat story!

Chapter 9 A few Individuals'

Memories of the South Park Area

The following individuals contributed to this book with some of their memories of "the way it was" in South Buffalo. They provided names of friends, places they hung out at and activities that occupied their time.

Marilyn (Sue) Lafko

Marilyn (Sue) Lafko like several of the folks you'll bump into in this book came from the Valley initially and it still has a very soft spot in her heart. Her dad's name is John and mom, Mary (Mraz). She has three siblings; Carol, Chris and Barbara. She and her siblings first attended P.S. 33 and Saint Stephen's Elementary in the Valley then, Holy Family after the family moved to Crystal Avenue, off South Park.

At Holy Family, her favorite teacher in 7th grade was Sister Mary Luke. That's where she established her first close circle of friends that included; Sue Padolic, Nancy Cole, Steve Nelson, Mike Grogan and Mike Gaughan.

Some of the best memories of her teens were; attending South Park High School, going to dances at Timon, Fazio's Hall, Tin Pan Alley at Bailey and Lovejoy and listening to music. Her favorite singers and groups back in the day were; the Four Seasons (with *Frankie Valli), the Temptations, Marvin Gaye and Chicago. Her favorite song was "December 63" recorded in 1963 by the Four Seasons.

*Frankie Valli was the front man for the Four Seasons beginning in 1960. He was born Francesco Stephen Castelluccio, May 3rd 1934 in New Jersey. His first successful solo single in 1967 – "Can't Take My Eyes Off of You."

One of her favorite things to do while growing up was spending most Sundays at her grandparents' house for family get-togethers. Other memories she has of her youth are places she frequented; the Neighborhood House on South Park near Tifft, Hempling's Drug Store, Corto's Baber Shop, Morrison's Deli, Dr. White's Office, Nick's Texas Hots, and Donovan's "Five & Ten" on the corner of Choate.

South Buffalo is special to Marilyn. Thinking about her time growing up, she said, "I remember everyone getting along back then, neighborhood kids playing together and all the neighbors knew each other. Large families like the Clearys with nine children provided the neighborhoods with a lot of kids to play with. Today, I only know a few close neighbors and don't see many kids playing outside like there used to be. Things have really changed."

For her career, she worked as a secretary, and subsequently, as a technician for Verizon.

Butch Wilson

Butch and his crew came from the area near PS #29. Several guys he hung with were:

Jack Gallagher, Billy Held, Bob Fulmer, the Burketts, Robert Clouden, Joe O'Holloren, Gerry Hurly, Ed "Stosh" Mendefik, Charley Pierce, Horst Sanders, Tommy Best, Jack "Jet" Jackson, Doug Kroll, John Ranne, Doug Alessandra, Tom Hurley, Dan Shea, Vinny Catanzaro, and Tom Rogers.

As teens, their hang outs were in front of Marge's Deli and Mary Bond's delicatessen. He remembers sledding at Lockwood Hill and playing Relievio at the Latona Court Apartments' playground. In his late teens he often patronized the Deco and Harry Aldridge's poolroom. Butch concluded his contribution to this project by stating, "I never regretted being from South Buffalo. There's no other place like it and never will be." Oh, the memories!"

Ann (Kenefick) Fitzgerald

When I asked Ann where she hailed from, without pausing she said, "I grew up in the Holy Family Parish." (Parishes were how people connected to the area they belonged to). She lived on Olcott and then Tifft Street with dad Joseph Kenefick (from 1st ward) mom, Catherine Barrett (from Crystal Ave), sisters; Teresa (Tess) Kenefick Sroda, Mary Kenefick McGrath, and brothers; Joseph and John Kenefick.

Coming from a large family myself (10 kids), I asked Ann about large families she knew around her neighborhood. She said, "The largest one I knew was the Kuebler family with 10 children; most everyone else had 5 kids; the Murphys, Dillsorths, O'Connells, and the Nowadlys,

She attended Holy Family under principals; Sisters Mary Gaudentia and Sister Mary Carole. After elementary school she went to Mount Mercy Academy. Her favorite teachers at Holy Family were Sisters Sharon Ann and Sister Joel. At Mount Mercy, it was Sister Thaddea, who by the way, taught her dad Joe Kenefick in the First Ward.

One of her favorite pastimes was Holy Family softball games. And, like so many of the youths back then, Ann hung out at Mulroy playground or at friends' houses on Alleghany and Folger, Caz Park.

Ann's circle of friends in her youth and teens were; Emma Mesanovic, Deb Griffin, her sisters, Dawn Dillsworth. At Mount Mercy; there was; (The "Herd" with Joan Kirchofer, Chris Fennie, Lenore Durenbeck, Nancy Wutz and Eileen Hanley.)

I wanted to know what her best memories of the 50s, 60s, or 70s in South Buffalo were, she said, "I loved playing softball, hanging around with my friends, walking to school (Holy Family and Mount Mercy) with friends, working at the Villa Pizzeria and later, at TOPS markets."

As I did with many people that I interviewed, I wanted to know what her first car was, the year and cost. She replied, "My first car was a Plymouth Fury III Automatic that cost me $500."

Her Life in the neighborhood

About what life was like in her old neighborhood in the 50s, 60s, or 70s, she said, "In the 60's -70s, Tifft Street was full of kids. Parents knew every kid - so you were careful how you behaved and were respectful.

With regards to kids in school, she told me, "In 1969, in my brother John's Kindergarten class at Holy Family, there were am and pm classes (totaling 4 classes) with 30 kids in each class; lots of Baby Boomers. One Saturday, it had snowed so much that on Sunday for the 9:00am Mass, the streets were full of kids getting to church; the nine o'clock mass was obligatory for the Holy Family students.

When thinking about what her old neighborhood is like today, Ann had this to say. "There are many changes; some good, cleaning up Mulroy Playground, for instance. Other changes, maybe not so good. The community has changed economically. Many families have single parents; not like the old days when most households had a moms and dads. The family structure has changed radically, making today's family life more stressful and demanding."

All of the Boomers enjoyed listening to early Rock and Roll or pop music. I asked Ann who her favorite singers were during the 50's, 60's and 70's. She said, "I liked the Supremes, the TOPS (Four Tops from the 50s and the Box Tops from the 60s), Aretha Franklin, the Beatles, and the Rolling Stones."

Her favorite song back then was, "It's Only Rock n Roll" (And I Like It - 1974) by the Rolling Stones.

As with all of the Baby Boomers, Ann grew out of the teen years into adulthood, got married to a former First Warder (Tim Fitzgerald) and had three great boys; Tim, Mike and Brendan. I had the privilege of teaching Tim and Mike at Canisius High School. Both were great young men.

Job wise, Ann ended up as an administrator for the Buffalo Public Schools.

Bobby Greene

Bob lived on Harding near the Deco#22 Restaurant. He treasures the memories of the old neighborhood; the stores, the playgrounds, the old pool room, the bars; but most importantly, all the people he came to know and hang around with. The numbers of people he actually knew and hung out with were well over 100 individuals. He knew and hung out with people from all of the four main South Buffalo streets. One name he mentioned to me several times was "Jeff Taylor" from Seneca Street.

His close circle of friends included: John Maxim, Dan Griffin, John Woodman, Allen Yox, Jim McCrory, Ray Wade, Mike Sperduti, Jerry Quinlan, Skip Ganger, the Cunningham and Jordan brothers, Ed Baun, and Billy Hillman.

When asked what he loved most about being a South Buffalo son, he said: "South Buffalo was one of a kind in the 50's, 60's and 70's. There was no place like it back then. It was very special. As I get older and talk to other guys from that time, the feeling is, we wish the old neighborhoods could be the way they were. Younger people today have no idea how great it was. It can't be put into words. It was something that had to be lived to understand. It was awesome!"

Kathleen Pugh

Kathy's clan first came from the Seneca/Babcock area – Orlando Street. Dad's name was Arnold (Buddy) and mom, Elizabeth (Tobin). Together, they raised six children; Patricia, John (Jack), Kathleen, Daniel, Rosemary and David.

Like so many young people living off one of the South Park streets and being Catholic, Kathy went to Holy Family where Sister Gaudentia was principal at the time and her favorite teacher was Sister Mary Austin. After elementary school, she was off to Mount Mercy High.

Her close circle of friends were; Barbara Buckley, Lisa Rainville, Nancy Nightengale and Linda McGee.

Like other kids where she lived, she was very familiar with certain stores and businesses. She mentioned Parson's and Judd's Pharmacy, Chat N' Nibbles Restaurant, Nick's Texas Hots, Woodside Furniture and the Deco Restaurant.

Some of her best memories were; going to drive-in movies, day trips to Crystal Beach in Canada. And her thoughts about the old neighborhood of days past, she said, "I remember how all the families looked out for one another and the kids."

Her views of how things are today in her old neighborhood, she said, "Things have really changed. You can see that it isn't as close-knit as it used to be. It's too bad! It was so different, so much better."

As an adult, Kathleen found work as an office clerk, later, as a Postal Service window clerk and eventually moved on to work for an insurance company and lastly, as company associate for a propane/welding outfit.

Ray Mattingly

Ray remembers a lot of the same things Butch remembered. He added that the guys would play steam ball behind the NU-Way Market and took swimming lessons at South Park High School on Saturday mornings. He gave me a neat bit of information about the purchase power of items costing less than 50 cents. For instance, he said that at Mary Bond's delicatessen he could buy a peanut stick, a small coke and a Superman comic for 25 cents and a liverwurst sandwich for 15 cents. "When you got to smoke cigarettes, you could get a pack for 26 cents."

Pat Nightengale

Pat's memories: "I was the fourth of seven children. It was more common in the fifties and sixties to have large families. South Buffalo had distinctive neighborhoods where the older kids looked after the younger ones. In my case, the neighborhood was South Park Avenue from Tifft Street and going south to about Ladner Street.

It was a time of families. Fathers worked and mothers were home taking care of everything. For better or worse, the older kids were in their own way, mentors. There was a stair-step approach from the older kids to the younger ones. Handed down were; the rules of ice hockey on frozen ponds, street games such as releivio, and kick the ricket. There were always pickup basketball, football and baseball games in the street and at Mulroy playground. Teams were picked by the older captains; the younger ones hoped not to be selected last. Paper routes were handed down from older kids getting their first real jobs. They got jobs at the Park Edge Market, or one the local pizzerias or other neighborhood shops. Many of us learned to smoke our first cigarettes as young as 13 years of age, to look cool.

These were happy times where simple victories were acknowledged, and losses were comforted by moms and dads. Lifelong friendships were developed with real community spirit and pride in being able to say, 'I'm from South Buffalo.' Although many have stayed and others moved away, we continue to embrace and share our learned values of community, respect, patriotism, honesty, and fairness. This was a place and a time that is hard to explain. It had to be experienced."

Billy McEwen and the Neighborhood

Billy remembered many things about the old neighborhood such as going to Ullenbruch's Delicatessen between Sheffield and Woodside on South Park as a teen. He mentioned that he never saw Norm Ullenbruch without a cigarette in his mouth. "He would treat all the kids as if they were his own."

If the boys perused the comic books too long, he'd say to them:

"Hey you, gonna buy those comic books?! This ain't no library you know!"

He remembered Broeker Motors at the corner of West Woodside that sold Ford Edsel cars in 1958 and 1959 as well as Studebakers and other used cars. Also, "Joe the Butcher" from Food Land at South Park near Altruria.

Bill said, "At noon, Joe would run across the street to Felong's Saloon for his liquid lunch. It was amazing that he never lost any fingers while cutting meat after coming back from those lunch breaks."

Another unique business Billy remembered was Cook's Shoe Store between West Woodside and Ladner. He said that he and others would go in and put our feet under a gizmo called a fluoroscope. It was an X-ray device "We'd put our feet under the scope, push the button and we could see the bones. I'm surprised after all the X-ray exposures we got that any of us are still alive."

He recalled Powers Drug Store between Ladner and Reading. He said Mr. Powers used to sell Wing cigarettes for 23 cents a pack. Billy would fib and score some smokes for himself. He would say "Yeah, they're for my father."

He also remembered La Hacienda Pizzeria at the corner of South Park and West Woodside. He said that he'd go in there, split a small pizza and two cokes with a buddy for 55 cents each. Speaking of good prices, he remembered Mangano's Bakery next to the railroad bridge before Lackawanna where you could get a donut for a nickel, or a dozen for 60 cents. Today, the average cost of a donut is about $1.10 each. Let's say it's $13 a dozen. That comes out to be 22 times the price from the old days. Doesn't it make you a little sick? Talk about inflation! It's kind of scary when you look at it that way. By the way, there was no sales tax on foodstuff like that, not even at the restaurants.

Nancy Zoldos' Memories

Nancy is the daughter of John J. Zoldos and Marilan (Stanton). She's one of five children; herself, Darwin, John, Scott and David. They were once citizens of our well-known Kaisertown until Mr. and Mrs. Zoldos moved their clan to Marilla Street in South Buffalo.

The children attended P.S. #72 on Belvedere St. behind Mercy Hospital, and for Nancy's high school years, it was baker Victory. The principal at the time was Willian S. Hubbard. Her favorite teachers were, Claire Wiest, Mrs. Steen and Art Schummacher.

Her close circle of friends were; Bridgid McDonald, Peggy and Eileen Herbst, Lynn Lyons, Patty Zappa, and Jimmy Morgan. Some of the friends she mentioned came from large families; the Herbst from Athol St. had ten children, the McDonalds from Cumberland had seven, and the Faheys from Edgewood had eight children.

Some of her fondest memories from her time back in the 60's and 70's are, her time in grade school, K through 8, patronizing the many small local businesses and knowing the people, and the neighborhood where she lived. At a young age, Nancy had an inclination for art, music, and athletics. Her hang-outs were on Athol Street, Abbott Road, Saint Thomas Aquinas Church, and school

When asked what she thought about her old neighborhood, she said, "It was a very cohesive place to live. It was great having a lot of kids around with which to play and befriend. Coming from Kaisertown where the majority was German and Polish, in South Buffalo, I quickly realized that it was filled with mostly Catholic Irish kids. Many of them became good friends."

Her thoughts about the way the neighborhood is today, she said, "A lot changed over fifty years, and although the neighborhood may not be as close knit as it was back in the day, it remains a very special place. I will always love South Buffalo, and although I now live in Hamburg, in my heart, South Buffalo will always be home".

Moving to Nancy's first car; she had a 1979 Thunderbird automatic; bought for the tidy price of $2000.

And, staying with the time period, I wanted to know what pop singer or group she liked back in her youth, she said, "I love the Rolling Stones and Soul Music. The songs I really loved to hear were; 'Color My World' from Chicago (1970), 'Stairway to Heaven' from Led Zeppelin (1971), and 'Sugar, Sugar' by the Archies.

After earning two College Degrees and doing a stint working for several large Buffalo Companies, Nancy quickly realized the "corporate world" wasn't for her. She spent the next twenty years working in an environment much more to her liking, The Left Bank Restaurant. Nancy is now enjoying her retirement, and still makes almost daily visits to South Buffalo, where much of her family still resides.

Joe Parisi

Joe is a former Holy Family school student who, with his older brother Sam, lived right across the street from the school. He still lives in South Buffalo not far from where he grew up.

One of the first things he mentioned was Harry's Pool Hall. "This is where all the young guys learned to play pool." He also mentioned a rival pool hall owner, Joe Licatta. As Parisi remembers, "That's where the big money games were played." He too, remembers Mulroy playground with George Hermann, where all who went there learned to play sports. He recalled the Sunday dice games as one of the less glamorous uses of the park. Besides the poolrooms and Mulroy Park, Joe spoke about the forts in the Tifft Street fields. Another fond memory was Fazio's Capital Hall where he went to Friday night dances. He talked about the sandlot tackle football games every weekend at Mulroy playground. He bragged that the "South Park boys never lost to any of the other neighborhoods."

He brought up South Park and Timon High noting that the people from those schools all meshed together from South Park, Abbott Road and Seneca Street. He remembered that there were a few fights between the neighborhoods. "There was nothing new about that. I think people from different neighborhoods always had some sort of territorial thing going on."

He noted that most of the guys from all areas of South Buffalo served in the Viet Nam War during that time.

Terry and Joan (Colern) Shanahan

Terry and Joan are both from the South Park area. Terry came from a relatively small family compared to Joan. Joan's parents were; her dad Sonny, mom, Gert (Curtin), the children: Catherine, Mary Pat, Trudy, George, Joe, Billy, Mike, twins…Jean and Joan and Patrick.

They talked about many of the same places already mentioned in the list of businesses along South Park. Some that came to their minds; the old post office, Pat's Shoe Store at the corner of Olcott with the A & P Market across the street. Horrigan's Meat Market at Choate, Sputniks Bakery, Abirigo's Pizzeria at the corner of Altruria where Joan's big brother Joe Colern worked. She did her Christmas shopping at Donovan's Five & Ten Store on the corner of Choate. She remembers the soda fountain at Parson's and

Judd's Pharmacy and Biddies Candy Store next to the Neighborhood House #3 not far from Tifft Street. At the Neighborhood House, they offered music lessons to Girls Scouts as an after school activity. Then, there was Murray's Deli, Chat Nibbles and next to that, Gene Wahl's Tavern at the corner of Amber. Joan and Terry remember Precinct 15 with Officer McDee being a favorite neighborhood officer on the beat when it was common to see them actually walk the main streets of the neighborhoods. Most of the folks got to know them personal and up close. It made for a better connection between the law officers and the locals.

James Shine

James (Jimmy) Shine, son of First Ward Richard (Red) Shine and Alice (Clancy) Shine was a resident of Alamo Place in South Buffalo. Jim said, "My dad came from Mackinaw St. and both of his parents were 'seawall beacher's.'" Jim Shine had cousins in the Ward; Tommy, Jack and James (Jimmy) Shine. The three brothers ended up moving to Mariemont Street in the early 60's.

Tim Bohen, in his book about Buffalo's Old First Ward called "Against the Grain," he talks about the seawall area beach dwellers (mostly Irish). He wrote that around 1837, about 1,000 "seawall beach residents" lived on a 3,770 feet long strip of Lake Erie shore near the present day Coast Guard Station on Fuhrman Boulevard. Tim stated that the area had "its own shops and amenities," and that there was even a church there – Mother of Mercy, along with an elementary school.

Jim also lived on Sheffield and Dorrance. He attended school #28 when he lived on Alamo. He is part of the Baby Boomer generation that enjoyed all of the things every other member of that generation did.

Like so many Buffalo area blue collar families, his clan experienced low times. In the late fifties, his dad was laid off from the grain mill and things got tough financially.

Jim said, "I remember that when it was time for a coal delivery to stoke the furnace, my dad could only afford a quarter of the load and the gas heater was turned off, and turned back on certain days of the week. When he needed to get a chunk of money quickly for whatever reason, he didn't go to the bank. He'd take us for a ride to some First Ward bar where a guy named "Stoney" would lend people cash that he kept in a cigar box behind the bar. My dad would pay him back a little at a time and Stoney kept track of who owed what in a little black book."

One of Jim's childhood hick-ups was that he and a friend once kept a large dog in his dad's garage. It was Mr. Morrissey's large Collie. After his mom found the canine and harangued the boys for having him in there, little Jimmy said to her, "We fed him peanut butter sandwiches and gave him water. We only rode him a couple of times!" After that confrontation, the dog was released.

Jim remembers his parents going out with aunts and uncles in the neighborhood. Cousin Ron Lystad would watch his own two brothers and him and while the parents were out. They weren't allowed to go out, but broke that rule every time. Jim said they'd head for South Park Avenue and check out the guys and girls hanging around the corners, the cool cars burning rubber. He recalls the neon sign at Sapar's Grill and a trucker unloading brand new '57 Chevys at the car dealer. What was unique about the new cars being shown off was that they would put out those huge spotlights that sent a beam of light to the sky as a way of drawing people in to check out the latest models.

At age 18, Jim worked at Buffalo Ornamental Iron Works 88 Beacon Street off of Hopkins, a business owned by the Kalenda family from Spalding Street and run by Art, Jack, Frank and Bobby. He remembers cashing his first paycheck at Teddy Swick's Hop Inn Tavern on Hopkins. He said, "Being 18, with a job, money, friends and my '60 Chevy, I felt I was on top of the world."

His first car was a standard transmission, stick shift, costing him $150.00 and $175.00 for insurance back then. So...what's your insurance costing you, today?

When asked if he knew any large families in his neighborhood, he said, "I lived next door to the Murtha brothers, eight of them! Come supper time, their grandmother would call each by name in her high Irish voice like a song. My dad would say, 'Here goes the alphabet song again.'"

Part of his family activities was to go to McCarthy's Bar on South Park where they had a juke box and he listen to the songs and watch his parents and aunts and uncles dance. He said, "Later in life, it was me and friends singing along to some of the best music ever, the 60s to the 70s."

Other memories he had of the 60s and 70s were; "Ash trucks going by, stinking to high heaven, a lot of boys carrying scout Swiss knives, the "rag man" coming through the neighborhood peddling rags, or sitting on his front porch on Sheffield and hearing stories from his upstairs tenant Harry Lindner, a World War I veteran born in 1899. We'd share beers and he'd reminisce about the war, Prohibition, the depression years, and the end of World War II.

Oh! We can't forget an incident that entailed, garage roof trespassing! Jim said, "Mr. Ciminelli on Good Street caught me running around the roof of his garage and dragged me all the way around the block to my mother...OUCH!!!!

A positive comment he made about South Buffalo was, "It's so good to see the ongoing improvements to the area. One of the more recent, the REAL NASTY "S" curve on Bailey Avenue that goes over Buffalo Creek near Mongavan Park.

When asked what his favorite singer or musical group from the 60s and 70s were, he said, "How can I pick just one from when the music revolution exploded all around the world? Some of my favorite artists back then were; Sinatra, Elvis, the Beatles and the Beach Boys." He also said, "When the singing group The Drifters released the song 'On Broadway,' I thought they were singing about South Park Avenue."

Pete Herman

Pete is the nephew of our beloved George Hermann, bar owner, Mulroy playground director/coach/overseer/sergeant-at-arms and "father" to all the boys who hung out there.

Pete had this to say:

"Growing up in South Buffalo was a great experience. All of us were so competitive. This brought out a fierce a sense of pride in our part of the city. I was taught how to play ball at the Caz diamonds and Mulroy Playground. Holy Family and Bishop Timon High set me up for a future in coaching. Lifelong friendships are always there. It was a blast growing up on Olcott and Choate streets.

Author P.A. Kane (Paul Kane)

Paul's family initially lived in the First Ward before moving to Lockwood Avenue. He is one of ten children. His parents are Patrick and Phillis. His siblings in order are; Maureen, Mary-Colleen, Joseph, Peter, Karen, (him-Paul), John, Gerald, Mike and Sheila.

About growing up in a large family, Paul stated, "Growing up in a three bedroom/one bath house with nine siblings in Buffalo, New York was just part life in South Buffalo; part of the assembly-line type of childhood."

While speaking to him, he was able to recall a couple of large families he knew on his street; the Colerns and the Velazquezs.

He didn't have much to say about pre-high school days, but had several stories to share about his teen years. Here are a couple…

First story: He said, "In high school back in the mid-70's my friends and I would catch the 16A bus for a quarter and go downtown to Memorial Auditorium (the Aud) and sneak into Buffalo Sabres games. There were a variety of methods to gain entry: sometimes we had a fake ticket (two old stubs glued together), sometimes we found an open door, and sometimes we would just hop the rope next to the ticket takers and run our butts off. We were a bunch of young unsupervised guys testing the limits of our prowess; seeing how much people would put up with our shenanigans. Obnoxiously, we would go down and sit in the gold seats—the most expensive in the Aud - and then argue with the ushers when they came to kick us out.

Paul was a great fan of the "French Connection." He said, "The Sabres team with the mid '70's French Connection with René Robert, Gilbert Perreault, and Ricky Martin - was fantastic! It was old-time freewheeling hockey at its best."

Second story: Some teens have ways to "shock" people. Paul and his buddies did a thing that could go sideways. He said, "We would stage these unbelievable fake fights between periods where a bunch of us would pretend to lay the boots to one of our friends. Our performances were so good that sometimes people came to the aid of our friend on the ground."

With that kind of background, you might ask yourself what any of these boys could turn out to be in the future. Well, Paul settled down, got a job and much later, he became an author. His first novel is called, "Written in The Stars: The Book of Molly."

Here are a few words from P. A. Kane. "Presently (2020) I am one neighborhood removed from South Buffalo in West Seneca, New York where I live with my wife, three college age children and a cat that hates me. I have a State University of New York background in English and I love to trade paperbacks, quiet black mornings and The Ramones.

I'm a middle aged guy coming to the end of his first career. It is a time of uncertainty for many people in my shoes. Writing gives me purpose every day, which is so essential as people like me take that long walk on the downward side of the bell curve."

One of my Memories - The South Buffalo "Beatle"

The guys on our strip got a preview of what was to become a fad all over South Buffalo and beyond. One of the neighborhood's young men, Dennis "Smokey" Wojciechowski went to see barber Tony Orsini for a regular haircut. His hair was long but always neatly combed. Tony thought he'd like to see what Smokey would look like with the "mop head" Beatle look. He commenced to cut and shape the hair, combing it down and blow-drying it in Beatle style. A side view of Smokey instantly reminded us of one of the Beatles. Before I give it away, for those who knew Smokey, guess which Beatle he resembled - John, Paul, George or Ringo? You'll need to read on to find out. Tony even bent Smokey's nose down a bit to get a striking side view resemblance. He left the barbershop after the cut and walked down South Park showing off his new hairdo. People took a look, made comments, laughed and made fun of it. It was only a joke at the time, but later, a lot the guys put away their Brylcreem and grew their hair long and added mustaches.

So.... which Beatle did Smokey resemble? It was Ringo. He never got the nickname "Ringo" though. To his friends, Smokey is still Smokey to this day. Another trivia item about the Fab Four... there were two "lefties" in the group, Paul and Ringo.

Beatles

More Trivia: Ringo was the oldest of the Fab Four

Richard "Ringo" Starkey, born July 7, 1940 - John Winston Lennon, born October 9, 1940

James Paul McCartney, born June 18, 1942 - George Harrison, born February 25, 1943

By the way, how many of you went out and bought one of those Nehru jackets the Beatles made famous in the 60's as they toured? The "fad" jackets were influenced by India's Prime Minister, Nehru Jawaharlal, who was in office from 1947 to 1964. Besides the Beatles, a host of other musicians and movies stars of the 60's donned the stylish Hindu waistcoat. That fashion only lasted a couple of years.

Chapter 10 The Valley - Little Hollywood

Valley sign

Three Valley Areas

The Valley covers an area of about one square mile with three distinct areas:

1. The western-most section west of South Park as you head north which ends at Buffalo River

2. The core of the Valley is made up of; Van Rensselaer, South Park, Smith, and Elk where you find St. Clare's Church (used to be St. Stephen's). PS. School #33 is just beyond that. The old St. Stephen's Catholic School was built in 1893. It is three stories high and had about 20 classrooms in it.

3. Then, there's the area they call "Little Hollywood." It takes in Smith, Milton, Clifford, Selkirk, Sordyl and Andrew Alley. I asked former resident, Joe Lucenti, if he knew how this area got its name. He said, "No one really knows for sure."

Naming the Valley

This section of South Buffalo which is a neighbor to the Old First Ward and the Seneca Babcock area came to be called the Valley after bridges were built to go over railroad tracks that crossed South Park, Elk, Seneca, Smith, and Van Rensselaer. A couple of lawmen; former Sherriff Higgins and Detective Richard Cotter, were credited with spreading the name, "The Valley," as they came to call it when they coordinated police investigations or attended to criminal activities there.

Railroad Tracks

To this day, a lot of Buffalo area folks have no idea where it is, and if they know, they don't know "why" it was/is called the Valley. The answer is… there once were five bridges you needed to go over to get into the area. The bridge at Smith and Seneca was removed during the years 1990 and 1991. The others are still very active with traffic and lets you see why it is called the Valley as you role down into it or role up and out of it.

Tour Guide of the Valley with Joe Lucenti on parents, residents, siblings

I connected with a man named Joe Lucenti who grew up in the Valley at 785 Perry Street. He graduated from Canisius High School in 1973. After college, he worked there for 19 years in several capacities; his last position there was assistant principal. He then went on to become principal of Akron High School in 1999.

We took a tour of the Valley for this project on January 18, 2015. As we made our way through, a thousand memories flooded Joe's head. I wrote things down as fast as I could. I could sense that although he no longer lived there, he's still a Valley son and very proud of it.

Joe said, "The Valley had a large number of Polish people as well as Irish. The greater number was Polish folks who dominated Perry, Fulton and adjoining streets located between Elk and Seneca streets."

He reiterated what was already said about the Valley being called the Valley. He stated, "This part of the city is bordered by Seneca Street, South Park, Van Rensselaer, the Buffalo River and the Selkirk Street side of the Valley where there are numerous sets of tracks behind the houses. You could not get in or out of the Valley without going over a bridge that went over tracks."

He added, "In its hay day, there were probably a dozen sets of railroad tracks on the south side of Selkirk Street with rail activity on every track."

One could argue that Buffalo Creek and the lift bridge near Lee Street and South Park is the actual southern border of the Valley area since there were several factories and plants where a lot of the Valley men and women used to work. But technically, it is the rail lines that mark its southern border.

Little Hollywood
Why it was called that?

Still curious about "Little Hollywood's" name, I continued to inquire about it. While on a solo visit back to the area, I asked several people. One younger man was Joe Dilivio. He lived on Minton Street right in Little Hollywood. He didn't know. I asked a postman who had delivered mail there for a long time. He wasn't really sure. The only thing he came up with was, "I don't really know. It might have something to do with the bridges the Valley has."

With that explanation, I didn't see the connection to Hollywood. I then asked Smith Street resident Rich Golden who has lived in the Valley for over 60 years. He didn't know either.

He said, "That's a good question. I never thought much about it. I really don't know how it got the name. Now that you mention it, I'm kind of curious to find out."

It wasn't until I went to the Seneca/Babcock Community Center and spoke to some people that I got an answer that made some sense. I was talking to Lynn Salomon, Jack Wagner, and Pat (Green) Lovern. I asked them the same question about Little Hollywood. Pat and Lynn from the Community Center didn't know, but Jack said that there are several stories as to how it got the name, but he wasn't sure. He told me;

"It is believed that there were several silent film stars from the 20's that were Buffalo natives or were Buffalo-connected and ended up living there. That was the connection with Hollywood."

I couldn't be sure with that account, so I did more research by following up on Jack's statement "…there are several stories as to how it got the name."

I called Peg Overdorf, Executive Director at the Valley Community Association Center on Leddy Street to see if she knew. I figured, "If anybody would know, it would be Peg." Here's the account of what she heard about the origin of the name.

"There are several stories about that area of the Valley. I'm not sure how true this is, but one of the stories I heard was that Andrew Sordyl owned property near the present site of the Larkin complex, and they (Larkin people) bought the land and moved the people (28 houses) over to the other side of Exchange Street in the area of Smith, Milton, Clifford, Andrew Alley, Sordyl Alley and Selkirk streets. Sordyl placed the houses in such a way (on Andrew Alley and Sordyl Alley) that the backsides of the houses from both streets formed a courtyard, and the way the staircases were built reminded people of Hollywood movie sets. So, for that reason, the area became known as Little Hollywood."

During interviews at Tilly's several weeks after I spoke to Peg Overdorf, Cheri Dolan, who is associated with Peg, agreed with her story via a cell phone interview.

Cheri's side of the story; "When people went over the Smith Street Bridge near the Little Hollywood area and looked down, the view of the buildings reminded them of the "West Side Story" movie set."

This story sounded pretty good to me but to check further, Peg gave me the phone number for Marge Starzynski so I could get another explanation about the area in question.

Peg told me; "Marge and many people in her family lived a long time in the Valley. She might know how Little Hollywood got its name."

I called Marge, asked her the question and without any hesitation, she said, "I don't know."

After a very short conversation, with a laugh in her voice, she said, "Maybe it was because so many of us 'Starz-ynskis' lived there during that time." And, there were indeed, a lot of Starzynskis who lived there at one time." Get it? Starz…ynski, as in movie stars - Hollywood.

So far none of the four people who gave me an answer were absolutely sure about the true story of Little Hollywood. I phoned Art Robinson, who is familiar with the Valley and has lived in the Seneca/Babcock community some 60 years. He didn't know either. I told him, "I won't rest until I get the answer."

He laughed and said, "When you find out, let me know. I'd love to know the answer to that question, myself."

Ken Seifert, a former Seneca Babcock resident thought it could be because not far from that area, as he put it, "There were several movie theatres." I could accept that somewhat but the area he spoke about was a bit removed from Little Hollywood to make a direct connection.

On January 30, 2016, I returned to the Old First Ward's museum - Waterfront Memories & More to dig up more information on the Valley, specifically, Little Hollywood. I was given a binder on Little Hollywood with a lot of newspaper clippings about it but there was nothing in it that talked about the origin of the name of the area in question. There were several older gentlemen looking over material on the Old First Ward who were somewhat familiar with the Valley. I asked them about Little Hollywood, but none of them had the answer. I figured that I had come to a dead end. If the museum didn't have the answer, local residents of the area didn't know nor did all those other people I talked to, then that was that.

I took a few notes about the Valley that I could add to the book and packed up. I made my way to the Larkin Complex (Larkinville) on Seneca Street where they were holding a winter-type festival and happened to park next to the fire station at Seneca and Swan streets.

I thought to myself, "While I'm here, I'll slip into the fire station to see if there's an older fireman here who might know something about the Valley from the old days."

Remember reading about Marge Starzynski a little bit ago? Well, by chance, the man in charge was Tony Starzynski. It took a while but then it hit me. I asked Tony: "What's your mother's name?"

He answered: "Marge."

What a fluke! I told him that I spoke to his mom the night before and recounted the conversation we had. He laughed. I got to the point and asked him if he knew how Little Hollywood got its name. He told me that he had asked his father a long time ago how that came about and here's what he said.

"My dad told me that way back when, in the area of Smith and Exchange streets, there used to be a bunch of younger guys in their late teens to early twenties that used to dress up real nice, wearing leather coats with the collars turned up, and slick hair. They had a kind of Hollywood look about them. So, people came to refer to them as the 'Hollywood Boys.' From the Hollywood Boys, the area became known as Little Hollywood."

Other people I spoke to about this topic for the sake of getting to the truth of the matter were, officers Jim Shea and Dan Redmond. (Both South Buffalo sons).

As soon as I asked the question: "How did Little Hollywood in the Valley get that name?" Dan jumped in right away. "My dad told me about that, years ago. It had to do with young people during the Depression raiding box cars that were stopped on the tracks near Selkirk Street on the southern edge of the Valley. The rail cars contained new dress clothes, and suddenly, a lot of young people turned up wearing very nice looking outfits. They were so well dressed that the folks in that area called the classy looking guys, 'movie stars.' From that, the area came to be known as Little Hollywood."

As we were talking, Dan called his father on a cell phone to confirm the story. His dad told the same tale about brand new clothes stolen from rail cars by youths in the Valley during the Depression.

Jim Shea added, "It was also noted that several young blond ladies from that same area were seen all decked out in new clothes, probably clothes the guys got from the box cars. Their sharp good looks added to the whole movie star thing of - Little Hollywood."

Now then, in October of 2019, I was speaking to Tony and Pat Orsini (cousins) about this very topic and wouldn't you know it, I got two more tales as to how "Little Hollywood" got its name.

Tony's version sort fits in with what Jim Shea stated. He said, "That area had quite a few blond-haired guys and young ladies; Polish and German. A lot of them wore sunglasses as part of their identity. Outsiders would look at them and remark, 'who do they think they are …Hollywood stars?!'"

His cousin Pat (Luke) Orsini said, "I was told that it was called Little Hollywood because the additions to the houses were built smaller and smaller and made them look like movie cameras when viewed from an airplane." (Telescopic houses.)

Dennis Starr and Digger Kennedy heard tell that it got that moniker because in the 20s and 30s, there was a group of young people in the Smith, Milton, Clifford, Selkirk, Sordyl and Andrew Alley area who dressed like "gangsters" - with greased-back hair, wearing suits and sunglasses. It made them look like "movie stars."

At Bob's Barber Shop on Seneca Street, barber Bill Holihan said, "Someone told me that it was named Little Hollywood because of two Puerto Rican actors that lived there and were always dressed real sharp with suits, sunglasses and dress hats."

Captain Bart (Beefy) Adams, a former Seneca Street area resident who became a West Seneca cop remembers hearing that Little Hollywood got its name because of …"a lot of pretty blonds in that neighborhood looked like Hollywood stars."

Just one more story…number 13! Mike Mazur said he heard that the part of the Valley's known Little Hollywood got that name, as Mike put it… "It was called that because a lot of actors and stage performers from the theatres and Burlesque shows that came to Buffalo made their way there after their performances. They were able to obtain inexpensive rooms (room and board) while they were in town. They all dressed and looked like movie stars."

The list kept growing as I did more and more interviews. There you have it folks, accounts of how the "Little Hollywood" name MAY have come about. There may be more, but I think you can deduce from the above which one[s] is/are closest to the REAL explanation.

[1] Bridges - [2] Retired silent Film Stars settling in the area - [3] Staircases of houses reminding people of Hollywood movie sets - [4] The Star…zynskis - [5] Several movie theatres in the area [6] Well-dressed, leather coat sporting youths, with slick-hair looking like "Hollywood boys" [7] Depression era youths raiding rail cars for brand new clothes, hitting the streets well-dressed and being called, "Movie Stars" - [8] Blond-haired guys and gals, wearing sunglasses and neatly dressed. [9] Additions to houses built smaller and smaller looking like 'movie cameras - [10] Young people that dressed like gangsters with greased-back hair, wearing suits and sunglasses - [11] Two Puerto Rican actors from there showing up on the streets dressed real sharp - [12] Pretty blonds in that neighborhood looking like Hollywood stars." [13] Stage performers from the theatres and Burlesque shows needing inexpensive rooms.

Which one of these do you think is the best to nail down the "real" story of how this part of the Valley got its name?

Valley Community Center

At South Park and Leddy streets, there is a facility known as the Father Carmichael Community Center. It is a day-care and senior center facility, headed by Executive Director, Peg Overdorf. The Valley has a public elementary school on Elk Street (PS #33) and next to it, Saint Clare RC Church (Used to be Saint Stephen's). The only businesses left in that neighborhood are a few bars and delicatessens. In the 40's 50's, 60's and 70's, the Valley was a lot more active with school, church activities, plants, factories and bars. For its small size, it once had a population of about 5,000 people; a mixture of people; Irish, Polish and Italians. Joe Lucenti is half Polish and half Italian.

Joe said he used to walk to St. Valentine Elementary School on South Park from his house on Perry Street. There, he served as an altar boy and in later years, played the organ for church services and events. The church itself was on the first floor and had around eight classrooms on the second floor. St. Valentine's was built in 1920 as a temporary church and school. Joe said:

"They were going to build a larger church and school, but, because of the Depression, there wasn't enough money to do it. So, a new church and school were never built."

The original building is still there but not used as a Catholic Church and school anymore. Like so many parishes in Buffalo and outlying towns, the parishioners and school children had to find other churches and schools.

Common Living Arrangements
Telescopic Houses

Joe stated that when he lived at 785 Perry Street, out of six houses in a row, four of them were occupied by his own family, grandparents, aunts, uncles and cousins. He stated that his parents lived there 49½ years; from 1953 till 2003. None of his family or relatives lives there now.

He said: "Even after leaving this area, a lot of people I know come back to visit. It's still their home. Even me, I like coming back here now and then. My heart is definitively - still here."

He also mentioned how many dwellings throughout his area and the old sections of Buffalo have what he called, "telescopic houses."

"As families grew bigger and bigger, one thing they did was, build additions to the existing homes to accommodate extra kids or for someone who got married and wanted to stay in the neighborhood near mom and dad. Some additions were built to take care of aging parents or grandparents so they would be near family in their final days."

When you drive down the I-190, take a look at the older houses on either side as you pass through South Buffalo and Kaisertown, you'll see a great number of telescopic houses. For a lot of people, back in the day, the idea of putting ma or pa, grandma or grandpa in an old folks' home was not an option.

For Valley folks
work was a short walk away

Joe remembered when he was young; most of the people in the Valley worked the local mills and plants. He said that his dad worked at General Mills in the Old First Ward for 38 years and that his brother John Lucenti is still there (2016) as well as his brother-in-law, Steve Spima. Other Valley people worked at Republic Steel, the Mobile Refinery on Elk Street and at National Aniline, Trico or other plants nearby. All were within walking distance.

Joe said, "Back in the 40's, 50's, 60's, and 70's, a lot of people I knew who lived in the Valley and worked the local places of employment didn't have a car. A lot of the workers could and would walk to work. It was so common back then."

Bars

He mentioned that there was a running joke about the Valley and its bars. He said, "People used to say that in the Valley, there was a bar on every corner. Not really, but there were a lot, that's for sure. Some of them were in the middle of residential blocks... not only on the corners."

Most of the nearby industries that hired many people from the Valley closed. When that started happening, many bars closed too. The clientele just wasn't there. In its hay day, the large work force supported the bars. Many of the local blue-collar workers were on one of three shifts in the grain mills, production plants and Republic Steel.

Joe said, "You have to realize that for many of the men working the 11PM to 7 AM shift, the bars would open at 8 AM and a lot of men ended up in there. That was their dinner time and a time to socialize."

He listed most of the bars that are or were in the Valley:

Tilly's Bar at Fulton and Smith, used to be Matikas and then Tuney's.

Other bars were: Tippie's Bar owned by the Kasowski's - Boot-Nose Bar at Perry and Van Rensselaer - Kelly's Bar - Johnny Hoar's Bar at South Park and Harvey - The Roaring 20's bar was a stone's throw south of Kelly's.

When I was at Tilly's Bar, I couldn't help noticing how great the place looked. Although it's an older building, owners Dan and Bernedette Concheiro did an amazing job upgrading the bar area...it looks very classy.

For my first South Buffalo book project, I found several friendly people there who were more than happy to help me gather material. Thank you and cheers to Robin Sanly, Dan and Bernedette Concheiro.

Joe talked about how most bars ran back in the old days. Here's what he said about his own family's gin mill. "John's Tavern on Perry Street was open from 7AM to 3AM. The whole family ran it and took turns working to accommodate the plant shift workers. People who worked from 3 PM to 11 PM could go out and stay at the bar till 3 AM to meet up with friends who worked that same shift."

Joe's family owned John's Tavern for 55 years. First, his grandparents owned it then his aunt and uncle on his mother's side. His grandparents, his mom, aunts and uncles lived above the bar. He literally grew up there.

He reflected back to his younger days, "I remember listening to the jukebox, live music in the back room, and eventually bartending at the age of eighteen. My first experience playing in a Polka band (accordion) was in the back room when I was twelve years old. I remember my grandmother with tears in her eyes. She was so proud of me because she bought me the accordion. I still have it almost fifty years later. I dazzle my nieces and nephews when I play it."

Valley Businesses

Businesses that were pointed out to me by Joe were; Ricotta's (Rix's) Deli on the corner of Elk and Smith streets and Frank's Barber Shop a little ways north and a deli at Fulton and Smith. At Elk and South Park, there used to be a Mobile gas station. On the corner of Smith Street and Elk was Dubois' Hardware and next to, it a Pittsburg Paint store and Ortiz's Deli at Milton and Smith. AT 755 Seneca was Jerry Brenner's drug store called Keller's Pharmacy and tucked in the backside of Little Hollywood was Basil Skorupski's Deli on Clifford and Selkirk.

He added: "We even had a 'bookie' down on Elk Street," and no deli was more famous than Kurzanski's in the middle of Fulton Street run by Eddy and Sophie Kurzanski. It was from an era long gone when everyone knew each other."

We continued our tour down Smith Street toward Buffalo Creek at the westernmost part of the Valley where it ends. We turned down Saint Stephen Place and headed toward a bright yellow house at 16 St. Stephen Place and could see the Coyne Seed Plant over the house.

In the Seneca/Smith Street area, there was Minton's Café and Beer Garden owned by John Pierszynski and a billiard parlor owned by Joseph Jagodzynski. You may have noticed several Polish names. It backs up the fact that there were a lot of Polish folks living in the Valley.

Joe said that at one time going down Seneca towards Main, there was a barber shop with apartments above it, an Overall Laundry, Boradzyk's Tavern, a soda shop, a shoe maker and Gladkowski's Bowling Alleys. He added:

"For basic necessities, we didn't have to leave the neighborhood. We had pretty much everything for our daily needs."

Valley Youth Activities

Joe talked about life in the Valley and some of the things the boys did to pass time away. We went down Perry Street and stopped at the old Niagara Mohawk Plant. Across the street is the embankment to the I-190 which was built around 1957 when Joe was a baby. He pointed to the near ground level windows on the Niagara Mohawk building where they painted a batter's box on the brick part of the wall. It served as the strike zone. Using a four foot long, one inch round stick and a small, hard rubber ball, they'd have at it. There was no catcher. The pitcher would throw the ball within the strike zone and if the batter hit it to the edge of the grassy area of the Thruway slope, it counted as a base hit. If the ball was hit to the middle of the slope, it was a second base hit and if the ball made it to the top part of the slope, it was a homerun. Joe never did say if they beaned any cars on the I-190 as folks zoomed by. What do you think folks? Should nailing a car zooming by on the Thruway have been a grand slam?

Joe went on to tell me, "Around the 4th of July, we would get fireworks and go over to the old Niagara Mohawk Sub Station on Perry Street. It was a huge brick shell with an incredible echo. Well, we'd drop a cherry bomb or an M-80 through an open window. It sounded like an atomic bomb. We were just boys being boys."

Joe and the neighborhood boys would play touch football in the streets or on several grassy areas. One such place was near the Swift Meat Processing plant on Perry Street, west of Van Rensselaer next to the I-190. He said, "The slope of the Thruway had these huge boulders and one day during a play, one of the guys knocked me into one of them, face first. I got fourteen stitches on my upper lips."

Joe said that they also played street hockey and basketball in a little park they called Best Field, across from the Swift plant. Besides Best Field, there was also Collin's Park where young people played the usual good weather sports and in the winter, they had toboggan chutes.

SPECIAL NOTE: Besides Jimmy Slattery, there was another Valley son that made a name for himself in the fighting game. His name is Peter J. Crotty. He achieved national recognition as a fighter. In the 50's, he became a county chairman in the Democratic Party.

On our tour around the Valley area, Joe pointed out where Allen Kaspersak, the Mayor of East Aurora used to live on Fulton Street and where former Buffalo Mayor Stan Makowski (1974-1977) lived on Roseville Street. We went to another street where the Smardz family lived. Joe said they raised chickens, pigeons, and had bee-hives.

Speaking of animals, this story was heard throughout Buffalo; so it's worth dropping it in here. Joe told me that his brother John woke him up one morning to tell him there was a cow in the street, on Perry Street. He got up to take a looked for himself, and sure enough, there was a cow right in the middle of the street.

On May 16, 1980, an old 2,000 pound gal along with a host of other bovines escaped from the P. Brennan Meat Packing Plant at 1010 Clinton near Fillmore, not too far from the Valley. I remember that event and that I had worked at that plant in 1964. It was Togg's Meat Packing Company then. The great escape made for a very funny 6 o'clock news item with Irv Weinstein at WKBW-TV. Cops and locals all joined in to gather the scattered herd. They got 'em all back to the meat company.

Some Folks from the Valley

The Cichon/Coyle clans

Steve Cichon and his family have been part of Buffalo for eight generations, and are connected to the Valley, the Seneca Babcock neighborhood and Seneca Street (south). He is very well-known in the Buffalo area as a; former radio newsman, historian, author, adjunct professor at Medaille College and producer at WNED-TV. He provided the following for this project.

For the Cichon side, Steve had this to say. "My great-grandparents came from Poland to "The Valley" in 1913. They bought a house at 608 Fulton Street in 1920. Great grandpa worked at Schoellkopf Chemical/National Aniline for more than 40 years. His son, my grandfather, worked at National Aniline/Buffalo Color more than 40 years at lived in his parents' house until he bought one across the street (from his brother-in-law's family) at 617 Fulton, where my dad grew up. He later moved the family to Seneca Street in 1966 but still had ties to the Valley, owning the bar at Elk and Smith.

The Coyles

On the Coyle side of his family, Steve provided the following. "The Cichons were in the Valley on Fulton Street until 1966 when they moved to Fairview off Seneca (near Caz Park). The Coyles were on Orlando Street (Sen/Bab area) until they moved at Hayden off Seneca in 1957 (St. Teresa Parish)."

My grandpa, Jim Coyle, was one of the guys who ran the (Babcock) Boys Club while Danny Neaverth, Joey Reynolds, Bill Masters Danny McBride were going there."

I asked Steve about how the Valley became known as the Valley, His response, "My dad always referred to the neighborhood as 'The Valley.' He always talked about having to cross a bridge to get in or out of that neighborhood. That's pretty much true now, but was even more so before they ripped out all of the old steel truss bridges... and didn't replace the ones on Smith and Van Rensselaer.

In talking with folks from the neighborhood about the Valley being called that, my best guess is that it was coined sometime in the 50s. It seems to be the generation that started referring to it that way. The city of Buffalo itself didn't use the name (Valley) in any of its planning or urban renewal programs in the 50s and 60s. In my research, I haven't been able to find any reference to the name in print in the Courier-Express or the Evening News until the time when the "Valley Community Association" was organized in the late 60s. One would have to assume, however, that the name was in some kind of familiar use leading up to naming a community association after it."

Long live the Valley!

Marie (Fitzpatrick) Ventura

Marie (Fitzpatrick) Ventura initially came from the Valley and now residing in the quaint Village of Blasdell. Her dad's name is Frank Ventura and mom, Hellen (Brooks). Common for the time, she too, came for a large family. Besides her (Marie) and her parents, there was; John, James, Williams, Ray, Francis, Helen (Fitzpatrick) Leach, and Jessie (Fitzpatrick) Riordan. That's a grand total of ten people vying for a place at the supper table.

Marie, in her late 80s at this writing, is a lady who has tons of memories of her beloved Valley, and when reflecting back on her time there, as her daughter Barbara (Ventura) Sherwood stated, "There is a glimmer in her eyes and a smile on her face," Her mother said, "Everyone was like family." Barb stated that her mother was referring to the fact that "...her precious community was 'family oriented' with tight-knit immediate family members and close relatives that lived down the street or a few streets away."

Marie went to Saint Stephen's on Elk Street where Sister Mary Bernice headed the school. Her favorite teacher there was Sister Marie Damian. Her close circle of friends back then were; Loraine Sala, Marcella Bakowski, Dorothy Slifka, and Hariette Kolaga. This crew of young ladies hung out at Harry the Greek's candy Kitchen on Elk Street, went or dances or took in movies at the Artistic Theatre located at the foot of the Elk Street Bridge.

Marie remembers well the "the way it was" in her old neighborhood and holds on dearly to the many memories she still has. But, when seeing that same neighborhood now, she only has one word, "Terrible." She still loves the Valley, can't help but loving it, but as Barbara stated, "Her sentiment simply reflects the reality that where she once lived and grew up is just no longer the way it was. Gone are so many stores, plants, specialty shops, stores, delicatessens restaurants and gin mills."

Tony Starzynski

When I spoke to Tony Starzynski in the firehouse, besides telling me about Little Hollywood, he told me that he was a good athlete in his younger days and that he would be invited over the bridge from the Valley to the Seneca Babcock neighborhood to play sports against the guys over there. Normally, the Valley guys didn't mix it up with the Babcock area boys and vice versa. He said, "People stayed on their own turf," Tony was an exception. As a matter of fact, Danny Neaverth, once from the Seneca Babcock area himself, reinforced that unwritten turf law. Dan said, "We didn't go over to the Valley and the Valley guys didn't come on our side of town. But, if they came to the "club, the Babcock Boys Club, there were no problems."

Both Tony and Dan alluded to the fact that stepping onto each other's turf could be taking a chance. Interestingly enough, Tony told me that Mr. Neaverth had coached him for intramurals at the Boys Club when he was younger. Small world isn't it?

Chapter 11 Seneca Street North (Route 16)

Seneca Street (Route 16) is not as long as South Park's connection to Route 62, but goes a fair distance. It starts near Lower Terrace in downtown Buffalo, becomes Route #16 and goes south through Buffalo, Elma, East Aurora and continues to Olean, New York. I found that there are several Route Sixteens in the United States. One is in Georgia which crosses that state and ends up at the city of Savanah. Below are the streets that intersect Seneca Street. If I've missed any, my apology; I believe most are there.

Lower Terrace	Walter	Avondale	Zittle
Delaware	Maurice	Remington	Peremont
Franklin	Orlando	Juanita	Cazenovia
Pearl	Wassor	Unger	Buffum
Main Street	Babcock	Sage	Seneca Parkside
Washington	Gorham	Riverview	Theresa
Ellicott	Imson	Pomona	Indian Church
Oak	Winona	Hammerschmidt	Fairview
Elm	Oakdale	Armin	Durstein
Michigan	Troupe	Paul	Cazenovia Parkway
Butler	Bradford	Roanoke	Warren Spahn Way
Elmira	Milton	Stephenson	Newman
Chicago	Harrison	Mineral Springs	Edson
Louisiana	Lester	Melrose	Mt. Vernon
Cedar	Hayes	Knoerl	Greymont
Spring	Keating	Haden	Maywood
Hamburg	Mergenhagen	Ryan	Manhasset
Larkin	Bailey	Geary	Burch
Van Rensselaer	Keppel	Yale	Wildwood
Hageman	Archer	Weyand	Chamberlin
Hydraulic	Pomeroy	Kamper	City Line
Griffin	Avon	Princeton	
Smith	Southside	Norman	
Peabody	Leamington	Kingston	

Seneca Street (North)

Custom Canvas - Chuck Guido

Going north on Seneca Street, I came to a business that's been there for decades: Custom Canvas at 775 Seneca. I stopped in to speak to the owner, Anthony "Chuck" Guido, a friendly older man close to 80. As of 2016, the business had been in operation for 55 years. He told me, "I opened on January 12, 1961."

He flashed back with me about the old days when he lived in the Spring-Swan Street area. He brought up that the old neighborhoods were so different from today and that most neighborhood folks in the baby boomer days didn't lock their doors.

"I never had a key for my house as a kid. Most of our neighbors didn't lock their doors either. I remember once when it was raining pretty hard, my mom said to me,

'Go across the street to Tripi's house and shut all their windows so the rain don't get in.'

I didn't need a key. They always kept the doors unlocked. Neighbors took care of each other back then." Sound familiar?

He also told me about the bars that used to operate back in the day. He said:

"Once, you could hit each bar going south, have one drink and by the time you hit 'em all, you'd be drunk. You'd start behind the firehouse at Swan and Seneca, go into Lee's Lounge, have one drink and continue south on Seneca to the next one, the Swan Lounge. Then cross the street to the Horse Head and afterward go to Big Joe Dudzik's place. Next, there was a bowling alley where you'd have another, and finally, you'd end up at Julia's Bar. By then, you felt really good!"

The Larkin Square Area and Hydraulic Street

Continuing toward downtown, I passed Larkin Square (Larkinville) at 745 Seneca Street where buildings in the area go back to 1827. There is a street down there called Hydraulic Street between Exchange and Swan streets. I wondered why it was called that. I learned that around 1827, the Hydraulic Canal was built which provided hydraulic power for factories and mills located in the Larkin complex and Exchange Street area. By 1832, there were several mills and factories, all run by the hydraulic power from the canal.

Located there was a saw mill, a gristmill (mill for grinding grain into flour), a brewery, a hat, pail and shoe factory. In 1867 John Larkin built a factory called, "Plain and Fancy Soaps." By 1902 there were at least 87 businesses in that area of Seneca Street.

The present day Larkinville was created by Sam Zemsky, owner of Russer Foods in 2002. Leslie Zemsky has been a huge part of developing many different ideas for events and welcoming a wide variety of Food Trucks that set up on certain days during the summer season. Huge crowds gather to hear bands or attend other special occasions such as "SOUTH BUFFALO NIGHT" - held in August. One of the very neat events has been the "Beatles' Tribute Bands" that play on top of a building across from Larkin Square. Bravo, Zemsky family for seeing the potential this area had!

DiTondo's, a Great Family Restaurant

I credit Robin from Chef's Restaurant for guiding me over to DiTondo's family restaurant which has been in business at 370 Seneca Street since 1904. Robin told me that it was the second oldest restaurant in Western New York. But, present owner, Alan Rohloff corrected that by saying, "It's the oldest continuing restaurant in Buffalo and has been operated by the same family for 113 years."

The "Swannie House," originally called the "Swanerski House" at 170 Michigan and Ohio Street having been in business 120 plus years, holds the record for being the oldest bar/restaurant in Buffalo. DiTundo's has always been run by the same family, but Swannie has changed hands a few times. Buffalo holds both in very high places in Buffalo's history.

DiTondo's had no break in ownership. No one else in the city has this distinction. It was started by Sabastiano DiTondo in 1904 and run by himself with the help of his sons Amedeo, Armando, John and Joseph. Alan Rohloff and wife Rose Mary DiTondo (Sabastian's granddaughter) were the owners prior to closing in 2019.

Alan and Rose Mary had a fairly simple menu that offered several tasty Italian dishes at very reasonable prices: Spaghetti for $6.75 or Stuffed Eggplant Parmesan for $5.95. It was a great place to eat. The only drawback is that they were only open for lunch Monday through Friday 11 AM to 2 PM; no weekends. On Fridays after a three hour break, they re-opened from 5 PM till 9 PM. By the way, it was a cash only kitchen.

The new owners, Rita DiTondo and her father, John (Sabastiano's son), were set to reopen in the spring of 2020. Anyone who had the pleasure of dining there before and were looking forward to return as loyal customers, were saddened by the closing, but thrilled that Sabastiano's legacy would go on.

Chef's Restaurant

Chef's Restaurant at 291 Seneca at the corner of Chicago is renowned in Buffalo as one of the city's best restaurants. It's been frequented by folks from all walks of life from blue-collar workers to lawyers businessmen, entertainers, and a hoard of professional athletes. It was open as a bar in 1910 by Gino Silverstrini and Lee Federconi, and in 1923, they opened as a restaurant.

Lou Billittier started out under Silverstrini and Federconi as dishwasher. He worked as a busboy, a waiter, and later became the restaurant's manager. In 1950, he was half owner and by 1954 became full owner. Today, it is run by his daughter Mary Beth and son Louis John Billittier.

Pierce Arrow Museum

The Pierce Arrow Museum located at 263 Michigan and Seneca Street was founded by James Sandoro and his wife Mary Ann. It is an absolute must see day-trip destination for all antique and classic car lovers. They have some of the most outstanding cars of days gone by. As one ad says, "It traces Buffalo's transportation history." To get more information go online. Also check out a great article written by Buffalo News writer Mark Sommer.

Buffalo Police Garage

The Buffalo Police Garage is located at 341 Seneca Street. Their main function is to do maintenance on Buffalo Police Department vehicles. I can't imagine the amount of miles they put on each vehicle in a year. Also, the amount of gas it takes to run their entire fleet.

Chapter 12 Seneca/Babcock Area:
people, businesses and more

Babcock Area Leaders

Some individuals whose names I was given that are or have been involved and committed to keeping the community alive and well are:

Dr. Daniel Alexander, longtime supporter and benefactor

Bob Kurtz, Director of the Boys Club until the 80's

Dennis Phillips, Director of the Boys and Girls Club

Carrie Sitarski, Community Center's Director

Brian Pilarski, Director of the Community Center

Peg Bougucki, Senior Director

Jodi Briggs-Garcia works at the Boys Club

Dan Neaverth, volunteer for intramural sports

Jack Wagner, Volunteered in various capacities.

Kari Colon, Youth Director of After School Programs

Rita Carluccio, Food and Pantry and Child Clothing

Lynn Salomon, After School Activities Coordinator

Carol Sylvia, ceramics class

Jackie Green is the cook for the kids' program

Another player who had an important role in nurturing the youths of the neighborhood was Dr. Richard Quinn (Principal of PS #26 on Harrison and Milton streets (the school no longer exists.) A special thanks to all of the administrators, teachers and workers at PS #26.

Pat Lovern and Jack Wagner wanted me to mention some of people who were part of School #26:

Rita Victoria, school cook

Betty Salomon and a lady named Joyce - cafeteria monitors

Helen Dibbles was a crossing guard for 60 years and a Brownie Leader.

Florence Mathers, crossing guard, whose house was a Buffalo Evening News newspaper drop point for the boys and girls with paper routes in the neighborhood.

Other community members and supporters of the area whose names came up as being part of the Seneca Babcock neighborhood are: Greg Vaughn, Jim McCabe, John Keller, Nelson Hughes, Dave Kleinesmith, Larry Soloman, Victor Victori, Pat Green, Moe Cochran, Eddy Cudney, the Sytarski family.

Little City

The Seneca Babcock area, about one square mile, is close in size to its neighbor, the Valley. It once was known as the "Little City within the City." Not anymore. The many changes have taken away the title. It got that name because it contained pretty much everything the people needed. "It was self-sufficient," as Lynn Salomon said. So much is gone now, and it doesn't look like it's going to return to its former glory anytime soon. The same goes for so many other parts of the city.

The Seneca Babcock area was more family-oriented a few decades back. A lot of families not only had their own home on a given street, but many had grandparents, aunts, uncles and cousins living on that same street or only a couple of streets away. There was greater unity among families. There was also the stay-at-home mom factor that proved to be a great thing in raising the Baby Boomers. There were indeed lots of children in the neighborhoods back then. It was a different time family-wise and socially.

It was common for families to be much bigger than in today's culture. The McCabe family had 16 kids, the Sitarski's with at least 12, and the Green's with 12.

The Community

What was this neighborhood like from the late 40s to the 70s?

I made a phone call to the Seneca Babcock Community Center and spoke to Community Center volunteer Carrie Sitarski in order to connect with people from that neighborhood who have been part of it. I told her I wanted information about the area; names of people, stores, and activities that made the Seneca/Babcock area what it was. She connected me with volunteer Lynn Salomon and a couple of other people who could help with my project.

I set up a date with Lynn for a Wednesday afternoon January 2016. As soon as I walked in and introduced myself, she led me to Pat (Green) Lovern and Jack Wagner who began unloading a ton of information about their beloved community.

I began by asking, "What was this neighborhood like from the late 40s to the 70s?"

Lynn said: "It was a great neighborhood. We knew everybody. If I wandered off four blocks from home as a kid, somebody would yell at me to get back home or they'd tell my mom. People looked out for each other, especially the kids. It once was a family oriented neighborhood.' It certainly isn't like it was. It's changed a whole lot.

We had everything anyone needed in this neighborhood. We didn't really have to go anywhere else for; food, clothing, barber and beauty shops, bakery, delicatessens, bars, entertainment, schools, churches, playgrounds or youth centers. We had it all."

I spoke of unity before. This also applied to the bars. Lynn and the others said that all the bars in the Seneca Babcock area used to get together and have a yearly vote to elect what they called the "Little Mayor" of the Seneca/Babcock area. I don't know why they used the word "little" but I surmised it was because of the small area that it represented; the Little City within a City thing. At any rate, this went on for a good while.

Community Center and Boys and Girls Club

This community had a ton of people who have either lived there for years or still live there and have great pride in their old neighborhood. They have a very strong connection to it and are involved in maintaining as much of the integrity of the neighborhood as possible. They are committed to keeping alive a community that has seen its best years go by. That's one of the reasons the Seneca Babcock Community Center and the Boys and Girls Club exist and are still going strong. They want to train the young people to "take over" and make it a better place, now, and for the future. There is a feeling of great loss among the older folks who lived there when it was vibrant. They wish it could be the way it was. For sure, they absolutely still feel great pride in being or having been, part of the Seneca Babcock neighborhood.

people, businesses and more

Seneca/Babcock Businesses
"You don't know what you've got till it's gone."

Corner store at Seneca/Babcock

The following will give you a look at what once was. Then, maybe you'll understand what was lost, and you'll gain a better appreciation of why the older folks are saddened with the condition of the neighborhood today. It's not the same with so much gone.

I asked my interviewees, "What about businesses in the Seneca/Babcock area in the 40's, 50's, 60's and 70's? What do you remember? What did you have here?"

Lynn Salomon, with the help of Pat Lovern and Jack Wagner, and a couple of people they phoned while I was doing the interview, did the best they could to provide me with information about their old neighborhood, the way it was. Starting north of the Buffalo Creek area, they went up to the point where you come to the bridge that leads to Smith Street. Here is the list of places, stores, shops, bars and other businesses that used to be. Very few remain from the old days.

Not all sites will be in order and forgive me for any that are missing. I only noted the ones given to me.

From Bailey

Angert's Auto Parts, Len-Co Lumber, Buffalo China and Ebb Plumbing Supplies on Hayes Street, the Thruway Inn, Tobin's Bar, a barber shop, Slim Boots Deli, a trailer lot, a gas station on the corner of Troupe, a credit union at Inson, a Methodist Church, Ford's Deli, Quality Bakery with a doctor's office upstairs, Teen Haven and a few pizzerias; Vic Victori's Pizzeria, Rita Maria's Pizzeria and, Moe Cochran's Pizzeria.

There was a dry cleaner's shop, a butcher shop, Chicks Hair Salon, Michael's Deli, the Boys Club, A & P Grocery, Cudney's Bar, Tobin's Bar at Harrison, Savris' Deli which later became a fast food place, Babcock Grill, Bradley's Bar & Bowling, Hank & Stell's Bar between Morris and Walters, Kentucky Cabin, Napoleon's and Cigars, a liquor store, Old Sod, Jean Machine (a pants store). Down Backcock Street going toward Elk Street, there was a bar that had a few other names: [1] Sally's [2] Sally's Split Decision [3] Sally's Daughter [4] Porkey's [5] Porky's II [6] Tigs and [7] Froggy's…WOW!!! AND then, there was Pristach's Bar on the street behind Froggy's Bar.

Saint Monica's Elementary School on Orlando Street, Ernie & Vy's Bar, South Side Club, Trico #3 Plant, South Buffalo Junk Yard, Woop-P-Doo's Bar and the Babcock Grill which later became Betty Boop's at the corner of Babcock. Other businesses were: a restaurant supply company, Quinn's Liquor Store, Bradley's Bar and Bowling Lanes, the Oakdale Theatre at Seneca and Babcock, the Atlantic Lumber Yard, Casey's Junk Yard, the Mullen Playground which is attached to the now demolished P.S. #26 on Harrison Street.

Youth Activities

I asked Lynn Salomon, Pat Lovern and Jack Wagner about activities that used to be a part of life in their community. Lynn stated that, aside from school and church activities, the youth played organized and non-organized sports of all kinds. A lot of these activities revolved around the Seneca/Babcock Community Center and the Babcock Boys Club which was known as "The Club."

For outside recreation young people in the neighborhood did pretty much the same things as other youths everywhere else. A lot of the young males played baseball, football and basketball in the playgrounds or on some sand lot. Many outdoor games were played such as hide and seek, kick the can, chestnut wars, steam ball, relievio and so on. Jack said that in the summer, one of the dares was to hop garages and in the winter it was, hitching on the backs of cars, trucks or busses.

Jack said, "Hitching cars was called 'Pogoing' and hitching busses was called 'Jarving.'" I never knew there were names attached to that activity.

It must be assumed that adults did their adult things: working to make a living and taking care of their families and homes, backyard B-B-Q's, birthday parties, bowling, mingling with neighbors and tipping a few pints at the many local gin mills. For many, there were Sunday dinners at grandma's house; an after church gathering that started around noontime and lasted into the late afternoon. It gave a chance for families to come together. This included aunts, uncles, cousins and some close friends. Thanksgiving, Christmas, Easter and the 4th of July were great times for big family get-togethers that kept families close.

By the way, the names of the meals used to be: breakfast, dinner, and supper. Somewhere along the line, dinner got replaced with lunch, and dinner went to the supper slot. Kids were told by moms: "Don't be late or you'll go to bed without your supper."

Hardly anyone uses supper any more to refer to the last meal of the day. If you speak to older folks, many will tell you, "That's right. Supper was the last meal of the day. It was always around 5 pm or 6 pm."

Who still calls it "supper" these days? Here are a few people that responded to that very question;

Mike Farrell: It's Supper for me
Sue Petrinec: Supper.
Clyde Leto: Over the years it has changed from supper to dinner. As a kid it was supper.
Jim Slattery: How about the living room? I still call it the parlor sometimes!
Jack Lafferty: Still supper here.
Connie Caruso: A little of both.

Dan Neaverth Memories

I connected with former resident of the Seneca Babcock area, radio and TV personality, Dan Neaverth. We first met at WKBW Radio back in 1966 and 1967 when I worked there as a mail clerk. There was never a dull moment at the radio station when Dan took to the mike. As some of you may know, he got his feet wet in radio broadcasting at the Seneca Babcock Boys Club.

Dan's dad was Herman and mom, Luise (Zeaska). Rare case here, living in the midst of families with a lot of kids, some as many as sixteen children, Dan was an only child. He lived on Keppel Street and attended St. Monica grammar school on Orlando Street a few blocks from the Boys Club of Buffalo. After St. Monica's, it was off to Timon High School.

A couple of his close friends back then were, Herky Shanahan and Bobby Herrington. Besides hanging out at the Babcock Boys Club, Dan played a lot of touch football in the street with his buddies.

Wherever you grew up, there's always a certain sentiment you have about it, no matter how long ago you moved away. For Dan Neaverth, it was the "Club."

I asked if he'd tell me about his memories of the old neighborhood'. Here's what he had to say.

From the sixth grade on, I would normally go directly to the Club. That's what we called it, 'The Club" (Babcock Boys Club). After school we'd get into some spirited games of Dodge Ball; a sport so violent that today's anxious parents would have forbidden it. In the scaled down area used for basketball, boxing, and other less violent indoor activities, we would stand with our backs to the brick wall, which was padded only in the area directly behind the basket. A ball was placed on the floor at half court and Mr. Kelly, who seemed to be about 100 years old, would throw a second ball at the one on the floor. Then all hell broke loose as we would scramble for the loose balls. If you were hit by a thrown ball you were out, but, if while holding a ball, you could deflect the thrown ball, you were not out and you continued to play. After a while it usually came down to a few guys left.

The most feared dodge ball player was Louie Saviano. He was left handed and if he hit you in the head with the ball, your head would bounce off the brick wall. The object was to slap your hand back and stop the ball so you could go after him if you were fortunate and he missed you, and if in your excitement you crossed the center line, Mr. Kelly would call you out. He always referred to me as Smiling Dan. The Club colors were blue and orange inside a Pennsylvania keystone.

During Easter breaks from school we had a tournament called the Blue and Orange. It was ideal for building relationships because you were teamed with guys you either didn't know very well, or didn't like at all. Now, you were on the same team. The event lasted almost a week and results of each day's events were posted and we anxiously checked them out. It was a competition of everything; basketball, dodge ball, shuffleboard, checkers. You played whatever you felt you were good at and could help the team you signed up for.

One of the highlights of being a team member was riding to other clubs in the Club car. It was a stretch Desoto that held about 12 kids. You felt so proud arriving at another club in that vehicle. On Friday nights we would watch movies and serials. I loved the "Fighting Marines." Each week, an impossible escape would arise and the following week they would escape.

Several guys decided we should start a radio station at the club. Danny McBride was the lead person and convinced Mr. Jenkins, club director, to let us broadcast from the third floor over the intercom to the other floors. We had a turntable and brought our own records to play. We even had a sponsor. Well, not quite a sponsor, but we did commercials for Vi and Emil's Casa di Pizza. We would occasionally get a free pizza. Later, Danny McBride convinced a local radio station to give us some newer records to play.

Also on our staff were Joey Reynolds, Bill Masters and John Sezpanik. We all had fake names for our shows; I was Joe DeMarco, Joey Pinto was Joey Reynolds, Danny McBride was Mickey Bride and John Sezpanik, was Jack Kelly. Only Bill Masters used his real name. At the Club, we MC'd dances and did play by play of football games while leaning out the window of the third floor that overlooked the playing field. We all went on to careers in Broadcasting.

Years later when my sons were interested in sports I decided to go back to the club and coach their football team. I could have had them play in a suburban little league but I realized that they had no contact with inner city kids. There were no African American boys in our south town neighborhoods. I wanted them to experience relationships with kids who didn't have a lot of the things they might take for granted. On our team we had kids from broken homes and one whose dad was in prison. We also had a great mix of city kids-Club kids. I still have memorable photos of our team. They were a great bunch of kids who listened, tried their best and enjoyed playing the game. We certainly weren't the best team but I think we all came away with something special. I have my dad's original membership card from when he was a kid. It wasn't the Boys Club of Buffalo then, it was the Wasson House."

Dan summed it up this way about his time at the Boys Club. "I think, if you talked to any of the members from the 50's and 60's, they would all agree that some of the best times of their lives were spent at The Club."

I bumped into Danny at a gym in March of 2016 where he told me a story about an accident he had a bit north of the Seneca-Babcock area when he was about 12 years old.

"I was riding my bike near the Larkin Building on the right hand side when this man came too close and hit me with the side of his car. I was lucky he didn't tear off my foot as he hit me. The pedal got bent pretty badly. I was okay but couldn't ride the bike with the pedal bent like that. He felt so bad that he put the bike in his trunk and drove me all the way up Seneca Street to Babe Boyce's shop at the corner Indian Church Road. He got it fixed and paid for the repairs. He put the bike back in his trunk and drove me back to my neighborhood. I was amazed a stranger would do all that."

That's the "old school" way of taking care of small incidents. Today, there might be a police summoned to the scene, the driver of the car ticketed, a police report written up and perhaps, a lawyer involved. Danny's story relates well to what Lynn Salomon said: "People in our neighborhood took care of each other."

Speaking of his neighborhood, a few businesses stuck in his head. He remembers, Ann's Red & White on Elk Street, Vallesses Soda Fountain, Angerts Auro Parts, and of course, Quality Bakery. I think the entire Southside, Kaisertown and many East Side folks knew about Quality Home Bakery; it was once, that famous!

When asked about his thoughts of his old neighborhood, he said, "Back in my time growing up the Seneca-Babcock area, everybody knew everybody. It was great! I came to know what a 'close-knit' neighborhood was. I lived in one and loved it."

As with others, posing the question to him about what he sees happening on his old home turf, he said, "The area went through a time of neglect for sure, but recently, there have been visible improvements made. I hope it continues."

Here's a bit more about Dan. Sports were favorite pastimes and so was music. And talking about music, most of you know that he was one of Buffalo's all-time best DJ on several local radio stations and also did a lot of TV work. More will be said about Dan as a DJ later.

people, businesses and more

All Baby Boomers had their favorite singers and music groups back in the day. Well, so did Mr. Neaverth. He could not name any one song that was his favorite. To that question, he simply said, "Many." He being a pop music DJ, he couldn't possible pick …one. Now, as for favorite groups or signers from the 50's and 60's, his favorite group was the "Four Aces" of the 50's with songs like the million sellers, "Love Is a Many Splendor Thing," - "Three Coins in a Fountain," - "Sincerely," and "Tell Me Why."

For favorite single artist, for a time, it was one of the following. I'll list a few and see if you can guess which artist was Dan's choice. Was it; Frank Sinatra, Dean Martin, Nat King Cole, Andy Williams, Perry Como, Sammy Davis Jr., Bobby Daren or Paul Anka. As you read much further in this book, I'll divulge which artist it was. Don't be angry with me, it's just a little game I'm playing. Hey, I gotta have fun too, you know!

Some Seneca/Babcock Neighborhood Folks

We talked about all the bars the Seneca Babcock area used to have, most of which are a memory, now. My three interviewees talked about a lady who owned one of those bars. She was more than over endowed. She had a fairly serious accident because of that physical trait. (Will call her "Jane Doe.")

Here's their story, "She was feeding birds or something from a second floor porch and as she leaned over to throw the seeds to the birds, the weight of her large chesty proportion caused her to lose her balance and sent her over the railing to a nasty plunge to the ground."

She survived. They didn't know if she broke anything but said that they took her away in an ambulance wearing a neck brace. A fall from that height had to have caused some injury.

I got a few stories of individuals you might find amusing. Let's go with "Mr. Fix-it" or "Scrooge."

Lynn told me, "There probably isn't a house in the Seneca Babcock neighborhood where he visited that he didn't fix something."

Someone joked that he used a lot of duct tape.

She added, "If he walked in your house and you said, 'this or that doesn't work.' He'd say, 'It's broke.' Then he'd fix whatever was broken."

He continued. "He went over to his sister's house one day and she complained that the washing machine didn't work. He took a quick look at it, smiled broadly and said, 'Did you ever think of plugging it in?'"

Scrooge was a character. They told me that he once shaved only the right side of his mustache and only the left side of his beard just to get people's reactions. Every neighborhood has someone like him to make life interesting.

Then, there was the "pop bottle" lady who would go around the neighborhood picking up empty pop bottles. She cleaned up the neighborhood by getting rid of discarded bottles, and got plenty of exercise. It also put a few dollars in her pocket. God bless people like her.

Lynn said, "A lady named Rita Harrington had a three wheel bike and would give little kids rides up and down the street."

According to my interviewees, there was another lady who they called the Cat Lady. Somebody said she had about a thousand cats. Another refuted that number and so they all settled on… "Okay, an abundance of cats."

Barber Louie Saviano

Lou Saviano was a Seneca-Babcock area son, born and raised at 61 Inson. The house burned down around 2018. He is married to west sider Angela Gardo from Busti Avenue. They have a son named, Joe.

Lou is a graduate of South Park High, class of '55. The principal then was Mr. McCarthy. He served in the Army during the Korean War from 1954 to 1959. He remembers enlisting for the service at the Greek's Soda Shop in his neighborhood with his buddy, Larry Klemp. Another guy, Jim Sember was supposed to sign up too, but, he "over slept." Thank you for your service, Lou.

At 83 years young (2020), Lou was still snipping hair in his shop in Kenmore with his son Joe. This was his 62nd years cutting hair, trimming beards and mustaches. One of his customers has been going to him for at least 39 years. When he first started at age 20, he'd cut some of the neighborhood boys' hair. One such young man was Greg Vaughn.

Greg said, "I was one of Lou's very first customers. He cut my hair in the basement of his house when I was ten years old for a quarter."

Before Lou made barbering his career, he worked at "Buffalo Pottery" at Seneca and Bailey. It later became "Buffalo China." His first barber shop was on Orlando Street, his second, at 2830 Elmwood Avenue, and his last, at 2828 Delaware Avenue in Kenmore where he's been for the last 32 years.

Getting back to some of his memories about a neighborhood he still holds dear, he said with a smile, "One of the things about our neighborhood was that we had, Quality Bakery."

He couldn't say enough good things about it. I told him that even though there was a bakery on South Park near where I lived (Altruria St.) that I used to come to Quality Bakery for certain items mine didn't offer.

He also remembered Mary's Deli on the corner of Orlando, Drew-s Drug Store at the corner of Imson, a barber named Karl, Slamber's Appliance store where they sold washer, fridges and TVs. That's where he saw his first TV program that the owner set in the store front window.

He also remembered his old elementary school, Saint Monica's on Orlando Street, and recalled that Danny Neaverth went there too. At that parish, Lou recalls that one of the priests was sort of mean.

He said, "Yeah. That Father Fitz... wasn't shy about yelling at the kids if they did something he didn't like."

One of his best childhood memories was that he got to go to the Greeks Soda shop with friends on Seneca from time to time. It was a treat. Back then, if a kid had a dime or a quarter to spend, he was fortunate. For some, treats were far and few in between. It was a favorite place for him and all of the other neighborhood kids. He remembers clearly how much he'd look forward to getting an ice cream cone, a sundae or one of the different flavored *phosphates.

FYI: *Phosphate soda is a type of beverage that has a tangy or sour taste. It came from old fashioned syrupy, fruit flavored "phosphate soda" recipes from the 1950s, and earlier. These drinks are called "Phosphates," or "Acids," because of the "acid phosphate" that is added to the beverage to enhance taste and quantity of fizz. (Source: Tiverylucky)

people, businesses and more

Some of the guys and gals he hung out with way back then were, Marge Dickman, Fran Tater, and another lady named Phyllis. In the guys' group was his best friend, Larry Klemp, Bill Masters, Ben McBride, Roger Hill, and Dan Neaverth.

His first barber shop was downtown, his second at 2830 Elmwood Avenue and his last, at 2828 Delaware Avenue in Kenmore.

Not all of his customers are locals. Besides customers who live near his shop now, he has friends from the old days that still come to him. Here's a list of names he gave me; Jim Sember, 84 year old (as of 2019), Jack Carry, Jim Senris (spelling), and Dave Phillips (deceased).Two outsiders I met while I was interviewing Lou were men from the west side of Buffalo. One was, Ken Sull who lives at Dewitt and Forest and the other, Russell Sciabarrasi, a Vermont Street resident. The latter two faithful customers make the trek regularly from the West Side to the Kenmore area to visit with their old pal and get a trim.

Greg Vaughn
Greg, in his own words

"I was born and raised in the Seneca Babcock neighborhood May 2, 1946. Growing up in South Buffalo, it was common for people to move at least a couple of times. Our own family moved four times; starting on Morris Street, going to Perry, then to Wynona, to Gorham and lastly, Babcock Street.

My dad was James Vaughn, originally from Medina and mom Clara (Fliss) was a First Ward lady.Our family was small compared to others we had in the Babcock area. In our family, there was, me, my brother Joseph and two sisters - Carol and Betty. We all attended St Monica's School on Orlando Street with principal, Sister Mary Armert. My favorite teacher there was Sister Mary Anita. In High School at South Park High, my principle was Dr. Hayes. My favorite teachers were Mrs. Brinkworth and Mr. Held.

I grew up with a ton of friends because of the Babcock Boys Club. Some of my closest buddies where; Mike Sullivan, Steve Woji, Pat Kehoe, Bob McBride Ron, and Don King. My favorite pastimes were; shooting pool, playing chess, diving, skiing, and doing any sports with a ball or gloves. The Boys Club kept us very busy. Our mentors there; were Mr., Jenkins, Mr. Nagy, Mr. Held and John Wojitowichs.

My neighborhood was full of life with a bunch of bars, an A&P Supermarket, a butcher shop, a movie house, a pool hall, Quality Bakery, Precinct 9 Police station before it moved to Seneca and Southside Avenue. If and when we had the money, I remember the soda bar me and my friends would go to as kids.

I have so many memories from my time in the Seneca-Babcock neighborhood, some good some bad or dangerous. Example: hopping trains, river rafting, and in the winters, hitching rides on back cars bumpers. In the summertime, we played kick the can, hide and seek and curb ball. Fridays nights were special times with movies and roller skating at the Boys Club.

Growing up in the Babcock Seneca neighborhood in the 40s, 50s, and 60s was great. It was a very safe area where everyone knew everybody and helped supervise and care for the neighborhood kids. There were a lot of kids to hang out with, especially with the fact that there were several very large families; the McCabes, the Greens and the Kehoes. I believe the total from all three came over to 40 children.

Like so many guys I knew in my neighborhood and from high school, I got drafted into Uncle Sam's Army. We all didn't go to Vietnam, but I was one of the unlucky few that did. I served with the 'Big Red One US Army Division.' Just out of Viet Nam, I bought my first car - a 1969 Chevy Malibu automatic at a cost of $3,800 dollars.

Reflecting back on having been raised in that neighborhood, I can say that I have no regrets. At times, things were tough, but it helped make me into a man that had the confidence to achieve my dream of becoming a professional photographer. I opened a successful photo studio at 682 Abbott Road near the corner of Red Jacket and Potter Road, 'Vaughn's Photography.'

After 44 years in the business, I'm enjoying retirement with my wife Joanne (Walkowiak) who came from Whitfield Street. We've been kept busy with and enjoying our grown children; Denise, Brian, Katherine (Katie) and our grandchildren."

Edward Standish

Eddy is a product of the Seneca-Babcock area from Imson Street. His father is Miles Donald and (mom) Patricia (Clark). He's from a family of six children; Donna, (himself) Eddy, Darcy-Lynn, Norma-Jean, Nancy-Denise and Doreen. They all went to P.S. 26 on Harrison Street.

He vividly remembers his childhood in his neighborhood. He related to me, "Our neighborhood was a safe place; people didn't lock their doors and we'd often eat lunch at the house of friends where we were playing. When I was a kid, my parents and other parents didn't worry about us if we stayed out till the sun went down. As a matter of fact, I remember my mom telling us after supper, 'Alright, go on out and don't come back till it gets dark.' That's the way it was for me and most of the kids in our area."

A side note here. Since the typical Baby Boomer household had anywhere from four to sixteen kids, there was a good reason for shooing the children out of the house. Mom needed some quiet time for herself, and most likely, time to tend to the babies – those in diapers and needing to be put to bed without the older children making noise and keeping them awake. Of course, it was usually the older girls in the family that helped moms tuck the wee ones in for the night.

As for going out to play, the Seneca-Babcock lads had the Boys Club where, as Eddy put it, "We'd play basketball, floor hockey and dodge ball inside. And, as long as the light would hold up, we'd often play football or baseball on the field behind the Club."

Little Eddy Runs Away

When growing up and being told "not to come home till it gets dark" may have been the impetus that gave Eddy the courage to run away from home when he was about 5 or 6 years old. Ed said, "Once, when I was five or six years old, I was upset about something and ran away from home. I remember putting together the kind of get-up you see in movies or cartoons where the kids or hobos have a stick with a sack at the end of it. I really did that. I began walking, but didn't get too far. Mr. Becker who lived a few doors down from us knew what I was up to and stopped me.

He said, 'If you're going to run away, you better come in and get a sandwich, first.' I went in, and after he and his wife fed me, the urge to run away was gone. I just went back home."

Ed's best friend in the neighborhood was Mark Castonguay. Other acquaintances were; Eddy "Jumbo" Newman and his brothers Preston, Dave, and sister Terry from Troop Street. Others Eddy hung with were; John and Rich Gravius, Mark Nieman, Donny Caldfield, Eugene and Bobby Soloman from Babcock, Lee Hooper, and Earl Mecklenburg, Debbie Frazier, Terri, Beverly and Tom Harris, Mart, Pat, John, Margie and Jackie Roasch, Lisa Verrastro, Russ Ortalano , Dan, Pat, Kelly and Jay Knoop.

people, businesses and more

Ed shared how the people of the Seneca-Babcock area were hard working folks that had jobs at the Trico Plant on Elk Street (closed in '80s), or worked at Republic Steel, National Aniline, the Mobile Refinery or other businesses close by. He ran down a few businesses he remembered: Not mentioning the names, he said there were four or five delicatessens, a dry cleaner, a flower shop, a Sinclair's Gas station at the corner of Troop and a trailer sales business next to it. Houdaille Industries, the ICR Company (International Railway Company), and Grady Building were also part of the commerce there. Ed figured there had to have been at least 40 or more businesses in his "Little City," made up of delis, bars, specialty shops, stores, beauty and barber shops, bakery and plants where he grew up. He also remembers several of the men working as "scoopers" at the grain mills in the Ward's Elevator Alley; some of the Scanlon men were part of that work force.

Larry "Bump" Kehoe

Larry was born at Mercy Hospital in 1950 and grew up for a time at 65 Perry Street, corner of Orham, next to Greg Vaughn's family. He had 5 brothers; one was Arthur, who he never knew. He said, "Artie was killed on Seneca Street near Babcock where a Model-T hit him after he broke away from my mom and chased a puppy in middle of Seneca. That was in 1936. His other siblings are; sisters Anita, Donna, and Maureen. His brothers are; Paul (lives in Florida), Mike, Dave (died in 2006) and lastly, Pat. He married a gal named Patty who came from the south side area.

From 65 Perry Street, the family moved to 716 Perry in the Valley neighborhood. During his 4th and 5th grade years, he was a member of the Babcock Boys Club. Larry also went to school 69 in Kaisertown and later when he moved to Altruria Street, he went to P.S. 29.

Growing up on Altruria, one of the memories he has goes back to when he was 16 years old. He said, "I remember a day in the summer of 1966 when the some of the guys in the neighborhood gathered to protest the lack of jobs for the young people. I went to the pool hall where there was a crowd and all of a sudden, everyone on the pool hall ran out and I took off toward my street. I didn't get any further than Nick's Texas Hots before a cop grabbed me and tossed me in a squad car and put me in a cell at Precinct 15. After things calmed down on the street, I was released and went home.

Larry passed away in May of 2020. - R.I.P.

Chapter 13 Seneca Street (South)

The Other Downtown

Seneca Street was like another downtown to us South Buffalo folks. It had shoe stores, clothing and department stores, jewelry stores, pharmacies, churches and schools, butcher shops, a library, doctors, dentists, banks and who can forget, the Seneca Theatre?

Shea's Seneca Show

Just about everyone in the South Buffalo area went there for the latest movies. It was once a "grand" theatre with a huge marquee that hung over the sidewalk and a 61 foot tall sign above it that said, "Shea's Seneca." It had 6,000 bulbs lighting their massive sign. It was said that the sign's lights "used enough electricity to light 75 homes."

It opened in 1930 with seating for 2,042. In its hay day they had double feature matinees with a cartoon or a newsreel between features. I believe the price of a ticket when I started going there was around 35 cents in the early 60's. You could do a movie with popcorn and a pop for less than a buck. It closed in the early 60' and reopened in 1965 with a reduced seating capacity of 1,332 seats.

Shea's theatre

Lobby

Seneca Theatre Comments

Here are a few comments from people who remember going to see movies at what we called the "Seneca Show."

(No name given) "So good to see they've revived the Seneca Show marquee! I loved that theatre! I remember walking home through Caz Park in the dark after seeing old horror movies and being a bit freaked out."

Jeff Frentzel – "I saw the first or one or the first James Bond movies at the Seneca Show in 1965. "Goldfinger."

Suzanne Hebert "The "Fly "and" Time Machine" were a couple of the memorable movies I saw at that theatre."

Kathy Plunkett Finn - "I went there when movies were 25 cents. I have many good memories of that theatre. One great treat was ...REAL butter on the popcorn!

Balcony at the Seneca Show – yes or no?

I polled people to see if they remember the theatre having a balcony or loges where smoking was allowed. Don't forget folks, those who reported back to me are going back 40 to 50 years or more. So...for some, the memories were a bit fuzzy. Here's what I was told by the following:

Fred DeVinney - "As best I can remember, the theatre didn't have a balcony or loges where smoking was permitted. For that, people would go down to the men's room. There was a chance you'd get hassled by bullies or a member of one of the local gangs if you did venture down there. It could be risky at times. But overall, it was a good time; no regrets."

Dan-Chris Ford –"Yes there were staircases; usually closed unless you smoked, then they'd let you go up."

Patti D'Anthony Nash – "I remember balconies because it was the first time I saw the word "LOGE" I remember it being a small dimly lit little sign. And yes, we snuck up there to see what it was. If you continued down the hall, past the entrances to the lower level (main) seating, there was a carpeted staircase that led to the balcony and off to a side "loge" - a small seating area of maybe 6-8 seats. I didn't know it was a smoking area though."

As a movie theatre, it was classy looking; certainly was one of the best in Buffalo.

Marilyn Tross Schrader pointed out an amenity offered to patrons. She said, "The ladies room at the Seneca Show was downstairs and I believe there were 'women attendants' down there."

When was the last time you went to the movies and had "attendants" in the restrooms?

The sad part about the Seneca Theatre is that in the mid-sixties, young people pretty much destroyed it. One source said, "It came to a point where all the seats were either sliced or torn by delinquents; both girls and guys. Some of the girls were worse than the guys!" What a shame South Buffalo lost such a gem.

Caz Pool and Park

Before we get to the businesses, let's check out Cazenovia Park, Caz pool, people and activities. The summers of the 40's, 50's, 60's, and 70's, Caz pool and the park were the places to be for little kids and teens. It is set between Seneca Street on the east side, Potter Road on the west side and on the north side, Cazenovia Street.

Once upon a time, it was a great place. There was that little pool for the tykes, the huge pool for the bigger kids and the three level diving pool for the athletic types who would go and show off their ability to do dives like the jack-knife, the swan dive, back dive, front one and a half, a one and a half with a twist, and so on. One stunt was called the Hawaiian. A guy would jump off the highest board which was 10-12 feet high, grab one knee, lean back a little, and hit the water. There would be this huge plume of water that would shoot up maybe twenty or twenty five feet in the air. I tried it a couple of times and leaned back way too far, smacked my back on the water and came up cringing with pain. Needless to say, once was enough. I didn't care to try the Hawaiian again.

I certainly can't leave out everyone's favorite, the Cannon Ball. To get the best results and impress the most people, the highest board was where you'd launched from. It had two purposes. First, it was to create the biggest splash possible sending water in every direction and as far as possible. And second, to splash the guys and girls who laid out on the concrete near the pool to dry off. If you got the lifeguards wet, that might have been your ticket out for the day. It's not that it wasn't refreshing, it's that, the shock of a sudden rush of water hitting them wasn't a welcome treat.

The tale of Cazenovia Pool would not be complete if I didn't mention two unique individuals; Herb and Joey Keane. Herb was a slightly older gent who hung around inside and out of the pool. He did this thing where he would allow anyone to punch him in the stomach as hard as they could. I never saw a really burly type do it to him, but he'd let any young buck have a go at it. He'd stand there and say: "Okay, go." I never saw him buckle. Amazing! The second and most memorable person for sure was our beloved Mayor of Seneca Street, "Your Honor Joey Keane." His parents were Richard and Catherine Keane. Joey was one of 16 children. He had 7 sisters and 8 brothers. Joey's siblings are; Nancy, Richard, Mary Alice, Sally, Thomas, Michael, Cornelius, Catherine, Connie, Daniel, James, Margaret, Peter, Maureen and William.

Joey, who was a special-needs individual, was a one of a kind, lovable character who was befriended by everyone in Caz Park and all along Seneca Street. All the guys had his back in case any outsiders messed with him. His great personality and friendly manners earned him the righteous title, "Mayor of Seneca Street."

As I was in the process of gathering material for this project, I was talking to Billy McEwen in April of 2007 at one of his singing gigs on Hertel Avenue. We were reminiscing about Cazenovia Park and Joey's name came up. Interestingly, about a week later, I saw in the newspaper that Joey passed away, April 13, 2007 at age 60. Later that day McEwen called me and said;

"Rog...., you won't believe who passed away!"

I said... "Joey Keane. I know. I read it in this morning's paper."

He said: "Yeah... Can you believe that?! We were talking about him just last Sunday!"

What Billy remembered about Joey was also what someone brought up during the eulogy at his funeral mass at Saint Teresa's Church. It was about a little game he would play with the ladies in the changing room at Caz Pool. He liked to run through there and freak out all the gals. He would either run in, then run right back out the door or run right through to the pool area and jump in. Billy asked him one day what he saw. Joey replied, "I can't tell ya" ...Requiescat in pace, Joey. (Rest in peace Joey.) You are missed.

For history buffs, on the topic of Cazenovia Park, it has been enjoyed for over 100 years. It all started 1890 when 76 acres of the Hart family was purchased and set aside for the development of a huge park. It was designed by Frederick Law Olmstead early in 1892 and construction began in October of that year. In 1896, a section of the park was dredged out and Cazenovia Lake was born. People were able to enjoy canoeing and swimming in the summer. In the winter, after it got cold enough for ice to form, before people were allowed to skate in the ice, it was test by having a horse walk across. If it held up, the okay was given for skaters to enjoy that winter sport.

In 1915, four baseball diamonds and three tennis courts were laid out. That's where the well-known "Bowl" came to be. Later, there was a combination of at least eight softball and hardball diamonds to accommodate the great number of teams needing their own "Field of Dreams." Remember that movie with Kevin Costner and the key quote, "If we built it, they will come." Well... thousands and thousands of players, young and old, have been coming to the "Bowl."

The pools and casino

In the 50s, 60s and 70s, the Cazenovia pools were a great way for people all over South Buffalo to play and cool off in the summer. Unfortunately, it was closed in the late 70s and stood empty for several years. In the mid 80's, two of the three pools were filled in. The only one that remains to this day (2019) is the tots' pool that only sprays water on the little ones. Although the pools and ball diamonds were great attractions, the park was also used though the years to host yearly Irish and Italian festivals, musical concerts, group picnics, farmers' markets and lots more.

As for the casino, after the pools closed, it sat unused for several years until the "Buffalo Friends of Cazenovia Casino" came together in 1988 and pushed to have it revived. In 1989, bids were approved to fix its interior and exterior. After the work was done, it again became a vibrant part of "the way it was" with numerous events throughout the summer months and into September where they hold a yearly "Irish Fest" that is enjoyed by thousands of proud Irish and many other non-Irish folks as well. "Érin go brágh! (actual phrase –"Éirinn go Brách") meaning, "Ireland forever" or "Ireland to the end of time."

The waterway eventually became, just Caz Creek that flowed down toward Lake Erie. As a creek, it tended to flood and still does after a thaw where ice chucks choke off the flow. When this happened in the past, part of the park area and the Potter Road neighborhood experienced flooding. To fix the problem, a levee was built. On that raised portion of the park, a stone foot bridge was erected. It became a favorite spot for young people to hang around, or under. They go under the bridge and do whatever things teens did; smoke cigarettes, drink beer or engaged in amorous episodes.

Some guys from the Caz Park area eventually formed a band and named it the "Stone Bridge Band" – after that Caz Park foot bridge. South Buffalo's Jim Slattery was a member of the band around 1992. The members included; Jim Slattery, Bobby Roof, Bob Wirth and Greg Moran. The band is still performing in the Buffalo. A couple of other people connected to the band were, Joe Head and Willy Shelkoff.

Tony's Barber Shop
Five Generations in the Hair Cutting Business

Tony's shop

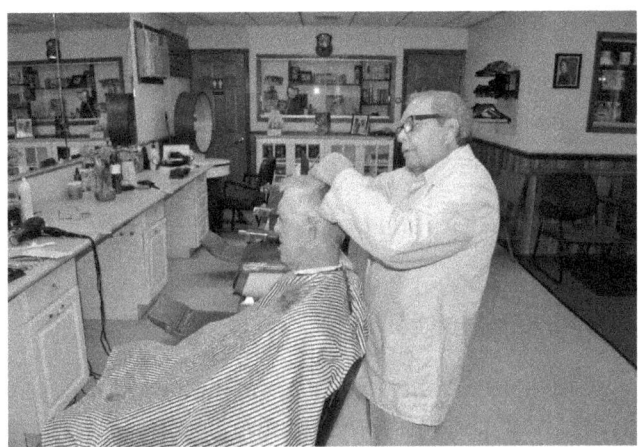

Tony & customer

Tony Scaccia comes into play a little before the official Baby Boomer generation. Originally from Sicily, he was born July 16, 1938. I spoke to him the day before his 78th birthday. At his present location at 2083 Seneca Street, he had been cutting hair for 56 years, since 1961. His family has been in the barber shop business for five generations. His father Charles Scaccia passed the trade down to him and his brother Charles. He still cuts hair along with his daughter, Maria Scaccia Gawronski. Even his wife Yolanda became a barber, not a beautician.

Tony said: "When I was sick for a while, my father told Yolanda that she should become a barber. And she did. She was one of the first women to obtain a New York State Barber's License. She trained under my father's tutelage as an apprentice."

I asked Tony how he felt about being in South Buffalo. His reply,

"Coming from Sicily to South Buffalo and starting this business was the best thing that could have happened to me. Seneca Street was a prime location."

When I asked what era was most special to him. He said:

"The '50s." Seneca Street had so much in the way of stores and businesses. We had Sears, Penney's, Western Auto, four liquor stores, three jewelry stores, flower shops, a liquidation store, a Deco and Your

Host restaurant and so much more. Fridays and Saturdays, the street was full of people. Besides the locals, we had people from Orchard Park, West Seneca and East Aurora who came to shop here."

Both Tony and Maria talked about their clientele. Maria said that even after some of their customers moved out of the Seneca Street area, they remained loyal. She told me:

"We have great clients. Many have moved away from here, but they still come to us for haircuts. It's about still belonging to this neighborhood. Even if they don't live here anymore, they won't totally disconnect themselves from the area."

Tony backed up the loyal customer phenomenon by stating that in his teens, Jimmy Keane, former Deputy County Executive, would come into his shop, sweep the floor and make coffee. He still does. Thanks Jimmy. (Note: Jimmy passed away December 2016)

He had many friends in politics. He mentioned people like Jimmy Keane, Mickey Kearns, Brian Higgins, Stefan Iwan Mychajliw, Jimmy Griffin, and Mark Schroder. He said that several of the politicians who launched a run for office, did it from his barber shop.

Of Mychajliw, he said that when Stefan was a teen, he would walk all the way from the Seneca Babcock area for haircuts in his shop. Jimmy Griffin became a regular after his barber passed away, Tony became his permanent barber.

He said: "Griffin was an early riser. He'd be the first one at my door, even before me!"

Maria jumped into the conversation and brought up the fact that a lot of the catholic school boys came to their shop for haircuts.

She said: "There was a time, everyone was known by what parish they were from. A lot of boys came in and had to have their hair cut 'just right'. We would even get a sheet from some schools that gave us specific instructions as to how the haircuts should be."

Tony added: "Our parochial schools lost so many kids between the 80s and 90s. In 1978 at Saint Teresa's school, there were 95 students who made their first communion. In 2016, only 5 students made it. Of course, today, Saint Teresa's School is closed. It's a shame."

I asked Maria's thoughts about the neighborhood. She had this to say:

"Do I see changes in our neighborhood, of course? In view of the fact that so many places have closed, people ask us how we've made it here for 55 years. Well, that's easy. Our customers became our family and are very loyal to us. During all the years we've been open, our family has been privileged of being part of the lives of so many of our customers. Hey, I even took part in picking out a few engagement rings for some of my male customers' girlfriends. That's the kind of relationships we have with our clients.
Another interesting thing about our barber shop is that some family members (meaning clients) actually meet up here as a group, for haircuts. While one of them is getting a haircut, the others sit and catch up about what's been going on in their lives."

She continued: "My dad knew everyone around here, and everyone knew him. That was good and sometimes, bad for me and my brothers if we did something we shouldn't have done. It meant that when we were out in the neighborhood, we needed to be on our best behavior. It was always expected of us growing up. You never wanted to disappoint your parents with a bad behavior report from one of the people in the community.

A well-known fact is that barber shops are sometimes like confessionals. Many of our close and loyal clients share all kinds of personal things about their family, their life or the neighborhood while sitting in our barber chairs.

Also, if we don't see a customer for a while, there's always a family member or friend who comes in and we can ask them about whoever hasn't been around. Then, the word usually gets out to those absentee clients via one of the regulars.

'Hey. Charley, they were asking about you at Tony's Barber Shop. You better stop in and say hi.'

You never lose that neighborly affection for South Buffalo and its people. When you want to know what's happening in the neighborhood, what happened to so and so, or who's running for office, you can always get an answer here at our shop. I think this is why our customers stay with us. We always ask about families, the neighborhood, or events in the lives of our people. Through the years customers have moved out into the suburbs, but always come back to reminisce about what used to be. A lot of happy and sad memories are shared.

Finally, Maria stated this about South Buffalo:

"What makes South Buffalo great is… our love and pride for the area, the memories we all hold onto and love to share. We were a strong community that helped each other. I am, and always will be, a South Buffalo kid."

Prior to interviewing Tony and Maria, I spoke to a customer named Kevin Nolan. I asked him how he felt about the area. He said:

"I wouldn't want to live anywhere else. I loved growing up here. When I was young, we were able to go home for lunch from school and had our moms there to prepare our meals. I remember going to Abbott Road to Jimmy the Greek's Texan Hots place for those great hot dogs. Also, I have old friends in the Old First Ward. We get together every Wednesday."

Bob's Barber Shop

Bob's Shop

Dan and Bill

According to a plaque on the front of the building at 2096 Seneca Street, built in 1922, there's quite a bit of history tied to it. At present, (2020) it houses Bob's Barber Shop. The hair cutting service on Seneca Street with Frank Campanile goes back to 1935 when he opened a shop at 1973 Seneca under the name, "Frank's Barber Shop." In 1951 he relocated to 2081 Seneca and in 1955, his son Bob, joined him. The last move in 1958 was at 2096. In 1975, Frank retired and left the shop to his son Bob and his partner. His son changed the name to "Bob's Barber Shop."

In 1987, Jack Gallagher began working at Bob's shop and in 1992, bought the entire building, including the barber shop, and continued cutting hair under the same shop name, "Bob's Barber Shop."

By 2015, the Hook & Ladder Development group bought the building from Gallagher and dedicated it to Frank Campanile. Gallagher turned the shop over to Dan Callahan who began working there in 1999. Dan became the fourth owner and kept the name - "Bob's Barber Shop." In 2019, he welcomed Bill Holihan aboard to share the workload.

I asked Bill what Seneca Street and South Buffalo meant to him. He said, "I'm from Ryan Street and living here gives me a sense of belonging. In the past, I loved the closeness we had with the people and the constant interaction with friends and clients. Another great aspect was that the neighbors who owned homes were proud of their neighborhood and took care of it. They policed it. If something wasn't right, something was said or done about it. Today, with many absentee landlords, it's not the same, but I see some of the old pride coming back. I love this neighborhood."

I don't know where the quote came from, but there is a fitting one at the bottom of the plaque for those who are - *"chirotonsors." (early 1900's term for barber.)

"To make a fine gentleman, several trades are required, but chiely, ...a barber!"

*Chirotonsor: (key-row-ton-sore) "One who cuts hair, especially, men's, and shaves or trims beards as an occupation."

Former Residents Remember

Gerald Regan

Baby boomer Gerald Regan, a retired teacher, spent his youth on Seneca Street and the Cazenovia Park area. He lived at 223 Seneca Street above his father's bar Regan's Bar & Grill and then moved to 2340 Seneca Street. At the elementary level he was taught by the Sisters of Mercy at St. John the Evangelist and then by the Franciscan Friars at Timon High School on McKinley Pkwy.

He said his front yard was Cazenovia Park. He remembers a chestnut grove in the park where he and his friends would gather chestnuts for chestnut wars and Caz Creek was where they'd fish and swim. Speaking of swimming, there was a water hole near the golf course. Gerry remembered that he and the other guys would dive for golf balls and sell them back to golfers for 25 cents each or 5 for a dollar.

Other activities that kept him and other Seneca Street boys busy were; climbing the Red Jacket Monument in Indian Park located between Indian Church Road and Buffum Street and hopping garages. Another dangerous pastime he and his buddies engaged in was to hop freight trains while they were going slow but then they would pick up speed and the boys had to wait till they slowed down again before getting off a few miles away. It was a long walk back home at times.

In the winter he and his friends would sled down Strickler's Hill behind School #70 on Buffum Street and skate on Caz Creek. They'd build fires by the banks of the creek, roast potatoes and warm their feet by the fire.

He remembers two neat parts of Cazenovia Park. One was "The Bowl." That's the part of the park where the baseball diamonds are. And the second, the swimming pools. He recalled that every warm summer day the place was packed with young people taking advantage of the facilities. He said: "It's a shame that all of that is now gone."

Besides sporting activities, families came from all over the area to have picnics and relax in Caz Park. Gerry and his crew would make rafts out all sorts of things that would float and sometimes they didn't float too far.

He said: "There was always something going on in that park. There was an archery range near the Caz Golf Course. We'd make and decorated our own bows and arrows. We also built model airplanes from kits and equip them with motors. It was great fun until they crashed or got caught up in some tree. We also flew home made kites. I'd save the strings from the linen supplies delivered to our tavern. I'd tie them together until I had several yards of it to fly my kites."

He remembered taking the Seneca Street bus number #14 heading downtown to Shelton Square where he'd take the "Canadiana" across Lake Erie to Crystal Beach, Canada. Once there, he'd ride the Comet roller coaster and swim in the crystal clear waters of the lake. His mom would pack a huge lunch for him which he hauled in his Radio Flyer wagon.

He said that when he was at Timon High School, he and some of the boys would hang out at Sullies on Abbott Road, drink cokes and meet up with the Mount Mercy girls. He worked as an usher at the Seneca Show which paid for his daily expenses.

For sure, he had to mention that the Friday night Timon dances were a must and people from all over South Buffalo attended. He remembers dancing to the music of Elvis Presley, the Everly Brothers, Fats Domino, and Jerry Lee Lewis.

On weekends he'd grab a pizza at La Bella's on Abbott Road, then go to listen to local bands at Mischler's Bar while having a few beers once he was old enough. Just a reminder, 18 was the legal drinking age in those days.

Peg May-Szczygiel

The May clan has long been a part of South Buffalo and very active in various social areas. Peg comes from a fairly large family; Bill May headed the family with wife Peg (Lavivey). Their children are: Bill Jr., Mary Rose, Mike, Peg, Ellie, Hank and Annette.

Their first resident was on Seneca Street and then McKinley Parkway. While living on Seneca, she went to Saint Teresa Elementary. She remembers a priest there that she liked a lot, Monsignor Toomey. When the family moved to McKinley, she went to P.S. 72. For high school, it was South Park High where Mrs. Brinkworth's history class was her favorite.

Everyone had a group of special friends growing up. For Peg, it was; Sue Lafko, Moe Masterson, June Burke, Maureen McCleary, Diane Macri and more, too many to list.

Passing time away for her as a teen and beyond was, dancing at Fazio's Club or hanging out at Chat N' Nibbles, George's Soda Shop and other areas in South Buffalo, the Valley and the First Ward.

For Peg, best memories of the old days, 50's to the 70's, she said, "I loved all of the places around the city with live bands, going out to Sunset Bay in Irving, Crystal Beach, the sororities and fraternities, and, I loved to travel." Some of that was done in her first car, a Ford Maverick. It was made from 1970 to 1977. Her favorite musical group was the Temptations.

Loblaws' parking lot served as a playground for the local kids, Peg said, "We could ride out bikes there, play handball, stickball, roller skate, and do go-cart races. The lot was right next to our house, my mom and other moms would sit on the porch to watch over the kids. Since it was well lit, we'd play past sunset while the moms would tap into their six-packs, sing songs and chat.

Peg brought up the "Blue Law" that was observed by everyone back then. She recalls that all stores closed at five or six o'clock and that on Sundays, all stores were closed. (More on the Blue Law later.)

As a teen, she remembers going to the Seneca Show and seeing teens necking. Peg said, "The ladies lounge (restroom) was kind of classy. I'd see girls smoking, talking about their boyfriends and touching up their makeup. They thought they were ~ hotsy totsy. "

As she got older, she experienced the teens' nightlife at Timon and Fazio dances. She said, "At Timon, there were more 'Squeaks' than 'Rocks.' There was address code and they played music (records) on turntables. At Fazio's, they had live bands, no dress code and there was more of an even balance of Squeaks and Rocks."

Once she hit legal drinking age, she went to bars for leisure time. She said, "For me and my friends, we hit different bars in the city; Tin Pan Alley at Bailey and Lovejoy, Glenn Park Casino, Southside Grill and Pal Tony's.

Reflecting back on good memories of the old neighborhood, Peg said, "I had great friends and really enjoyed the holidays." And as for today's thoughts on where she grew up, "It isn't as friendly as it was when I lived there since so many people that made the neighborhood it was, moved away."

As a working adult, Peggy worked for the Health Department and helped create the 1st Ward Community Association Center. She helped Peg Overdorf with the yearly Shamrock Run and the Saint Patrick's Day neighborhood parade, events at Riverfest, the River Festival and she is one of a force of four ladies taking care of the Waterfront Memories and More Museum at 41 Hamburg Street in the Old First Ward; Bert Guise-Hyde, herself, Joan Graham Scahill and Marilyn (Sue) Lafko.

Bob Williams

Bob Williams was another Seneca Street area lad who lived through the Baby Boomer years. He was from 64 Edson and like so many of the guys and girls in South Buffalo, grew up a bit on the poor side, not poor; it's just that it was time when there weren't any frills or luxuries for most. That's the way life was for the majority of the families all over South Buffalo. He said:

"Most of the guys I knew and hung around with didn't have much. No one had any spending money. Most families I knew lived from paycheck to paycheck."

Neighborhood Credit System – the Tab

Another one of Bob's memories from his youth was moms and dads could go to the local butcher shop, markets, delicatessens and pharmacy and put their purchases on a tab. That's right! No papers needed to be signed; a person's word that the bill would be paid in a timely manner was enough. That was real community living. The store owners kept a book with names and amounts, and when customers got paid at the end of the week, the bill would be taken care of. Ulrich's Butcher Shop located between Edson and Durstein was one such place.

Here are a few people that remember their family running tabs, and in what stores:

Kathleen Flattery from the Ward, "My grandma Sullivan ran tabs at her deli on Katherine Street for the neighbors."

Jim Slattery, "At 15, I ran a tab at the Columbus and South Park deli to buy cigarettes."

Jean Ralston, "In the 30's and 40's, my mom had a tab at the corner store of Hayward and South Park. She would send us kids there and it was understood that she would pay what she owed ~ when she could."

Margaret Brockman and John Silvestri remember running a tab at Bob Senco's Gulf station on South Park.

Bonnielee Matjuchin, "Our family had a tab at Wendley's on Abbott and Hubbell; also at the A&P Market."

Rich Fisher, "Our family ran tabs at the deli at Seneca and Riverview and at a nearby meat market.

Kathy Garlock, Edwall's on Abbott. "He would put our orders of bread, milk on a tab. My husband Tom would stop by every Friday when he got paid and settle the bill with the store."

And...that's just the way it was for a lot of South Buffalo folks. The days of setting up tabs in any store are long gone.

More on lack of money...

Bob Williams remembers one guy in his crew that didn't have a good dress shirt, so he borrowed one of his sisters' hoping no one would notice the buttons on the opposite side. He also remembers that when some of the kids' shoes had holes at the bottom, they'd put a piece of cardboard on the inside to patch them up. He also said that he once saw a girl who wore plastic bags over her shoes one winter day because she had no boots. Times were very tough for a lot of the kids back then. How many of you had similar experiences?

Bob recalls when he was a kid and would go shopping with his mom, She'd put aside $1.25 so she could treat him at a soda bar after the shopping was done. They'd get a sandwich, a drink and dessert. The fact that his mom paid for all this with a budget of only $1.25 is pretty amazing. Today, you can't even get a cup of coffee for that price. By the way, a cup of coffee back then was a dime.

Activities experienced by many of the Seneca Street guys were about the same as those who lived in the surrounding areas of Abbott Road, McKinley, Hopkins and South Park. There were sports in the local playgrounds, Cazenovia pool in the summer, ice skating on Caz Creek in the winter, roller skating at

Skateland on Orchard Park Road, bowling, and Timon dances. A lot of spare time was spent by Bob's crew hanging around in front of Joe's Delicatessen near the corner of Edson across Caz Park. According to Bob there was never a behavior problem hanging out there. He said that all the guys respected Joe and watched out for him. When elderly folks came down the sidewalks, they'd make way for them. They had a sense of respect and politeness. Today, I've seen older folks having to sidestep young people hording the sidewalk and having to walk in the street to get around them. That's just wrong!

Bob said that in the summer some young guys would raid gardens and fruit trees; not so much because they were hungry but just to have something to do. The plum, cherry and apple trees were the more desired targets. Well, at least they ate healthy. There were a few times when one garden owner came out and yelled, "I've got a shotgun. You better get out of there or I'll shoot!"

No one ever got shot, but the kids never knew if the man actually had a gun and would he actually shoot?

Hopping garages was another fun thing to do, like the guys from other areas did. In his crew, one of the guys taking part in the garage hopping was a little on the heavy side. As Bob told it, their hefty friend broke through one of the garage roofs and landed on the car below. Now inside, in a little bit of pain and very panicky, he had to get out of there. The door was locked. He kicked the door open and fled the scene. That incident curtailed the garage hopping outings for a while.

Seneca Street Remembered

Bob remembers a lot about the neighborhood. In my conversation with him and his wife Jeannette (Sirolli) Williams, he recalled places starting from the "city line" where George's Hot Dog stand has been there since the mid-50s. He said that there were three hot dog places at one time, all near one another. It was also known as the "Slimeline" by the locals because it was at the city line. Texas style hot dogs were called "slime dogs" because that tasty sauce toping would often "slime" all over your mouth and hands. The other hot dog places were a bit north between Georges Texas Hots and Wildwood Street. Bob couldn't remember their names or exact locations. Speaking of Wildwood, he mentioned the bowling alleys that were there and Trautwein's Fish place near Daly's Bar at 2423 Seneca. He said that people used to form long lines outside of Trautwein's on Fridays to get a fish fry at a cost of around $1.25.

City Line Texas Hots

At the corner of Buffum and Seneca, Bob said there was Mohigan's Market and at Birch, a bowling alley that featured "duck pin" bowling. These were smaller pins knocked down with a smaller ball that didn't have finger holes. It was a bit larger than a softball but made of the same material as the regular bowling balls.

Across from Indian Church Road, there was Dr. Hanzley's office and directly across Indian Church Road was the original Full Gospel Taberbacle, now located in Orchard Park on Route #20 near Union Road. He also mentioned the Parkside Bar near where he lived and at Durstein Street, a bar called the "Zoo" by its patrons.

He said: "Two very different crowds made these their main hangouts. The Parkside Bar had people who just drank while at the bar we called the Zoo, there were those who drank and ingested 'recreational medications' and inhaled smoke from another substance that didn't come from cigarettes."

There's a funny story about one of the guys who used to hang out at the Zoo.

"Joe" went in the Army for two years, did his stint and when he came out, he went back to reconnect with his old crowd at the Zoo, only to find out that some people didn't realize he was gone that long. He walked in, sat down, and one of the guys said to him:

"Hey Joe. Wow, man? I haven't seen you in here in quite a few days. We're you been, man?"

Anyway, Joe picked up from there and got back to whatever his old crew was doing.

He pointed out other businesses that are or used to be on Seneca Street. There still is Cannan's Funeral Home near Caz Park. There was a Twin Fair, Parkside Lounge at the corner of Edson Street and Berst Furniture on the corner of Indian Church Road. A bit further north was Kimaid and Matter men's clothing store where, even I came from South Park to shop for pants and shirts. A pair of good dress pants then cost between $10 and $18. They would take measurements and do alterations. It was a great store. I went to grade school with Mr. Kimaid's son Ronald who is a Timon grad.

Seneca Show turned to night club

Bob Williams had great memories of the Seneca theatre which became a night club called "Club Helene" and then renamed, "Psychus." He said that top music groups performed there such as; The Buckinghams from England (Kind of a Drag), the Zombies, (She's Not There), Bob Seger (Rambling Man) and Country Joe and The Fish (Rock and Soul Music). Both clubs featured a ton of Buffalo's top bands.

Chapter 13 Seneca Street (South)

He also recalled that there were bowling alleys upstairs from the theatre. One was known as Miller's Bowling Alleys, and another as, the Marx's Bowling Alley. He said that he and seven other guys would sometimes chip in $1 each and bowl for the pot. Hey, at 50 cents a draft, eight dollars in those days could provide a drinking guy beer for a few days. It depended on how much he drank, of course. There was a bigger bowling alley at Wildwood and another named Southside Lanes near Buffalo Creek. Eventually, the bowling lanes above the theatre were demolished and it became the Sky Room and then the Roof Top Bar.

Staying in the Seneca Theatre vicinity, Bob mentioned there was Fishman's Five and Dime Store, complete with a lunch counter and soda bar. A couple of doors down, there was a clothing store, a shoe store, Your Host Restaurant, an auto parts store, doctors' offices, lawyers' offices, flower shops, delicatessens and several other businesses.

I can't forget to mention Saint Teresa's Church at the corner of Seneca and Hayden Street and one of Buffalo's 50 Deco restaurants located right near Buffalo Creek.

Some other businesses that have been there many years and are still there today are; the Corner Florist at Yale, Bank of America and an M & T Bank near the corner of Cazenovia Street (names have changed). Further north, there is McCarthy's Funeral Home between Knoerl and Melrose, Artone's Pizza Subs & Wings place (once owned by Tony Augustine), and next to that, Lomis, Offers and Lomis Memorial Chapel. Across Buffalo Creek on Seneca Street still stands the very well-known Len-Co Lumber Company.

Bob's Crew

Bob named some of the guys that made up his crew of red-blooded American South Buffalo lads; Bucky Kerns, Dan Smith, Bobby Fitzgibbons, Tommy "The King" Riley, Pat "Shiner" Shine, Pete "Pops" Geary, Dan Patschuk, Phil and Larry Williams, Pauly, Bobby, Billy and Ricky Bugman, Jeff and Jim Taylor, Chucky Held, and "Tuffy" O'Neil. It was rumored that "Bucky" Kerns was related to pitcher, Warren Spahn, for which Cazenovia Parkway was renamed -"Warren Spahn Way."

He and his crew played touch football against other teams in the South Buffalo area. According to him, the games turned into tackle football resulting in abrasions, lacerations and contusions along with a few broken bones and rattled brains. Speaking of rattled brains, a couple of those guys might have had the capacity of becoming nuclear physicists if their brains hadn't been so rattled. Only kidding folks.

Bob said: "For the 8 or 10 years we played, we had 150 wins, 2 ties and 1 loss. Our best player was Pete 'Pops' Geary. He was a bit older than the rest of us and served as our coach for these grueling, body damaging matches. It was fun. We had a great time."

Driver's license and cars for Seneca Street folks

While I had Bob's ear, I thought I'd inquired where and when did he and his wife Jeannette got their driver's license. He told me, "It wasn't until he got out of the Army in the mid-sixties. I didn't have to take a driver's test like everybody else because he had an Army driver's license that I simply present to the folks at the auto bureau and got my New York State license."

Jeannette said, "I didn't get my license until I was 18 years old and had to make the trip to Williams Street in East Lovejoy to take the driver's test. Glad I got it done the first time around. Some of my friends had to do it more than once."

Noteworthy Cars and their Owners

Bob's first car was a 1967, 8 cylinder automatic Coronet 440 Magnum. Some other cars that were well-known on the Seneca Street strip were Phil Williams' Road Runner and Pauly Bugman's Mach I.

In the sixties and seventies, Baby Boomers who were fortunate enough to own a car got to go to drive-in theatres. Back then, the local drive-in theatres were the "Park Drive-in" on Orchard Park Road, the "Star" on Lake Avenue in Blasdell, and the "Sky Way," on Saint Francis Drive in Hamburg.

He talked about some of the car owners stuffing a few guys in the trunk to sneak them in. Cars back then had huge trunks. I think, back in the 60s, the ticket price was about 50 cents a head if you were an adult. Saving 50 cents back then could buy two gallons of gas, two packs of cigarettes or a quart of beer. Now can you see why those nice young lads snuck in the drive-in theatres? They had a better use for the fifty cents they saved – like cigarettes and beer. A pack of smokes was 25 cents and a quart of beer, 50 cents.

Bob said that he knew a guy who took his fifteen (nearly sixteen) year old girlfriend to a drive-in theatre one night and the following ensued: (To protect the innocent, we'll call her, Suzy).

"After parking the car, mounting the speaker on the window, the guy lit up a joint with all the windows closed and smoked away. His girlfriend Suzy didn't smoke and became overwhelmed with the effects of the smoke. After a fairly long time of exposure to the second-hand smoke, it was enough to give her a buzz! It put her out. Suzy fell asleep."

Some Seneca Street Bars
Daly's Bar

I heard tell that Daly's Bar is the oldest bar on Seneca Street. According to Tom Kelly, the building had been in the Daly family since the late 1800s and was opened as a Veteran's post by Bill Daly around 1923 during the time of Prohibition. He got a license to operate it as a soda bar. A customer I spoke to said that during Prohibition time, it also served as a Speak Easy and had a couple of bowling lanes in the back. In 1956, a sec-ond William (Bill) Daly, a South Park High grad, bought it from Uncle Bill Daly and ran it as a neighborhood gin mill and worked it to the age of 91.

Tom Kelley owns Daly's now as well as Kelly Expressions Photography which is a stone's throw from the inn. When you walk in to Daly's Bar, you sense that you are in a place that still has old time charm. It's been a popular watering hole for over 60 years for local retirees, politicians, firefighters, cops and area hard-working men and women who meet there to socialize. It's a great community tavern.

Hopper's Rush Inn

Rush Inn /Hopper's Bar

Hopper's at 2104 Seneca was once owned by Billy Klass who also owned the Caz Grill. From around 2016, Rick O'Sullivan owned Hopper's had been there for three years when I stopped by to gather information on the pub. Rick has many faithful patrons that meet up on a regular basis to tip a few pints of the brew.

There, I met John Czechowski who lived in the vicinity of city line off Seneca. He said, "When I lived in the city line area, we had two zip codes; 14210 and 14224; one for South Buffalo and one for West Seneca. And, I had to attend West Seneca West High. My grandparents came from Poland and lived in the First Ward for a time. My family had deli at the corner of Seneca and Bailey called Spencer's Deli. It's boarded up now."

Larry Brooks, a man in his early eighties and longtime guest at the Rush Inn had fond memories of days gone by. He's originally from Wichita Road located just south of city line past the Texas Red Hots Restaurant at 2949 Seneca. He brought up the "rag man" going down Lilac Street where he lived at one time and went to P.S. school #28. He recalled that the man would come rolling down the street in a horse-drawn wagon.

Of Seneca Street, he said, "The sidewalks on Seneca were so full of people back in the 40's, 50's and early 60's that we'd have to walk on the street; especially the during holiday shopping season."

And, about the Seneca Theatre, "I used to go to the Seneca Show in the 40's every Saturday and pay 10 cents for a matinee. I loved the 'Flash Gordon' series with Buster Crabb and 'Tarzan' movies with Johnny Weissmuller."

According to a man who wanted to remain anonymous, he said that the Seneca Theatre was owned by a man named Harry Lots and that he owned several other buildings in the Seneca Street area.

I spoke to another patron in Hopper's who also did not want to have his name in print, but was willing to speak to me. When I asked him what he thought about the Seneca area, he simply said, "It was a great place years back. Although it went downhill, I see it's trying to make a comeback. I hope it happens."

Blackthorn Restaurant

Black Thorn bar

Further down the street, still going strong is the Blackthorn Restaurant and Pub at 2134 Seneca.

In 2016, I stopped in the Blackthorn Pub at 2134 Seneca Street owned since about 1976 by Pat Lalley and Larry Adamy. I spoke to bartender, Jerry Shea and a patron named Lou Dingledey. Jerry was originally from Peabody Street. He said that the bar had a long history and that it changed names and owners from the Early Times Tavern in the fifties to the mid-seventies, to Blackthorn Restaurant and Pub. It has had the following owners; Tom Gang, Tim Leary, Dan Nostrandt Kevin Gould, Pat Lalley and Larry Adamy. It is a great venue for all sorts of celebrations; baptisms, birthdays, showers, weddings or any other event where one needs a place to have parties. Besides indoor space, the Blackthorn Pub offers outdoor amenities; outdoor bar, a fire pit, horseshoes and shaded seats and tables to enjoy the open air in warm weather.

Jerry flashed back a bit and mentioned some of the bars that have gone out of business in South Buffalo. He came up with the Golden Nugget near the city line, Parkside Grill across from Caz Park, the Southside Grill near Riverview and Seneca, the Schupper House that changed to Ireland's Own, the Thruway Inn at Harrison Street, Eddy & Wally's at Keppel Street, Charley O'Brian's at Elk and Seneca... which became Tobini's and then Luther's. There was also a Babcock Grill at the corner of Babcock and Seneca, at Morris Street, there was Old Sod. At Walter Street, there was, Cigars, then Hank and Stelle's, and another gin mill known as the Kentucky Tavern. There once was a bar called O'Neill's at 2454 Seneca, which became the Shanahan House in 1959.

As you can see, there was never a lack of watering holes on the Seneca Street strip or anywhere else in all of South Buffalo. The structures for the bars were in many cases were modified homes that were turned into restaurant-bar establishments. Way back then, many housed the owners and their families that lived upstairs. Going to work was real easy; a little trip down the stairs and into the bar they went. Most had family members who worked there bartending, or doing the cooking (if they served food). The job of cleaning up before opening time was done by one or two family members, wives, sons or daughters. Such was the case with Joe Lucenti's clan who owned a bar for fifty plus years on Perry Street in the Valley.

As you cross the bridge over Buffalo Creek going south, on the right, there was once stood the Pomeroy House on the corner of Pomeroy Street. That bar eventually became the Bridge Inn. It caught fire and was never rebuilt. Only an empty lot remains.

Other Seneca Street Area Folks

Art McLaughlin

I got to sit down with Art McLaughlin, another Seneca Street area resident of days gone by, and gathered more information about how things were. Art lived at 136 Parkview and still remembered his old telephone number – 828-5131. He went to McKinley High School and knew a guy (I knew from South Park) by the name of Vinny Catanzaro. Vinny was from the Marilla Street area of South Park. Art used to take bus #15 downtown and get a transfer to get to McKinley High at 1500 Elmwood Ave in Buffalo.

He remembered a lot of what life was like growing up in that part of South Buffalo as a kid. Like Bob Williams, he remembers the many activities the young men used to do like playing football and baseball at Caz Park in the bowl, dances at Fazio's Hall on South Park and Timon High on McKinley, hopping garages, drinking at what they called "70 Fields" (behind PS #70), tobogganing down Strickler Hill and ice skating on the Caz Creek.

He brought up how Caz Creek used to rise high enough to flood surrounding areas with chunks of ice going as far as Potter Road and breaking through basement windows. They eventually did some flood control work in that area to prevent that from happening.

He recalls Lawn Fêtes at St. John the Evangelist Church at Seneca and Parkside. He said that since gambling was illegal, they worked in some other phrasing so the games of chance could take place. Wink. Wink.

One activity in particular that was somewhat dangerous was hitching on the back of cars in the winter. Art told me he did that too. It was fun until he got caught by his dad. He said that he was hooked onto a car one winter day... not knowing the car that was following behind him was driven by his dad. Oops! He didn't say if he got a lickin' for that or not. I wonder if his dad had done the same when he was a kid. He did say that Seneca Street was not a good place to hitch onto cars. It was usually cleared of snow and taking a tumble onto asphalt was not appealing to any of the guys.

He thought that swimming at the Caz pool in the summertime was one of the great pastimes. The older guys would go to the diving pool and show off what they could do. Art and his buddy Ernie Colern were normal teenagers who liked doing exciting and interesting things. One of them was, getting on the highest board at the diving pool, Art would get on Ernie's shoulders and they'd do whatever dive or trick they could come up with. Only one thing wrong with this, they got to do it only once. The lifeguard's duty was to tell them, "Don't do that again." or "Get out."

The guys would think, "What's the big deal with doing a double man jump off the high board? What could possibly go wrong?"

Art's Crew

Here are some of the guys Art hung around with as well as some he only knew casually.

Ernie Colern, Bob and Ricky Chapman; Ricky became the mayor of some town in the Midwest. Mike Ciglia, Jimmy Stephens, Terry Collins, John, Paul and Fred Rich, John Denecke, Don and Ron Felchow, Jack Sherry, Al Gang, Billy "Weed," Gand and his brother Tom Gang (Blackthorn Tavern related) Jack Eustace, Ray Swartz, Mike Davis, Gary Canal and Dave Melisio. (I was in the same division at Fort Riley Kansas in 1966 with Jack Eustace (9th Infantry Division). Jack passed away around 2018.

Terry Collins and Dennis Sears from Art's crew also served our country.

Small World

In my conversation with Art we discovered we both knew Greg Vaughn the photographer (Seneca-Babcock area son.) He did the photos for Art's son's wedding, Daryl. I told him that I knew Greg years ago at South Park High.

Cars

I talked to Art about cars he and some of the guys he hung around had back then. His first car was a 2 door, 1962 Plymouth automatic 6 cylinder. He worked for the South Buffalo Railroad and made $2.30 an hour. With that he was able to make car payments of $28.88 a month. Some of his next cars were a 1966, four-speed, two door V8, Chevelle that he took on a trip to Florida for his honeymoon with Bev Williams May 25, 1968. After that, he had a '69 Chevy Sports Coupe and a '71 Olds Cutlass.

Bob Chapman, who Art hung with, had a 1959 Chevy Impala convertible. It was a great looking car with huge fins. John Rich had a souped up 1952 Ford and Denny Sears had a 4 cylinder Triumph convertible and a '69 Olds 442 automatic.

Stores Art Remembers

We talked about some of the stores from back then. The stores won't be in order along Seneca Street and most have been mentioned but there are a few new ones.

A central point was the Seneca Theatre at Seneca and Cazenovia. Next came Dunn's Pharmacy, Penney's Store, Kimaid and Matter's Men's clothing store, Etore Photographer and Inglegerg's Jewelry. There was a Woolworth 5 and 10 store to the left of the theatre, Erie County and Buffalo Savings banks, Papa's Restaurant, a flower shop, Western Auto, Your Host Restaurant, Melrose Bar, a pizzeria next to Blackthorn's Tavern and a hobby shop. Berst Furniture at Indian Church Road used to be a Hens and Kelly's Department Store. Then, there was, Babe Boyce's Auto and Bike Shop on the other corner, Coolie's Deli next to Parkside, the Southside Grill, Precinct 9 at Southside and the Julieta Ice House at Avondale and Seneca streets. Everyone remembers George's Texas Hots at city line.

Art said, "What a lot of people don't know is that George also had a hot dog stand near the Peace Bridge in Front Park. It once was another Ted's Hot Dogs. He bought it and served hot dogs for a while till it caught fire. He never re-opened the business."

At this writing, Art is semi-retired and enjoys family and friends along with golfing and his 1946 Chevy Fleetline Aero Sedan that he rebuilt pretty much from scrap.

Donna M. (Witczak) Shine

Donna lived at 208 Indian Church Rd as a child and young lady. With her, there are ten people in her clan. Her father is Stanley T. Witczak and mom, Lilliam (Lee) Ayers. Her siblings are; Linda, Danny, Jamie, Robin, Eddy, Nanette, and Aimee. The family's parish was St. John the Evangelist on Seneca Street where she went for catechism classes.

She has great memories of growing up as a South Buffalonian and playing in Indian Park on Buffum St. She also remembers the unwritten rule of "staying on your own turf"- a lesson she learned in the 60's when she strayed from Indian church and ended up on Frank and Ryan Streets to sell raffle tickets for her church. When they knocked on a man's door on Ryan St. in St. Theresa's Parish, they were told, "Go home and stay in our own neighborhood!' Donna said, "As a kid, I wondered where that line was?! Living there was a bit troublesome for me."

A "lefty" at a Catholic School

Being a student from a public school in a catechism class, she had to contend with unsympathetic nuns. One problem was, being left-handed. She said, "I got the ruler across my knuckles from a nun who didn't like "lefties!" Another problem with a nun was a misunderstanding she had about sitting with her public school catechism class for the 9 o'clock mass. She said, "I got in trouble for not sitting with my class. It happened when I went in and the church was so over crowded that I needed to sit in the back instead of being with the other children. The nun made an example of me by not allowing me to sit with them. I got so embarrassed. I faded to the back of the church and sat there."

On a better note, a few good things she remembers about living in the old neighborhood was; going to the city line's Texas Red Hots Restaurant owned by George and Joe and enjoying great hot dogs, sledding down Strickler's Hill behind School #70 on Buffum Street, and hopping trains with her brothers on the Pennsylvania Railroad tracks across Mineral Springs Road along Hillery Avenue.

Artwork at Saint John's

Donna loved her church. She said, "I loved looking at the beautiful artwork of paintings and statues, especially of Jesus on the Cross. By November of 1970, St. John the Evangelist Church walls were painted over with a light blue paint when I got married there.

My grandfather on my mother's side, Mahlo "James" Ayers, had repainted the inside of St. Patrick's Church on Emslie during the Great Depression. The statue of St. Patrick from that church greets all who enter the library at the Buffalo Irish Center at 245 Abbott Rd. It's the only thing that remains from Saint Patrick's that I am aware of. I always think of my grandpa when I see it."

"Crick" or "Creek"

I'm sure many of you have been pulled into a conversation about the pronunciation of 'creek' when talking about Cazenovia 'Creek.' It's one of those South Buffalo things; a funny one at that!"

Donna relates to it this way, "I frequently spent time at my aunt and uncle's house on Sage Avenue and while playing there, I remember being strictly warned by one of them saying, 'DO NOT go down by that crick!'

Someone had recently drowned there." (Buffalo Creek is located at the end of Sage)

Donna said, "If you referred to the water, it was pronounced 'crick.' If you were talking specifically about Buffalo or Cazenovia, it was referred to as 'creek'. It seemed each neighborhood had a little different take on pronunciations. All I know is that my brother and I used to play down by the - crick!"

That's "the way it was", and that's the way it still is with the locals and ~ Caz creek/crick.

Christmas Time and Stores on Seneca Street

Of Christmas time on Seneca Street, she said, "It was magical along Seneca Street in the early 1960s, from Babe Boyce's store at the corner of Indian Church to Parson & Judd's Pharmacy at Cazenovia Street. My first job was a floor-walker at Fishman's, and working the soda fountain with friend my Elaine. She remembered Western Auto where she bought her first 45 rpm records of Sonny and Cher's "Baby Don't Go' and "I Got You Babe."

Donna and the Seneca Show

Donna was one of thousands that enjoyed being a patron of Shea's Seneca Theatre. She remembers its brilliant marquee outside flashing in the dark, the echoing foyer of mirrored windows along the inclined mezzanine floor, the darkness of the theater, the balconies elevated above the crowd on each side, and the largest red velvet curtains.

She said, "I remember seeing James Stewart and Maureen O'Hara's "Mr. Hobbs Takes a Vacation" played in the early 1960s. Other movies I remember seeing there were, "Robinson Crusoe" ~ "Goldfinger" with actor Sean Connery, and the Beatles' 'A Hard Day's Night.'"

The upstairs area where the bowling allies and dance classes used to be, was remodeled and reopened on November 7, 1970 with two weddings in the new SKYROOM, 2186 Seneca Street. I remember that date very well because it happened to be the reception of my own wedding! It was divided into two halls for our event. One side had my reception and the other was for the reception of Buffalo Bill's Tom Sestak and his new bride, Patricia Smith. So, I always say that Buffalo Bills' Jack Kemp, Ed Rutkowski and Tom Sestak were all at my wedding reception."

Donna eventually moved to Orchard Park and became Senior Payroll Manager for the Town of Orchard Park for over 23 years before retiring.

Buffalo Irish Genealogical Society

Donna, her husband Jim, and high school classmate, Kevin J. O'Brien, co-founded the "Buffalo Irish Genealogical Society" (BIGS) in October 1997. Jim and Donna have been volunteering two to three days a week at the Heritage Discovery Center (HDC), 100 Lee Street doing genealogy for others and help organize and run the HDC Research Library.

Mary Heneghan

Mary's clan hails from Seneca Street. Her father, John Breen, comes from Kilmihil, Co. Clare, Ireland and mom was, Katherine (Scanlon) Breen. Mom and dad Breen raised three children; Mary, John Jr. and Noreen (Orr). This family belonged to Saint Teresa's Parish. She went there for her elementary school years and then on to Mount Mercy.

Like all of the Baby Boomers who walked to school, she remembers that the walk to Saint Teresa's was half a mile and to Mount Mercy, two miles. After the Mount, she pursued a degree at Buffalo State College where taking a bus number 15 and getting a transfer from downtown to hook up with an Elmwood Avenue bus.

Everyone remembers their close circle of friends growing up and Mary had hers too. They were;

Peggy Moran, Cathy Carey, Monica Bruenn, Nellie and Brigid Moran, Pat Scanlon, Cathy Breen, Barbara Clark, Pat Maloney, and Mary Margaret Lahiff.

There were always large families spread throughout the neighborhoods. Like so many people, Mary remembers the Keane family with sixteen children. Those were the days when people didn't pay much attention to the fact that certain families were large. It was just a common part of South Buffalo life. It's just "the way it was."

Finding something to do to pass time away for a lot of Baby Boomers wasn't very easy. A lot of youths had no outlets for their interests or to develop talents they may have possessed. I'm a prime example of that as well as most of the guys I hung out with. For Mary, it was Irish step dancing. South Buffalo was and still is very rich in Irish culture and she found her way into the Irish dancing world.

Besides dancing, she got to experience family trips to Rockaway Beach and New York City. But, her most treasured outing was her first trip to Ireland with her father in the 60's.

Music was a big part of most teenagers' life, and Mary's favorite era for that was 50's music. Her favorite artists were; Elvis (of course), Wayne Newton, the Beatles, and the Irish Rovers. She loved Elvis' "Blue Suede Shoes (recorded 1956 by Elvis but written by Carl Perkins 1955). She also liked the song "Black Slacks" recorded by Joe Bennett and the Sparkletones in 1957. Another song she liked was called, "Down in the Old Neighborhood." It was written by Mary Jane Moran, probably in late '50's. She performed at the Top Hat Grill, Lackawanna Hotel and throughout Western New York.

Lastly, thinking of her old Seneca neighborhood, Mary cherishes memories of her youth there. She said, "I loved the strong family ties, the great work ethics practiced by most people and the great freedom all of the kids had in playing outside without worrying about their safety."

As for what's going on today, she said, "I feel it's still family oriented with a diverse population and I'm pleased to see Seneca Street making a comeback."

As a working member of the Baby Boomer generation, she worked as a teacher, and later, as a business owner (Tara Irish Gift Shop on Abbott). She's kept busy being the "Director of the Irish Heritage Center" on Abbott Road (aka) "The Buffalo Irish Center."

Joe Head

Joe's childhood was spent in the Seneca Street area. His dad, Tom, mom Dorothy (Caverly) and brother Mike first lived South Ryan, and at an early age on Chamberlin Drive. As was the norm back then, he had cousins living not far from his family on Armin.

For his elementary education, he went over to Saint Williams on Harlem Road. He and his friends spent time playing boys games and shooting their toy bows and arrows with the rubber tip. No danger there, however, one of the fellas named Joey, got a 30 pound bow from his mom as a gift. Not a good idea!

As Joe tells it, "Joey shot some neighborhood guy with an arrow he made out of a straight branch to fit his bow. The tip was really pointy. Not thinking it could be dangerous, he aimed, let the arrow fly and hit Hank Baker right in the nose. The weird thing about it was that the arrow went through the cartilage of the nose just above the lip and got stuck there. Hank freaked out, turned toward the boys, roared like a lion, grabbed the arrow with both hands and snapped it off at both ends, leaving the middle piece still sticking through the cartilage. He screamed at the boys and wanted to chased them to give them a beat-down, but needed to get home quick to get help taking the remainder of the arrow out of his nose. It wasn't funny then, but kind of a funny story now. I'm glad it wasn't a worse injury; he could've been hit in the eye or worse! "

After they grew up, Hank went to Vietnam and came back with a Purple Heart. A Salute to you, **Hank!**

High school for freshman Joe Head was at the Timon Annex on Como Street, an old phone company building. As Joe told me, "For special events or assemblies, as freshmen, we went to the main building on McKinley. The problem was that the seniors there took liberties in pranking us. One day when we were entering for an assembly, some of the seniors gathered up a bunch of the dirtiest chalk erasers they could find and as we walked in the door, they began "powder-buffing" our neat sports coats. They only got away with that for a short time as Father Tim grabbed one of the seniors by the shirt, lifted him up about six inches from the floor and began to tell him, 'This isn't the way to treat our freshmen, now is it?!' I better NEVER hear about you and your friends doing anything like this again! Understood?!'

"Not that a little bullying or taunting never happened again, but the chalking thing didn't. Father Tim was not someone you messed with."

Since his high school years, Joe has been a very active singer/guitarist since the sixties and still going strong. Musicians that he's been associated with were/are men in the "Stone Bridge Band" and the "Blue Ox Band" with Willy Schoellkopf and Charley O'Neill. Later on, he formed another band called, the "Third." (or 3RDS) with himself, Charley O'Neill, and Jim Brucato. After Charley passed away, Billy McEwen joined Joe and Jim. These last three are members of the "Buffalo Music Hall of Fame."

When I mentioned Seneca Street to Joe and asked for his thoughts about the strip, he said, "Seneca Street was IT! It was great! Back in the 50's and 60's for me, Seneca Street was something to see. It had it all. I remember all the stores and shops we had. It was phenomenal! My mom giving me 50 cents to go to the Seneca show and with that, I'd buy my ticket, get a popcorn, pop and candy and still have change left over sometimes. To get in, the cost was 25 cents for matinees, pop 10 cents and a candy bar, 5 cents.

For school clothes and for a lot of the students, Joe said, "We'd go to Kimaid and Matter's Men Shop. They also sold school uniforms and would tailor them if needed."

About Joe's thoughts comparing what Seneca Street was like when he was young man and now, he said, "There's no comparison. Back then, Seneca Street was like going to downtown Buffalo in many ways. Today, it's not even close to what it was; it's somewhat depressing being that I remember vividly how great it once was. But, there is a bright side. I see they've made a lot of improvements. I hope it keeps going that way. I was especially excited when they renovated what's left of the Seneca Theatre along with a few other buildings next to it. I'd like to be optimistic and think that in my lifetime, I'll see real positive improvements to that great street."

Bart Adams

Bart, along with parents Earl "Porky" Adams and Betty (Johnson) - and siblings Denny, Karen (Kohlbacker), Sally, Betty, Eve and Michael, came from 22 Kamper Street off Seneca. The Adams kids went to school #70 on Buffum Street, South Side Jr. High and South Park High School. All were well acquainted with the Seneca Street area.

Growing up, Bart either hung out with or knew members of the Bell family, the Szchactas, the Gearys, the Wagners and, Rick Gianonni. Other close friends of Bart's were; Nancy Moore, Lynn Keenan, Debbie

Howard, Debbie Fraccia, Joanne Siverella, Adranne Ruff, Patty Aquilla, Bill Hollihan, Ned Lamarte, Renée Jakubik, Dave Carderella, Tom Kenyon, and Donnie Phillips.

He named a few large families in his area, the Moores and the Marinaros. Then, there were the Callahans with 8 children, the Scheck with 6, the Adams 7, the Lewis 6, the Whelens 6, the Keanes 16, and the Gastals with 7.

Somewhere along the line, someone in his circle of friends dubbed him, "Beefy" Adams. Some of those friends included; Bill Hollihan, Ned Lamarte, Dave Calderella, Tom Kenyon, Don Lee, Danny Pacella (aka) "Chochi", George Lukas, and Joe Scholl (aka) "Boat."

Bart and friends often hung at the Caz Park Casino or Your Host, Santora's Pizza, the Seneca Show, and the Coffee Pot at Seneca and Kamper owned by Rick Elliott's dad; also at Mario's Pool Hall on Seneca and Princeton.

Bart said, "Another hangout for Seneca Street youths was a place at Seneca and Kingston we called "The Island," next to a diner run by a couple of guys (names lost). They didn't want us hanging out in front of their place, so they set up a couple of pool tables in an attached building they owned. That solved the problem of loitering in front of their business."

Bart had a 1964 Dodge – push-button transmission (his first car) to go to work or go to bars to hear local bands. One that he enjoyed a lot was the "Fugitive" with Billy McEwen. Besides the local musicians, he liked all of the singers and groups of the 50's and 60's. He singled out the following: The Rascals with songs like "Good Lovin' (1966) - "Groovin" (1967) – "How Can I Be Sure" (1967). Early Beatles music with songs like "Love Me Do' (1962) - "I Saw Her Standing There" (1963) - "She Loves You" (1964) - "Eleanor Rigby" (1966). Dion and the Belmonts', "A Teenager in Love" (1958) - "I Cried Before" (1959) and "The Wanderer" (1961).

Thinking back about life in the Seneca Street area, he said, "In the 60's, the area was vibrant but in the mid to late 70's we saw a lot of businesses being boarded up. Bart said, "Seneca Street, from Buffalo Creek to the city line, once had about 17 bars. I'm glad they're starting to revitalize part of Seneca Street. The people mostly responsible for is a group called, "Hook and Ladder Development."

Bart remembers Father Bill Gallagher who served at Saints Tommy's, St. Martin's and later, at Saint John Vianney's in Orchard Park, and has a connection to a major name in police work. He said, "Father Bill's brother, Joe, was an officer in New York and worked with Serpico of the New York City Police Force. That's the Serpico of the 1973 hit movie "Serpico," starring Al Pacino as Frank Serpico."

Career wise, Bart served on the West Seneca Police Department. His son Bart Jr. followed in his footsteps and became a Buffalo detective, working in narcotics. Bart Sr. came to know a lot of Buffalo law enforcement people and politicians – Jimmy Griffin, for one. He mentioned Sheriff Tom F. Higgins (1930 – 2018) and Buffalo Detective Richard Cotter (1927-2011). Bart's own brother, Denny, was a detective on the Buffalo Burglary Task Force.

Of Sheriff Higgins and Detective Cotter, Bart said he heard a story about naming the Valley, "the Valley." He said, "What I heard was that Sheriff Higgins and Det. Cotter were in the same squad car as they headed into that section of Buffalo and that Cotter was the one who made the statement that they were 'going down into the Valley." As many folks know, anyone going into that area had to come down a bridge, no matter which street they took, to get into it; South Park, Van Rensselaer, Elk, Smith or Seneca Street."

Bart added, "Detective Cotter's son became my partner on the West Seneca Police Department."

While talking about law officers, he said that I should mention the most highly decorated lawman in Buffalo, Joe Ransford (1942 – 2017). The Buffalo News referred to him as a, "Cop's cop," - a "Gentle giant," - a "Legend." He served the Buffalo Police Department for 29 years. He passed away from cancer at age 75. Thank you for your service, Joe.

Dennis Adams

Dennis Adams is Bart's brother, also raised 22 Kamper Street off Seneca with parents Earl "Porky" Adams and Betty (Johnson) and siblings, Karen (Kohlbacker), Sally, Bart, Betty, Eve and Michael.

Dennis' career in law enforcement took him to many locations throughout Buffalo. His first duty was at Precinct 9 as a CPO, after that, on to the Police Academy and then, duty at Precinct 12 on Genesee Street, Precinct 13 on Hertel Avenue in 1971, next, Vice Investigator on the West Side, six weeks of detail with TPU and lastly, 13 years on the Burglary Task Force at Precincts 15 and 16.

Dennis was part of the force that was present when the Chippewa Street's Fisherman Warf's night club got shut down. He said, "Every major law enforcement agency were on hand; (SLA) State Liquor Authority agents, TPU guys, Narcotics agents, city police, and even some of Rocco Diina Sr.'s security men.

According to Dennis, the place was shut down for having engaged in illegal activities. He said, "Some guy was thrown through one of the plate glass windows and an officer going by the name of "Bull Dog" wound up having $1,800.00's worth of dental work." He added, "When it was all over, there wasn't one bottle on the shelf that wasn't broken. The place was destroyed."

Ralph Batchelor Remembers

Ralph lived on Wildwood Avenue, right off Seneca. He remembers the soda fountain place on Seneca between Wildwood and the city bus loop. He stated:

"That was a fun place to hang out. There was the Greek hot dog stand right there at the bus loop. I used to go in there a lot, especially after partying; to munch up a bunch of those delicious Greek hot dogs with their secret sauce."

I asked him about memories he had of Caz Park. He stated, "Cazenovia Park is where I played a lot of sports and enjoyed the pools in the summer. Besides the pools and the great ball diamonds, there were several gang fights from time to time; some small and some very big ones. They ranged anywhere from a few guys on to hundred or so. Most of the time, the cops heard about it and arrested a bunch of us. There were a few times when some of the guys ended up in jail for a few days. I remember one guy who stood out from the rest of us. His name was Joe. We called him "Little Joe" because he was a bit on the short side, but boy was he tough. He originally came from Hungary and I remember him telling me that he and his father had to fight off invaders every once in a while."

One of the guys was more or less the leader of the South Park/Seneca Street gang. He hung around or associated with 40 to 60 guys. We'd get together on occasions hanging on street corners, swimming or playing baseball at the park, big parties or gang fights. The main group had about 10 guys who generally hung around together. The gang fights happened on rare occasions, not very often at all. Usually, each group pretty much stayed in their own territory. After a while, the confrontations faded and people got along okay, for the most part."

He mentioned that some of the boys from Seneca Street were the hoods (hard guys) with black leather jackets and motorcycle boots and used to fight with the Squeaks from Abbott Road. Abbott was closely linked to Seneca Street with some side streets connecting one to the other. Cazenovia Park and Cazenovia Creek separated those areas.

Ralph eventually moved away from street activities and taught himself to play the guitar. Within a year or so, he put a band together with friends who hung out together at a foster home he lived in. He taught some of the guys how to play. The drummer was a natural. They played at school talent shows, some dives and parties. When they turned 18, they started playing in some of the best places around the Buffalo area like, the Silhouette Club and Mel's on Broadway.

Of the Seneca area, he said: "Seneca Street will always be special to me, lots of great times and many good memories."

Mr. Edward Miller

In 2016, I was able to catch up with one of South Park High School's teachers, Mr. Miller. I remembered him from when I went there in starting in 1962. He was very happy to share several memories of his younger days as a resident of South Buffalo and his South Park High teaching career. Being able to speak to someone who was up in age was a great addition to the project. At the time, I believe he was around 87 years old. Thanks to his daughter Iva who put me in touch with her dad. I was able to gather interesting information about his past, the high school strike, and his career as a teacher.

Mr. Miller's life covered a lot of ground. He was born in 1927. He, along with siblings, Paul, Donald and Suzanne, lived in Lackawanna, the Old First Ward and on the following streets in Buffalo: Eden, Tifft, Mesmer, Columbus, Durstein, McKinley and Edson. He ultimately settled on Tindle Street on the edge of South Buffalo in West Seneca where he, his wife Iva and daughter Iva have lived for many years.

In his youth he attended PS #34 elementary in the Old First Ward at 108 Hamburg Street. That school was demolished around 1976. He then went on to Hutchison Technical High School on Elmwood. After high school, he obtained his teaching credentials from Canisius College.

For those of you who went to South Park High where he began teaching in 1958, you probably ran into Mr. Miller somewhere along the way. He was a Social Studies teacher and swim coach. Some of his best memories come from his time as swim coach in the sixties and seventies. He replaced Mr. Bill Sweeney and coached for twenty-three years until 1981. He said this about South Park High School, "Once, South Park High was the elite school of Buffalo."

His daughter Iva, named after her mom, remembers her father would often drive half the swim team home after practices and swim meets. Then, for a celebration after swimming season was over, he'd have the entire team over to his house for (you won't believe this) L.S.D. As his daughter Iva said this, I wasn't sure I heard correctly and quickly exclaimed, "L.S.D?" Relax folks. It's not what you're thinking. She proceeded to explain the acronym she used. It meant, Luscious Spaghetti Dinner. Mrs. Miller would whip up a huge pot of spaghetti with sauce, meatballs, bread and salad. Everyone would have a great time eating and talking about the season and reliving some of the great and not so great meets they had during their competitions. One of the swimmers was Abbott Road area's own, Kevin Caffery.

Iva also told me that the swim team felt close enough to her father that they took the liberty of throwing him in the pool. Mr. Miller had been wearing white pants and guess what appeared through those white pants? Valentine boxer shorts with hearts! She related another story about the boys on the team calling all night every ten minutes, and hanging up.

I don't know if he ever got back at the team for doing that or not. If it had been me, they all would have had to swim many extra laps in the pool. "Keep me up all night? I'll show them." But, I'm not Mr. Miller. He was a nice man.

Things Mr. Miller Remembers about South Buffalo

-Horse shoe pits at the Timon High School site before the school was built – pre 1946.

-The Seneca Show where he was an usher.

-He spoke about going to Mohigan's Market on Seneca Street where he loved to get their custard filled eclairs.

-Tommy Wright's Tavern on the corner of Zittle where he'd go and tip a few glasses.

-The building of the Caz Creek flood-control banks.

-As a teacher at South Park High- cookouts at in Taylor Park

-The teacher's strike at South Park High in the early 70s.

-Teachers who crossed the picket line having their car tires flattened.

-Dock in pay for being on strike.

-Fined for being on strike and money taken out of his paychecks. One paycheck he received was for a meager $5.00.

I asked Ed and his wife, who he met at the Seneca Show while he was an usher: "What do you remember from the old days that you wished was still around?"

Mrs. Miller responded right away: "Quality Bakery in the Seneca/Babcock area and Sullivan's Ice Cream Parlor on Abbott Road where, in my time as a young girl, you could get a large hot fudge sundae for 10 cents. Iva also remembered, Mum's Bowling Alleys above the Seneca Show." (That was before others took over and changed the name).

Mr. Miller agreed. They often frequented those places.

Like most of my interviewees, I asked both Mr. and Mrs. Miller what they felt about having lived in South Buffalo area in the 40s, 50s, 60s and 70s.

Mrs. Miller: "I wouldn't want to have lived anywhere else. So sad Seneca Street isn't what it was."

Mr. Miller: "It was great living here. I have many fond memories of this area."

Dave Miller

First off, although the above Millers lived on Edson, they are not related the following Miller clan who also live on that street.

Dave Miller's clan began in the Seneca-Babcock area with dad, Joseph Anthony Miller and mom, Elizabeth (Pugh). They eventually settled on Edson Street and had six children; Julie, Joseph, Rosemary, Dave, Chris and Michelle.

The Miller children went about their lives like all other kids in their Seneca Street neighborhood. They went to the nearby church and schools, had their own special places where they'd play; on the street and

Caz Park. They shopped at the numerous stores on the Seneca Street strip and took in as many movies as they could, if the money was there.

In the sixties, twelve year old Dave and his buddies were into shooting their BB guns. One of their targets was to hunt pigeons. It was one of those things the local and other area boys did. A lad could stay occupied firing hundreds of BBs in a day. The favorite brand of the time was the; Daisy Company's "Red Ryder" BB gun. It was introduced in 1940 and cost between $2.59 and $3.00. If you increased the cost to bring it up to 1960's prices, it was probably around $12 to $15. A lot of young Red Ryder BB gun totters got into different kinds of trouble firing those "dangerous" toys. Dave did!

Dave and a President Kennedy incident!

On a warm summer day in the early 60's, Dave and friend Pat Mc'Cooy just happened to be in the wrong place at the wrong time.

In Dave's own words, "It was the inaugural day of the opening of the New York State I-190 part of the Thruway. Me, and my friend Pat Mc'Cooy, got together to shoot pigeons under the Elk street bridge with our BB rifles like we often did. We were around twelve years old and didn't realize that a motorcade with President Kennedy aboard was going to be passing by for the event. We climbed up on top of the bridge and as we were sitting on a fence talking, suddenly, Federal agents in an unmarked car pulled up."

They asked us, 'What do you guys think you are doing?!'

We quickly tried to unload the BB's out of the guns so they would just be air rifles; thinking we were in big trouble! They got out of the car and one of the men said. 'Don't you know the President is going to go by here?!'

We didn't know anything about that. We were just hunting pigeons! To us, it was no big deal, but to the Feds, it was real serious business. They took our guns away, gave us a stern warning and sent us on our way. It was one of those freak moments when the unexpected happened. I still get a kick out of it when I relive the moment. (Busted by Feds at age twelve!) I wish they hadn't taken out guns away. We didn't have money to go out and get new ones right away."

That's the way it was for Dave and his buddy Pat on their "pigeon-hunting excursion."

Martin Denecke

Martin Denecke's family hails from the Seneca Street area. In all, it'd be safe to assume there are over a hundred people connected to the Denecke clan; whether they be Deneckes, or part of the clan associated through marriage. The family is scattered throughout the U.S. and foreign countries.

His grandfather, George Denecke was a City of Buffalo Parks worker back in the 30s and 40s, and his grandma Agnes was from the Bamrick clan; another big South Buffalo family. She was one of nine children. George and Agnes were born around 1905.

Marty's father Charles's siblings include; Gerry (wife Pat), Ann (husband, George Faltyn), George (wife Nancy) and John (wife Joanie). Ann and George are still living. Former Buffalo Police Officer, Sergeant Joe Denecke Jr. is Marty's dad's first cousin. His parents were Joe, Sr. and Charlotte (Geary) Denecke. Joe & Charlotte had 9 children.

His mom Ellen (Strong)'s siblings were; Rita (husband Chet Horner), Kate (husband Jack Sheehan), Margie (husband Bob Kelly; owners of Kelly's Korner in N. Buffalo), Dan (wife Nancy) Strong and Billy Strong.

Charles grew up in a home on Parkview, off Seneca Street. He went to Timon High and mom, to Mount Mercy. His mom grew up on Ryan Street, only five blocks away from his dad's family. They met at Caz Pool at age 16, married 5 years later in 1954 and had 10 children.

The Denecke house on Parkview became the family residence for several years for young Marty and siblings, Tom, Ellen, and Mike. His other siblings, Pat, twins Colleen and Susan, John, Charles Jr. and Jennifer were raised in Hamburg where they moved in 1961.

While living on Parkview, Marty remembered Caz pool and childhood friends Ricky Palucci and younger kids of the Joyce family. After the Deneckes left the Parkview home, Marty's cousins, the Faltyns, moved in for a time.

Frank Avery

Frank Avery was not an official South Buffalo resident until he was older. He was born and raised in the Riverside section of Buffalo and eventually, as an adult, resided on Indian Church Road in the 70's where he, his wife Lori and their children became part of the South Side population. They were all Baby Boomers that got to experience life on Seneca Street and other parts of South Buffalo.

Growing up, he did pretty much what other guys did; hanging around street corners, at friends' houses, going to record hops, and going to see the latest movies. Besides the above-mentioned, he also filled spare time listening to music, playing the guitar, singing, reading the Bible and holding Bible studies. He also collected a large amount newspaper articles that dealt with the Seneca Street area, Caz pool, South Buffalo articles of all kinds on the Irish Center on Abbott Road, and Irish festivals, Kaisertown, and even, news items relating to the Village of Blasdell.

As with all of the young men, getting a car was an attainable goal and Frank's first set of wheels was a Chevy II – automatic he got as a gift; a thing very, very few Boomers could ever hope for.

When asked about his memories of life in the Indian Church neighborhood, he said, "It was very different from what is it today; it was a place where I knew everybody around my area. Today, a lot of neighbors don't know the people three houses down the street from them. That's not the type of neighborhood I want to be part of."

As mentioned, Frank loved and still loves music. When reflecting back to what group and songs he liked, he leaned heavy toward Bob Dylan and the Beatles. His favorite Beatle song is "A Day in the Life" that was released in 1967 and was part of the album, "Sgt. Pepper's Lonely Hearts Club Band." For those of you who are familiar with "world renowned" guitarist/singer Phil Keaggy, he became a close friend of Frank and Lori and stayed many times at their house on Indian Church Road when doing concerts in Buffalo. How good a guitarist was Phil? Someone asked Jimmy Hendrix, "How does it feel to be the greatest guitarist in the world?" Hendrix replied, "You better ask Phil Keaggy that question."

As a bread winner, Frank became part of that elite segment of the work force that dealt with computers. He was a soft wear technician.

Karen (Adams) Kohlbacher

Karen lived at 22 Kamper Street off Seneca with dad, Earl and mom, Betty (Johnson). This fine couple had seven children; Denny, Karen, Sally, Bart, Betty, Eve and Michael. Karen went to school #70 on Buffum

Street and remembers that her principal was Ms. Ethel Hopkins. Her favorite teacher in 5th grade was Mrs. Denz, and best friend back then was, Debbie Stevens.

Like so many of the young ladies in the neighborhoods, Karen's favorite ways for passing time was; hanging with friends and listening to the current top tunes on 45 records. She loved watching American Bandstand, seeing all of the stars and hearing the latest songs. She said that she also spent a lot of time with the Callahans and Whelens on her street.

Speaking of the Callahans and Whelens, she said, "We were nine in our family, the Callahans, with parents were ten, and the Whelens, nine."

She has fond memories of certain stores on the Seneca strip. She remembers; Fishman's, Norbans, Liberty Shoes, Western Auto, the Sample Shop and Woolworths and of course, the "Seneca Show," as we called it. She recalls seeing Patty Duke films there as well as the Beatles' "Hard Day's Night movie back in the 60s.

Thinking back about the great music and singers/bands we had back then, some of Karen's favorite entertainers were; the Supremes, the Beatles, the Platers, the Surfers, and Ann Murray. She loved Murray's song, "Could I Have This Dance" - an 80's tune.

For some reason, this is a question that I feel I need to ask most of the people I interview; "What was your first car?" This is probably because we had so many really cool-looking cars back then. By the responses I get, the folks who lived and saw many of the machines then, can search their mind to see if they can picture the classic beauties we had. For Karen, it was a 67 Ford. With the different models available, you can only guess what it looked like …but, you have some idea because back then, you could tell one car maker's product apart from the others.

As she flashed back about the old days and the way neighborhoods were, she had this to say, "It was wonderful back then. The neighborhoods were alive with kids playing hopscotch, jumping rope, playing tag; we were outside till the lights came on. It was great!"

Her thoughts about what she feels the neighborhoods are like now, "I find that a lot of properties are in deplorable condition. They are filled with mostly renters; many of which run down the houses and park on what used to be – lawns. It's just not the neighborhood I remember."

Karen's line of work was in medicine - as a Registered Nurse

Chapter 14 Life in the Abbott Road Area

People and Businesses

Abbott Rd sign

List of streets crossing Abbott Road

According to a local street map and an Atlas Road Map, Abbott Road doesn't have a route number tied to it. It starts at South Park and Bailey Avenue, goes to Bayview Road in Armor NY, does a quick left then a right turn where becomes South Abbott Road and ends at (old 219) Boston State Road, New York. Here are the local streets that cross to it - up to the Lackawanna City line.

Heussy	Ruthland	Alsace	Narragansett
Alamo	Kennefick	Meriden	Hollywood
Kimmel	Milford	Lorraine	Shenandoah
Dash	Como	Cazenovia	Dundee
Midland	Portland	Red Jacket	Kimberly
Southside	Eaglewood	Magnolia	Cushing
Mumford	Tamarack	Oakhurst	Eden
Robbins	Strathmore	Peconic	Densmore
Lakewood	Athols	Wheatfield	Whitehall
Stephenson	Columbus	Coolidge	Carlyle
Clio	(Timon H.S.)	Woodside	Downing
Melrose	Edgewood	Ramona	Turner
Hubbel	Salem	Minnetonka	Dorrance

Abbott Road - The Triangle Area

Not many folks know that Abbott used to be known as Abbott's Corner Plank Road and South Park was White's Corner Plank Road. This junction along with Bailey Avenue, South Park and Abbott Road is also referred to as the Triangle. A bit to the south of that where Southside, McKinley and Abbott Road meet, there is a park known as the Heacock Park area.

The Murthas

Before I move down Abbott Road, I want to introduce you to a very unique Irish family from the Triangle area known as, the Murthas.

In this book, I bring up large families a lot, but there is one that is absolutely amazing! In my family, there are five girls and five boys, in the Seneca Street area Keane family, there are 7 girls and 9 boys. What are the odds that a family of eight children would wind up with all of the siblings being - BOYS? That's exactly what happened to Mr. and Mrs. Murtha. Number five son of that family is Larry. Here's what he had to say about his lineage.

"My grandpa Thomas Murtha came from the poor section of Dublin called "The Liberties" and landed in Ellis Island in June of 1921. He changed his name from Murtagh to Murtha following the advice of his Uncle Ned (Ed).

Typical of that era, he saved enough money while working at Republic Steel on South Park Avenue to bring his fiancée Margaret Hughes over to the states. They were neighborhood sweethearts having lived only two doors from each other back in Dublin. They married here in Buffalo and had 6 children; Michael, Margaret, Thomas, Rosemary, Patricia, and Daniel.

My dad, Thomas (aka Jay), married Bernadette Fitzpatrick from north Buffalo and settled in South Buffalo where all of their children were born. From oldest to youngest, they are; Tom, Jim, Mark (deceased), Marty, (me) Larry, Matt, Mike and Patrick (Trick). The "Y" chromosome still runs strong along my own family; I have 4 sons - and 7 out of 8 of my grandchildren are boys."

He continued, "My father worked very hard to provide for his 8 sons while mom stayed home. He worked 3 jobs; as a full time Postal Carrier, a full time baker and a part time Parcel Post employee. These jobs totaled 100 hours per week.

Up until March of 1966, we had grown up at 34 Alamo Place in the Triangle. Back then, where you came from was known by your Parish. We were from St. Agatha's. The 1st 5 boys went to school there until my

Mom and Dad couldn't "entertain" one more call home as the nuns complained one too many times about our behavior. The straw that broke the proverbial camel's back and caused us to transfer to P.S. 28 was the fact that the oldest brother Tom was caught having a pen in his mouth while mimicking smoking a cigarette."

Young Larry Murtha and Chestnut Wars

Larry and his seven brothers spent a lot of time hanging out in Heacock Park, located at Southside Parkway and Abbott Road. He spoke of an event he and his compadres used to do every chestnut season. They took part in the yearly ritual of chestnut battles. Many, if not most of you (yous guys) know how that went. You'd gather chestnuts (the bigger the better), drill a hole in the middle, slip a string through the hole, (usually, an old shoe laces), tie a knot at the bottom of the string and go to war. Larry shared how his crowd decided who would go first.

He said, "After a quick two-out-of-three rock, paper scissors preface, the winner would select whether or not to attack or to defer."

The object was taking turns, back and forth, hitting the opponent's chestnut and breaking it apart. One guy would strike, and if he failed to break it, it was the other guy's turn. Larry, being one of the combatants, tells how one of those battles unfolded between him and a challenger named Toby. Here's his story of that battle.

"We took turns, back and forth, back and forth, until the outer shells were decimated and nothing remained but the cream-colored fruit exposed to enfilading fire. I let go a fierce and final fling and sent Toby's chestnut sailing over the crowd in a spray of splintered slivers."

After such battles, Larry described how the boys kept track of their wins. "Like the notches in a gunfighter's handle the contestants would garrulously display with bellicose bravado, the long chain of victories represented by chestnuts necklaced onto a different shoelace; usually tied to his waist belt."

I believe this game was played all over the Buffalo area. Heck, when I lived in Welland, Ontario in the 50's, my friends and I did the very same thing. I usually didn't do too well. There were always guys who had given their chestnuts some special treatment to make the shells and inside pulp harder. They would easily destroy the average virgin chestnut and, there was always some guy who would show up with a monster chestnut. Right way, you knew you were doomed. It was fun, simple good fun.

Larry's Basketball Story

When the weather was good, basketball courts were filled with Baby Boomers, especially, in the summer months. It was common for players from other playgrounds around the city challenged each other. Larry witnessed a game he's never forgotten. Here's his account of the match.

"There was a pickup basketball game that took place in the 60's in South Buffalo at Mungoven playground. It included my heroes from South Buffalo versus a team from Riverside. My team included such players as Dan Murtha (my uncle), Paul Grys, Paul Fitzpatrick, Mike Kull, and a few others of South Buffalo's best players.

When the Riverside team showed up, they arrived in two cars. The lead car emptied out quickly. All black players. The second car had fewer players. The back seat was occupied by only one guy who emerged slowly. As he came out I was shocked to see the size of his feet and the length of his legs. I had never seen a man so big. I was awed as I watched the Riverside team annihilated my heroes.

A few years later I watched three of those players on national TV vying for the NCAA national championship. Paul Grys, Mike Kull, and Bob Lanier!"

Abbott Road Residents

Abbott Road isn't as long as South Park or Seneca Street, but it too, has a lot of great South Buffalo history. As in all other South Buffalo communities, Catholic parishes played a central role in educating so many of its young people and offered many other functions that brought its parishioners together. The churches along with their elementary schools on Abbott were:

Saint Agatha's near the Triangle – (formerly at Germania and Mystic) Saint Thomas of Aquinas between Athol and Tamarack Streets Saint Martin of Tours between Downing and Dorrance. Saint Martin of Tours School later became Notre Dame Academy on July of 2006.

The Leahy family remembered the priests who served at Saint Thomas in the 60s and 70s: Fathers O'Loughlin, McNichols, Masser, Beichler and Swich.

The nuns they remember at Saint Tommy's were: Sisters Marie-Bernard, John-Elizabeth, Dionisha, William-Marie and Mary Austin

Abbott Road has its own unique place in the hearts its people. Not only for those from that area, but also for others who spent time there and have various connections; it may be friendships, relatives, businesses, night clubs that had great bands or restaurants that were special to them. That area, like the Ward, is very Irish-oriented; what with the "South Buffalo Irish Center" located there, Doc Sullivan's Pub and the street names in both its English and Gaelic. For instance, Hubbell Avenue is written with a sort of upside down "Q" – QRONN.

The Irish Center

Irish Ctr.

Irish Monument

Past Heacock Park, you'll find one of Abbott Road's favorite places to hold "Irish Pride" events of all sorts. It used to be the South Buffalo YMCA. This facility at 245 Abbott is known as the "Buffalo Irish Center," (BIC) but technically, it's the (GAAA) "Gaelic American Athletic Association of Buffalo New York," established in 1970. At this writing, Mary Breen Heneghan is its director.

It is also the place where several Irish organizations meet or have met. As stated in one of their information sheets,

"The original mission was to provide a base where Irish American organizations could gather, and a home where the Irish Emigrants could share their culture and network as they were woven into the community."

The center has over twelve non-profit Irish American organizations promoting Irish culture. Here are some of these organizations: the Knights if Equity - Court 5, St. Patrick's Irish American Club, Daughters of Erin – Court 5, Irish Cultural & Folk Art Association of WNY, Ancient Order of Hibernian, the Ladies Ancient Order of Hiberians, Innisfree Ceili Dancers, and the Shamrockettes dance group of the then "Penrose Quealy School of Irish Dance." This group was invited to put on an Irish dance show in Hollywood, Florida in March of 1964 and performed at the World's Fair September 25, 1965 in Flushing Meadows – Corona Park, Queens, New York.

Other groups at the BIC are; the Buffalo Fenians Football Club, School of Irish Culture (teaches Gaelic language), Fir Doitean (Buffalo Irish Firefighters), Sheriff's Pipe and Drum Band, the Buffalo Bagpipe Band, the Woodgate School of Irish Step Dancing, and the Daughters of Erin.

Since 1970, the Buffalo Irish Center has had many devoted supporters. One of its greatest supporters and patron was former Buffalo Mayor James "Six-Pack" D. Griffin – (mayor from '78 to '93). Griffin loved South Buffalo. Names that came up in an article written by Buffalo News writer Karen Brady in 1986 of people associated with the Irish Center were; John Carney ('86 president), Mary Breen Heneghan, Marge Reilly McDonnell, John T. Marren, William Lorigan Brady, Vincent "Vinnie" Murphy and James J. "Jim" Finucane. Other people tied to the Center are; Mike Byrne, Tom Johnson, Fred Conway, Denis Sullivan, Kieran Harrington, Jim Brennan, Kevin Dunphy, and Jack Fecio.

The main yearly event at the Buffalo Irish Center happens in March; the Saint Patrick's Day celebration. For many years it's drawn folks from all over western New York. Afterwards, it's a grand old Irish party called a "Hooley," with live music, dancing and drinks well into the night. A couple of past Grand Marshalls of the parade were; John J. Marren and William Loringan Brady ('86).

There's a second Irish celebration that month at the Center, that of the "Rince na Tiarna" and "Clann na Cara" dancers. That event draws hundreds of folks from all over the south side of Buffalo and beyond.

Karen Brady, a Buffalo News writer, mentioned comments made by two of the people mentioned above. Vinnie Murphy stated, "This is a neighborhood that is pretty much the same as it always was – with nice, friendly, neighborly people. I wouldn't live anywhere else. I'd be lost living anywhere else."

And, Jim Finucane said, "I was raised here and hope to die here. I think there are thousands in the area who feel the same way." Jim is a retired fireman from Engine 4 at Abbott and Hollywood. Thanks for your service, Jim.

Tara's shop

Mary Breen Heneghan is the owner of TARA'S GIFT SHOP across the street at 250 Abbott Road with son Tom managing the store. Mary and Marge Reilly McDonnell had an Irish goods store on Union Road in West Seneca. Between that store and Tara's, it's been in business for over 40 years.

It carries great Irish themed items from the Emerald Isle, from local Irish product suppliers, and artists. One can find such articles as special Irish occasion cards, posters, T-Shirts, hats, scarves, jewelry, *shillelaghs, **blackthorn sticks and more. During the "Saint Paddy's Day" celebration, the shop is mobbed with folks buying up their merchandise.

FYI... in case you didn't know, although it is used as a walking stick, technically,*the "shillelagh" was/is a weapon item, while the "blackthorn stick" is a walking stick.

Past and Present
Businesses/Bars

Abbott Road was almost as business-packed as South Park or Seneca Street, once. Right behind the bank at the corner of South Park and Abbott was Smilly's South Buffalo Café and Deli. Across the street at 18 Abbott Road was Ruthy's Pub also known as "The Bucket of Blood in the 60s and 70s." I was told it was called that because of the many fights that would go on there. It was somewhat the counterpart to Seneca Street's bar known as "The Zoo, or South Park's Pal Tony's." At the time I stopped in, the new owner of the property was, barber Esteban DelValle. He was cutting hair in the backside of the building. He told me that his plan was to remodel the front where the bar was and make that space his barber shop.

At 20 Abbott, there used to be a tire recap business owned by Fred Bates. It is now Koepnick's Collision Shop, first opened by Howard "BoBo" Koepnick in 1969. His sons, Joe "Yogi" and Mark, have been running it since the early '70s.

Koepnick's neighbor/business is Dennis Starr's "Side by Side Antiques" at 26 Abbott Road across from St. Agatha's. Heading down Abbott on the other side of the street, there are other watering holes.

The closest bar near Saint Agatha's is Griffin's Irish Pub at 81 Abbott, open since 1996. It had a few previous owners dating back to the '50's. Presently, it is owned by Ross Catalino. Back a ways, it was known as, [1] McDowel's, [2] Klavoon's, [3] O'Neill's run by Rory O'Shei, [4] and lastly, Griffin's Irish Pub. Dan Griffin was a partner in 2002. Other names that came up for people connected to that particular saloon were; Francis J. O'Connell and Barry Snyder Jr.

At Griffin's Irish Pub, I met Baby Boomer bartender, Joe McCarthy. He has a very interesting family...all law enforcement men. His grandfather John McCarthy, was a "police inspector" in the 60s, his dad Joe, a sergeant on the Homicide Squad, uncle John, a patrolman, brother Tom, a detective on the robbery squad, and brother Pat, a lieutenant at "A" District on South Park. One of Joe's nephews, John, became an Erie County Sheriff.

At the end of my short interview with Joe, he said, "Make sure you put in there that it was my mom Mary (Shanahan) McCarthy that kept the family in line. She was the boss!"

A pub that's been around for years and is a stone's throw from Griffin's is Jordan's Ale House at 107 Abbott. It too, had a few name changes. It goes back to the Dash Inn in the 60's, then, Dick Keane's, and Stanky's for forty years before it became Jordan's.

One of the bars near the Irish Center that is no more was, Mischler's. I went there many times to hear bands in the 60's and 70's that provided cover tunes of the latest pop groups. One such group was Billy McEwen's "Stix and Stones Band." It was the house band for a while.

Some of the locals back then that frequented the pub had this to say.

Richard Fisher – "Loved Mischler's! Ceil was the best cook. Her chicken and salad dressing were so good!"

Tony Zucarelli – "I used to hang out there with my older brother."

Peggy Redmond – "The girls couldn't go to the bar in front. They had to stay in the back room. I was 16 when I went there."

Alvin Puskalka – "Right! No girls were allowed at the front bar. I remember that a lot of nurses from Mercy Hospital used to come in and hang out in the back."

James Campbell – In Ireland, they called it the 'dirty bar' (front bar where some of the men would get a bit crude). That's why the women were barred (pun intended) from the front."

Tom Miller – My parents, aunts and uncles all went to Mischler's for fish fries on Fridays. It was a pilgrimage."

Stone Murphy from Meridian Street – "I was introduced to my brother-in-law's future wife in the front bar in '66' or '67."

Between Mischler's and former Smitty's, now Doc Sullivan's, is Conlon's Bar and Grill near Hubbell.

Marty's Collision Shop

Every car owner, at one time or another, needed and still needs a good collision shop to straighten out dings, dents, and do extensive auto body work. Marty's Collision at 334 Abbott has been doing that since 1950, that's 70 years as of 2020. It was started by Joe Cardamone then turned over to his son Mike with brother Marty sharing the load.

People and Businesses

Doc Sullivan's at 474 Abbott went through several hands. Way back (50's, 60's), it was once [1] George Hermann's place, and subsequently bought by [2] Eddy Smith, hence the name "Smitty's." He ran it for about 10 years or so in the 70's and 80's. A lot of the area's Baby Boomers remember that when the "chicken wing" craze hit, Smitty's was one of the best places to get what became known as "Buffalo Wings." After Ed Smith, [3] John Losey took it over. [4] Next, Jim Morrissey and Dennis Dargavel took a run at it. Dargavel was Morrissey's partner for only about a year. [5] After that, Jimmy Travis partnered with Morrissey. In 1999, Jerry "Doc" Sullivan and Donald Howell took over the establishment and changed the name to [6] Doc Sullivan's. All the owners kept the chicken wing recipe that made Smitty's famous throughout South Buffalo. Lucky number "7." Around 2004, Tommy Cowan took over the restaurant/tavern with landlord Matty "Burkey" Burke being very accommodating to the new owner with regards to upgrades and building maintenance.

At the time of my interview, Tommy's crew consisted of Tammy Sibley, a cook and waitress who hails from the First Ward's Hamburg Street and had worked for Smitty's and Doc's for the past 20 years. Two of Tom's barmaids/waitresses that I met were, Alyssa Klein and Grace Welsby.

Point of interest: Smitty's/Doc Sullivan's was rated for having the second oldest restaurant offering chicken wings after the Anchor Bar made them popular by (mom) Teresa and son, Dominic Bellissimo, March 4th, 1964. Doc's restaurant won the "Best Wings" award four years in a row at the Buffalo Wings Fest. It was also featured twice on the "National Food Networks."

A few more bars along Abbott were, Molly McGuire's near Woodside and the Ounce and a Half at Abbott and Hollywood. It was once owned by John Curran and Charlie Smith, then, Jim Pongo and Terry Brown. Lastly, there was Bachelor's II near Carlyle Street - the last one before you hit Dorrance.

Mercy Hospital

The Sisters of Mercy opened a 30 bed hospital on Tifft Street in 1904. Today, it is the biggest resident on Abbott Road along with the Sisters of Mercy Convent and Mount Mercy School on Redjacket. The hospital has gone through numerous expansions throughout the years. Many of you Boomers and your children were born there.

The Leahy Family Remembers

Abbott Road People and Businesses

To get good information on what businesses exist or once existed on Abbott Road, I turned to Eileen Leahy Stack, an early 70's Mount Mercy Academy girl who grew up in the Abbott Road area. It was her family of Baby Boomers' main stomping ground. She sat down one day with her clan, brothers; Pat, Bill and Dan, sister, Susan and her parents, Tom and Peg. They came up with all sorts of memories of people, events, activities, and places of business from the Triangle to the Lackawanna City line. Everyone there had a blast reminiscing.

They came up with a ton of names of people they knew; way too many to list, but here's a good number of them: The Byrnes family on Red-Jacket, the Asteks, Boris, Breens, Campbells from Hubbell, Comerfords from Strathmore, Carrs from Whitfield, Carrigs from Oakhurst, Conrads, Fitzgeralds and Jacksons from Ruthland, Chellas from Abbott, Cronins, Coughlins, Devines and Faheys from Edgewood, Dickman's from Alsace, Fortis from Tamarack, Freedenburgs from Oakhurst, Hannons from Strathmore, Henault from Eaglewood, Klines from Cumberland, Leahys from Abbott, Learys from Edgewood, Maloneys from Cumberland, McGraths from Tamarack, Myers from Eaglewood and Tamarack, Mustellos from Edgewood, Quivilands from Tamarack, Quinns from Como, Ransfords from Oakhurst, Recktenwalds from Abbott, Reddingtons from Abbott/Magnolia, Shanks from Oakhurst, Snyders from Abbott, Stutz from Ruthland, Sullivans from Ruthland/Egdewood/Belvedere, Suto's from Tuscarora, Vivians from Cumberland, Waltons from Lorraine, Rathkes, Canaans and Boo Higgins from Edgewood, and the Websers.

The Leahys' talked about growing up in the area of Abbott, Whitfield and Red Jacket. The kids had a church parking lot to play in that belonged to the Salem Lutheran Church. They named it Stone Lot Stadium because it wasn't paved; it was gravel. The local kids played baseball, relievio or hung out to pass time.

People and Businesses

There were two empty lots on Whitfield where some would gather. They were named First Field and Second Field. Some of the kids made forts in those fields.

Eileen remembers a beloved pine tree that graced McLellan Circle at Red Jacket, Choate and McKinley Parkway. It was decorated every Christmas until somebody cut it down.

She stated: "It looked so beautiful when it was decorated. We were very, very upset when it was cut down! We really missed it."

Area folks were upset for a long time with whoever did it. This was their neighborhood and someone came and messed with it. It is still a mystery to this day as to… "who done it."

Eileen mentioned other activities that kept them busy. Such games as; you're it, pies, mother may I, tag and PIG. Basketball was played in every playground and even at St. Tommy's during the summer. They would open the gym for basketball from 6 PM to 9 PM under the direction of Mike Breen, Vic LaDiscio and Mike Dickman. There were also various grammar schools from South Buffalo that would compete in track races on Saturdays at Cazenovia Park under the supervision of Mr. Head.

The Leahys came up with as many stores as they could remember that operated on Abbott Road including; the L.B. Smith Plaza at 1234 Abbott Road. I found it interesting that the address number was: one, two, tree, four Abbott Road. It's unique; hard to forget.

They sat around and began reminiscing about the numerous businesses that existed in the 50s, 60's and 70's. For those of you weren't around in those days, the list will at least give you a glimpse of what was there.

The stores will all be on Abbott Road and will not necessarily follow in order down the street. Sorry for any of the stores missed or any misspellings.

Bete's Tire Service, Howland's Esso Service, Mister Doughnut at Abbott and McKinley, Quinn-Amigone Funeral Home, Heat Moffett Heating Service, The South Buffalo Branch YMCA which became the Irish Center at Lakewood, a laundromat, Mischler's Bar, M & T Bank at Melrose and Stevenson, Liquor store at Como, Jimmy's Meat Market, Park Edge Candy at Hubbell, Shanley's Dry Cleaner at Salem, Fred Walter Jewelers, Haft's Fresh Cut Meats, Downer & Till Automotive, Bob Rigby's Sport Store at Edgewood

Trophy Shop between Alsace and Edgewood, Pete Snajack's Sporting Goods between Meridan and Salem, Parson & Judd Pharmacy (est. 1923), Papa's Pizzeria and Jimmy's Texas Hots near Cazenovia Street, Lawanda's Linoleum, Kulp's Hardware at Eden, Frank's Shoe Repair at Portland, Kennedy Mortuary, Hoff's Paint and Wallpaper, Kelly Photography and Bridal Shop at Potter Rd. Cecile's Dress Shop at Robbins St., LeTeste Red Goose Shoes at Ruthland, McKay's Work Clothes 851 Abbott at Ramona.

McKay's Clothes (est. 1973)

I need to pause here for McKay's. I've past that local business a thousand times and never gave it much thought. It has a neat history. From the outside, it looks like a little mom and pop neighborhood shop. After you enter, it's almost like you want to step back outside to look at the building to see exactly how big it is from out there. Once inside, I was amazed to see how deep the store is. It is easily a hundred feet long and has a huge inventory of quality work clothes from "brand name" companies. One that caught my eye right away was the "Carhartt" brand. Others are; Levi, Lee, Timberland, Irish Setter, Dickies, and they also sell school uniforms.

At this writing, the store is owned by Bruce and Nancy McKay. I spoke to owner Nancy McKay who was very busy on this Christmas Eve day (2019). Between taking care of customers, cashing them out, answering the phone and speaking to one of her employees, she was very gracious in taking time to provide information about the store.

She said, "We go back to 1973 when my father-in-law "Mac" McKay took $1,200 and opened this place to offer inexpensive used work clothes for the men that worked the steel mills, construction or various other plants where their clothes would get very dirty or wear out due to the nature of the job. Back then, Mac would sell used pants for $2.00, and shirts, for $1.00. When they got ruined, they would come in and buy another set.

As the store expanded with more offerings of work wear, Mac's son Bruce came aboard and eventually became the owner."

All I can say about the McKay's Work Clothes Store is that it is a "top shelf" shop for anyone looking for quality work wear.

Heading further south on Abbott

Other stores and businesses as we head further toward the former L.B. Smith Plaza, there was; Runner's Roost, Brooke's Drug Store at Portland, Thompson's Bridal Shop at Potter, Coniglio's Drugs Store, Hortman's Music at Woodside, Trend Furniture at Woodside, Lamps Pharmacy at Densmore, Rexall at Stevenson, and Karn's Flower Shop at Mumford, Joseph's Flowers at Shenandoah, Louis' Cleaners at 1083 Abbott (run by Louis Pacifico), Henry's Hamburgers (Into the 70's - maybe the last Henry's in Buffalo which became Dino's Bocce Club and then Imperial Pizza), across the street was Bachelor's II bar, Dairy Queen at Downing. Between Downing and Dorrance Avenue, one would find a Prudential Insurance Office.

The area south of Dorrance Avenue is technically Lackawanna territory but most South Buffalonians treated it as if it was part South Buffalo, especially those living in the South Park, Abbott Road and McKinley Parkway areas. They would shop at Robert Hall Men's Store across the L.B. Smith Plaza (1234 Abbott), bowl at the Lucky Strikes Bowling Alleys, eat at Crean's Restaurant and see movies at the Abbott (Town) Theatre.

More Businesses before Hitting Ridge Road

In the same area before hitting Ridge Road, there is O'Daniel's Bar-Restaurant, a Texas Red Hots. It used to be the Knotty Pine Restaurant in the mid-fifties with operators Nick and John. In 1989, it became Abbott Texas Hots. Lastly, there was, Laurel and Hardy's Nightclub near Ridge Road.

Old First Ward born Tim Fitzgerald and wife, Ann Kenefick Fitzgerald came up with a few businesses that were missed by the Leahys. They listed; Coffey's Deli, Harry's Deli, Ko-Ed Candies, Smitty's Irish Pub which became Doc Sullivan's, Campanili's Barber Shop, Roots Collision, and Pinarpo's Market. (Spelling could be off, sorry.)

People and Businesses

The L.B. Smith Plaza (est. 1951)

Before the Seneca Mall existed, a lot of people from South Buffalo came to the L.B. Smith Plaza on Abbott Road near Ridge Road to take advantage of a variety of stores not found in their neighborhoods. As you see the list below, you'll understand why.

When the Leahy family came to what was called the L.B. Smith Plaza at 1234 Abbott, in their reminiscing, they pretty much got all the names of the stores that made up that plaza in the 50s, 60s, and 70s and a few into the 80s.

AM & A's, Brand Names, L.B's Men Shop, Bell's Quality Market, Century then Naum's Catalogue Wholesale, Columbia Market, Hen's & Kelly's (gave Green Stamps), Kresges, Marine Midland, Liberty Shoes, Scott Del Children's Clothes,* Zawadzki Jewelers, Zilliox Optical.

Tim and Ann (Kenefick) Fitzgerald came up with a few more in the Plaza: Loblaw's Market, Page's Restaurant and the ACME Market.

According to sources who worked in the trade, the following car dealers that were at Abbott and Dorrance: L.B. Smith Ford in the 50s, next, Sherwood Sheehan Ford which later became Anderson Ford, then Atkins, and one of the last - Basil in 2000, which lasted 5 years.

Only one of the original stores left in the Plaza

There is only one business left from the old days in the L.B. Smith Plaza. That's ZAWADZKI JEWELERS. In January of 2020, I spoke to Randy, a fourth generation family member. He told me that the store was first set up in the early 40's by his great-grandfather, Casimer "Casey" Zawadzki, on Ridge and Ingham in Lackawanna's First Ward.

Around 1946, after WWII, his grandfather Casey Jr. and his wife Emily (Gonsiorek) paired up to manage the business. When the L.B. Smith Plaza opened in 1951, they relocated there and have been there ever since. His sons Mike and Dan along with Randy are part owners. To date, the family has been in business over 75 years. That's a great legacy. Bravo!

People's names sometimes have interesting meanings. When Randy mentioned his grandmother's maiden name, he chuckled and said, Gonsiorek in Polish means, "goose."

Knowing that jewelry stores are one of the prime targets for robberies, I asked, "Has the store ever been robbed." Randy said, "Yes. On Christmas day in 1989, some guy stole a truck and crashed it in the front of the store. Since we were closed, it was normal procedure to place the valuable merchandise in our safe. He didn't get much; only a few inexpensive items."

CHAPTER 15 ABBOTT ROAD FOLKS

The following individuals are a few people from the Abbott Road area I had the pleasure of interviewing. They spoke to me about their time in the old neighborhood and their ongoing love and ties of where they came from. They spoke warmly about friends, schools, activities, the neighborhood itself and accomplishments. First up is Kevin Caffery.

Kevin Caffery, "The Legend"

Photo: Courtesy of Kevin Caffery

Captain Kevin Caffery's family was originally from the Valley before moving to Pries Street. His father worked for Nickel City Railroad. Kevin went to Holy Family and then to Saint Thomas Elementary School on Abbott when the family moved to Milford Street.

In his teens, he hung out at the South Buffalo YMCA (now the Irish Center). He was a member of the swim team there for many years under coach, Bob Mullens. He praised Mr. Mullens for being a "nice guy and great coach." In good weather, he spent a lot of time at Caz Park playing baseball. His grandmother Margaret worked at the Caz's shelter building during active seasons.

Throughout his high school years at South Park High, Kevin was on the swim team with Mr. Ed Miller as the team coach. His skills as a swimmer earned him the honor of making All High.

After high school, he joined the Erie County Sheriff's Department in 1969. After twenty-three years of regular duties, he headed the Erie County Sheriff's Department's Aviation Unit as their prime helicopter pilot. Twenty-two of his forty-five years of service were spent in the air. He retired in 2014.

He, along with Flight Officer Art Litzinger, was often seen on newscasts as part of the helicopter crew that took part in risky rescues of Lake Erie boaters who capsized, or ice fishermen who found themselves stranded after the ice had cracked and separated. When I spoke to him in June of 2016, he told me:

"I took part of literally hundreds of such rescues during my career, of men stranded on ice flows. I remember that in one day my crew and I retrieved over 20 stranded fishermen. One of the guys we rescued wanted to be pulled up with all his fishing gear. We told him no!

We brought him up and put him in the co-pilot's seat. As we flew away from the rescue site, I noticed out of the corner of my eye that a fish was flopping on the floor of the helicopter near the guy's right foot. Can you believe it? This guy had slipped a string of fish down his snowmobile suit."

"Well that was it! My partner and I had enough of this character, and at about 1,000 feet, we dropped him out of the helicopter. We kept the fish, of course!"

Only kidding folks! Kevin and his crewman didn't do that. They saved this very imprudent angler's life and let him keep his fish. What a great rescue team.

Kevin said that in his helicopter, there were usually two men; himself and one other crewman for the easier emergency calls. At other times, there could be as many as three or four crewmen aboard to take care of more complicated airlift needs and rescues.

One of the duties called for Kevin and his crew to do flyby sweeps over rural areas where possible marijuana growers were known to try their hand at farming. He and his partner would scout out fields for any signs of marijuana plants and report back to area law officials. Local law enforcement and State Troopers would in turn move in, make arrests and destroy the plants.

He's was also called on to fly over areas where there were reports of people shining laser lights at air aircrafts. One such case led to three men from Kaisertown being arrested.

He and his crewmen even joined Canadian authorities from time to time by flying across the lake to join them chasing down criminals.

On occasions, Kevin and his crew in the helicopter used infrared cameras to track suspects. He would coordinate operations from the air as officers on the ground pursued bad guys who were on foot. "The infrared equipment was a tremendous tool," he said.

Another incident he was involved in was when he chased two guys in a stolen SUV. He stated:

"I took part in a number of car chases, but this was the longest one I was ever involved in. We were running out of fuel and had to turn back. It was very disappointing that we couldn't continue the pursuit."

He also shared the heartbreak of having to pull out of rescue missions. There were times he had to abort situations that were deemed too dangerous to the victims and/or the helicopter crew. Other means had to be used to finish certain rescues he and his crew were forced to abandon.

He told me that he nearly abandoned a rescue once when a man contemplating suicide had waded into the Niagara River near the falls. He said:

"It was a very scary situation. This was one of those rescues where I was afraid I might have to pull back and not attempt an air rescue. I was hovering over a man who had waded into the river. My crew was getting ready to snag him out of the water, and I could see that the blades of my helicopter were creating a situation that made him very unsteady on his feet. My heart was pounding. I thought the turbulence would surely knock him over and the river would carry him over the falls. I could literally see him mouth to me 'Help me!!!' This guy didn't really want to die. Thank God we were able to get him out of there. I came very close to pulling away from that one."

That rescue and many more were often lead news stories featured on TV, not only in the Buffalo/Erie County area but also on TV stations in neighboring states and Canada. Having made a name for himself as an "Ace" helicopter pilot who constantly risked his life to save others, Kevin and Deputy Chet Krupszyk were guests on the Oprah Winfrey Show in 1999 to talk about their rescue of nine year Anthony Trigilio who fell into freezing water while his seven year old friend Rich Burst held on to his hand.

Sheriff Howard

Sheriff Timothy Howard, head of the Erie County Sheriff's Department said this of Caffery. "He's a legend. Kevin is a very humble man, but he's got to be one of Erie County's greatest heroes. He's an asset, not only to the Erie County area, but to the whole region. His reputation is nationwide. I've gone to many police events all over the country and had other Sheriffs walk up to me and ask about our helicopter pilot." (Source: Dan Herbeck, Buffalo News)

If you spoke to Kevin, he would have hundreds of stories to tell you; some funny and some very sad. I asked Captain Caffery to give me his thoughts about the South Buffalo he remembers from the 60s and 70s.

"It was a great life. I established long friendships. It was a time and place of close knit families and safe neighborhoods to grow up in. Our local police and firemen were wonderful models. I knew I wanted to be a cop at the age of five. And, I can't forget the guys I could count on in those days; the Operating Engineers, iron workers, and scoopers. If you ever needed anything as a young kid, you only had to ask those guys."

Kevin's father, Frank, served as a New York State Assemblyman. He has two brothers, Mike and Fran.

Captain Caffery, thank you for the many lives you and your crew helped save, and for the many critically injured you got to the hospital on time. You will indeed be remembered as a hero and as your boss called you ~ a "legend."

Tom Best

Tom and his six siblings first came from the Abbott/Choate area and then moved to 18 Densmore Avenue in Saint Martin Parish. When I spoke to him about his days in South Buffalo and what he felt about the area, he said:

"If I could, I'd go back and live in the Abbott Road area in a heartbeat. I loved the camaraderie we had."

I asked if he could provide names of some of his neighborhood comrades of the past, he gave me the following names:

Buffalo police officer Joe Denecke, John Pavlovic, John Hamilton, Ray Jerge, Mark McNichol, Paul Fabian, Jim Quinn and Bobby Russell (Timon guys) also, Michael Caffery (lawyer and brother of Kevin Caffery, Erie Co. Sherriff helicopter pilot)

I asked him for names of some of the girls who hung with them during his teen years on Abbott. His statement rang true for most of the Baby Boomer guys who hung out at their favorite gathering spots.

Tom said, "Oh, there were no girls in our group. It wasn't like today where girls and guys all hang out together and guys treat the girls as their equals. It's wrong. It was pretty much taboo for any girl in my day as a teenager to hang around with us guys. If she did, she was looked upon in a negative way. It wasn't the proper thing to do. The girls had their own places to hang out. It wasn't on the streets in front of some store or pizzeria. That's the way it was. As the guys got older and had girlfriends, they'd date them but never brought them to hang with the guys."

Tom was in law enforcement for 34 years. He spent his first two years from 1967 to 1969 with the Blasdell Police Department then the rest of his career, with the Town of Hamburg Police Department from 1969 until his retirement in 2001. During his stint with Hamburg, he started off as patrolman, went on to become a detective and then, Detective Chief. After his retirement, he entered politics and was elected Hamburg Councilman from 2007-2008. In 2009, he ran for and won the post for Superintendent of the Hamburg Highway Department.

Dennis Dargavel

Dennis lived on McKinley and attended Holy Family until he moved to Edgewood and subsequently, to Turner Street where he attended St. Martin's. After grade school, like a ton of South Buffalonians, he attended South Park High. I asked Dennis who were some of his close friends and where they hung out back in the 60s. One of the main hang outs was Papa's Pizzeria near Mercy Hospital on Abbott Road. As for a close circle of friends, he mentioned: Jack Reville, Mike and Paul Grys, Mike Griffin and Buddy Harbicheck.

After graduating high school, Dennis went to the Buffalo Police Academy. He made it all the way through training and was ready to be sworn in as patrolman when a more appealing opportunity presented itself in Real Estate. He's been in that field since 1971. His longstanding success in realty has earned him the prestigious recognition of Realtor Emeritus. That means he's been a member of the National Association of Realtors for 40 years or more. One of Dennis' ventures also took into the "pub" business. He once partnered with Jim Morrissey to run the famous Abbott Road inn called Smitty's.

Jim and Diane Mahoney

Jim, like so many people who lived in South Buffalo has very fond memories of the Abbott Road area. As I spoke on the phone with him and his wife Diane, they both expressed great disappointment about the way the whole area has changed, all the stores that have closed, the lack of real community feel that existed, and the fast-changing demographics. Jim and Diane said:

"It's really sad to see how much of what we had, is now gone. It was great growing up there."

Jim remembers some of the guys he hung out with. Here's list he gave me. (Forgive any misspellings): "Biff" Fabe, John Schreier, Bill Fisher, Dan McNaughton, Dan Honan, Jim "Moose" Kelly, Steve Nelson, Mike Grogan, Jim Stillwell, Gary Matteson, Mike Walton, Paul Culligan, Jim and Dave Comerford, Vince Lonergan, Pat Stanton, Pete Carr, Fred Ode, Tom Gang, Pat Hurley, Paul Fitzpatrick, Rick Mozdzier, Billy Botten, Jack Smith, Fred Pannozzo, Steve Munson.

I'm sure he could have come up with a ton of other names of people he knew, but these were the guys who made up his main group.

He mentioned that he went to Saint Martin's for grade school, Timon High, then on to Lemoyne College in Syracuse.

As he got older, a couple of his main watering holes were Ounce and a Half and Early Times. Also, he remembers the Irish Center where so many events took place that related to Irish heritage and culture. Like all of the others mentioned so far in this project, he remembers the activities he and his friends took part in at Caz Park, baseball, the pools and ice skating. He was very fond of the Tosh Collins Recreation Center at 626 Abbott Road where he played basketball with many of the guys in the area. At first, the center only had a gymnasium and some exercise equipment. Later on, they added the enclosed ice rink where Black Hawks star Patrick Kane of South Buffalo honed his skills.

Katheen (Byrnes) Aures

Kathy… lived on Mariemont and Dundee, then on Red Jacket Pkwy. He dad's name is Patrick and mom's name Joan (née Sim). She has two brothers; Patrick who lives in Ireland and is an actor, and Kevin, who resides in Texas.

She attended PS #67 and #72. The Principal then was Mr. Hubbard. During her elementary school years, her best friend was Donna Greenan (now deceased)

One never knows what future connections you'll make later in life. Such is the case with Kathy. You see, she's married to Gary Aures, my wife Donna's brother who once lived on Hopkins and Good Street. Kathy's dad (Partick Byrnes) also lived in the Hopkins area and as a boy and delivered the newspaper to Gary's father Gene Aures' house. After Kathy was born, the family lived on Red Jacket and Gary's clan moved out to West Seneca near Saint John Vianney Church on Southwestern Blvd. Lo and behold, many years later, somehow Gary and Kathy met up somewhere, dated and got married. What are the odds of that happening?

She went on to Mount Mercy Academy for four year. She said, "The best memories of my youth were the four years I spent at Mount Mercy were I had fun and made lifetime friends. My favorite teacher was Sister Wm. Marie and Denise McKenzie."

Her list of friends and associates from high school is big. She listed the following and the parishes they belonged to. As Kathy put it, "Friends from high school were associated with a parish. Just mentioning what parish they belonged to told me what part of South Buffalo they were from."

Here's Kathy's list of friends; Eileen (Leahy) Stack, Jean (Cronin) Cassidy, Kate (Coughlin) Lynch, Mary Ann Myers, and Terri O'Connor, all from Saint Tommy's parish, then there was Linda (Sieckman) Dugan/ Saint Martins. From Saint Theresa's, there is; Lynn Adamczyk and Sue (Quinlivan) Walters. From Saint John's parish at Cazenovia Parkway, there was: Theresa (DiLuca) Vallone, Margie (Fiztgerald) Ostrander, Trish (Gallagher) Casillo, Margie (Martin) Michalski, Linda Howells, Catherine Gorman (deceased), Annie Bugman (deceased) Mary (Leak) Ward and Nancy (Huson) Allen. One of her old friends, Liz Hughes, lives in Australia.

Some of the ladies Kathy knew were from West Seneca but were considered being Saint Martin parish girls. They were: Pat (Hess) Cannan, Pat Quinn, Giovana (DiBiase) Germain, Sheila (Masterson) Scanlon and Sue (Kivisits) Creighton. She ended the list by saying, "I'm still in touch with several of them."

When asked what her favorite pastimes were, she said, "Playing softball, relievio, and hanging around what we called the 'Stone Stadium.' It was part of the Salem Lutheran Church's property at Whitfield and Red Jacket. Another hangout was at Saint John's on Seneca Street or at friends' houses."

I asked her if there were large families in her neighborhood. She said, "Oh, we had several. The Gallaghers had ten kids, the Stack family had fourteen, and the Germains, twelve. She couldn't provide the children's names, but one of her best friend, Eileen Stack, had them all. Thank you Eileen!

The Gallagher family roster: Joe, Bill (aka Monsignor William Gallagher), Mike, Bob, Jim, Steve, Ann, Mary-Therese, Mark and Trish.

The Stack Family kids were: Rosemary, Billy (deceased), Nancy, Maureen, John, Mark (deceased), Beth, Kevin, Dennis (Deceased), Karen, Kathy, Lori, Therese, Ginny.

The Germain Family lineup: Don (deceased), Tom, Ray, Elaine, Jim, Joan, John (deceased), Mary Ann, Michael, Bob, Joe, and Patty Ann.

The Stack and Germain families belonged to Saint John the Evangelist Parish.

As for stores and businesses Kathy remembers frequenting in 60s and 70s, she mentioned the LB Smith Plaza (Abbott Plaza) as well as Henry's Hamburgers which became a Dino's Bocce Club Pizzeria and now, the booming Imperial Pizzeria. She listed several stores where her and her family shopped. On Seneca Street there was; Twin Fair, Kresge's, Liberty Shoes Norbans, Pangels, Best Furniture at Woodside and Abbott, and of course, Coniglio's delicatessen on Abbott.

When you got to the age where you could drive, getting that first car was a real treat. Kathy said, "My first car was a '69 or '70 Galaxy 500 automatic. It cost $100.00!

I wanted to know what her old neighborhood was like in the 60s and 70s. Her response, "Things were really different from what they are today for kids. For one thing, we walked everywhere we had to go. And when we went to someone's house to get them to come out and play, there was always that annoying (to parents) calling out from outside, "Oh Molly! Oh Molly!" (or) "Oh Joey, Oh Joey!" I think my old neighborhood today is pretty much the same as it was. Although a lot of people moved away, many are actually starting coming back."

Being interested in music, I wondered what her favorite artists and songs from the past were. She said, "I really liked Billy Joel, Carol King, James Taylor and Elton John. As for favorite songs, that would be James Taylor's – 'You've got a Friend." (released 1971)

Career-wise, Kathy took time to raise three children, Ryan, Kyle and Chelsea. Once they were grown enough, she taught school at St. Bonaventure on Seneca Street and St. Martin's/Notre Dame Academy on Abbott and Downing.

Tom McDonnell

And Dog Ears Book Store and Café

Tom McDonnell, who hails from Carlyle Street, has been a tremendous supporter and promoter of South Buffalo. His parents, Kevin McDonnell and Marguerite (Reily) had four children; Tom, Lynn, Jean and Meagan. Tom is the Executive Director of "Dog Ears Bookstore and Café."

He attended Saint Martin's Elementary, Timon High, Buffalo State and Canisius College and UB. At St. Martin's, his principal was Sister Mary Eymard and his favorite teachers there were Moe Myers and Barb Ryan.

His close circle of friends were; Boots, Moose, Mikey, P.J. and all of the Carlyle gang; Danny, C.J., Wills, and Toni. His activities included playing hockey, baseball, reading, martial arts, and any street games like, hockey, red rover, relievio, hide and seek...etc. A few of his hangouts were, Dorrance Avenue, Caz Park, and gathering with friends behind P.S. School 67.

When asked about large families he knew of in his neighborhood, he named; the Kents having seven children, the Milligans, seven, and the Hillerys having eight or nine kids.

As for businesses that were close to him that he recalls were; Danny Sansone's Tavern, Miranda Liquor, Lamps' Pharmacy, Kulp Hardware, Henry's Hamburgers. One of his favorite stores was Convenient Food Mart run by Mr. Reeses.

One of Tom's best memories of the 60s and 70s was as he put it, "Playing outside until the street lights came on." When asked about what the neighborhood was like, he said, "It was the last of great American childhood existence because we were 'free from the media' influences."

At "Dog Ears Bookstore and Café" at 688 Abbott Road, Tom has been running year round programs where children can be children and not be so influenced by the world outside. He does "Story Time," where he reads to children, while often dressed in various costumes to fit the characters in readings such as, Dr. Zeuss' "Cat In The Hat" book. At Christmas time, he has involved his entire family in playing parts in the store-front window at Dog Ears wearing costumes that depicted the well-known Christmas movie, "A Christmas Story," (1940's setting), with Ralphie dreaming of getting a "Red Ryder air rifle" and dodging school bullies. Oh, I can't forget the one prop in the movie that dad, actor Darren McGavin is so proud of, and that his wife hates, but puts up with ...the "leg-shaped lamp."

Chapter 16 McKinley Parkway

Queen of the South Buffalo Streets

Here are the intersecting streets tied to McKinley Parkway, starting at Bailey Ave and moving south. It ends at South Park where it comes to the Buffalo Botanical Gardens near the Lackawanna border.

1. Kimmell	11. Strathmore	20. Whitfield	30. Cantwell
2. Midland	12. Columbus	21. Sheffield/Coolidge	31. Downing
3. Almont	13. Tifft/Edgewood	22. Woodside	32. Latona Court
4. Lakewood	14. Richfield/Alsace	23. Mariemont/Ramona	33. Aldrich
5. Mesmer/Cleo	15. Loraine	24. Harding	34. Dorrance (McKinley Circle)
6. Hubbell	16. Bloomfield	24. Culver	
7. Kenefick	17. Belvedere	26. Ridgewood	
8. Como	18. Choate (McClellan Circle)	26. Okell	
9. Eaglewood		28. Arbour Lane	
10. Olcott	19. Red Jacket (McClellan Circle)	29. Eden	

McKinley Parkway has always been an awesome street to me. I call it the "Queen Street of South Buffalo." It has remained relatively unchanged. Ninety-eight percent of it is residential with some of the grandest houses in Buffalo. The only non-family dwellings on the Parkway are; Podiatrist Dr. Barry Fitzgerald at 843 McKinley, the South Park Presbyterian Church at 519 McKinley, Timon-Saint Jude High School at 601 McKinley, the Salem Evangelical Lutheran Church at 10 McClellan Circle, and yet another at 231 McKinley called Our Lady of the Rosary RC Church at Kimberly where they have a 10 AM mass on Sundays in Latin.

Timon/Saint Jude High School

Timon High School at 601 McKinley was established in 1949. It became "Timon-Saint Jude High School" in 1993. The original Timon High was located on the 3rd floor of Our Lady of Perpetual Help in the Old First Ward. It opened in 1946. Their moto is "Fortes in fide." (Strong in faith).

The new location on McKinley Parkway between Columbus and Strathmore is where they've educated young men from several Buffalo boroughs since 1949. At one point, there were so many students enrolled (over 1,100) that the freshmen attended classes in an annex known as Nash Hall. That was an old telephone company building on Como Street.

The McKinley school building was a huge center of activities that included Friday night dances, bingo games, lawn fêtes, special performances and karate tournaments in the 70's. Just about everyone in South Buffalo and beyond attended the many events held there.

I read something about one of the dances held at Timon in the 50s where Paul Anka made an appearance. Of course, he sang "Diana," a hit at the time.

Timon prided itself, and still does, in providing a well-balanced education, complete with great book knowledge and spiritual exercises as well as sports and clubs to allow students outlets for their talents; be it on the basketball court, track and field, baseball, football or hockey.

One of their alums, Joe Kempkes, set a record in track when he ran the mile in 4:53 minutes in 1962. One of the well-known clubs was the Radio Club where Danny Neaverth was a member and became one of the top Buffalo DJs heard for miles via WKBW Radio. By the way, he started his professional radio career in Coudersport, PA.

While speaking to Steve Banko in 2020, he told me that he set a shot-put record in 1962 or 1963 that he believed still held at Timon High.

Timon and Religious Instructions for South Park High Boys

Any of the Baby Boomers who attended Timon came in contact with Father Tim. He seemed to be ten feet tall. He would have made a great drill sergeant. I remember once when we South Park High School boys attended religious instructions and some of the guys acted up, he kept us after and made us sit and stare at the clock for a half hour. Do you know how slowly time passes when you're staring at a clock?

I was told by a former Timon High student that back in the 60's, some of the good friars weren't as benevolent toward guys from the South Park Avenue area as they were toward the Abbott Road scholars who were perceived to be more gentlemanly. Perhaps, this was because a lot of the South Park Avenue area lads had a "less than favorable reputation." All in all, it boiled down to a, "boys being boys," thing, that's all. Most of the Timon High guys were relatively the same – no one better than the other. And...that's the way it was.

At the time I was putting this project together (2020), the principal at Timon was Dr. James Newton, assisted by Dean of Students, Eugene Overdorf.

Dr. Newton grew up in the Seneca/Babcock area with dad, Preston, mom Phyllis (Herbert) and siblings; Carol, Theresa, Dave, Barb and Donna. He went to St. Monica's and Southside High. Like most young men in his neighborhood, he spent a lot of time at the Boys Club. His favorite music group was U2, an Irish rock band from Dublin that was formed in 1976. The group consisted of Bono, the Edge, Adam Clayton, and Larry Mullen Jr. Rock on, Jim!

The McKinley White House

One of the greatest houses on the Parkway is a white three story house at 60 McClellan Circle. I call it the "White House of South Buffalo." It is majestic and has these great, tall pillars at the front. It's been my favorite South Buffalo house since I was a kid.

While I was taking pictures of it for the book, a man in his early forties who was walking his dog said to me: "I've lived here since I was little and have always loved this house. It's fantastic."

Ed and Lori Cudney

I wanted to speak to the present owners, Ed and Lori Cudney in May of 2016 but got no answer when I knocked. I went across Choate to Jack Heitzhaus' house at 54 McClellan. He wasn't home either but his daughter Mary Heitzhaus-Lombardo was there visiting her dad. Unfortunately, he had stepped out to go to the store. When I asked Mary about the white house, she pointed to a young mom with her daughter sitting in a chair across from her.

"You can ask her. That's the owners' daughter, Alexa."

Alexa Cudney Zippier wasn't able to give me details about the history of the house and said that I would need to speak to her parents. I came back the following week and spotted Mr. Heitzhaus sitting on his porch and figured I'd talk to him before going to the white house. He didn't have a lot of facts about it and directed me to Margaret Nash Richards' house around the corner on Choate. He told me:

"She's related to the people who used to live in that house. She would know a lot about it."

I went there and found Margaret and Lori Mortellaro Cudney sitting on the front steps. Between Lori and Margaret, I was able to find out that the deed dates back to 1913 for a Jeanette Baron. It then went to Thomas and Anna Crotty until, at least 1921. In 1921, it wound up in the hands of Doctor James and Mary Nash. (Margaret Nash Richard's grandfather) from 1921 until the 1940s. The next owners were Elizabeth (Nash) and husband John Gormley. It has remained in the Nash family until, 2005. From 2005 to the present, Ed and Lori Cudney have been the proud owners. I thought the house might be a historical landmark but found out from Lori Cudney that it wasn't.

She stated, "I wish it had that distinction, but it doesn't. However, McKinley Parkway is part of the Olmstead Park Conservancy, and that Park/Parkway system is on the National Register of Historic Places."

She added: "The Conservancy has Design Guidelines for the Parkway but they won't interfere with the home owners' properties with regards to remodeling or upgrades."

Lori continued:

"They (Conservancy people) stated that there is no need for approval from them to make changes, but that our front porch was under their guidelines, meaning that if my husband and I want to make any changes that are visible from McKinley, they have to be approved by the Conservancy."

In short, Ed and Lori are to a certain degree, under the Conservancy ruling with regards to changes to their fantastic home. I asked Lori what she and her and husband Ed felt about living in South Buffalo. She said:

"There is no other place we would rather live than right here in South Buffalo. It's a wonderful place; close to theatres, green space, and our awesome waterfront. We even like the winters."

Talking to Cudney's Neighbor

McClellan Circle

Looking to get more information about McKinley Parkway, I went back to see the Cudney's neighbor, Jack Heitzhaus. Although a pre-Baby Boomer, he was more than able to relate to my inquiries. He was very interested in talking about the area. We laughed at the confusion of the intersecting streets that make up McClellan Circle. Mostly everyone figures that all of the houses have McKinley addresses, but that's not the case. The houses that face McClellan Circle have addresses that are not McKinley Parkway addresses. The white house is 60 McClellan Circle, not 60 McKinley Parkway. Jack's house is 54 McClellan Circle, not 54 McKinley Parkway. Interestingly, the house to his left has a McKinley Parkway address. I found out that McClellan Circle was once known as Woodside Circle. Jack Heitzhaus, his wife Patricia and their eight kids originally came from Pries Street and have lived on McClellan Circle for the past 29 years. When I asked him what he felt about living in South Buffalo, he said:

"It's the most wonderful place you can live in. The people here are magnificent. I wish that it would stay the great place that it is…but, things are changing. Right now, it's still good but I worry about our children and what they may have to put up with in the future."

Sitting on the porch with Jack felt very comfortable. We were looking out toward McClellan Circle. It was quiet and peaceful. As I left, I could see that he looked relaxed and totally enjoyed sitting on his porch taking in the comfortable 75 degree day and watching people and traffic go by.

John (Jack) Gallagher

I didn't get to interview many people from McKinley Parkway, but did get a bit of info on one former resident, John "Jack" Gallagher. His parents were John Gallagher and Angnes (Quinlivan). His siblings are, Aileen, Karen, and Michael.

McKinley Parkway is fairly good in length and people in streets between Abbott and McKinley are covered by four parishes. Working from north to south, they are; Saint Agatha, Holy Family, Saint Ambrose and Saint Martin/Our Lady of Notre Dame. John and his siblings attended Saint Ambrose, which is now part of a group three churches; "Our Lady of Charity Parish, Holy Family - with offices at Saint Ambrose."

John's high school years were spent with the Franciscans at Timon. His close circle of friends included Butch Wilson, John Ranne, Mike Cunningham, Bare Pelligrino, and Jim Jackson.

A couple of Jack's pastimes in good weather was playing baseball and basketball in the area parks on organized teams as well as numerous pickup games that happened every day during summer vacations when challenged by the many different crews that were around back then.

His memories of the state of the neighborhood when he was growing up, he said, "We had a close-knit neighborhood with a lot of activities that were done through St. Ambrose. I feel the neighborhood is still very nice today (2019), but not as alive as when I grew up there. There used to be a whole lot more children back then."

The reason for the lack of large groups of children not being out and about playing anymore is due to the fact that today the average family is made up of two to four children compared to the Baby Boom years when families easily doubled or tripled those numbers.

Jack enjoyed the popular music back then like most young men. He said, "I loved Jerry Lee Lewis and his song "Great Balls of Fire." (recorded October 8, 1957 on the Sun Records label in Memphis, Tennessee).

His working days were spent at Bethlehem Steel Plant in Lackawanna and U.S. Post Office.

Our Lady of the Rosary Chapel

In 2916, I spoke to a lady named Angela who lives near Our Lady of the Rosary Chapel, 231 McKinley Parkway which was established in 1993. She told me:

"It used to be a Methodist Church. They've been doing masses in Latin on Sundays for several years now. A priest comes in from Rochester or Syracuse to say mass. They do things the old traditional way. For example, some ladies cover their head with veils. The mass usually lasts about forty-five minutes."

I asked what the attendance was like. She replied: "It's usually packed most Sundays."

This church has traditional Latin masses on Sundays at 10 AM. It is headed by Father Adam Purdy. I was told by parishioner, Maryjean Kraengle in the summer of 2016 that Father Purdy came in from Syracuse for the services. One half hour prior to the mass, those who congregate said the rosary and also did confession during that period of time. There were two altar boys for the mass dressed in their cassocks and surplices (altar boys' robe and top garment) with their hands folded. The priest faced away from the people as in the old days.

Maryjean was very gracious in providing me with information about the church. I asked her about head covering for the women and girls. She said,

"Head covering is required to attend mass. Some women wear hats but most girls and ladies wear chapel veils.

She pointed to two signs with the rules of the church affixed to the doors as you enter the sanctuary. One states the dress code:

"Men and women need to dress modestly. All women need to cover their head as is the code for Apostolic Custom and Church Law. No slacks, shorts, sleeveless dresses and low cut dresses are allowed that do not meet the norm of Christian modesty. Dress that is too casual is inappropriate. Proper dress is done to honor the Lord.

I noticed all the women and young ladies were appropriately dressed with hats or chapel veils.

The second sign explains the rules for taking communion:

"Fasting is recommended three hours before communion, but one hour is presently binding under the church law of Apostolic Custom and Church Law."

You older Baby Boomers who were altar boys and had to respond in Latin might find it interesting to attend a mass at that church, for old time's sake. It brought back a lot of memories of - the way it was.

Chapter 17 The Roman Catholic

Church & Parishes (Memories)

OLV Church

Since I just covered a bit about a church and Latin masses, the fact that South Buffalo was predominantly Catholic at one point, I thought it would be a good idea to look back and see the way the Church functioned in the 40s, 50's and 60's. Those of you that are Catholic and lived through those years might find it interesting to look back and reminisce. Here we go.

Sign of the Cross

Remember having been taught that when you walked or rode by a Catholic Church in a car, you would make the sign of the cross? And, being a good Catholic meant that you went to church every Sunday and holy days of obligation. On various holy days of obligation, if parochial schools were in session, it was very common to see the entire student body march from the classroom building, escorted by the full habit clad nuns, or teachers. It was always in two lines; with the girls going ahead of the boys "in silence, please!" After mass the students marched right back to the classroom.

Back then, people put on their Sunday best to go to church or at the very least, wore neat-looking clothes. And the churches were packed. I mean packed. In fact, ushers would have to go up and down the aisles on Sundays and special mass days to see if there were seats available for people standing at the back who had not found an open seat. Today, in some large churches, you can have a whole pew to yourself since services are not well-attended anymore. Due to poor attendance and low contributions, many had to close.

As I remember, Christmas and Easter were the two most attended days. Midnight masses on Christmas Eve were always standing room only in several churches I attended. Yes, it was good seeing people do their religious duty, but it was sad to see a few people in attendance that had too many drinks before coming. Some folks would start celebrating Christmas Eve a few hours before midnight mass. When standing or kneeling, you'd see half a dozen or more tipsy people sway a bit, and as mass went on some seated parishioners nodded off to sleep. I remember on a couple occasions when ushers had to escort out men who were talking too loud during the liturgy. Apparently, they were too drunk to realize that sound travels. Other than that, midnight masses ran smoothly. After mass, a lot of the adults went home to celebrate with relatives; eat moms' famous special Christmas dishes, have a few drinks and open presents. The general rule for the little ones was to be in bed.

Entering Church

In the past, folks followed a strict decorum or sets of dos and don'ts when going to church. Most of it is still practiced. The procedure for entering, being at mass, and exiting the church, used to follow guidelines. First thing, females had to have their head covered with a hat or chapel veil. As we well know, a lot of the rules have been changed and women do not have to cover their heads any more. You'll also see many young females in dresses with plunging necklines, wearing shorts, halter tops, tube tops and ripped jeans. It seems anything goes.

Reverence for what should be considered sacred ground as well as showing self-respect does not seem to be a concern for some. In the past, there was an understood dress code that went with going to church to honor God's fourth commandment, "Remember the Sabbath day, to keep it holy." Some things should not have changed. A lot of guys also miss the mark with regard to proper dress when going to spend time in the "House of the Lord." By the way, this goes on in non-Catholic churches as well.

As one entered a Catholic Church back then, silence was one of the first things observed. Then, one would bless themselves by dipping their right hand fingers (usually the first two) into the holy water bowl and making the sign of the cross. This relates to the Bible in Deuteronomy 28:6, "Blessed shall thou be in thy coming in, and blessed shalt thou by in thy going out."

The Jewish people place a mezuzah on the door posts (mazuzot) of their houses. It holds a piece of parchment containing Hebrew verses. They touch it, bring their hand to their lips and kiss it to honor God as they leave and enter their home.

Once in church and people found their seat, they genuflected in the aisle and again made the sign of the cross. When mass started everyone stood when the priest entered. After that, there was that series of sitting, standing and kneeling as well as spoken responses, and making little signs of the cross on one's forehead, mouth and heart at a point in the mass. After the mass was over, exiting your pew was also done with reverence and in silence; again genuflecting and making a sign of the cross. On the way out, attendees again dipped their right hand fingers in the holy water and made the sign of the cross.

The Mass

There used to be daily masses; 6:45, 7:15 and 8 a.m. at Holy Family and other churches. For a long time on Sundays, there were at least six masses. Eileen Leahy from Abbott Road said that Holy Family used to have a 7am, 8am, 9am, 10am, 11am, and noon "high mass" with the 6 highest candles lit on the altar.

Steve Banko added that there was a choir and organ player filling the church with music and songs at high mass. For people who worked weekend day shifts at the plants, churches began having a 5pm, 5:30 pm or 6pm mass Saturday afternoons that would count for Sunday observance. Steve reminded me that Holy Family students were required to attend the 9am mass on Sundays during the school year. One of the staff nuns would be there to oversee them. They were expected to sit in a designated area with the boys separated from the girls.

Masses in Latin

In the 40s, 50's and 60's, Baby Boomers heard all masses in Latin with the altar boys responding in Latin. I was one of those altar boys.

After the Second Vatican Council of 1962-1965 it was decided people should hear the mass in their native language and have the priests facing the people. Today, the masses are said in all different languages. Not all Catholics agreed to the change. The Society of St. Pius X still has masses in Latin.

Communion

Up until the 60s, people had to follow very strict guidelines in order to receive communion in Catholic churches. Fasting from midnight until after communion the next day used to be expected until the rules changed in 1964 to fasting three hours before taking communion. Now, one must abstain one hour, consuming no food or drinks with the exception of water. The elderly and the sick can have something to eat even if it is within the hour time frame before communion.

Before taking communion, remember the right fist action of lightly striking your chest three times and saying, Mea culpa, mea culpa, mea maxima culpa - "By my fault, by my fault, by my most grievous fault." It was a moment to get right with God before receiving communion; reflecting on one's sins and asking forgiveness.

Catholic Boomers remember when everyone came to the communion rail and knelt? Yes, knelt. You'd wait with hands folded for the priest and the altar boy with the communion plate to approach and serve you the wafer (the communion plate was to catch fallen wafers). There was no such thing as receiving the host in your hands at one time. Only priests were allowed to touch the hosts and gently put them on the parishioner's tongue. The priest would say in Latin: Corpus Christi "Body of Christ" and you'd respond "Amen", open your mouth, and receive communion.

You were not supposed to chew the host or even have it touch your teeth. You were expected to let it soften on your tongue until you could swallow it. Lots of changes, eh? Today, the priest either places the communion wafer in your hands or if you'd like it done the old fashioned way, you can still have it placed on your tongue, and you may chew it.

Lent and Fasting

According to (Canon Laws 1251 & 1252), refraining from eating meat on Fridays was once a church law for all Fridays until 1966. In 1983, the Code of Canon Law was revised and stated that eating meat would be prohibited for Catholics on Ash Wednesdays, Good Fridays and all Fridays throughout Lent, but the Catholic Church still recommends not eating meat on Fridays. During Lent, people were urged but not required to fast and to do one's best to give up something. For young people it was giving up candy or TV programs, going to the movies, dances, or some other things they enjoyed having. Adults might give up a meal, not see a movie or eat out, give up cigarettes, drink fewer beers or deny themselves some other things that were meaningful to them on a daily basis. Would you believe a guy once actually said to me?

"I'm gonna try giving up 'swearing' for Lent?" What?! Like that was really something that belonged in the category of things to give up for Lent.

A Bit of Cultural Stuff

Easter was and is as revered a Holy Day as Christmas for most Catholics and other faiths. People took their outfits up a notch on Easter Sunday. You'd see adults decked out more than usual. How many of you remember men in suits, shirts, ties and buffed shoes; ladies wearing colorful dresses and coats with fancy hats? Then, there were the little girls wearing pretty dresses, patent leather shoes, bonnets and colorful jackets with white gloves. Little boys wore their neat suits, white shirts and ties and spiffy shoes. It was a time for celebration and family time. At the house after church, men were to stay out of the kitchen. It was time for moms and grandmas to shine.

For the Irish

"Beannachtaí na Cásca ort!" ~ Happy Easter

"Barr an mhaidin duit. ~ Top o' the mornin' to you.

"Sláinte" ~ Cheers!

"Éirinn go Brágh" ~ Ireland forever.

Irish moms' and grandmas' menu included their famous Irish stew, corned beef with unsliced bacon, boiled with cabbage and potatoes, "farl" (a bread), maybe,"boxty" (Irish potato pancake).

Desserts were perhaps, Irish tea cake, Irish apple cake, plain or with custard, Irish whiskey cake, or maybe Bailey's Irish Cream cheesecake.

For the Italians

"Buona Pasqua." ~ Happy Easter

"Mangia bene, ridi spesso, ama molto." ~ Eat well, laugh often, love much.

"Mangia e statti zitto!" ~ Eat and shut up.

My Sicilian wife has that one on the kitchen wall.

Italian moms' and grandmas' menus included huge pots of spaghetti sauce with plenty of garlic (I love garlic.), meat balls, mushrooms and sausage, beef "braciole", lasagna, manicotti or chicken cacciatore. They'd fit twenty or twenty-five people at tables put together.

Desserts would be pizzelles (of course.), "cucidatis", anisette cookies, anise biscottis, cheese cake, maybe a ricotta pie and for sure, cannolis. Mmmm, quello è buono -"Mmmm, that's good."

For the Polish

Wesolych Swiat Wielkanocnych ~ "Happy Easter"

Na zdrowie (pronounced ~ Na sdrovieh) ~ "Cheers!"

Smacznego (pronounced ~ smachnego.) ~ "Enjoy your meal"

Polish moms' and grandmas' menus always had tons of pierogis, golumbki (stuffed cabbage) potatoes, cabbage, kielbasa (sausage), klopsikis (meatballs).

Desserts were paczkis (doughnut), piernikis (spice cookie), babka cakes, karpetka cakes, faworkis, szarlotka cakes.

Mmmm, to jest dobre. ~ "Mmmm, that's good."

Chapter 18 Common Life

South Buffalo Neighborhoods

Safe Neighborhoods

One of the unique things I remember about living in my neighborhood was that it was safe. Many people kept their doors unlocked. No one in our family had a key to the house except our parents; I never saw them use it. The house was always unlocked, day or night. It seemed that it was that way in most of the homes all over South Buffalo, especially, houses with large families. There was no need to lock up since somebody was always home. People knew each other up and down the street. For the most part everyone got along, even with so many different nationalities on every street. That's the way it was in most of the neighborhoods throughout our area. It was great!

Nationalities

Our family was French Canadian. In the duplex we lived in, in the early 60's, the next door family was Polish (the Smiths) for a time. A Hungarian family (the Nagys) moved in after they moved out. To our right, we had Puerto Ricans (the Rodriquezes), on our left, an Irish family (the McDonald's) and across the street, Italians (the Morabitos and the Marianos) and Mexicans (the Villalobos). Down the street, on either side, we had several other Irish and Italian families. Joe Nigrelli, (Italian) down the street from us needs to have a special mention. He went to mass every morning at Holy Family. You couldn't find a nicer "gentle man" than him on our street. No one had anything bad to say about him. He was one of my sponsors when I got my United States citizenship in 1968 along with Officer John Swietek. He was a detective for the Buffalo Police Department with 39 years on the force. Joe and wife Margaret (McCarthy) had four sons; Stephen and Michael who became State Troopers, Peter served on the Buffalo Police Force and another son, Joe Jr., went to work at the Police Dispatch Center in Indianapolis. Their only daughter, Susan, married State Trooper Joseph Denahy.

Families and Mothers

The neighborhood was also a place where a lot of moms fed other kids along with their own. Some kids were sent out and told: "Go out and play and don't come home till it's time to eat." Some families with so many kids in the house had to shoo them out so they could get housework done or entertain a guest without having interruptions from their four, five, six or more kids. Neighborhood parents had each other's backs concerning raising kids. There was a sense of real community and was very family oriented. Moms watched over their children and neighbors' children as well. If children were playing at someone's house that was somewhat far from their own at lunch time, it was a given that the host moms would feed their children's friends too.

If a neighbor saw a problem, he did not hesitate to straighten out a kid who was out of line. You might say neighborhoods were self-policing. Neighbors got involved and respect for adults was expected. A kid who disrespected an adult neighbor would usually result in the neighbor and parents resolving it quickly. The outcome was never good for the child. Moms and dads got things resolved pretty quickly by loud chastising or the sting of the belt. The child would get straightened out and apologies followed. That's the way it was.

Hardly any family was above the other status-wise. Most of the dads were blue-collar, hard-working men with a lot of stay-at-home wives. Many of the men worked the local grain mills, the docks, sanitation department, mail delivery, Bethlehem Steel along Route 5, (I worked at Gate 6 myself – '66) or Republic Steel on South Park near Allied Chemical on the other side of Buffalo Creek. Then there was the Donner Hanna Coke Plant, the Trico Plants, Buffalo Tank Division in Blasdell, the Woodlawn Ford Stamping Plant, the Chevy Plant on River Road, Buffalo Railroad, Buffalo China on Seneca Street, the Westinghouse Electric, Worthington Pump near Clinton and Bailey and a number other plants throughout the area.

Discipline

Stay-at-home moms would watch the roost and if she had trouble with one of her own, there was always that threat,

"Do you want to go to Father Baker's?" or... "Wait till your father gets home!"

Father Baker home... (home for defiant children and teens)

In those days it meant something. You would be in trouble. I know a lot of kids were dealt with harshly by parents for having done something wrong. In many families punishment was, "No supper for you tonight. Go to your room," Or... losing one's allowance, not having friends over, being grounded or no going out on the weekend. Sometimes kids got a double dose', a lickin' and they couldn't go out for the night or weekend. It depended on the infraction. In really bad situations, a kid got all of the above, but that didn't happen very often. There was usually order in the neighborhood homes.

I lived next door to a large family and hung out with their sons George (Jorge) and Joe (José). More than once I saw their dad George Sr. come out the door chasing Joe or George with his belt in one hand and holding his pants up with the other.

Bleeding hearts who think this was brutal, relax. They were never vicious beatings; just enough to get the boys' attention and adjust their attitudes. Not only did dad take care of business with the leather belt, ma too, would often be seen coming out that same door wielding the menacing piece of leather. Apparently, the boys thought that running outside would offer some form of safety, but they always had to go back in. They had to eat, sleep and bathe. If they ran too fast and too far, mom and dad knew they'd catch up with them later. That's the way it was.

If you still think that was bad, you should've seen the action when their grandfather or grandmother would come after them with the belt.

Margie Weber from Altruria told me:

"I remember a family near my house where one of their dad's belts was kept on a hook in the kitchen by the stove. It belonged there as much as the pot holders next to it and served its purpose for any of the kids who got out of line or mouthy, as we used to call it."

In our own family when we were younger, our dad, Leo, would sting the defiance or attitudes out of us when it needed to be done. For the most part, we minded. Mom and Dad were the bosses, not us. It was that way for our neighbors, our family, and a ton of other South Buffalo Baby Boomers. We didn't think much of it. We didn't like getting a lickin' but we knew that if we broke the laws of the house, it was very likely there would be consequences. None of us became so traumatically damaged that we couldn't handle life.

If anything, as José told me" "It taught us about respect for parents and consequences for bad actions. I believe I was successful in life because I had parents who taught me discipline and respect."

Respect and Manners

For most of us, there was no talking back or arguing with our parents. In my house, none of us ever talked back or argued with our parents. Today, a lot of the kids lack respect for parents. Many simply have little or no idea what it is to have values, manners and respect. There was another code of conduct among most of the kids I grew up with. It was always Mr. or Mrs. so and so when we addressed older folks. Today, kids think they are at par with everybody, of any age. Using an older neighbor's first name was not an option for us as kids. Even as we became adults, we still used Mr. or Mrs. It was all about respect.

If company came over, children were expected to show respect for the guests and use proper manners. They were expected to greet them and communicate with them when spoken too. If a child were sitting in an armchair or sofa, it was understood that he or she would give up the seat for the adult.

If you were at your own house, a relative's house or even at a friend's house back then, it was considered very rude and improper to put your feet on the couch, armchair or coffee table. As kids, we were taught that feet belonged on the floor not on the furniture. Even today, on my own couch, I'm very conscious about not doing that. Therefore, I certainly wouldn't do it anywhere else.

Oh, and if you went into a house where the mom had custom-fit plastic covers on the living room furniture, that room was out of bounds for children and their friends. Only adults could sit there and only on special occasions. It was weird, but that's the way it was.

Large Families

Most family men and their wives focused on living as good a life as possible by making a living and raising a family. It was very common for a couple to have 10 or more children. In the Seneca/Babcock area, the McCabes had 16 kids, the Sitarskis had 12, the Greens 12. The Caz and Seneca area Keanes had 16 kids, the Murthas from the Triangle area had 8 boys, the Halls on Whitfield had13 kids. There were ten in the Gannon family on Woodside, as well as in my own. The Bankos from the Valley had eight kids, the Cloudens on South Park Avenue with twelve kids, the Pughs down the street from me had six, the Smiths next door to us had five children and the Colerns on Lockwood Avenue, also ten kids. The Rodriguez family to the right of us ended up with at least ten. To each of those families, add moms and dads. Many of the homes only had three or four bedrooms and - one bath! Picture that for the morning rush when all the kids had to get ready for school! That's the way it was.

Having a bunch of kids was so common back then. That's the way life was; you got married, had children, and didn't worry too much about how you'd feed them all. It would all work out, and work out it did. What's interesting is that back in the 50's and early 60's, the average yearly income was $3,500 to $5,000. This put anyone with a big family in a low to very low income bracket. When it came time to fill out the tax forms though, large families had DEDUCTIONS. Between 1917 and 1920, the tax deduction was $200 per dependent. In 2016 it went up to $1,000 per child under the age of 17.

Extra Special Kudos to the Baby Boomer Moms!

God bless the Baby Boomer moms and grandmas. I mean that very sincerely. If you could ask the moms of the Seneca/Babcock McCabe family with 16 kids, or the Hall family on Whitfield with 13 kids what they went through to maintain the household and their sanity, they'd have stories to tell you that would make you cry. Think about it. In those huge families, a lot of moms breastfed their babies and still got all the house work done. If they were not breastfed, that meant bottles for the little ones. Now, imagine twins or triplets! Before baby formula was around, a lot of babies were given whole milk in bottles that were warmed up on the stove with water in a pan.

And when they were old enough to eat, how many of you remember Pablum? I did a bit of research on that. Pablum was invented in 1939 by Drs. Alan Brown, Fred Tisdall and Theo Drake. It was the first "ready-to-eat" baby cereal. It was a mixture of; precooked wheat (farina) oatmeal, yellow corn meal, dried brewer's yeast and powdered alfalfa. Mmmm good! Check out "alfalfa." It was primarily grown as a food for livestock. YIKES! Like millions of other tykes, I was fed that and survived.

"Hey, the baby's diaper is wet!" In large families, moms probably had at least three little ones at a time in cloth diapers; a new born, the one year old, and the two year old. There were no disposable "Pampers" diapers back then.

Wringer Washing machine

With three in diapers at a time, you have to figure they needed five or maybe six cloth diapers for the day and night. That's at least 15 diapers in a 24 hour period for the three wee ones. At the end of the week, 15 a day times 7 days gives you a whopping 105 dirty diapers. Moms needed to rinse them out in a pail or the toilet, wash them in an old style washing machine, put them through the wringer, hang them up on a clothes line outside and finally, go get them when they were dry. The job still wasn't done! Moms had to fold them and put them in a drawer or cupboard. The cycle would go on and on - day after day, after day, and didn't stop until all their kids were potty-trained. Imagine adding the rest of the family's laundry. By the way, the "standby" if moms ran out of diapers was kitchen towels or smaller bath towels. Think of it, those items were then washed and put back in the towel drawers. Again, YIKES! GROSS!

Doesn't it get you tired just reading this? Moms' daily routines were unending and exhausting! God bless all the moms and grandmas of yesterday that had the chore of keeping their little angels dry.

Enough about diapers, let's see what else those incredible moms from the Greatest Generation had to do to manage their family. I'm not leaving out the dads, but I'm sure they'd have to agree that the wives had the harder job taking care of the families.

Food Handouts

Back in the day, a lot of large families got one kind of handout or another. I can remember families drinking powdered milk and getting butter, margarine, peanut butter & jelly and cheese from the Federal Food Distribution Centers. In the 60s, moms (mine included) would buy day old bread for ten cents a loaf from the Wonder Bread Bakery on Clinton and Adams Streets. It was fine. Day old bread was just as good as fresh.

When you think of the many families with dads who went to work and kids who went to school, all needing lunches, a whole lot of bread was needed. If you factor in bread, lunch meats or peanut butter/jelly and lunch bags; it took quite a chunk of a family's budget. For the most part, it was the moms who put lunches together at night or got up early to do that task. Those of you who were from very large families, do you remember mom writing your name on the lunch bags and lining them up in the fridge? This too, was done day in and day out. PHEW!

School Lunches

Even if they had cafeterias in their schools, a lot of kids from large families couldn't afford to buy lunches. Let's look at the McCabe (Seneca-Babcock), the Keane (Seneca Street area) families with 16 kids and the Halls with 13 kids from Whitfield. Hypothetically, if only 7 of the 16 kids and dad needed a lunch, at two sandwiches each, it meant 4 slices of bread per person per day. It comes to 32 slices of bread a day for lunches. Multiply that, times 5 days a week. It comes to 160 slices a week. Based on an average of 22 slices per loaf, they probably needed over 7 loaves of bread a week just for lunches. Oh yeah, don't forget toast for breakfast. Maybe 10 loaves or more were needed a week to keep the Keane, McCabe or Hall families in bread. And, the budget said, OUCH! I can remember my own mom buying seven to ten loaves at a time for the week for 10 kids and dad. Very often, it didn't even last to the end of the week.

Chapter 19 Education for Baby Boomers

Elementary and High Schools

Right or left handed?

Right off the bat, some students had problems as they began learning to write if they were "left handed."

Right-handedness was the norm, while left-handedness was very often discouraged by nuns and secular teachers. This was partly due to the Latin word for left, sinistra. The Latin word also means evil. Then, there is "dextro" and "sinistro", meaning right and left. Also, there is the Bible passage of Matthew 25:31-46, referring to Christ putting the righteous people at His right and the unrighteous at His left. A lot of Baby Boomer students were forced to change hands. Not me. I'm still a lefty. You've already read in the Seneca Street section about Donna M. (Witczak) Shine who had her knuckles hit by nuns for being a lefty when she was in grade school. It was an ongoing problem for many back then.

Now then, I believe the educators that harassed, belittled, or punished left handed students weren't mean by nature, but were, themselves indoctrinated into the same thinking. It goes way, way back when somebody came up with the notion that "lefties" had some sort of evil spirit in them.

After polling South Buffalo Baby Boomers on Facebook who are lefties, in February of 2020, I got 42 responses. Out of those 42, 24 were ladies; that's over 50%. Here are some comments I chose of what some baby Boomer lefties had to say about teachers (mostly nuns) that tried to discourage them from using their left hand in school.

Note that about 10% of the people in the world are "lefties."

Dennis Starr - "I'm one of those lucky 10% ers. I did just fine all my life being a lefty."

Linda Larson - I'm 68. It happened to me so many years ago and I can't remember the Sister's name. I do remember coming home crying because of being forced to write with my right hand. I am still left handed and proud of it. We left handers are a strong breed.

Gerard Weitz - I didn't have problems being a lefty, but 4 of my siblings did. The Nuns at St. Thomas Aquinas tried to cure them, but didn't. 40's to late 60's.

Peggy Morrell - My sister had problems at St. Martin's, in the 60s. They tried to break you of it. The nuns didn't win, nor did it make my sister ambidextrous.

Daniel D. Banko - In the early part of the 70's at St. Agatha's, I got the yardstick. I'm glad to say, I'm still left handed.

Amy Dabar - All three of my kids are lefties and went to Catholic schools. If they were reprimanded for it I don't remember.

Johnny Pal - At P.S. # 33 and St. Stephens Religion classes, I was told I had the Devil in me and my Dad set them straight! That was in the 60's

Mary Gavin - I went to St Martins up to 67 and never had a problem until I went to the Mount.

Toni Full Hillman I went to public school and didn't have any trouble until I reached 6th, 7th and 8th grade. When writing I didn't turn the paper the right way and didn't have the correct slant.

John Brown - I Graduated from St. Thomas Aquinas in 1966. I was hit with a ruler on knuckles for writing left handed. I also heard about sign of the devil back then. I was forced to write right handed in lower grades.

Mary Ellen - I went to BPS #26 and I was never made to change until I got into third grade the teacher (Miss Royter) made me hold my hand behind my back and grab the chair so I would not write with my left hand.

Tom Kostusiak - Saint Teresa's had my arm tied to my side. When I started writing mirror image my Mom put a stop to that.

Others that responded about the trials and tribulations of being left handed: Carol Gaspar (St. Thomas Aquinas in late 60s) Larson Linda (At Holy Family), Steven M Kellerman (PS 27, PS 33), Maryann and Rusty Rueger (Holy Family), John Heffron (St. Martin School), Lisa Devine (Saint Theresa's first grade), Sara McParlane Hibbard (St Teresa's), and Dan Ford.

A South Buffalo Lefty's Military Story

Paul K. Mullen

"I didn't experience any issues because that nonsense ended by the time I entered school in the late 70's at St. Ambrose. But, here is a true story of a slight advantage to being left handed.

I served as a Gunners Mate in the Navy and was a small arms instructor (SAMI). Although I'm left handed, I shoot right handed. While deployed to Kuwait in 2008 we were at the range and the other SAMI in my unit didn't know I was a lefty. He broke his thumb on his right hand and could only shoot left handed. So he challenges me to a competition to see who can shoot better with our weak hand. Of course I took up the challenge. What I didn't tell him was that I can shoot pistols either hand equally as well. Needless to say that was an easy challenge to win. We just laughed afterward. Sometimes it pays to be a lefty and not tell anyone." Thank you for your service, Paul. ...Salute!

Writing Tools

Many Baby Boomers didn't have ballpoint pens when they started school. It was either pencils or pen and ink with pens that had steel tip nibs that were inserted into pen tip holders, then, dipped into little bottles of ink that were located at the right hand top corners of students' desks. I believe all those desks were designed for right handers.

Writing Cursive

Lots of Baby Boomers have the special ability to write excellently in cursive. My sister-in-law Diane Noody and my daughter-in-law's aunt, Donna Pasquarella, write incredibly well. Here's sample of Donna's cursive writing:

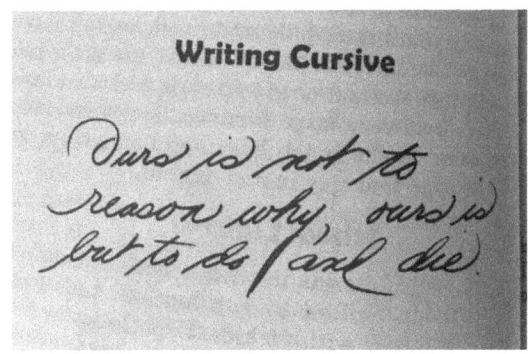

Sample CURSIVE phrase:
("Ours is not to reason why, ours is but to do and die.")

How many of you remember having to perfect the grownup way of writing around the second grade level? In Québec in 1952 when I went to school, no kindergarten, I started in 1st grade and went directly into writing cursive. As a matter of fact, I didn't learn how to print until I went to college....later in life.

As I taught languages at Medaille College in 2012, I wrote something in cursive on the board and a student actually asked me, "What does that mean?" Folks, I'm talking college level, here. That student along with many others, were never exposed to cursive. What happens when someone says: "We need your signature to finalize these very important documents. Please print your name on this line and sign your name on the line below."

If all they know how to do is print, isn't it a problem for non-cursive writers when it comes to signing checks, credit card receipts and documents. Grade schools need to bring back teaching cursive to the classroom, don't you think? I asked a friend of mine, Ray Colpoys who is in his 70s, if he still wrote cursive.

He told me, "I don't mean to brag, but my penmanship is excellent. The reason for that is because when I was a kid, my mom made me go to Mount Mercy every Saturday morning for a year, where her sister (a nun), had me practice pages and pages of me writing cursive. I'd even have to go home and practice all week and the following Saturday bring back the sheets. I got really good at it. Even to this day, my wife comments on how good my handwriting is."

Writing in shorthand

Before moving on, how many of you ladies took "shorthand" in high school? Here's a sample for those that never learned or those that have never seen it.

Shorthand samples

Pen and Ink Dilemmas

There were two big problems for the Baby Boomers with the pen and ink system. First, people could only write a few words at a time before having to dip the tip of the pen into the ink bottle, again. They had to be careful not to load too much ink in the tip. If they did that and started writing, they could end up with a blob of ink on their paper and smear their work. If they had a blob of ink, there were blotters to soak up the excess. Lefties had the worst of times with pen and ink and couldn't avoid lots of smears. I'm a lefty. I know. I used the pen and ink system for a couple of years back in the 50's.

If you had a couple of dollars, you could buy a fountain pen that had a self-contained bladder that you'd fill by moving a small lever to deflate the bladder, dip the tip of the pen into an ink bottle, release the lever and the ink was sucked into the bladder. This allowed for uninterrupted writing of many words. How many of you used those?

A modification of the fountain pen was the cartridge pen. Those pens were even easier to use than fountain pens. You'd buy a pack of ink cartridges, unscrew the tip portion of the pen, slip in a cartridge into the hollow part of the pen, screw back the tip and the cartridge would automatically get punctured by an inside tip orifice, and away you went. By the way, cartridge pens are still in use today. Cartridges came in black, blue or red ink. The down side is they too, could smudge up your writing if you were a lefty.

The ballpoint pen came into common use in the late 50's and early 60's. We are all familiar with those, so I won't go into any details. Not too long after ballpoint pens came to be, felt tip pens came along. They were good writing implements. From there, all different kinds of ball point and felt tip pens flooded the market.

Parochial and Public Schools

People in South Buffalo and throughout the City of Buffalo were very much connected to a parish as a way of establishing what part of Buffalo they were from regardless if the children went to a public or parochial school. The parishes covered certain areas and that became what people were associated with. If someone said "I belong to Our Lady of Perpetual Help," you knew right away that they lived in the Old First Ward. If someone said: "I belong to Saint Teresa's," that would mean he or she was from the Seneca Street area between South Side and Mineral Springs.

Parishes with Schools

Saint Brigid on Louisiana Street ~ Saint Valentine on South Park (OFW) ~ Our Lady of Perpetual Help (corner of O'Connell and Alabama, OFW) ~ Saint Monica's on Orlando streets ...Seneca/Babcock area ~ Saint Agatha/All Souls near the Triangle Abbott Road ~ Holy Family on South Park & Tifft ~ Saint Ambrose on Ridgewood ~ Saint Thomas on Abbott Road) ~ Saint Teresa on Seneca Street ~ Saint Martin became Notre Dame Academy on Abbott Road ~ Saint John on Seneca Street near Caz Park ~ Saint Bonaventure both on Seneca Street... Tim Russert's second elementary school.

High Schools

Mount Mercy Academy on Red Jacket Parkway (all girls' school)

Timon High School on McKinley Parkway (an all boys' school).

Baker Victory High where quite a few of the local guys and gals went to.

Being predominantly Catholic communities throughout South Buffalo, it was the Sisters of Mercy who taught kindergarteners to eighth graders in the parochial schools. Learning the three "R's" was one part of their agenda. The students learned values, discipline and morals. Their objective was to guide their students to become educated, respectful, virtuous adults. Being realistic and understanding the nature of boys and girls, I know that a lot of the teachings of these good sisters didn't always stick in the minds and souls of their pupils. Many a former parochially-educated individual either disregarded or discarded the good teachings of those ladies. Overall though, the sisters did do a good job and planted good seeds in order to set their students on the right path to become well-educated, productive individuals. For the most part, their efforts were not in vain. That is to their credit, and I for one, salute them. They affected a lot of lives in many good ways.

Holy Family School

After PS #29, I attended Holy Family School at the corner of South Park and Tifft streets from September of 1960 to June of 1962 for 7th and 8th grade. It was a great school for the Catholic kids who attended there, as were all of the other Catholic grade schools in the area. Tim Russert, nationally known political analyst, was our most famous student. He attended Holy Family for a few years then transferred to Saint Bonaventure on Seneca Street after moving away from Woodside Avenue. In his book Big Russ and I, he speaks very fondly of his experience and mentioned that many of the people with whom he had made friends with, continued their friendship for many years, and some remained his friends until his passing.

One of the things I still remember about the school was that there was no mixing of the genders in the school yard. Girls had to stay on one side and the boys on the other. That's the way it was for most grade schools back then. When the bell rang for class, we formed two lines. The command was given to march, and in we marched. The girls entered first, then the boys. There was no talking in line. Violation of this rule meant an immediate tongue-lashing or perhaps some sort of corporal punishment.

The girls were under a bit more scrutiny than the boys. They had to wear skirts, at or below the knees, with a white blouse, socks and shoes. The nuns were very aware that some of the girls would try to wear their skirts a bit too high. If and when one of the young ladies would dare break the rule, you can be sure Sister would attend to the problem, post haste. The boys on the other hand didn't have a problem. We had to make sure we had on a dress shirt and tie, dress pants, and shoes. The neat thing about the ties was that they could be string ties like the cowboys wear.

All of the classes were taught by the Sisters of Mercy in the upper grades. Some of the students would dispute the word mercy in their title. Several of the nuns put the fear of God in many a young man or woman who wanted to test their patience. One of the nuns there was Sister Mary Clementia, an elderly lady. She seemed to us to be about seventy years old but could be as mean as a cornered wildcat if you didn't do things her way or crossed her.

Sister Jeanne Marie was my eight grade teacher. Maybe my memory does not serve me quite right, but it seems to me that she hardly ever got out of her seat to teach. Everything was done from her desk. She was pretty stern and didn't put up with any nonsense. I may have seen her smile twice the whole year I had her for 8th grade. She did smile when I graduated. Draw your own conclusions.

I can remember vividly one guy I used to trip on a regular basis when he came down the aisle. His name was John "Jack" Lafferty. I don't know why I did it; maybe to break the monotony. I wasn't a bad student. I guess, I just wasn't focused enough – you know …ADD or something like that.

Another memory is how one of our classmates would pass out from time to time. He would intentionally hold his breath until he passed out, and of course, got a free ticket out the door to go home to convalesce.

There was another guy who came in one day beet red. He looked like he had been to Florida. The only problem it was the middle of winter and he hadn't been to any warm climate to get the sunburn. He had fallen asleep under a sunlamp. Ouch!

Then there was the boy who had no winter boots. His father ruled that he wasn't going to walk to school through the snow and ruin his shoes. He was made to wear his mother's brown, zippered rubber boots with the fur piece around the top. Baby Boomers know the kind. Well, he thought that if he flipped the fur pieces up on each boot, no one would notice; they did, and of course, they laughed. He didn't see any humor in it, just felt the embarrassment. Poor guy! He didn't wear them for the walk back home after school. He tucked them under his arm hiding them as best he could. That poor schnook was me.

The Gym

Anyone who went to Holy Family remembers the Gym which was not even close to a regular size gym. It had a very low ceiling and pillars. You had to be sharp when playing basketball there. A few of the players came to an abrupt stop because of those pillars. They weren't padded either. I remember once when we played a game against another Catholic school, we won. It wasn't so much because we were better than they were, but because we were used to practicing in that gym. Going in for a long shot, we knew how low to aim while the opposing team would arch their shots more and hit the ceiling. Of course they complained that it wasn't fair. We laughed. We basically didn't care how we won that game as long as we won. Needless to say, there were no more contests played in our gym. We always had to go to a school with a real gym for our games.

Lunch Breaks

I remember going home for lunch each day. There were no cafeterias in grade Catholic and Public schools when I attended. You had to wait until you got to high school for that. It was interesting seeing all the South Buffalo Catholic and public school Baby Boomers filling the streets at noon. I'm talking about hundreds of kids.

It was good for students who lived relatively close to their school but for the kids who had a long walk, you have to wonder if they had much time to finish their meals. My walk to and from school was only four blocks. Some of my friends had to walk nearly a mile, one way. In good weather, it wasn't bad, but in foul weather, it was down right, miserable. I do remember that they made some accommodations for kids who live really far or who had no adults home to prepare food for them. They'd have a long table in or near the gym area where those students ate lunch. Some of the kids didn't have stay-at-home moms and still went home had to fend for themselves. Who knows what some of those poor kids ate or if they had much to eat at all.

Today, with so few stay-at-home moms and bussing, most all grade school students pack a lunch or buy from their school cafeteria. Someone brought up setting up neighborhood schools again and having children go to those schools instead of being bussed across town. I'd be for that but it's a different time with different family dynamics. It wouldn't work well. But, wouldn't it be nice to go back to neighborhood schools, stay-at-home moms and children being able to go home for lunch with moms and siblings like in the old days? Oh, the good old days.

True Story

After I had graduated 8th grade from Holy Family and attended South Park High, I had a school break for some reason. Joe Predergast and I were shooting baskets at Mulroy playground right behind Holy Family School. From one of the windows, we heard this elderly voice telling us to leave the playground; that the basketball bouncing was distracting her students. Well, being in high school and no longer under the authority of the good sisters, we decided we weren't going to leave. We kept playing. Suddenly, we saw this little lady in her habit, with a sweet look on her face coming towards us. It was Sister Clementia.

As she got near Joe and me, she said with a smile in a very sweet voice, "Could I see your basketball for a second?" Not thinking, Joe handed it over. She tucked it under her arm, promptly turned and walked away. My reaction was, "Get the ball back!" I followed her and asked for it, but she wouldn't give in; just wouldn't give it back.

Brash as I was, I tried to grab it. She quickly twisted away so I wouldn't get it. I can't believe I did this - forgive me Sister! I made a quick move and popped the ball out of her hands as though I was doing a steal during a game. Got it! She put her hands on her hips and stared at me with one eye shut tight and her teeth clenched. It's been nearly sixty years and I can still see that stare. We shot a few more baskets and left. Maybe it was fear, I'm not sure - but we left.

Public Schools

The other side of the coin here is the public school system. Not very far from where the parochial schools were located, there where public elementary schools also. Starting from the same general area as the parochial schools, some of those schools were/are:

P.S. #4 in the Old First Ward on South Park

PS #34 elementary at 108 Hamburg Street in the Old First Ward (Demolished around 1976.)

P.S. #33 on Elk Street in the Valley

P.S. #26 on Harrison Street in the Seneca/Babcock area

P.S. #27 on Pawnee

P.S. #28 (South Park and Abbott)

P.S. #29 (South Park and Okell)

P.S. #67 (Abbott Rd and Naragansett.)

P.S. #70 on Buffum

P.S. #72 (on Belvedere St. behind Mercy Hospital)

Although religion was not part of their curriculum back then, public school teachers instilled the same code of conduct and moral convictions in their Baby Boomer students as did their Catholic counterparts. If you were a Catholic student attending a public school, you attended Religious Instruction Classes once a week. It wasn't mandatory, but parents made the call on that. Most of the Roman Catholic students attended the classes.

Discipline and Corporal Punishment

Anyone from the Baby Boomer era remembers full well the practice of corporal punishment. It was all about teaching consequences for bad actions. There were rules and regulations. Anyone guilty of not following the school rules were aware of the possible meting out of some sort of punishment by the administrators. All in all, most schools ran well with few incidents of applying the dreaded ruler to the knuckles or the yardstick on the behind. Parochial schools had the kneeling down in a corner remedy on a nice, cold, marble floor for a half hour or so as one of the ways of curing a defiant student.

For severe infractions, a young lad or lass needed to go to the principal's office. Some of those sessions were the worst. Many students entering a principal's office for a major offense never left. No one knows what happened to them. Only kidding! But... in such cases, the parents were often consulted and that's when the rebellious child might have gotten a double dose of corporal punishment. The school administrators dealt out their punishment and the parents got a shot at their kid as well when he or she got home. God only knows what some of the kids got when they got there.

For the most part, parents trusted and backed the school administrators and accepted the discipline their children got. As a matter of fact, when students got in trouble and were punished for it, they didn't want mom or dad to know about it. Parents knew it meant their sons broke a rule and probably got what they deserved. Since the school already took care of the discipline, they didn't want mom or dad to dish out their own brand of punishment. I won't say that the punishment students got was right in every case, but most of the time, it was. Rules were in place and were expected to be followed. "That's the way it was!"

School administrators and teachers were in control back then. Today, a lot of schools have discipline problems. Some schools are even chaotic at times. Many of today's schools are in shambles because of students' rights. There is no fear of repercussions for bad behavior. It's a shame. Today, corporal punishment does not exist. If a principal or teacher should put a ruler to the knuckles of a student or a paddle or yardstick to their backside, they would tell their parents and all hell could break loose. Cops and lawyers would be called and heads would roll. The principal or teacher would most likely lose their job. In some schools, teachers are afraid for their safety because of student threats. There's really something wrong with that picture. It boils down to, disregard for authority.

P.S. 29

I remember only a few guys with whom I became friends and still talk to from PS #29. Bob Regan is one I mentioned before. To this day, I can still see him in my mind's eyes. He was playing handball behind the school and seemed to me to be a tough hombre. He wasn't big, but I could see that he was packed tight like a stick of dynamite and could blow up big. I noticed the guys in the yard paid attention to him when he spoke. Apparently, he was one of the guys you minded. He was tough and direct, but he loved to laugh and had a great sense of humor.

Bob recalls that they would often station one of the spectators of the handball matches on top of the roof connected to the handball playing area. Rather than having people climb up every time the ball ended up on the roof, they thought it was a good idea to plant someone up there for the duration of the match. Poor guy!

There, I also became friends with Mickey Guzda from Lockwood Avenue and Eddy Dacey from West Woodside when I first moved from Orchard Park. As a matter of fact, Eddy saved me from some young guy who wanted to thump me. For some reason, I don't know why, either I said something or he said something, I responded in a manner that pushed his button and it lead to the threat of me being roughed up. Eddy Dacey happened by and said: "He's okay," leave him alone."

I was a runt at thirteen. The guy who gave me trouble was a bit taller and stouter. Thank you Eddy! Years later, that ruffian and I became great friends.

South Park High, est. 1915

South Park High School on South Side Parkway was known for having teachers and administrators who were highly dedicated, with strong values and no-nonsense attitudes. A former teacher, Edward Miller, said this about the school:

"Once, South Park High was the elite school of Buffalo."

Administrators and Dress Codes

South Park High was a fairly big school with lots of students. When I attended, the principal was Dr. Norman Hayes with Mr. Raymond J. Schanzer as assistant principal. It was filled with young men and women from many neighborhoods of South Buffalo. As with all of the Catholic and public high schools back then, we had a dress code. All the guys showed up every day wearing a shirt, neck tie, dress pants, socks and dress shoes. No male student was allowed to roll up his shirt sleeves during school hours. If Dr. Hayes passed a student with sleeves rolled up, he was known to get a grip on one of the sleeves and rip it off at the cuff. Now, that meant the student had to go home and explain to mom and dad why his shirt had one sleeve shorter than the other. It was understood; you will come to school in proper attire and breaking behavior or dress code rules will not be tolerated.

The girls were expected to dress like ladies. Their dress code was simple enough. They wore neat blouses, skirts of an appropriate length, socks or stockings and shoes. Most didn't wear much makeup. Only a few would put on lipstick and maybe some rouge. There certainly were a lot of puffed up hairdos back then. You would see a whole lot of the girls with "teased hair," always kept in place with hair a ton of hair spray…brands such as; Helen Curtis Spray Net, Aqua Net, or Hidden Magic hair spray perhaps.

Assistant principal Schanzer was one man you didn't want to toy with. He was the school's sergeant-at-arms in charge of discipline. From time to time, there were guys who got to have a bit of special time in his office for one infraction or another. Some came out a bit sore but had a better understanding of the policies, rules and expectations of the school. No one wanted a return visit to his office for misbehaving.

It was a good school, but not perfect. There were occasional incidents of lack of respect for a teacher, too much clowning around in class, harsh words between students, bullying, shoving matches or even a fight now and then. Any misbehavior happening in the school was dealt with post haste.

Class Incident

One day, Assistant Principal Schanzer received a list of names of about nine young scholars from Mrs. Lewis' math class who needed an attitude adjustment. It all started one winter day in 1963 when Greg Vaughn, one of our fine young men discovered that he could do a rapid-fire tapping with his foot that he could keep up indefinitely. Mrs. Lewis, who was a bit hard of hearing, heard the racket at a lower tone. She stopped teaching and yelled: "What is that noise?"

The young tapper pointed toward the windows where the radiators were located and said, "I think it's the radiators knocking, Mrs. Lewis." He even kept the tapping going as he gave her this information. She sort of believed him. He continued the tapping on and off during the class and we'd laugh. Again, Mrs. Lewis stopped teaching; looked toward the radiators, turned to see us laughing, frowned at the class and continued the math lesson. I'm sure she figured it out after our class left and the noise stopped. I suppose we weren't smart guys - just wise-guys.

Learning the Hard Way

As students, we knew if we messed up there would be some sort of consequence. Here's the account of the group session we had with our beloved assistant principal for misbehaving in Mrs. Lewis' class in 1963. In our group was Mike Catanzaro, Greg Vaughan, Clyde Leto, George Amplement, four other guys and myself. I'm glad I wasn't one who got one of Mr. Schanzer's best shots. Clyde Leto was his first target. Schanzer walked up behind him with the list of names and comments to address the conduct unbecoming of young South Park High School scholars. Bang! He got hit from behind. George Ampleman was next. Our dear assistant principal twisted his ear pretty hard. He then said a few words to Mike Catanzaro followed by a back hand to the side of his face. Mike didn't say a word. He took it like the tough Old First Ward boy he was. He didn't move. I believe Greg got a few hard hits on the head with his knuckles.

I must've had a kind face or the list had me down as a lesser culprit; he only flicked his finger at my left ear a few times and began reading us the proverbial "riot act."

At any rate there were no more problems in Mrs. Lewis' class for the rest of the year. There's probably something to be said here about the effects of corporal punishment. I know that with the kind of discipline we received at South Park, things ran fairly well for the size school it was. We didn't have the problems we see in some of the high schools today. We all knew who was in control at South Park and it wasn't the students. The teachers and administrators ran a tight ship.

A True Story

Lunchtime at South Park was uneventful for the most part, but a few things stick out in my mind. One item is; the boys and the girls did not sit together. It was probably a good thing. You know... hormones and all.

The great "Smokey" (Dennis Wojciechowski) never brought a lunch to school. He would come to our table, wait till all the lads were settled in to eat, then he would go out and see who had what in their lunch. He'd simply ask guys for something they could spare. He'd come back to the table with sandwiches, cupcakes, drinks and even, ice cream!

Another True Story

Daniel Arthur Shea was a great guy and a cut-up who loved to laugh and joke around. One day, he came up with a hoax to pull on Mr. Curry, our lunchroom monitor. Dressed in his shirt, tie, sports coat and glasses, he passed Mr. Curry and cordially greeted him; "Good afternoon Mr. Curry," then walked away past a point where he couldn't be seen. He took off his glasses and sports coat, and a few minutes later, walked past Curry and asked:

"Mr. Curry, did you see my twin brother Arty Shea? He's wearing a sports coat and glasses."

"No, I haven't," was the response.

Danny went back, put the glasses and sports coat back on, returned and asked, "Mr. Curry, I heard my twin brother Danny Shea is looking for me. Have you seen him?"

At this point, Mr. Curry had enough; gave Danny an earful and threatened detention. The twins never reappeared from that day on. Good one Dan!

Recycling is Not New

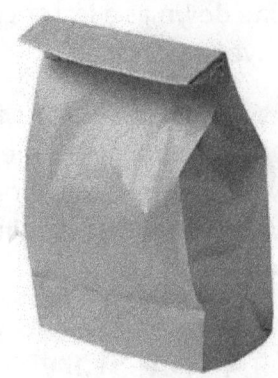

Recycling of lunch bags was part of the norm for many who took lunches to school, offices or plants. Many of them brought back their empty lunch bags. Tim Fitzgerald who went to Timon High remembers that a lot of students would regularly re-use their lunch bags.

He said: "Sometimes, we'd use the same bag all week long."

When I was in school in the 60s I would fold the bag and bring it back home for reuse as long as it held up. I found that I was able to reuse each bag at least three to four times. With five of the older children in our family needing lunch bags, one bag a day for each person would require 25 bags a week. Multiply that 40 weeks of school and by the end of the year we would use up about 950 lunch bags. That would have been a lot of wasted paper, had we not recycled. We didn't waste things back then. If it could be reused, we would. It was like the jelly jars that became drinking glasses or old orange crates and the empty cigar boxes that were used for storing things. We even saved the strings the butcher shop used to tie meat packages with.

How many of you Baby Boomers remember saving every brown paper grocery bag mom would get from doing the weekly groceries? That was before plastic grocery bags. The bags were all neatly folded and put in a pile or stacked in a certain place to be used in the kitchen trash can. Once full, someone took it to the trash cans out back. If you remember, by the end of the week, you'd throw out five or six grocery bags full of trash, maybe more, depending on the size of your family. Most families had two galvanized trash cans out back. With twelve people in our family, we had three cans.

How many of you remember that when you took out the garbage, you often didn't quite make it to the trash cans? The bottom often fell out dumping the contents on mom's clean kitchen floor because someone placed a liquid or slimy substance near the bottom of the paper trash bag? Sometimes, some of you in that situation would make it outside your back door and almost make it to the trash cans. If a neighbor happened to be watching and saw the trash blow right through the bottom of the bag onto the front of your pants, your shoes and the yard; he'd laugh, and laugh, but not you. You'd find yourself using several expletives, right? All of the above scenarios happened to me.

Great Book Covers

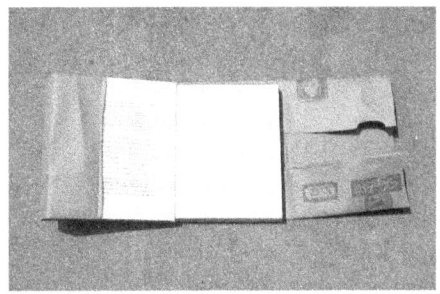

Covered book

Remember using those saved grocery bags to cover your text books. I'd get a bag and cut it large enough to have folds that went inside the hard-bound front and back covers. Those folds would act as slots to slide about an inch and a half to two inches on the insides of both covers. They were rugged enough to withstand almost a year's worth of use. People would write and draw on them. Of course, the names of the subjects were written on the front and the spines, and the student's name was usually on the bottom. People would draw all sorts of things on the fronts and backs. The girls would write their boyfriend's name or initials somewhere on the cover with hearts and an arrow through it. You know what I mean, the common puppy love kinds of things.

No Backpacks

Speaking of books and school, remember not having backpacks back then? The boys carried their books under their arm and the girls held them in front with one or both arms. School supplies were very few. We were only required to have pencils, pens, rulers and erasers. That was about it. No calculators back in the 40's, 50's, or 60's, folks. That's when we used our brains to do basic math in our heads or on paper.

Demographics

The great thing about the school was that people from all over South Buffalo and beyond went there. Our knowledge of other people doubled, tripled, and even quadrupled. One of the things that happened for the first time to a lot of students was that they would be integrated with African-Americans. Most of us from the South Buffalo neighborhoods had not attended grade schools that had black students. But, at South Park, that all changed. For the most part, people from the various neighborhoods got along. Some good and lasting friendships even came out of that experience.

I remember one of the black students I came to know and befriend; his name was James Thomas. The homeroom teacher kept mixing up his name when taking attendance and called him Thomas James. He would tell the teacher:

"The name is not Thomas James, it's, James Thomas."

Guess what? He still messed it up from time to time. When it happened, James Thomas would look at me and smile as if to say: "He did it again."

Cultural Experience

In October 1962 I met a very pretty girl at South Park named Carol Gardon, who I liked a lot. She lived on Clinton near Bailey in the area known as Kaisertown. I went to a dance with her at a school on Clinton. When the music started playing, it was a moment of instant culture shock! They were playing Polka music and Carol wanted me to dance. "Wait a minute!" A French Canadian boy from South Park did not dance the polka. Why? Because it's the Polka! It wasn't what we did in our neighborhood at Timon or Fazio's Hall. But in that neighborhood, there was great pride for their Polish heritage. I found it interesting that the young people were - into it! That's what they did ~ polka music and polka dancing. In South Buffalo, we were into the music of Elvis, Roy Orbison, Ricky Nelson, Bobbie Vinton, The Drifters, Dion, Ray Charles, the Four Seasons, the Everly Brothers, Del Shannon, and Chubby Checker. The dances we were into were what you'd see on American Bandstand; not polka music or polka dancing. I wasn't a good dancer anyway. I was lucky I could slow dance, let alone do the polka! I did manage to get in a few slow dances with Carol though.

Chapter 20 Downtown Shopping

Entertainment and Money Matters

In 1940, Buffalo's population was ranked 14th in the United States; in 2016 it fell to around 26th. It certainly has seen better days. There were a lot of stores in South Buffalo during the Baby Boomer era, but downtown Buffalo had many more and different ones.

Getting to Main Street in downtown Buffalo was easy from all three main South Buffalo streets. You took the #15 bus from Seneca Street, the #14 bus from Abbott Road or the #16 from South Park at a cost of 15 cents a ride in the 60s.

Old metro bus

Going downtown back then was like any big city in the United States. There were all sorts of department stores, specialty boutiques, lots of theatres, restaurants, bars, the Hippodrome poolroom, great nightclubs with great bands and very well-known performers.

Just about everyone from any of the eight main South Buffalo areas went downtown, either regularly or occasionally. You could do serious shopping there or have a choice of over half a dozen movie houses: Shea's-Loew's Tech, Hippodrome, Center, Shea's Buffalo, the Century, the Lafayette, Broadway or the Palace.

Buffalo could once boast in having the largest night club between Chicago and New York City. One of the biggest venues for entertainment was the Town Casino Restaurant and Night Club 681 Main Street right across from Shea's Buffalo Theatre. It closed for a time and reopened as the Town Ballroom. Back in the 40's, 50's and 60's, some of the stars that came through were; Frank Sinatra, Sammy Davis Jr., Danny Thomas, Louis Armstrong, Milton Berle, Mae West, Perry Como, Mile Davis, Dizzy Gallespie, Nat King Cole, Bobby Darin, Johnny Ray, and many big bands.

Before the malls existed, the big attractions were department stores like AM&A's, Hengerer's, Berger's, Hens & Kelly's, Kresges, Kleinhan's, Woolworth's and of course, Sears and Roebuck. During Christmas time, these stores were packed with shoppers. Main Street was full of cars, busses, cabs, and sidewalks were jammed with pedestrians. The great choice of stores provided excellent competitive prices. You could shop cheaper or go high class if you could afford it. By the way, those were the days most of the purchases were done in cash. These days, we're very close to the predicted, "cashless society."

A Bit of Credit Card History

Credit cards first came into play in 1946 but it wasn't until 1959 that American Express introduced the first plastic credit card. There were other cards prior to the plastic American Express card but they were made of cardboard or celluloid. In 1959, we had Master Card followed in 1966 by Bank of America. Visa and Discover followed. With all those credit cards available, they came to be known as plastic money. It was very convenient to make purchases but created a very slippery path to bankruptcy." Many got into deep debt back then and today also because of credit card use. Some people have multiple cards and use them all. That's not good! I have one but I still prefer paying in cash.

The Blue Law

It's very nice that we can shop seven days a week these days, but once upon a time, shopping on Sundays was not possible. How many of you Boomers remember the "Blue Law" that was around in the 40's, 50's and part of the 60's? It dates back to 1755.

Historically, it is believed the term was coined by Reverend Samuel Peters of Connecticut back in the 18th century. The term was first used back in 1755 and described as…"Legislation that prohibits or restricts certain activities in order to support religious standards."

In rare instances, blue laws affected activities on days other than Sunday, but the most common use was in reference to Sunday, in which case they were also known as "Sunday laws." It was all about the "faithful" who honored God by following the fourth commandment – "keeping the Sabbath holy."

"The Puritans were probably the first to enforce Sunday laws on the North American continent, banning many commercial and recreational activities on Sundays during the 1600s." (Source: Article Library)

If you remember, all stores used to be closed on Sunday. Even the essentials like milk, bread and ice, weren't delivered. Milkmen, bread delivers and icemen usually had the weekend off. If there was a local deli on your block and the owner lived in the back of the store, you could knock on his door and ask if he would go into the store to get you a couple of quarts of milk or a loaf of bread to see you through till Monday when deliveries resumed.

Businesses eventually saw that a lot of people who worked on Saturdays couldn't get to the stores; especially after many women/moms who once stayed home, joined the work force. That was money lost for the businesses. So, the Blue Law was relaxed and stores (except liquor stores) opened on Sundays around noon and closed between 5 PM and 6 PM.

The law prohibiting the sale of alcoholic beverages on Sunday lasted longer. Eventually, the problem of… "What to do about people who worked on Saturday and are only off on Sunday?" The Blue Law was again relaxed and liquor stores were permitted to sell their goods - but, not until noon. Sunday mornings were still held sacred so people could attend church before imbibing!

A little levity…Check out some funny restrictions New York State once had connected to the Blue Law.

-Citizens may not greet each other by "putting one's thumb to the nose and wiggling the fingers".

-A fine of $25 can be levied for flirting.

-The penalty for jumping off a building is death.

-A man can't go outside while wearing a jacket and pants that do not match.

…All I can say is…WOW!

Home Delivery – Bread, Milk and Ice

Milkman

Going back to the fifties in Québec, I remember home delivery services for of bread, milk and ice Monday through Friday. I'm sure some of you older South Buffalo Baby Boomers still remember when you had an "icebox" rather than a refrigerator. The iceman would bring in a large 40 or 50 pound cube of ice and set in the icebox. Keeping ice cream in one of those was not an option. As a matter of fact, what we call junk food today was not known to us. Ice cream was a once in a while treat for special occasions only that we could buy at the corner delicatessen for a nickel. Also in the fifties in Welland, Ontario, we still had a milkman delivering milk in a horse-drawn wagon. When we moved to South Buffalo in 1960, we had one of those little milk compartments at the back of the house where we left our empty quart glass bottles and the milkman would replace them with a fresh supply.

Very Hard Times

When the Lackawanna Bethlehem Steel Plant, employing over 20,000 men, went on strike in June 10, 1959, many South Buffalo family men who worked there were in dire financial straits. The paychecks stopped. It was a very bad time. It was called "The Big Fight." The strike lasted 116 days (nearly four months) and people suffered greatly. One such family was the Smiths next door to us with seven mouths to feed. The Lackawanna plant produced steel from 1922 until 1983. Little by little, all 20,000 lost their job. The plant stopped most of its operations on October 15, 1982.

Not only did Bethlehem Steel close, eventually, several other mills; Republic Steel on South Park, Ryerson Steel in the Lovejoy area, and Buffalo Tank Division on Lake Avenue in Blasdell.

When many families lost their paychecks, many of them lost their homes as well. A lot of folks relied on family and friends to help them get through those tough times; some received food stuff such as powdered milk, flour, cheese, peanut butter, and can food items from government food relief centers to sustain their families. With plants closing, the Buffalo area lost a large number of people. Many had to resettle elsewhere in order to find work.

No Cash on Hand

How many of you Baby Boomers remember neighbors borrowing bread, milk, sugar, butter, cream, coffee, money or cigarettes from each other? We called it borrowing, but it was really a handout; except for money, that is. Most of the time, moms would replace a bottle of milk, a loaf of bread or cigarettes they borrowed.

Your mother might have said to you, "Hey, Shamus or you, Katherine, go over and ask Mrs. Milligan next door if I can borrow a cup of sugar and a couple of dollars? Tell her I'll pay her back when dad gets paid from the plant at the end of the week. Oh, and tell her I'd like a couple of cigarettes if she can spare them." Back then, those two dollars could buy a fair amount of necessary foodstuff for the family.

In our neighborhoods, we were pretty much equals, financially. So many folks were broke by the time payday rolled around. Dads worked steady jobs and a few moms too, but not many. They didn't over spend, and learned to stretch the dollar. Our parents went through the Depression years (1930s) when they had to do with a whole lot less than we Boomers ever did. Many of them knew about soup kitchens and soup lines. We never experienced that, thank God. When it came to budgeting money, most moms were experts. And... for the most part, it was the moms that handled the money.

What Money to Spend?

Money was tight. I don't remember many Boomer kids having any steady pocket money back then. Some of us had a couple of coins, but it was an exception to see anyone with a few dollar bills on them. In some households, there was the special treat of an "allowance." Those of us whose parents didn't make this one of the benefits of being part of the family corporation were a bit jealous of those fortunate individuals who did get it. If a teen got a two, three or maybe five dollar allowance a week, they were fortunate. If we figure conservatively, that $3.00 a week allowance came to $150.00 for the year. That was a lot of money for any kid/teen. A lot of us were lucky to have a quarter in our pocket. Most kids asked their parents for enough money to cover a ten cent ice cream cone, a bottle of Coca Cola, the price of a movie ticket, fifty cents to skate at Skate Haven on Orchard Park Road or attend dances on Friday nights at Timon or Baker Victory High.

Admission to dances was fifty cents and a movie at the Capitol or Seneca show was around thirty-five cents in the late fifties and early sixties.

You might have heard from your mom, "Okay, you can go to the dance. Here's the fifty cents, but don't ask for any more money this week! We've got bills to pay and can't afford too many of these frill."

Very often, the answer would be, "Sorry Jimmy, I really don't have anything to spare this week. I only have four dollars to make it to the end of the week. And, with us seven to feed, it's gonna be really tight."

I knew quite a few families that lived from paycheck to paycheck. Things were tight. A lot of people didn't have a dollar left by the time Wednesday or Thursdays rolled around. Many of those families ran tabs at local stores for milk, bread or baby food.

There weren't many snacks around the house either. The cupboards had staple foods, not snacks. The meals we had were usually very basic. I remember my mom own opening up a huge can of pork and beans for supper for the ten of us. We'd have that, a couple slices of bread and a glass of milk. "What's for dessert?" was not a question we asked. And forget having a snack before going to bed. That luxury wasn't part of most of the Baby Boomer perks. That's the way it was!

Allowances
And peoples' comments on the subject

I never knew about allowances until I moved from Canada to the United States. Once our family landed in South Buffalo, I heard that some friends on my street got a one or two dollar a week allowance. The word "jealous" would describe my feelings. But, I also found out that it was a pretty common thing for the average kid on the block to NOT get an allowance. Any cash most of us had in our pockets was usually provided on a…"as needed" basis. For most families I knew, there wasn't any spare cash in the family budgets for us to tap into. Most of the kids went to the "boss of the family" - moms (usually), and if they could accommodate them, they would. If not, they just went without. Who were the lucky Baby Boomers to get THAT "perk" growing up?

I put the word out on Facebook to Baby Boomers about this subject. Here are a few responses I picked out. Please keep in mind that things cost a lot less back then. So… a quarter or fifty cents for a kid went pretty far for penny candy purchases and a dollar for a teen usually took care of a day's expenses for movie with popcorn, soda pop and candy.

Mary Barry Oring – "I was given $1 a week for chores. That was enough for me to take a bus to Caz pool, buy a movie ticket at the Seneca Show, buy a coke, and sometimes, more than one candy bar."

NOTE: Realize that in the late 50s, early 60s, a bus fare was 15 cents, a movie ticket 25 to 35 cents, a coke 10 or 15 cents and candy bars, 5 or 10 cents. Do the math. Total on the heavy side comes to around 75 cents.

Bill Masters - "No allowances. I delivered the Courier Express to earn spending money."

Eileen Schott – "No allowance! I was the youngest of 8, and when I turned 11, I began baby-sitting to earn spending money."

Eddy Standish – "There were six kids in our family with both parents working. We had a list with the names of the chores that were numbered one through six. Number one was for the oldest in the family. We switched jobs during the week; cleaning rooms and doing the laundry. But…taking out the garbage was for the boys only - because, as we were taught, it was a man's job.'"

Debbie Rysczynski – NEVER! And …I was expected to clean my room and help around the house.

Bill Conwall - "NOPE! If I needed money, I had to work for it."

Joyce Roman – "Fifty cents a week was my allowance …only if I did chores. I was one of nine children. Once I got a job, I paid room and board."

(Baby Boomers…explain "room and board" to your children and grandchildren. They just might not know what that is!)

John J Warden – "I got 25 cents a week for taking the trash cans out to the street and cleaning my bedroom."

Janine Gavin-Pokrandt said, "I got 25 cents a week as a kid…and when I turned 18 and got a job, I paid $10 a week to stay there, and …did house chores!"

Bill Sexton – Yep! I got a $1 a week from my dad and I would run to the corner store to buy the latest Superman comic book."

Marjorie Heilig Sours was a good budgeter. She said, "I got $2 a day for school lunch. I only spent $1 and had $5 saved by the end of the week."

Lynne Gould said, "I Born in 1957. No allowance. If there was a chore to be done, I had to do it before going outside to play with my friends. None of my neighborhood friends got an allowance either. There were 6 kids in our family and my dad worked two jobs. When I was old enough, I babysat for 50 cents hour for two bratty kids …lol. At sixteen, I started a regular job."

Judy Knoop stated, "I grew up in a family of twelve children in the 70s and 80s. No allowance for us. We never expected one and we all had chores to do."

Kathleen Byrns Mendola – "Born in '57. No allowance, and I wasn't alone. I can only remember one kid that did get an allowance. One day, the boys were out in front of school before it opened, Sr. Mary Richard walked by and heard this kid (the one who got the allowance) say his father owed him $5. Sister got in his face and told him his father owed him nothing! She said, 'You have food, clothes, a roof over your head and it's all because your dad goes out and works hard every day!' You could have heard a pin drop when she was done with him."

Rebecca Couturier - "As a kid I received $0.25 per week. Got my first job at 14 working in the concession stand at the Buffalo Zoo. They didn't hire girls for paper routes back then.

Chris Riley - One of the very fortunate kids. He stated, "I used to get $5 to $10 a week." Bet he had a lot of friends!

Cathy Hannon Druckemiller - "No allowance! I was one of nine children. We earned money by returning bottles for deposit and babysitting.

Nancy Ogorek - "I was born in 1963. No allowance. The seven of us kids were allowed to live there (our house). We all did chores for that privilege."

Rick Thomas - "I got 25 cents a week in the late 50s"

Beverly Tate - "I think I got $2.00 a week for putting dinner in the oven and setting the table when I got home from school. I also helped my mom canning tomatoes and peaches."

Linda Larson - "No allowance as a kid, but as a teenager, I got $10.00 a week, but I had chores to do before I received it. It was not a handout there were rules attached to it. It was my mom's way of teaching me how to budget money and I am thankful I learned this. So many kids grow up not having a clue about handling money."

I believe you have enough examples to see *"the way it was"* regarding allowances.

More on youths earning money

When we were pre to early teens, we could make $1 or $2 shoveling snow in the winter. Nobody, and I mean nobody - had snow blowers in the 50's and 60's. We'd grab whatever shovel the family had and go knock on doors to see if people wanted their sidewalk and driveway shoveled. The shovel I remember using was an old coal shovel from the 30's or 40's. I still have it. For the girls, the primary way of making a few bucks was babysitting.

As teens, many of us had a paper route. It was always good for a bit of spending money. I delivered the Courier Express seven days a week (1961-62) to houses on South Park between Choate and Bloomfield and I also had all of Bloomfield and Richfield streets. I had maybe fifty or sixty customers.

Other guys I knew who delivered the Courier Express were Joe Prendergast from Sheffield who he delivered on his street. Tony Pacella from Columbus delivered on his street and Tifft from South Park to McKinley Parkway. Joe Liberti from Tifft Street had about a hundred-sixty customers. He handled part of Tifft from South Park to Hopkins, Folger, Payne, Garvey and some of Hopkins Street. John Carney from Crystal delivered the Buffalo Evening News. We Courier Express delivery boys were up very early every single morning.

Prendergast said he was up around the time the Courier truck dropped off his bundle of paper around 4 AM or so. He said, "I was a bit lazier. I'd get up at five or five-thirty. I didn't like it at all but like I said, it was a bit of pocket money."

The better paper route was delivering the Buffalo Evening News because it was an after school thing. There was no getting up in the wee hours of the morning. Not only that, the Buffalo Evening News didn't have a Sunday paper; only Monday through Saturday. Those carriers didn't have to deal with inserts or a super heavy load. A daily paper back then cost only 7 cents and the Sunday paper with all the advertising inserts, comics and special magazine sections was 20 cents. By 1963, the Sunday paper had gone up to 25 cents.

Price Check

It seems to me that the price of items was more reasonable back in the day. Here are prices of what some things cost back in 1946. Keep in mind, minimum wage was 40 cents an hour; a $16.00 paycheck for a 40 hour week.

A first class postage stamp was 3 cents, bread 10 cents a loaf, a quart of milk 18 cents, a gallon of gas, 21 cents, a cup of coffee, a nickel, a phone call from a telephone booth could be made for a nickel, a newspaper was 3 cents, a car $1,650, and a house, $12,600.

In the fifties and sixties a good size candy bar was a dime, a pack of Juicy Fruit gum, a nickel; large pretzel sticks, a penny each and a bottle of Coke cost 10 cents. It was 8 cents cents for the liquid and 2 cents bottle deposit. There were no cans or plastic bottles then, only glass. And…..you didn't find them littering the streets, vacant fields or roadways.

Speaking of pop/soda pop, I may be wrong, but I could swear Coca Cola tasted different in the fifties and sixties than it does today. There was a rumor going around that you could remove rust from chromed bumpers with Coke Cola. I never tried it myself but heard the rumor more than once.

Back in my teens, things were made in America. I don't remember reading the labels on my shirts or pants and seeing "Hecho en México" (Made in Mexico). Nor did I have anything made in Pakistan, China or some Central American country. Pretty much, everything we had was made in the States. A decent pair of shoes cost about $12 to $20. A pair of "US Keds" high top sneakers could be had for as low as $2.50 and basic girls' sneakers could be bought for $1.00. A good white, dress shirt cost $2.50 to $5.00 and pleated dress pants, $8 to $12.

Gasoline was around 23 to 26 cents a gallon and the average car cost between, $1,500 and $1,600. A new house at the end of my street went for $15,000 - $17,000 in the early sixties. That same house now is between $70,000 and $90,000; maybe more. The cost of a regular postage stamp is quite high compared to the five cent stamp of the sixties. When I was in the Army in 1966, I used to send a lot of letters back home. A regular stamp was five cents and airmail was seven cents.

Cost of Treats – the way it was

Pizzas were one of the major takeout treats in the 50's and 60's at a fairly low price. Today, for some families, it has become a scheduled meal of the week - and not so cheap. I remember working for the Bocce Club Pizzeria in the early 60's on Clinton and Adam Street. A large 18 inch cheese pizza cost $1.80. If you wanted pepperoni the cost was $2.10. Today, that same size cheese and pepperoni pizza is over $20. Buffalo's East Side Bocce's was THE pizzeria to go to back then and people would come from all over; the West Side, East Aurora, Eden, West Seneca, Lackawanna, and even, Fort Erie, Canada.

South Buffalo and most neighborhoods had hot dog restaurants. The price for these tasty treats was around 20 cents each back in the late 50s and early 60s. Today, at Louie's Texas Red hots, they are around $2.39 each. Comparing prices to today's makes Baby Boomers cringe. A regular cup of coffee which once cost a dime is now $1.50 or more.

Along with pizzerias and Texas hot restaurants, in the early sixties, "Henry's Hamburgers" came along. It was located across from the Park Edge Market on McKinley near Abbott. It was the first "fast food" joint I ever saw. And the prices! How about 15 cents for a hamburger, 20 cent for a cheeseburger, 12 cents for French fries and twenty cents for one of those super thick milkshakes? How many of you remember how hard it was to draw their milkshake through a straw before it had time to soften? Man, you could see the veins on people's foreheads popping out trying to get that tasty vanilla or chocolate" ice cream up the wax-fortified straws. In December of 2019, I paid $2.98 for a cheeseburger at McDonald's. From 20 cents at Henry's back in the 60's to nearly $3.00 for a burger is a tremendous jump in price. Of course, back then, hourly wages were $1.00 an hour compared to today's $15.00 an hour minimum.

Great Trash Pickup Service

Talking about money, we got a lot for the taxes we paid to the City Sanitation Service back in the day. We had curb service for trash day.

Tim Fitzgerald who, in his younger days, worked for the sanitation department said, "We had what we called Rollers. These were the guys who went into your yard starting at 4 AM, take the metal garbage cans from the back of the house and bring them to the curb for pickup. A lot of them used hand carts with wheels to roll out the heavy cans. Hence the name, "Rollers" After the trash pickups were made, the same guys or a different crew would come around and return the cans to the sides or backs of the houses."

I remember one of our own, Jack Pugh from Altruria Street who was big and very strong. He could pick up six full cans at a time and take them to the street. He'd put one under each arm, then, grab two cans by the handles, two in each hand and off he'd go to the curb. That was a great service.

According to Jack, that lasted from around the fifties to the early eighties. He remembers that for a long time the city of Buffalo had over 600,000 residents. It whittled down to less than 300,000 as the city and surrounding areas lost a lot of manufacturing plants and people headed elsewhere to make a living. That is an immense drop. He also remembers that when he started out in with the sanitation department in the 1960's there were around 400 men working there. By the time he retired in the mid-eighties there were only about 85 men needed to take care of garbage pickup. The reason for that was the department got mechanized garbage trucks and didn't need so many men. The new trucks were equipped with a hydraulic compressing mechanism to cram as much trash into the truck container as possible. Only two men per truck were needed, same as today.

Hey Baby Boomers, remember in the old days, they only had open-bed dump trucks for our trash pickup? There were usually two guys on the ground and two guys in the dump-truck. Those on the ground would toss the cans onto the truck and the guys in the truck bed dumped them and threw the empties back down to the men on the ground. Also, do you remember your trash cans looking a little beat up after months of use and because the men dumping the trash often had to BANG them against the edge of the top rails to shake off items that were stuck on the bottom? On and on it went, up and down each street. Now, that was work. I always respected what they did. Those men really earned their money. There was a running joke among them with reference to their pay:

"We don't make a lot of money, but we have all we can eat."

Bad joke. God bless them."

NOTE: John J. "Jackie" Pugh left us much too soon at 65 years of age on January 27, 2012.

Chapter 21 Baby Boomer

Activities, Friends and Hangouts

As with all of the South Buffalo areas, the South Park area had a ton of Baby Boomers on every street. The young people didn't have a lot but managed to stay busy doing one thing or another.

Baby Boomer, Margie Weber remembers and said, "Who can forget Mr. Softee and his jack-in-the-box music? Ninety percent of the time he came at dinner time. And the carnival rides-remember the bumper cars on the back of a flatbed that went from street to street? Who needed Darien Lake or Fantasy Island? We had our own amusement park and refreshments out front. Talk about curb service. Then, there was the man who drove down periodically in the summer with comic books in his trunk for free. And, the man who hollered out of his truck window on hot summer days: 'Rags, rags for sale.' They were used as dust cloths and our Moms who would run out to get them. With the red smoke dust from the Coke Ovens blowing around all windowsills had to be wiped down daily in summer. There were many times the sheets and other laundry had to be pulled off the line while drying outside and rewashed when Bethlehem Steel spewed out its red soot."

Friends

All the kids made many friends and knew a slew of the neighborhood people. A lot of the young folks formed their own little groups which was natural. Despite the groups that existed, just about everyone interacted and would play sports in Mulroy park behind Holy Family School, go to Timon dances on McKinley Parkway or at Fazio's Hall (also known as the Peppermint Lounge for a short while) at the corner of South Park and Southside. I went to school at Holy Family with Mr. Fazio's son. There was a soda shop across from Fazio's where we'd spend time drinking a malt and talking. In the winter, there was always the Cazenovia ice rink for outside open skate. The rink drew a lot of people from Seneca, Abbott McKinley and South Park.

Hopping Garages

Not all of the kids read books, belonged to groups who did creative things or spent their time constructively. A lot of the Baby Boomers did not have much direction, or goals they were working towards at that age. One of the summer activities some of the young men used to take part in was hopping garages. If you're not familiar with this activity, you're in for an eye-opener. There were only select individuals who took part in this activity. It wasn't a sport or a game. It wasn't even logical. It was a dare thing. I remember one of the streets where they would hop garages was Whitfield Street. The first dumb thing was they started on the roof of the firehouse that was right behind the Precinct #15 Police Station. The second dumb thing was that the first garage was a ten-foot drop from the roof of the firehouse. They could have broken a leg, twisted an ankle or worse, gone right through the roof and landed on who-knows-what inside the garage.

The game plan here was to go from one garage to the other as they alternated left, right, left, right. Most were close enough that it would take only a short jump to get from one to the other. They could go to a certain point then have to go back because the next garage was not close enough to jump onto. Once though, they went as far as they could and all sat on the roof of the last garage and pondered whether or not they could make it to the next one and continue down the street. The only problem was that it was at least a twelve foot leap to grab the edge of the flat-roof. Then, they'd have to do a pull-up to get on top of the roof. No one bit on that idea except one guy. He chewed on the idea for a few minutes, then, took a run, leapt and slammed his entire body against the side of the garage as he tried to grab onto the ledge. It didn't end there. Down on the ground with his knees killing him from the crash, he was stuck. The only two ways out were the driveway where a lady was screaming at him, "Get out of my yard" alongside her barking, growling German shepherd or take route number two; escape over the neighbor's fence where there were thorny rose bushes. You have to ask yourself a question at this point in the story. Which option would you have chosen? Which one do you think our flying ace chose?

Choice number #1 - the driveway where the dog was, that could have chewed him up a bit?

OR

Choice number #2 - go for the fence with the rose bushes and receive cuts, lacerations and abrasions?

The sanest thing to do in the minds of the guys atop the roof counseling him was for him to take the bushes. He struggled for a few seconds in the middle of his confusion and pain with the dog barking, the lady yelling and the guys telling him to go for the fence; he finally took the advice of his loving buddies and over the fence and through the bushes he went. Yes, he got some nasty scratches and cuts but was spared dog bites. We kind of wondered what would have happened to him if he had taken the driveway toward the lady and the dog.

Groups of friends

A lot of the kids from different streets met at someone's house with their circle of friends and played all sorts of games or hung out and talked about anything and everything imaginable. Some would play catch or baseball on some lot, wrestle, hop garages or play basketball if they were lucky enough to have a basketball net in their yard. My neighbor, Brian McDonald had a basketball net on his garage and I played there for a while till I moved into another group of friends as did Brian.

A couple friends of mine and I would meet up at the Cazenovia ice rink with a few of the girls from our school, Margie Morrison, Anne Schneeberger and Karen Lobuglio. We would also go to CYO group skate nights at Skate Haven on Abbott Road in Lackawanna. Skate Haven became Lucarelli's Banquet Hall. Skates were the old style four-wheel roller skates with two wheels in back, two in front and a rubber stopper at the toe. It was always funny watching people who couldn't skate well, crashing into the side railings or the walls to stop.

Some of the guys and girls we mixed with were:

Sam and Joe Parisi, Bill Nicholson, John Lafferty, Brian Moran, Joe Prendergast, John Tevington, Bill Graber, Jim McDonald, Nick Vertalino, Lenny Weber, Joe Calabrese, Marilyn (Sue) Lafko, Rosemary Stebbins, Marjorie Weber, Adele Petrilli, Marcia Miniri, Mary Bussman, Phyllis Palmieri, Carmela and Danny Giganti, Susan Padolic, Barbara Buckley, Kathy Pugh, Diane Macri, Maureen Masterson, Patricia Nigro, and Margaret Tomasello.

The Playgrounds

A lot of the guys went to schoolyards or playgrounds to meet up with friends and pass hours chatting and playing. Those who went to local parks played sports like softball, baseball and basketball and football. Most games were pick-up games. They weren't organized by adults. Guys got together, picked sides and played, just for the sake of playing. That was nice, lots of good times.

There were several parks in South Buffalo that kept the youth occupied: Mungovan Park on South Side Parkway/Bailey Avenue near the present site of Southside Elementary School. Hillery Park on Mineral Springs Road, Mulroy Park behind Holy Family on Tifft Street and the Okell Playground behind School #29. They were busy from morning till night in the summer time. Some baseball, softball and basketball games were often organized by park athletic directors all over the area. Caz Park had great baseball diamonds in the bowl that were enjoyed by teams from all over the area.

Mulroy Playground Games

As parks go, Caz Park was the gem of parks for South Buffalo. The biggest draw, for sure, were the pools and casino for the kids, and a golf course for adults where tons of kids and teens from all over spent hours there. Mulroy playground was also very special. In the summer, George Hermann was in charge of the park building that had bathrooms and a section for sports equipment. He would hand out the equipment. The park had horse shoe pits, a half and full basketball court, swings, slides, teeter-totters, a small pool for the kids, and baseball diamonds. I can't forget the picnic tables under the tree near the equipment building where guys would congregate and play cards, mostly pinochle. I watched them play and tried to catch on but I was too dumb I guess. I could never follow what they were doing. I heard terms like:

Aces or Kings around, Bare run, Bid up, Meld bid, Runs and Marriage, Common marriage, Royal marriage, Lead back, Round house, Trump, Trick, Jack of Diamonds and Queen of Spades. I just couldn't process all that.

Crap Games

Shooting craps was much easier to follow. The games went on everywhere in Buffalo. In our own area, breaking up crap games was one of the activities that kept the local police busy. Some played at Mulroy Park and other crews would go behind PS #29. The games usually took place in the summer months after the parks closed and all the little kids were gone or on Sunday afternoon. The bets weren't usually very large. Normally they were 25 or 50 cents or dollar bets. No one had very much money to gamble with. At Mulroy, if someone yelled, COPS, everyone would scramble to pick up their money and run like hell. As you can imagine, some of the guys weren't very choosy as to what part of the pot they picked up in their rush to pick up and run. The games would go on all summer long. A few guys were scooped up by the police, interrogated a bit then, let go. I don't remember anyone having to go to court for this. It was one of those things that was considered harmless, but still, against the law. Guys as young as twelve to grown men played. I remember Pat L, an Italian teen guy the cops had in a lineup in the park. When the police asked his name, he said with a Spanish accent: "My name...José Jimenez." He was imitating a Hispanic comedian that was popular at the time. The group got yelled at and released.

One dice player I remember had a short scruffy beard - wore a baseball cap and metatarsal shoes from the steel plant. He was only known as "Pops." He spoke very little, and when he did, he was soft-spoken, saying only what needed to be said to place his bets.

As the legend goes, according to Tony Szymkowiak and Ron Wentland from the Taylor Park crew, they said, "Pops lived in one of the spaces under the Tifft Street Bridge and worked at Bethlehem Steel. We heard that he didn't cash his paychecks when he got paid until some of the guys from the plant found out about his situation and every six months or so, someone would take him to the bank and have him do that. Because of where and how he lived, no bathing facilities, a foreman at the plant got him to take a shower at least once a week."

Let's get back to the park. Today, Mulroy Park is a shadow of what it was. Too bad! It once was a great place to meet up with friends, hang out and play sports, a lot of sports.

Some kids stayed beyond the park's closing time. The police would come by and shag them out as it got dark. Of course, kids would be obedient to the law officers - until they left. Then, some would go back in. For the most part, it was to sit around, chat and smoke cigarettes.

Speaking of the police, COPS (Constables on Patrol) rode in cars, usually in pairs. I also remember policemen walking a beat back then. Many of the officers walked up and down South Park, Abbott and Seneca. A lot of them got to know the locals personally. I can't deny that a few of our young men got to visit their local Precinct on occasion where they were detained for inappropriate behavior and had a time out inside a jail cell. The south precincts back then were; Number 7 at 355 Louisiana Street in 1935 and later at 300 Louisiana and Miami. Number 9 station's first location in 1191 Seneca in the Seneca-Babcock area and then moved to Seneca and Southside. The southernmost station was Number 15 at 2028 South Park and Whitfield and then to P.S. School 29 at 2219 South Park and Okell. The last place to house the South District (A-District Headquarters) is at 1857 South Park Avenue. In 1938, there were 19 precincts throughout Buffalo.

Dumb Fun Winter Activities

About the only readily available winter activities we had were: ice skating, sledding, tobogganing and skiing. Well, don't you know, for the guys, there was one more fun thing to do when the snow fell. Those of you who lived during that time must remember hitching a ride on the back bumpers of cars, trucks or busses when there was snow on the streets. You'd hook onto a bumper, do boot-skiing, and go as far as you dared. If the car was going fairly fast when you let go, your legs couldn't keep up with the momentum and you'd end up rolling around like desert tumbleweed; and the guys watching you would laugh and laugh at you. It was really funny to watch. It was the same for the poor schnooks who would be seen hitting dry pavement during their joy ride. They would end up with road rash. Again, the guys watching this would have a good laugh - but the bashed up victims didn't find it funny.

Police Involvement in the Neighborhood

For the most part, the neighborhoods were safe and peaceful. There were very few incidents that would be deemed as criminal or posing a danger to the general public. Most of the problems came from too many young people hanging out on street corners during the warm weather with nothing to do. Remember, the Baby Boomers were numerous and hanging around the house with siblings wasn't fun. Hanging around with people their own age, usually on street corners, provided them with a way of passing time, have a few laughs, and talk about whatever was on their mind. Guys shared a lot of useful information among themselves, as well as bad. It was the same for the girls wherever they congregated. Let's be honest, that's probably where most teens learned about the bird and the bees.

Now and then, since there were so many bars on all the main strips, there were times a drunk would be confronted by law officers and maybe taken home in the squad car or sent home in a cab. On street corner hangouts, police would sometime come by and break up groups when they got too large or boisterous. Some even got hauled off to local precincts when the requests to move along or disperse weren't obeyed.

Group Arrested

One such incident happened when a group of older teens got arrested in front of PS #29 back in 1963 for loitering and rowdy behavior. They were put into three squad cars, hauled off to Precinct 15 and put in their cells. Then, the lads got a ride downtown in the Paddy Wagon to the Holding Center for the night. The next day all nine stood before the judge. It was one of those cases that should not have gone that far. I believe the Cops were a bit frustrated with so many young guys loitering on so many corners that they figured it was time to make an example of this crew. The case was dismissed with a strong warning from the judge to "Stay off the street corners."

The law officers proved their point and the boys now had to deal with mom and dad. By the way, all nine made the Buffalo Evening News with names, ages and streets they lived on. How embarrassing. From then on, they made better choices as to where they hung out.

Chapter 22 People around the Neighborhood

Just about everybody in these neighborhoods could relate to a ton of people from their respective area. Bob Greene sent me a list of 75 names of people he either hung around with or was familiar with. Eileen Leahy, along with her brothers and parents came up with over 72 friends and acquaintances from their immediate area from the old days.

One of the guys who moved from Lackawanna to South Buffalo was Chuck Aldridge. His brother Bobby was a Golden Gloves Champ boxer and New York State champ. We called Chuck "Elvis." He lived on my street (Altruria) and was known to walk right down the middle of the street when he left his house. We all knew that. From a distance, even at night in the dark we'd see a figure walking towards us and we knew... here comes, Elvis. We came to call him that because he looked a little like Elvis and had a certain swagger when he walked. To us, he was cool. He wasn't arrogant and didn't play the tough guy although he had some size to him. He was soft-spoken and friendly but we knew not to say anything stupid or mess with him. He'd walk by and we'd say "Hi Chuck." He'd come back with something like: "How yous doin'?"

We got along fine. He was one of us, an Altruria guy; a South Buffalo, South Park guy. I'm sure that in all the other sections of South Buffalo it was the same. Kids had older popular guys and girls they looked up to for one reason or other.

Several guys from our neighborhoods passed way too soon. One was Roger Brennan. He lived right next to Ullenbruch's Delicatessen. He was a real nice guy, quiet, always pleasant and probably one of the few guys I ever met that didn't have a mean bone in his body. He passed in his early twenties maybe. Another guy from the neighborhood who passed was Mike Knezevich who lived on Richfield and died in a car crash. Ted Pasiecznik from Aldrich Street also died in one on McKinley Pkwy around 1971 when he hit a tree near the Erie County Fairground. Ted married a girl name Brenda, served in the armed forces as a paratrooper, trained in Panama and went to Viet Nam.

Speaking of Vietnam, I must mention Tim Nightengale, a marine from Altruria Street. He died in one of the Vietnam fields on 4/6/68 - five months shy of his 19th birthday. His mother Peg was given Tim's Purple Heart. There were several more South Buffalo area soldiers who died in Nam, I'm sure. Whoever they are, I salute and commend them also.

Another guy from the neighborhood who passed away was Richie Yox. He is well remembered by an awful lot of guys. If you mentioned Richie on the South Park strip, most guys would know who you were talking about. He lived near the Harding Street area. He had trouble processing information. I remember that he had to carry a pad and pen to keep track of things. His short-term memory wasn't good. One of the neat things about Rich was that he could play the guitar. He often brought it out on the strip, sat down on a store front stoop and began playing and singing.

Eventually, that playing paid off. He hooked up with Chuck Carr (Crystal Ave), one of South Buffalo's many talented musicians. They formed a group and had gigs all over the Buffalo area. One of the bands Chuck formed was "Flashback." In his youth, before music, he was a top basketball player. There weren't many in the area who could match his court skills. Chuck passed away in December of 2016.

Neighborhood Groups

There were frat groups. The Esquires consisted of older guys like Johnny and Tony Orsini. The Little Esquires wanted to emulate the older guys and tagged on little in front of Esquires. They consisted of Pat and Joe Liberti, Andy Collura, Tony and Mario Pacella, Sam Parisi, Bobby Domzolski and Tom Willard. They had frat jackets with Greek lettering for the Latin version of Veni, Vidi, Vici "I Came, I Saw, I Conquered". There were a few other such organized groups. It was all done as a way of belonging to a group, doing things together and having fun; much like Sam Accordino's group near Taylor Park.

Sam Accordino

Sam Accordino was born in the early 40s and lived on Heussy Street near Saint Agatha's. He went to school 28 elementary adjacent to South Park/Abbott. After eighth grade, he enrolled at Burgard High. After Burgard, he enlisted in the Army and did a stint from 1961 to 1963.

Going back to his earlier years, he didn't have much to say about his pre-teen years, but stated that when he and his friends were around fifteen, they hung out mostly at the Greek's and Taylor Park on South Park. He and his friends formed a "gang" called the "Gators," complete with the gang's emblem on their black and powder blue jackets – about fifteen to twenty members. The girls connected to them also wore gang jackets – pink ones.

Sam stated:

> "We weren't the kind of gang that got involved in typical "hard gang" activities. It was just a thing to do; to hang out together and have an identity as a group. We weren't in competition with other gangs, frats or clubs and, we weren't into gang fights. Seneca Street also had a couple of gangs, I believe; the Cougars and the Rebels. Anyway, we just hung out as a group to have fun".

Gater colors

I asked Sam if he remembered any of the people he hung with. Here are several names he came up with. He was sorry that he couldn't come up with more or remembered the correct spellings for a few. Here are some: Gussy Carmani or Carmanis, Vinnie Antonelli, Chuck Rambino, Gerald Marchain, Carmen Sabastian, Joe Simmons, Tom Gombos, Diane Charlton, Sandy Nappo, Jeanne Shank, Pat Balonio, Rosie Backman, and Bob Moffitt.

Having attended Burgard High where a lot of Baby Boomers learned to work on cars and many became top mechanics. Sam and I got on the subject of cars he had. He said that his first was a 1950 Mercury. His favorite was a 1956 Ford two door automatic with a "Continental kit." (A Continental kit is that awesome looking shelf and spare tire accessory at the back of many classic cars of the forties, fifties and sixties) It was first seen on Ford's Edsel Lincoln Continental in 1942.

Ford with continental kit

More Friends & Neighbors

Right across from our house lived a couple of cousins; Frank Morabito who lived downstairs and Frank Mariano who lived upstairs and were friends with my brother Jacques. They had their own crew that hung out. Some of the names connected to them are Mike and Corky Hess, Neil Curtin, Bob Ulrich, Ray Colpoys, Tom Tighe, Tommy Ford, Dick Kemp, Paul, Owen and Gail Roland, Tommy and Jimmy Lasker and Dick Brown.

They would gather at the Deco at the corner of Harding and South Park. From there, they'd go wherever there was an event or a place to meet up with others for car races, boxing matches, and billiard games downtown, parties or bars where bands were playing.

A few of the guys who come to mind as some of the first to ride motorcycles down South Park Avenue were Mike Hess, Joe McGir and Bobby Fulmer. Joe once came down the strip a la Evel Knievel at about thirty miles an hour, jumped up on the seat, stood up, arms up to the side and coasted for a while doing what was called a Flying Eagle. A couple of the guys were connected to Buffalo motorcycle clubs, the Leathermen and the Road Vultures. That lifestyle lasted only a short time.

Joe was a fairly good golfer. One of the ways he kept a supply of golf balls was to dive into South Park Lake and scoop up all the balls he could find that the less talented golfers either hooked or sliced into the lake. He made a few dollars selling dozen to golfers who frequented the South Park Golf Course.

A list that Dennis Wojciechowski "Smokey" gave me of guys who hung out together between the Deco, the pool room and a few bars were Danny Shea, Jimmy "Stanley Stingray" Wilczak, Earl "The Duke" Thompson, Danny Jordon, Bill Nicholson Mickey Guzda, Mike Colern, Paul Aquisto, Carmen Nappo, Frank Daliusio, Carl and Dave Villalobos, Jimmy "Shy" Shine, Angelo "Sonny" Ferrari from Hayden Ave (off Seneca Street), Jim Buckley, Dan Manley, Rick Gianoni, Bill Clancy, Paul and Denny McDonald, Eddy Dacey, Billy McKuen, "Fingers" Walnicki, Harry Everly, Joe and Jim Syracuse, Dave and Jim Gianonni, and Smokey, himself.

Very often, individuals from different groups would mix in with others for a while then reconnect with their original crew, while remaining friends with past acquaintances. The whole phenomenon was great.

On summer nights in the early sixties, a group of fourteen to sixteen year olds hung out at the *Hartman's house on Lockwood Avenue. This crew included Sharon Pieczynski her twin sisters, Jeanne and Joan Hartman, Jerry Bonafede, Pat and Joe Liberti, Sam Parisi, John Carney, Tony Pacella, John Harmon, Tom Willard, Bob Domzalski, Paul Williams and Mike Banko.

Chapter 22 People around the Neighborhood

One of the largest South Buffalo families was the Hartmans ~ with thirteen children. In order from the oldest to the youngest of these Baby Boomers were: (dad) Walter, (mom) Charlotte, and children: Dolores, Rita, Mary, Phillis, Charlotte better known as "Sis", Dorothy, John, Ron, Sharon (Pieczynski), twins Joan/Jeanne, Betty and Bob.

Another group that hung out in the neighborhood near Tifft and South Park included Roger Pasquarella, Sam Bambrick, Lou Sprague, Bob Duke, Jimmy Miller from Pries Street, Jim Patterson and Sam Parisi.

Chapter 23 Several Well-Known

South Buffalo Connected Individuals

Pitcher Warren Spahn

Spahn was born in April of 1921 and spent his formative years in Buffalo's Kaisertown. He played ball for South Park School. That led to him signing with the Boston Braves in 1940. He was a southpaw, the best left-handed pitcher, ever.

One of his trade-marks was his high kick as he got ready to pitch the ball. The famous sports writer Al Silverman wrote, "Watching Spahn for the first time go into his delivery was an esthetic experience The Spahn windup was the most picturesque, most graceful, the most beautiful windup I had ever seen." (Source: Buffalo News Feb. 29, 2016)

Buffalo honored him by changing the name of Cazenovia Parkway at Seneca to Warren Spahn Way. Former Mayor Jimmy Griffin was very instrumental in changing the street name. Besides boxer Slattery, Spahn was one of Griffin's top sports' heroes. He died in November 2003 at the age of 82 in Oklahoma.

Steve Banko

Highly Decorated Vietnam Veteran

Viet soldiers monument

Steve Banko III, born in 1946, is another South Buffalo son. His father, Steve Banko II was of Czechoslovakian descent, and his mother Pauline (Post) Banko was from Texas. The family first settled in the Valley on Elk Street and moved to Koester Street when he was five. He is second in line of eight children. The list goes like this: Jim, Steve, Mike, Paula, Margaret, Mary, Tom and Danny. He attended Holy Family

School, Timon High, Saint Bonaventure College and then to UB to earn his BA degree in 1973. He also took journalism courses at Buffalo State College in 1976.

Pre-war and pre-college, Steve had friends from South Park, Abbott, McKinley Pkwy, Seneca Street and a few other close neighborhoods. Some of the memories of his younger days in South Buffalo include hooking up with his crowd of friends at Holy Family Parochial School such as: Jim Bausch, Joe Leary, Bob Domzolski, Jerry Bonafede, Bob Duke, Judy Conrad, Janice McGrath, Mary Zucarelli, and Jane Ward.

Friends from Timon High years include Mike Kull, Mike Grys, Paul Fitzpatrick, Greg Calveric, John Collins, Suzie Bradley and Sue Gallagher.

Some of his favorite hangouts during grade school were Mulroy Park, Parsons Judd, Friday night Timon dances and during high school years, it was LaBella's Pizzeria on Abbott. When he hit legal drinking age, he could be found at Mischler'sBar on Abbott Road. By the way, he readily admitted that during the time of the Squeaks and the Rocks, he was a - Squeak.

Playing basketball was one of his passions. He played a lot at Mulroy Playground under the watchful eye of playground supervisor, George Hermann. Here's what he had to say about Mr. Hermann,

"The role of George Hermann in the lives of many young men in the South Buffalo area can't be overstated. He was equal parts; coach, teacher, mentor and surrogate father; the latter, because so many of our own fathers were working in back-breaking, mind-numbing jobs like those in plants and mills. They rarely had time to see us play, to help us get to games, or guide us. They were too busy earning a living and keeping us food, clothing and shelter. So, men like George at Mulroy, which is now George Hermann Playground, and Paul Head at Hillery Playground on Mineral Springs, went way beyond the call of their profession and really impacted our lives."

So many of the guys around Steve's age spent hours playing ball on the playground courts. He related in an article that he witnessed one of the best games ever played at Mulroy Park. Some of the players were, Billy Roberts, Louis McManus, Duke Forsythe, Tony Bevillaqua, Whitey Martin, Mike Marley, Bob Duke and Kevin Milligan.

In 1967 he was drafted and went to Fort Benning, Georgia for basic training and then, to Fort Dix for advance-training. On January 20, 1968, he shipped out to Viet Nam for his first tour of duty. He saw a lot of action. One of the most terrifying and heart wrenching things he experienced was seeing his entire company being wiped out. Many of his close Army buddies died on the battle field.

He said, "Having made it out alive and having to live with that was a very hard thing to do."

Time may heal all wounds, but scars remain. He was seriously wounded in December of 1968 when he sustained a shattered leg being hit by shrapnel. He also suffered burns to his hands. From the Vietnam fields he was sent to Yokota, Japan for his medical care. He did a second tour starting on October 1, 1969 to January 28, 1970. In all, he was wounded six times during battles.

For his wounds and service to our country Steve was awarded Four Purple Hearts, two Bronze Stars for valor and two Bronze Stars for service and a Silver Star, our nation's 3rd highest award for valor. Although he was highly decorated as a soldier, here's what he had to say concerning those medals.

"I had the misfortune of being in a lot of action that resulted in a lot of wounds and a few medals. The wounds are more of a reminder of my service than the medals."

He listed some other guys he knew who served our country; not all went to Nam; John Ranne, Jimmy Riley, and Gerry Nostrant from his class of '65 at Timon who were "grunts" along with Mike Kapture and Tom Glavey. He said that Joe Duffy O'Connor from Baker High was a decorated MP. Duffy was another grunt from St. Ambrose and Timon (class '65.) Other guys Steve knew that went to Nam were Dave Fennessey from St. Theresa's. He was in the 101st Airborne and was killed in action during his second tour on May 20, 1967. Then, there was Bobby Smith from Seneca Street, also killed in action as was Jimmy Cummings from Good Avenue and Tim Nightingale from Altruria Street. Others guys who served were: Paul Schaeffer from the Seneca-Babcock area, one of the Fitzgibbons boys and retired Buffalo firefighter, Phil Ryan from Seneca Street.

He mentioned that he served with another South Buffalo man, Jim "Mo" Maloney and that he knew his brother Dan and his mother Annie who worked at Mischler'sTavern. He also remembered another guy who was a Marine, Terry Cannan, who went to St. Tommy's and Baker Victory High. Steve said: "Terry took a bunch of shrapnel in his legs."

After Nam, Steve went through some rough times as did many of the men who returned after having experienced the hell war brings. He saw a lot of gore and death all around him during battles, especially when his company got wiped out.

Here's what he had to say about that, "I survived because of a lot of guys and a lot of heroism. That in itself creates other psychological issues, including 'survivor guilt'; feeling bad about living when so many of your friends died."

In Nam, he battled the Viet Congs and when he came back, like so many other soldiers, drinking became his enemy. After several years fighting that battle, he "won the war!" To date (2020), he's been clean for well over 40 years and enjoying his family and friends.

He attended the University of Buffalo and St. Bonaventure. He was in government for three decades. His first position was as advisor to former Mayor Anthony Masiello. He then held a position with New York State's HUD Department as Field Supervisor. He oversaw 48 of New York's 62 HUD operations.

He hosted the Viet Nam War Memorial Moving Wall when it came to the Buffalo area. It was first displayed at Chestnut Ridge in 1989 and again in 1995 at the waterfront's Naval Park.

In 2009 he delivered a speech to a Veterans' Expo in Utica, New York. It was judged as "The Best Speech of the Year" by the Cicero Foundation. In 2009 he spoke again at the Purple Heart Memorial on the Memorial Walk of Buffalo's waterfront. That speech was published on Memorial Day and Vice President Joe Biden quoted Steve by name at the National Address at Arlington Cemetery. He has spoken to audiences in more than twenty cities across America.

"Thank you Steve for your heroic actions and faithful service to America. Those who went with you know firsthand how it was; and what horrible memories you all carried back home. A special thought to the many that may still be tormented by it all. God's best to you. We salute you." ~ RRR

Tim Russert

I certainly must include Tim Russert in the lineup of South Buffalo-connected achievers. He was the most notable individual from our neighborhood. The son of Timothy "Big Russ" and Elizabeth Seeley Russert, he grew up on Woodside Avenue near McKinley. Tim was honored by Woodside being given a second name, Tim Russert Way. He too walked the very same streets many of us walked. He frequented the pharmacies, delicatessens, soda shops, library, movie theatres, parks and eateries that most of us did. He went to the same elementary school I went to, Holy Family.

One of his childhood friends, Ralph Palmieri lived at 116 Woodside. Ralph said, "Besides all of the street and neighborhood games we played, one thing I remember doing with Tim was playing Davy Corckett. He even had one of those coon hats with the tail."

Ralph and his sister Phyllis got to enjoy his company only a short time as kids. The Russerts moved to West Seneca and Tim went to Saint Bonaventure on Seneca Street after his family moved from Woodside.

And according to Tom Gannon who also lived on Woodside, he said that when his brother Bob needed to give up his Buffalo Evening News paper route, Tim Russert took it over. That means that all of the families he delivered the paper to, after he made it big, were able to say with pride and glee, "Tim Russert was OUR family's paper boy when he was a kid."

Like most of us from the area, he came from a blue collar family, having strong values, faith, ideals and convictions. Much of those qualities can be attributed to having had loving parents, living in a great neighborhood, and attending Holy Family and Canisius High School.

The one difference about Tim Russert and most of the guys he hung with was that he was able to look way beyond what any of us did. No one I knew from the neighborhood had any notion of becoming a nationally known celebrity. I'm sure Tim didn't know this as a teen or young man in South Buffalo, but he took steps that led him on to achieve celebrity status. He established himself as one of our nation's top TV commentator, reporter and show host. He became a political analyst/commentator and hosted the very well- known show "Meet the Press," for NBC.

He visited Buffalo on a regular basis and expressed his great love for South Buffalo on many occasions. In his book written in the early part of 2000 called "Big Russ and Me," he mentioned some of the very same places I've already mentioned. It was apparent in his story that he felt very much at home in the neighborhood and had a great time being raised there. He left us suddenly when he suffered a heart attack in Washington on June 13, 2008. The ceremonies and memorials that took place to honor him were simply amazing. His funeral was attended by numerous notables such as; President Bush, former President Clinton, a great number of TV colleagues, senators, singers, actors and other famous people. One of the state politicians proposed a bill to name part of Route 20A near the Bills' Stadium, after him. For a South Buffalo boy who did extremely well, that was a fitting and honorable tribute. He was one of the Buffalo Bills biggest fans. At the end of his Meet the Press shows, when the Bills were scheduled to play, you'd hear him say, "Go Bills!"

Dave Caruso

BPD 60's squad car photo: courtesy of Det. Mark R. Stamback

David was born and raised in the South Park-Hopkins area of Saint Agatha's Parish. He lived on Lilac Street with parents, Vincent and Jennie; brothers, James and Michael and a sister, Connie. He went to elementary PS #28 and Hutch Tech High where he graduated from in 1964. During his teen years there were a few people he hung around with who were close friends. He stated that he probably associated with at least a couple of hundred people his age back then but couldn't possibly remember them all. That's the way it was with most of the guys and young ladies in South Buffalo. Everyone knew a slew of people outside their immediate circle of friends.

Some of the people he hung out with were, Joe Morganti, Dan Podgorny, Greg Collins, Barry Russell, Bill McCooey, Jim Parks, Rick Jones, Karen Maroone, Sue Jindra, Jeanne Grosjean, and Bonnie Eich., Places his crew hung out as teens were, The Villa Pizzeria, Timon dances, Capitol Theatre and Caz Park.

He did what all of the South Buffalo guys did, swimming and baseball at Caz Park and football at Mungovan Playground. Cazenovia Park was one of the common hangouts among all of the South Buffalo guys I interviewed. Everybody went there mainly for swimming and baseball; no matter what area of South Buffalo they were from.

In 1964, Dave went to Buffalo State Teacher's College where he majored in English. After a short stint as a college student, he changed his mind and pursued a career in law enforcement.

He began as a Police Cadet in 1966 and worked out of City Hall's Police Athletic League (PAL) Office. In 1967 he started his police duties as a patrolman out of the Old First Ward's 7th Precinct. For several years he also supervised PAL leagues at the Summer Street Youth Center in the Walden and Bailey area.

In 1980 he was promoted to Lieutenant and was stationed at Precinct 15 on South Park. In 1983, he became a Captain and worked out of Precinct 3, the downtown station that was located in the old Grey Hound bus station on Main Street near Tupper. In 1990, he was again promoted to the rank of inspector. Until his retirement in 1996 he was then stationed at the old Precinct 15 which was South District Headquarters on South Park. I asked him if he thought cops should still be walking a beat in the neighborhoods like in the old days. He said:

"Walking the beat is one of the elements of community policing the Department still uses to some degree."

I asked him for names of some of the men on the force that were close colleagues or served with him. Here's a short list:

Bob Carey, George "Hobie" Amplement, Norm Appleford, Pat O'Brian (Abbott Road lad) Bill Vivian, Joe O'Shei, John Montondo of the Old First Ward, Joe and Lenny Weber from Crystal Street, John Brill of the Old First Ward and the Harmons, Kevin Sr., Kevin Jr, and John from Crystal Street.

The topic of precincts came up. I asked Dave what he thought about the closing of precinct houses the Baby Boomers were used to having in their neighborhoods. Was it a good or bad idea to do that?

He said, "The time was right. With the population shrinking and the fact that most of the precinct houses were old and in poor condition, I believe the decision to go to larger district headquarter facilities to accommodate a modern police force was a right decision."

The five main district headquarters that resulted were: District A,B,C,D, and E. Focusing on the South Buffalo area; District A presently covers what once was Precinct 7 in the Old First Ward and Valley areas, Precinct 9 is the Seneca Street and the Seneca-Babcock areas, and Precinct 15 handles the South Park, McKinley and Abbott areas.

I asked David to give me an example of something that made him wonder about his career choice. He said:

"During my rookie year on the Department, UB along with many other college campuses was experiencing some unrest due to the Viet Nam conflict. One evening, several patrol units were dispatched to the campus. Lines were formed with police and demonstrators facing each other. The atmosphere was very tense and unfriendly. I noticed some acquaintances were on the other side and I wondered whether or not I had I picked the right career. That thought hit me even harder as the order was given to move in to disperse the crowd. As we did this, we passed a demonstrator with crutches sitting on the ground. As we moved along, he got up and hit an officer with one of his crutches."

As with most of my interviewees, I asked Dave what his feelings were about the South Buffalo he knew as a Baby Boomer

"South Buffalo was a great community with strong family values and family ties. It was a place where everyone had numerous friends from diverse nationalities."

Daniel Shea

Dan hailed from Evanston Street, off Downing. He went to PS #29 and South Park High. Like so many of the Baby Boomers, he too hung out with a crew of guys on several of the street corners, mixing it up with people he knew from other crews or areas of South Buffalo. He mentioned that he hung out at Harry's pool hall between Choate and Bloomfield and that he spent a lot of time there with many of the guys from his area and others from up and down the South Park Avenue strip.

He felt that most of the guys from South Buffalo had an advantage over guys from the suburbs in the way of moxie, meaning: cleverness, having skills or street sense to deal with the kind of life people experienced in South Buffalo. This was not so much the case during elementary school age but was more as he got into high school and encountered people from numerous areas of Buffalo. He learned about different ethnic group mentalities, different crowd mentality, drinking, drug problems, and respecting turfs. He, along with everybody else, learned early on about boundaries.

Part of his crew were Jimmy Reidy, Vinny Catanzaro, Mike Catanzaro (OFW), Earl (St. John) Thompson, Jim "Stanley Stingray" Wilzak, Pete Chmura, Gary Williams and a few older guys, Tom "Bull" Kate; at one time considered the toughest guy in South Buffalo. Billy Held agrees.

Then, there was Bill Held and Butch Wilson who he hung with once in a while. He remembered that a lot these guys and others would gather behind School #29 to play craps.

As for growing up in South Buffalo, here's what he had to say, "I was always proud to say I was born and raised in South Buffalo. We had deep roots and a sense of pride in the neighborhood. Good old South Buffalo. It was sacred."

As Dan got into police work, his street knowledge came in handy when he had to deal with all sorts of behavioral and criminal cases. He made his mark in law enforcement on the Hamburg Police Department. He began as patrolman and moved up the ladder to Detective, Lieutenant and finally retired as a Captain.

Billy McEwen - Music Man

Billy McEwen lived on West Woodside Street and went to Public School #29 with a lot of the other South Buffalo boys. He too, hung out with his own crew of guys but mixed it up with numerous other crews. By the age of sixteen, Eddy Dacey prompted Billy to start a band. That's when his singing career in the Buffalo area started. He remembers playing in the "Stix and Stones Band" in 1965 at Mischler's Lounge, 410 Abbott Road and Portland as the house band. He said:

"We'd play Friday and Saturday nights and got $12 a night."

The very first time I saw Billy singing, barefoot no less, was in 1965 at one of the bars out at the lake called the Grand View Casino on Old Lakeshore Road. The place was packed. This was a time of the music revolution. We were into The Beatles, The Rolling Stones, Sly and the Family Stones, The Animals, CCR, The Monkeys, The Young Rascals, Jimmy Hendrix, Paul Revere and The Raiders, Donovan, Bob Dylan, Neil Diamond, The Who, The Guess Who, The Beach Boys, Crosby, Stills, Nash and Young, Peter, Paul and Mary and so on. New bands were springing up all over the country. Billy did great cover tunes and some originals. He quickly developed a following that stayed with him for years.

Checking proof at the door back then was slacker and there were many under-aged individuals who slipped through. There were hordes of full of energy young people looking to drink, have a good time in nightclubs and find good music groups to dance to. Billy's bands were of that caliber.

Billy said he used to play the Grand View Casino five or six nights a week and made $75. He was paid in single dollar bills that came from the dollar a head cover charge. The owner was a man by the name of Eddy Monin who also owned a couple of other bars in the area where Billy and his bands got to play also. Monin told Billy that his gigs had earned him $250,000 in the summer of '65 at the Grand View alone. Billy wondered why he didn't get a bigger share of the take. Oh well, as they said in the Godfather movie: "It's not personal. It's business."

He also became the lead singer in the bands Bo Diddly, Posse and, Billy McEwen and the Soul Invaders. The bands were some of the best known in the Buffalo band circuit. His soulful singing and great harmonica playing became well known throughout the Western New York area. He's also pretty good on conga drums.

Besides singing engagements all over Western New York and beyond, he was the voice in a number of radio and television commercials. You may have heard him in commercials for; AM&A's, Tops Market, City Mattress, Holiday Valley Ski Resort, Buffalo Raceway, Delta Bingo, Keyser Cadillac, Auto Place, Dick's Sporting Goods, Skill Buick, Heritage Stove Shop and several more.

To his credit, he is in the Buffalo Music Hall of Fame along with Seneca Street son, Joe Head. Billy and Joe did a lot of gigs together with another great Buffalo Music Hall of Famer and one of the best base players around, Jim Brucato. One of the places they often graced their listening audiences was Talty's Bar.

Ask most people of the 60's generation in the Buffalo area who regularly went out to listen to local bands if they ever heard of Billy McEwen, and 90% of the time you will get the answer:

"Oh sure I know him. My friends and I went to hear him sing many times."

Billy Held

Bill Held, another notable from South Buffalo, along with brothers Larry and Dwayne, came from Cantwell Street. As crews go, he was part of one with such individuals as:

Doug Kroll, Doug Alessandra, Butch Wilson, John Ranne, Billy West, Bob Regan, Vinnie Catanzaro, Lloyd Hogan and Bob Fulmer and Ted and Mike Pascieznik.

He was a colorful character with a great personality. One of the things I remember about him is that he was a bull. I mean that in a flattering way. He was built. He was one of the guys that if there was trouble, you'd want Billy by your side.

Besides those qualities, he loved to sing. He took some guitar lessons at the Park Ridge Music Store on Ridge Road until he got good enough to form a band. I remember him bringing out his guitar at Deco 22 one night and showing us what he could do. He and his band played in such places as Ann's Inn on the corner of Bloomfield and South Park, the Astro Lite on Ridge Road in Lackawanna and the Ground Round at the Seneca Mall. I believe I also saw him play at Mischler'sBar. He had many other gigs in other establishments in the Buffalo area.

Like so many in South Buffalo, Bill worked at the Bethlehem Steel plant as did his father. As a matter of fact, his dad died there in a most unfortunate accident. He went on to drive tractor trailers for Sealtest Dairy Products and became their top salesman. His next driving job was for Riverside Trucking which is where his driving career ended. As he drove his truck one day, the transmission blew up and parts of it tore through the floor of the cab, causing major damage to his leg. After he healed, rather than going back to driving, he started his own business, Held's Janitorial Service. He eventually had contracts in Buffalo, Rochester, Syracuse and Naples, Florida. The Florida business was called King of Clean. It was the largest janitorial service in Florida. He sold that part of his business interests but maintains services in Buffalo, Rochester and Syracuse. His sons Bill Jr. and Mike now run the family businesses. Billy's son, Bill Jr., is in charge of running the janitorial services part of the Held Corporation and his other son, Mike, is in charge of the Gulf Club Protector business. (see video on youtube.com)

The Gulf Protector business was born when Billy Sr. became interested in golf and eventually joined the Orchard Park Country Club. An idea struck him as he played the game and got caught in a few downpours. He saw golfers throw coats, towels, blankets or some sort of tarp over their golf clubs, or hold large golf umbrellas over their expensive clubs. That idea proved to be extremely rewarding. In 1982, he invented the Golf Club Protector which is a golf cart enclosure. His invention sold very well and sales are still going strong nationwide. He even established a maintenance service for Golf Club Protectors and provides services to all country clubs. Sales and service keeps Bill's son, Mike very busy. They have a West Seneca office.

Covered golf cart

Roger Pasquarella

Roger was born in 1946 and lived through all of those glorious years this book is featuring. He lived in Orchard Park as a kid in the area they called "The Hill," located across from Sacred Heart Church and Capriotto Auto Parts on Abbott Road. He was raised there by his grandparents until he went to 7th grade and then they moved to 109 Amber Street.

He finished elementary school at PS #29 and attended South Park High where he graduated in 1964. That's where he met his wife, Donna Williams, from the Seneca Street area. It was a two mile walk for her and many others to South Park High. Roger was not a mean guy, but he told me that he locked his girlfriend, Donna, now his wife, in a locker at South Park High.

He said jokingly, "I paid for that little stunt with 49 years of marriage."

They're doing fine. They have a boy, Jayson, who is the owner of Lucia's Restaurant on The Lake across from Hoak's Restaurant along Route 5.

During his preteens and teen years, Roger hung out at Mulroy Playground, Chat and Nibble's Soda Shop, Harry's Pool room, the Deco Restaurant, Capitol Theatre which became Fazio's Hall and on a rail (for sitting on) in front of an electric building near Tifft and South Park. His crew comprised of guys like:

Jimmy (Pries Street) Miller, who was best man at his wedding later on. Then, there was Jim Mahoney, Fran Manzella, Jerry Bonafede, Tim Regan, Billy Heilich, Pat and Joe Liberti, Sam Parisi, Steve Banko, Mike Grys, Bobby Duke, Danny Shea, Jack Carney, Lou Sprague Tom Willard and, Norm Appleford.

He said that when he and the other guys hung out on South Park that they were always respectful to older folks who needed to walk by their group.

"We were brought up to do that, respect our elders." and added

"But sometimes, we would tease and mock certain individuals our own age as they passed by, doing what teenagers do for the fun of it; not necessarily being malicious."

He also remembers gravitating to other groups for a short while, to check out other people he knew, then hook back up with some of the same guys from his former crew.

In his mid to later teens, Roger remembers some of the boys were into sipping a bit of wine. Yes, they were all under age. People in all the other crews on the strip and the other neighborhoods were doing the same thing. Anyway, he reminded me of the close to rot-gut wines the guys would drink such as Wild Irish Rose, Ripple and Thunder Bird. Colt 45 was the beverage of choice for the beer drinkers in the group. After high school, he went to UB for Social Studies, then, enrolled at Buffalo State College for his master's degree in Exceptional Education. He taught school for a short while before getting into the transmission business. He started out with Cottman's Transmission and later –became the owner of a franchise of six "Continental Transmission" shops. He also owned the "Macaroni Company" on Pearl Street and "Garcia's Irish Pub" near the Buffalo Convention Center. It became the Pearl Street Brewery.

I asked him how he felt about having lived in South Buffalo:

"It was one of the best neighborhoods because of friends, locally and from other neighborhoods, and other schools. There was a strong camaraderie.

Chapter 24 Baby Boomer

Hair; Clothing Styles, Fashions & Smoking

Ladies' Products and Hair Style

Before you dressed up, you took care of your hair. Many ladies, young and older ones, had "tall hair" styles back in the sixties. Ask the young men today what teasing hair means, most won't have a clue. It was very common to see women with teased up hairdos that were three, four or more inches high. If you look at old high school yearbooks of that time, you readily see what I mean.

Margie Weber from Altruria remembers the girls would use, "Spoolies" at night. They looked like a little rubber disk that snapped open. You wrapped a strand of hair around the stem portion then folded the top portion over the bottom to curl hair. They were fairly painless to sleep on.

Margie said, "In High School girls used empty frozen orange juice cans to get the bouffant look along with lots of "teasing" with a rattail comb. Aqua Net was the hair spray brand of choice. To lighten the bangs (the first attempt at streaking) we used straight peroxide on the bangs."

Guys' hair styles and products

How about the guys with the slick hair in the 40's, 50's and 60's? There are still a few around today. It wasn't natural oil keeping that slick look for the guys who became known as "greasers." If you styled your hair back then, the product of choice for the guys was "Brylcreem." You might remember the TV ad: "A little dab'll do ya." Well, it was never a little dab for most of the guys. It was more like a glob of Brylcreem. "Vitalis" was another male hair product. It wasn't as greasy as Brylcreem. If you had a crew cut, you'd use a waxy product called "Butch Wax" to keep all the hairs standing at attention; even with a 50 mile an hour wind coming at them.

Speaking of hairstyles, the Rock" types had something we called a D.A. (a duck's a**) as part of the hairstyle and, a spiffy little twist of hair in front. The D.A. part of the Rock hairstyle was where you would comb the hair back at each side and bring it together at the center of the back of the head so the hair met. You would then, take the comb and run a line from the crown of the head down to your neck. You needed grease to keep that look. A lot of guys would spend more than a few minutes in front of a mirror getting the hairdo just right. I'm talking guys here. A bit weird but, that's the way it was.

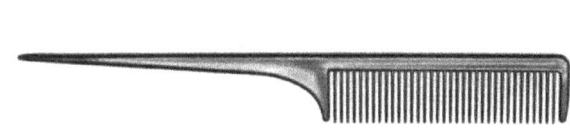

Rat tail comb

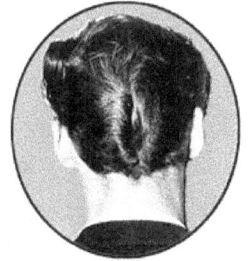

back of head with D-A

One instrument to coif the hair was a rat-tail comb. It had regular teeth but had a handle on it that tapered off to a point. The rat tail helped control the comb for the best hairstyling possible. A lot of the guys would snip off the sharp end for obvious reasons; like it was a bit dangerous.

We had all kinds of ways to express ourselves in our looks. Quite a few white guys even had afros, not the huge out-of-control types, but enough to make you look twice. If a guy had straight hair, many got perms to sport the look. Some of you will remember the TV show "Welcome Back, Kotter" with Gabe Kaplan and John Travolta? Gabe had an afro but he was just a Caucasian guy with bushy hair; afro-style.

The Girls' outfits

In the mid-50s and very early 60s girls always dressed with more self-respect and modesty. I don't remember ever seeing a girl looking sloppy. The casual dress for the Baby Boomer girls in the warm weather was cotton type pants that came to their knees, called pedal pushers. They had zippers on the side or the back. A trend for them for a while was wearing one of their dad's or big brother's white dress shirts with the tails hanging out and collars up. For school and church, girls wore dresses or skirts with nice blouses and dress shoes. For certain events, some wore nice slacks with good-looking tops.

The Guys' Fashion

One of the unique things about guys in our time was that we all dressed nice as we got to a certain age. There was a certain self-respect that drove us to do so. It wasn't like today. A lot of today's kids, young adults and some adults look very untidy compared to the way we dressed. It seems as though some of the kids today dress as sloppy as they can. I don't get it. I've joked with some of the young people today that if they were to walk down South Park, Hopkins Street, Abbott Road or Seneca Street in the 40's, 50's or early 60's with their underwear showing, shirt untucked, baseball cap on sideways or wearing pajama bottoms and slippers, they might have a problem, just for looking goofy. It was about self-respect and being part of what the neighborhood was all about. We weren't rich, but we didn't walk around looking like oddballs or slobs. Looking untidy was not a goal for anyone on our strips. Today, it seems, the worse they look, the cooler they think they are. There's really something wrong with that mentality.

Fashion Influences from Movie & Music Idols

In the summer, a lot of the guys wore t-shirts like you see in older 40's and '50's movies. Some of the guys would roll their pack of cigarettes in one of the sleeves. That practice goes back to at least the 2nd World War. GIs did this for easier access and to keep them from being crushed in their pockets. You could see or imagine Marlon Brando in the 1951 "A Streetcar Named Desire" movie and possibly again in the 1953 biker movie, "The Wild One." where he had a pack stashed in his T-shirt sleeve in some of the scenes. Another iconic star who could be seen doing this was James Dean in the 1955 movie, "Rebel Without a Cause."

In the warm weather in the 50's and early 60's, a lot of the guys wore a neat T-shirts along with neat looking pants. Those were the days when moms actually ironed the t-shirts, usually at the request of the young man wearing it. It was not acceptable if the t-shirt was all wrinkled. You would be mocked for it. Most guys wouldn't dare go out looking sloppy. Being mocked for poor street dress was an absolute. Hey, we had an image to uphold. We weren't rich but we had self-respect.

Fashion Influences from a Song & TV

In the late 50's there was a song entitled "Black Slacks" by Joe Bennett and the Sparkletones. Those pants became a very popular thing to wear for a while. Besides black slacks, we wore other color pants as daily wear. It became the grown up thing to do, looking presentable no matter what you were doing or where you went. Most of the guys I knew had dress pants and knocking around pants, other than dungarees. A few greasers I knew did wear jeans, but most, dressed up well enough to walk into a church for Sunday mass looking acceptable.

When the Dr. Casey and Dr. Kildare medical TV shows aired in the 60s, young people bought and wore doctors' scrub tops some fashion designer came up with. I think that only lasted one summer. They weren't that cool.

Dressing up vs. Dressing down

When we reached a certain age, gone were the dungaree jeans and tennis shoes/sneakers to go hang around the corners or to the various spots we'd gather to spend time talking, going to a show, a restaurant or an event. In our minds…. jeans were for work; for laborers, farmers, cowboys and bikers. As a matter of fact, my grandfather who was born in the late 1800's and worked in plants, never had a pair of dungaree; neither did my father (born in 1919) or any of his six brothers that went through the Depression years and worked various laborer jobs. All the time I was growing up through the 40's into the 70s, I never saw any of them sporting blue denims. It was the same for any of the older men in the South Buffalo area that worked in plants, hardly none of them wore blue jeans – except Mr. Morabito who lived across the street from me. He wore denim overalls for work.

For any Baby Boomer who was/is a laborer, greaser, farmer, cowboy or biker, as you well know, the "dungaree" - Denim, Levi, Wrangler jean industry didn't go away. As a matter of fact, it is still a huge business. By 2019, it grew to a 6.6 a billion dollar a year industry.

It was started by Levi Strauss and Levi's brother-in-law, David Sterns in the 1870's in San Francisco. The first pairs of "Levi 501" jeans were made in 1890. FYI…The fabric itself was first produced in France in a town called **"de Nîme"** and the word "jean" comes from a town in Italy called **"Gênes."** I didn't research any further to find out how the two entities got combined to give us "Denim jeans." I'll just leave that for you to do. Just know it's a European thing.

Now then, between the 50's and the 70's, there was what was called, the "Blue jean craze." For the Baby Boomers, if you think back, you remember the greasers, the mods, the rockers and the hippies; they bought up a whole lot of Levi 501 products.

Going back a bit further, the "Levi" company had competition for a while, the "Wrangler" Kontoor Brands Inc. of North Carolina. They made jeans initially for cowboys in rodeos. In 1947, they produced overalls ("13MWZ" style) mostly for plant workers, farmers, auto mechanics, train engineers and railroad linemen.

In 1897, a man by the name of CC Hudson worked for the Kontoor Company sewing on buttons on their overall for 25 cents a day. After the plant closed in 1904, he and others bought the plant and named it the "Hudson Overall Co." and later renamed it the "Blue Bell Overall Co."

If you look around these days, sporting denim jeans has become the choice pants wear for men and women. It became the "casual wear" of the late 20th and 21st century. "Dockers" pants have become a strong second challenger for the type of pants young and older men wear. That's another subject altogether.

Skinny Dress Pants

One of the styles that came in for a short while in the early 60's was skinny peg leg-fit pants. These pants were so narrow at the bottom that if you had large feet, you could barely get them on. Some guys couldn't even wear them. After you had them on, you might actually struggle to get them off. How do I know? I had a couple of pairs. I could force my feet through the bottom but when it came time to take them off, it was always a fight. I remember falling to the floor a few times trying to get them off. I was so glad when that style went out. So when bell bottoms came in style in the mid-sixties I was a very happy guy. They had lots of room. And who can forget the Madras shirts with the wild designs and large collars?

Denim pants took a break for a while, but came back really big in the late sixties and seventies as stated before. Hey! I'm sure many of you can remember the denim suits, complete with nice neat pleats and a matching vest. Speaking of dressing up, the ties in the 60s were narrow but in the seventies they got real wide.

Dry Clean Only

Our shoes were shined and our pants had pleats. We took care of our dress pants. We didn't have mom wash them in her washing machine - especially, sharkskin pants. Those shark skins were brought to the cleaners. For the South Park guys I hung with, it was Belvedere's Cleaners next to Precinct #15 on South Park Avenue or Cadet Cleaners at Woodside. On Abbott Road, it was Louis' Cleaners, and on Seneca Street the Helpee Selfee Laundry and Dry Cleaning got it done. Dress shirts were okay for moms to put through the wash and then iron.

You have to remember a lot of moms had washers that did not treat the clothes very nice. Once the washing cycle was done, all the clothes went through the wringer process. That's when moms would take the clothes and send it through a set of the wringer rollers to squeeze out the water. Most were hung out to dry on the clothesline in the backyard. If your folks had money, your mom might have had an automatic washing machine with a spin cycle and then, she would put your clothes in the dryer like the laundromat had.

Ironing

Ironing was another whole process. Let's see how many Boomers remember this. Before they came out with irons that gave you steam to help take out wrinkles, moms would sprinkled waster on t-shirts, shirts and pants. The water in the clothing articles would steam up as mom ironed and the no-wrinkle end result was accomplished. Thank God for "steam irons," one less step for mothers, especially in cases where the families were large and the ironing chores could take hours. Think of the Culver Street Gilmour family of twelve children plus mom and dad, or the Keane family of sixteen children. God bless those moms.

One more thing about large families and clothes, there were times when the few clothing items you did possess didn't get washed and you needed a shirt or a pair of pants, you'd go through your closet or a pile of clothes on the cellar floor that mom separated for the wash, and you'd find a shirt that didn't look too bad. You picked it up, looked it over, shook it out and put it on. It reminds me of country singer Kris Kristoffeson's song, "Sunday Morning Coming Down." The lyrics go like this: "I fumbled through my closet for my clothes and found my cleanest dirty shirt...." That's just the way it was for a lot of Boomers.

Dress shoes

Back in the Baby Boomer days and way before that, the average kid only had two pairs of shoes; sneakers and "school/church" shoes. That was it. I didn't know anyone I hung with that had more than one pair of dress shoes …I mean, no one! A lot of the guys wore lace-up shoes, while quite a few went with "penny loafers."

Although we had a shoe store in the neighborhood, when it came time to get re-shod, many of us would get our shoes downtown on Main Street in a store called Hardy's Shoes at $7.77 a pair and no tax. We Rocks liked the Cuban-heel look. By the way, we would walk everywhere we went before we got cars. Not many got rides from mommy or daddy in those days. Our shoes wore out pretty fast and the need for a new pair came up quick.

In an effort to save our heels from wearing out too fast, a lot of us would go to Louie (Louie's Shoe Shine and Hat Shop) to have him put on steel cleats on our fine kicks! You can only imagine the sound of a few of us walking down the street with our Cuban heal cleat-clad shoes …click clack, click clack. Weren't we cool?

Louie, the owner of the shoeshine and hat shop was known by about everybody on the strip. He was a small, older, Italian gentleman with the accent to go with it. A lot of the guys got their shoes fixed there and got them shined on a regular basis. I remember when he was done shining our shoes, he'd get this little bottle of white substance, put a little dab on the tip of each shoe and do one more buffing. I asked him one day what that white stuff was. He replied; "Is a pigeon milk."

I had to ask him where he got the pigeon milk. Think about it. Did you ever in your life hear of pigeon milk? When asked, he simply said, "Is a secret. I no can tell you."

We never did find out where he got it from. Anyway, the shoes looked really nice when you stepped down from the two-seat perch with the metal footrests. Louie old friend, you are not forgotten. Thanks for the great shines.

Sneakers

As teens, we wore sneakers mostly for playing basketball and other sports. We paid about $2.50 to $3.50 for a basic pair back in the late 50's and 60's. For a while, we only had the black hi-top style. U.S. Keds and Converse All-Stars were a couple of the favorite brand names. Do you Baby Boomers remember when they introduced the low-cut style in the sixties? We thought they were so cool. They were still made of canvas with the rubber bottoms, though.

A precursor to sneakers dates back as far as the 18th century. In 1882, the US Rubber Company manufactured a rubber sole, canvas top sneaker called Keds. By 1917, they were mass produced. The rubber-soled shoes got the name "sneakers" because you could walk real quiet and "sneak up" on people.

Today, sneakers are the primary foot gear to wear. Some kids today don't even own a pair of dress shoes. Some go to weddings and funerals dressed in a suit and, you guessed it, their sneakers. Nikes and other name brands cost more than $100 and way beyond in some cases. Some of the kids can't even conceive of the idea of putting on a pair of dress shoes. Wait till they have to go get a real job in the real world and have to grow up, clean up and dress up. By the way, back in the day, most young people only had one pair of shoes and a pair of sneakers to wear; not three four or five pairs of both items. Owning multiple pairs of shoes was unheard of.

Lifestyles of the Rocks & Squeaks

Do the terms Squeaks and Rocks ring a bell? The Squeaks or Collegiates had short hair, usually parted and combed over flat in front and wore lighter colored clothes than their counterparts, the Rocks. You can't forget the penny-loafers and the brand-name shirts the Squeaks wore; Lacoste with an alligator logo. There was a whole look to them. They were squeaky clean-cut. They sported no sideburns, mustaches or beards, and definitely, no engineer boots or Cuban heel shoes with cleats. However, I think I remember a few Squeaks having cleats on their loafers and clickity-clacking down Abbott Road or South Park Avenue. After all, they also walked everywhere and shoe bottoms wore out quickly.

The Rocks had the idea that the Squeaks thought they were better than them. There definitely was a difference in looks and to a certain degree, attitudes. There was an air about those Squeaks, according to the Rocks, that is. The Rocks displayed a look and attitude of the James Dean rebel; not in a bad way you understand. The whole look with longer slicked-up hair, sideburns, pack of cigarettes rolled up in the T-shirt sleeve, belt with the buckle worn to the side, the Cuban-heel shoes with cleats and all was the image of the Rock....the original "Fonzies." We were just teens that picked a style to identify with.

Whether Squeak or Rock, the time spent together amounted to little more than talking about cars, jobs, a problem at school or at home, planning a party, goofing with each other, throwing zingers at people they knew who were passing by, or talking about what someone did. For sure, there were conversations among the guys about girls or girlfriends and among the girls, chats about boys and boyfriends.

It was the same for the girls but not on the corners. They usually met at someone's house. I never saw a group of girls on any of the major South Buffalo main streets hanging out on corners. It wasn't acceptable. It was a guy thing. The Latino culture used to have a saying, "Las calles son para los hombres, no para las mujeres." "The streets are for men, not for women."

A few times, there were some foolish problems between the Rocks and Squeaks with a fight here and there, but the bad blood didn't last long. One reason for short feuds was that within the groups, there would always be somebody who was related to or knew someone on the other side. For the most part, it was a pretty good co-existence. After all, we were all people from the same neighborhood. After thinking about it, I reasoned that the whole thing was nonsense. We were all South Buffalonians.

Most of the Squeaks I knew were headed for college or some career in a trade or a business. The Rocks, from what I saw, did the best they could to do at what they did best. Many dropped out of high school.

I don't want to leave you hanging here with a bad thought about Rocks. Most of us got steady jobs with fair to good salaries. We married, bought houses and had kids. At this writing, many are retired and enjoying the fruits of their labor. Several retired from the police force, the fire department, the steel plants, auto plants, utility companies and a host of other jobs.

As a Rock, I along with crews I hung with wasted a lot time on street corners. We weren't looking ahead very far. But, most of us did land on our feet later on. Personally, I worked many jobs. I was one of those drop outs but got my GED and eventually went to college earning a bachelor and master's degree in education. I taught French and Spanish for twenty-three years at Canisius High School and taught part time at Medaille College for twenty-one years.

Smoking

Living near numerous plants that spewed out polluted air day in and day out in many of the South Buffalo neighborhoods, we Baby Boomers breathed in a lot of nasty, unhealthy air. Picking up the smoking habit fit right into our polluted life.

Lucky Strike pack

Lighter

A lot of the Baby Boomers smoked Lucky Strike cigarettes at first. They were only 23 cents a pack when I started smoking in the early 60's. (I quit in '75) Another favorite brand was Pall Mall, and the real tough guys would smoke Camels or Chesterfields. Quite a few of us had Zippo lighters and would do these little tricks. With one sweep against our thigh we'd open the lighter lid, then, we'd slide it the other way so the striker wheel would roll to ignite the wick. Some guys would flip the lid open against their thigh, then, do a snap-of-the-finger on the lighter wheel and "Voilà," the flame would come on. Oh yeah… they were so cool!

No Restriction Smoking

Smoking was real crazy back then. It was allowed everywhere with no restrictions. In people's homes, it was rampant. Children grew up breathing in second-hand smoke on a daily basis. In cars with children aboard (even newborns), unthinking parents smoked away without concern for their kids' health. People could smoke anywhere in public. Bars and restaurants were filled with smoke. In theatres, there were loges (balcony seating) equipped with ashtrays where smoking was permitted. If you rode on any of the public transportation modes including buses, cabs, trains and airplanes, you could light up any time!

Some high schools even had designated places for their seniors and teachers to light up. In colleges, you could light up in most of the classrooms. I went to Buffalo State College in '73 and every class room had clouds of smoke hanging in the air. The absolute worst places that smoking was allowed were hospitals and hospital rooms where patients were recovering from operations or illnesses. What the hell were we thinking?! Today, the policy everywhere is – NO SMOKING! I even heard a news story where in Belmont, California, smoking was prohibited on public streets where someone's smoke could be smelled and breathed in by non-smoking passers-by. We've indeed come a long way, baby.

Chapter 25 Life and Times of Baby Boomers

With Simple Technology

The early Baby Boomer days were times when life was technologically simpler. There were no calculators, boom boxes, Walkman radios, computers, cell phones or I-pods. Heck, only accountants, businesses and banks had adding machines as far as I know. We knew how to do basic math in our head. When you were a cashier it was all manual. You needed to know how to make change. Today, if an item cost $5.87, and you give the cashier a $10 dollar bill and 7 cents, he or she might freak out. Computing giving back $4.20 in their head would be challenging for many of those who are used to letting computerized cash registers do the work for them. We've gone from using our brains to letting machines do the work. Not that it's all bad, but it goes to show that we're not using our brains as much as we used to. The song "In the Year 2525" from the 70's singers Zager & Evans,' is scary! It talks about the future when machines will be doing everything for us. It's happening more and more these days.

Telephones

Boomers from the 40's, 50's and 60's remember the rotary dial telephones, party lines, and the way phone numbers were given out. I still remember my old phone number from the 60's and 70's as TA 5-8527 or 825-8527. If you called the "South Buffalo YMCA" at 245 Abbott Road back then, their number was TA 3-1984. How about a phone call to "F.M. Sound Equipment Company" on Main Street in Buffalo? The phone number there was TT 2-6223, and for "The Ideal Pharmacy" in the Lovejoy district, it was TX 3-1110.

Rotary phone

Phone History

The rotary dialing system was introduced in 1904 and came into common use in 1919. It was phased out and replaced with push button dialing after it was introduced at the 1962 Seattle's World's Fair by the Bell Telephone company. For those of you who used the rotary dial phones, do you remember when you miss dialed, and had to do it all over again? What a drag that was, huh? I still have three in my house that actually work and are connected. Now and then I'll phone people on one of them. My grandsons asked:

"What is that, Papa?" It's become one of those items that the very young can't relate to at all. The touch tone dialing system was indeed a great and welcomed innovation. Thank you Ma Bell.

Also, those were the days you could actually speak to an operator right away by dialing "0." It was great! Today, just about every business, local, state and Federal office you call, you don't get to speak to a "person!" NO! You have the drudgery of having to select from a list of "options!" I loved the old ways so much better… speaking to a person. I don't want "options!" I want people on the other end of the line, don't you?

How about those old phone booths with a door, a seat and 5 cents a call? It kind of bummed us out when they hiked the price to 10 cents. The good thing about the calls back then was you could talk as long as you wanted to. Several years later, the phone companies found a way to make more money by raising the price of a basic call and charging by the minute after three minutes. Back then people had private conversations by using a phone booth with the door shut. Today with everyone using cell phones, you can hear everybody's conversation. I find it very annoying.

Oh, to go back to the good old days with private phone conversations when in public, using phone booths. Back to the idea of having phone booths today, cities and restaurants should set up old style booths with doors and a seat for people who want to be private when out in public. Hey, if it ever happens, remember, it was my idea.

The Radio
and
Disc Jockeys

Neaverth

Reynolds

You couldn't go any more basic than a crystal set as a means of listening to the radio. I latched onto one around 1962. You could only get one AM radio station on it. For me, it was WKBW radio. It had no speaker. There was a single ear piece and the sound was not very loud. It was cool at night when I went to bed. I could listen to KB without disturbing my other four brothers in the bedroom. KB had a very powerful output from its towers located in a field off of Big Tree Road in Hamburg. It put out a 50,000 watt signal that covered the greater Buffalo area, ran down the east coast as far as Florida and was received as far as Europe. Can you imagine that? WKBW was regarded as one of the top AM radio stations in the country.

If you were a normal teen or young adult of the fifties and sixties, you listened to some kind of (pop) music. For most of the younger generation rock was the choice. It was new, different and somewhat of a phenomenon compared to what our parents listened to. In the fifties, there were only AM radio stations. FM stations came in a bit later. For a lot of us WKBW 1520 AM radio was the most listened to radio station. DJ's such as Joey Reynolds, Tommy Shannon who attended Bishop Ryan High on Clinton St., *Danny Nevearth, Jeff Kay from Baltimore, Stan Roberts from New Jersey, Sandy Beach and several others were popular voices on the AM airwaves at the time. The theme song for the Tommy Shannon Show on KB was done by the "Rockin' Rebels" with Kipler brothers Mickey and Jimmy from Aldrich Place in South Buffalo. The theme song did so well that it was recorded as "Wild Weekend". It was heard throughout the nation and is still played today. No one from that era can forget George the "Hound" Lorenz who attended South Park High. He joined WKBW Radio in 1955. I remember the howling sound that became a trade mark for the Hound as the show got started and ended.

*Remember me asking you which artists were Dan Neaverth's favorite back in the 50's and 60's? Here it is ~ it was Perry Como and the Four Aces.

Going back to WKBW as the number one station in Buffalo back in the day, here's a broader list of that crew from the 50s through the 70s, even into 80s on AM radio. See if you're old enough to recognize all or most of the names; Dick Biondi, Jack Armstrong, Jay Nelson, Fred Klestine, Jon Summers, Jack Kelly, Doug James, Rod Roddy, Lee Vogel, and Bob Diamond.

Other popular pop music a.m. stations that were available back then (before we got FM radio) were, Buffalo's WBNY where Dick Lawrence worked and established the first Top 40 list, WJJL from Niagara Falls with the unforgettable George "Hound Dog" Lorenz.

For the Boomers who can remember, although never a Buffalo resident, another DJ we all listened to on the radio was, Robert Weston Smith (aka) Wolfman Jack. I can remember tuning into his show many times. He was born January 21, 1938 in Brooklyn, New York and died of a heart attack on July 1995 in Belvedere, North Carolina. His great trademarks were his Wolfman howl and his gravelly voice. It might interest Wolfman fans to know that he was an ordained minister in the Universal Life Church and was known as "Reverend Jack."

I feel it wouldn't be right if I didn't mention the "Dean of Talk Radio," John Otto. He was the absolute best at his trade. He hosted a talk show from 10pm to 1am starting in 1962 on WGR and WKBW radio until December of 1999.

Music Contraptions

Way, way before even the crystal set, there was the 1877 Thomas Edison phonograph that would have a turntable and a huge funnel-shaped horn where the sound came out.

RCA w/ dog

Retro phonograph

What's interesting is what people are using today to listen to their favorite tunes. Forget the Hi-Fi stereo system which was an expensive and bulky piece of furniture that sat in your living room. Many were combination radio-record player-liquor cabinets. It was larger than most TV's in a lot of cases. It only played the radio and records; no tapes, eight track cartridges or CDs. In case you were too rough with the needle you, needed to have a spare on hand. When it went, the music was over.

78 Records

The 78 RPM speed record I listened to in the 50's first came out in 1925. It was close to a foot across and only had one song on each side. There was the A side which played the popular hit and the B side which played a less popular song. They were made of various brittle materials and coated with shellac. If you dropped one it could easily shatter and if you scratched it, it would skip and repeat the line before or skip forward to another line in the song. The needle would follow whatever groove it caught. I first heard Elvis Presley around 1956 on one of those 78's. I can remember resetting the play arm on the record player over and over again to listen to "Don't Be Cruel" which I memorized and loved singing along.

Reel to reel tape players

Reel to reel tape players were available for our music listening pleasure since the 1930s. One could buy pre-recorded music of various artists from music companies. They were usually 7 inch reels, containing several hundred feet of acetate magnetic tape usually played at 30ips (inches per second). Later, the units offered various play speeds: 7½, 3¾ and 1⅞. One could have several hours of uninterrupted music. Reel to reel was somewhat popular in the late 60s and early 70s. Some of you readers had one of these, right?

The 45 Records

Baby Boomers also had a smaller and flexible vinyl record; it was nearly seven inches across and like the 78 record, it too had only one song on each side. It was called the 45 RPM record complete with a large hole in the middle where you needed to insert a plastic disc in the middle of the record to fit onto the spindle of the record player or the Hi Fi. Hi Fi stands for high fidelity as in high quality sound. I remember buying the Beatles' Hey Jude 45 record around 1969 and playing it over and over till I wore it out.

As with the 78, you could stack several 45 records on top of each other on your stereo system where there was an automatic gadget that would release the next record when the previous one finished. It repeated that process till the stack was all played out. It was a nice invention. To listen to the flip side of the records, you needed to take that entire stack and flip it over for another half hour to forty-five minutes of songs

The LPs – Long Play Records

Around the same time the 45 came out the LP was introduced. People would buy stereo Hi Fi players with stereophonic sound. They had big, bold sounds that could fill a room with never before heard separation of sound. If your sound system was a good one with the right speakers or headsets, you could hear horns on the left, drums and vocals in the middle and guitar and bass on the right. It was like you were right there at the concert. The LP was over a foot across and very flexible. If you scratched it, it too would get to skipping and repeating lines. You had about five to eight songs on each side of the LP album, depending on the length of each song.

"In-a-gadda-da-vida" by a group called Iron Butterfly Evolution came out in 1968. I heard the title was derived from the phrase "In the Garden of Eden." The long version of the song runs something like seventeen minutes and seven seconds. The featured drum part alone is around three minutes long. That sort of song length wasn't done by many other groups. The movements were repetitious but moved well from one movement to the other for a more or less psychedelic song. One thing that rings true, the musicians could actually play their instruments well. Much of the rock music after the mid 80's and the 90's became muddy and not much in the way of distinctive sound for any of the new and upcoming bands.

The LP format lasted a good while but then two other ways of listening to music became popular the tape cassette and the eight track tape cartridge. Both formats existed along with the 45s and LPs. They became the preferred means for listening to music by most young people. Cassettes could also be played in your battery powered boom boxes also known as Ghetto Blasters. Boom boxes were a hit in the sixties and seventies. Some were quite large and put out very loud sounds; hence the moniker, "boom boxes." Some people would carry them around on their shoulders with the speaker right next to their ear. It wasn't very good for the hearing. In a study on sound pollution I did while attending Buffalo State College in '72, I came across a report that stated:

"By the time a person realizes he or she has a hearing problem, he or she could have as much as a forty percent hearing loss."

The auto manufacturers quickly incorporated both the eight track and tape cassette players along with the AM and FM radio into their cars. You may know someone who still has a functioning eight track player at home and even plays it regularly.

The tape cassette marketed in 1962 is a 2½ by 4 inch format that held the same amount of songs as any album. Blank cassettes were available in 30, 60, 90 and 120 minute formats. All sorts of cassette players with combination AM/FM radio were made. They played continuously till it hit the end. Then, flip over to get another side's worth of tunes. Eventually, manufacturers made tape players that would hit the end of one side, then, click over to start playing the other side automatically.

The idea behind Eight Track Cartridges was to offer better sound; much like the LP's did with separation of sound. The eight track endless loop cartridge became popular and you didn't have to flip it over. It would simply go to the beginning again. One of the nice things about it was that if you had a good player, you could pick out certain song selections by pushing a button. With cassettes, you had to search to find a favorite song. Eventually a cassette tape player was made that allowed going back to previous selections with the push of a button.

Films and Technological Visual Apparatuses

Before we were able to watch movies and see our favorite movies stars on television, we need to remember people that filled movie theatres for that. The first film for the public was shown in Paris, France in 1895 in a place called the "Grand Café." It was produced by the Lumière brothers, Louis and Auguste.

Films have intrigued and entertained everyone in a grand way since the 20's. People had their favorite genres; dramas, crime and gangster films, regular and slap-stick comedies, war stories, Sci-Fi movies…etc.

A lot of the early films were comedies with such stars as; Charlie Chaplin, Harold Loyd, Fatty Arbuckle, Buster Keaton, W, C, Fields, Laurel and Hardy, the Marx Brothers, Abbott and Costello, Leon Errol, Ed Wynn, Our Gang/The Little Rascals

Everyone remembers certain films they saw, their favorite stars, and unforgettable lines. Baby Boomers, see if you remember any, or all of the following.

Charlie Chaplin as the Little Tramp did silent films at first, then on to "talkies." In the movie, "Modern Times" (1936), it was the first film in which he spoke. He sang a song labeled "as gibberish." His first all talking film was "The Great Dictator" (1940). It was a mockery of Adolf Hitler.

Clark Gable in "Gone with the Wind" (1939) Famous line…"Frankly my dear, I don't give a damn!"

Edward G. Robinson, as gangster in "Little Caesar (1931). Famous line… "You want me, you're going to have to come and get me!"

W.C. Fields – with his unique, nasally delivery…in the film, "Never Give a Sucker an Even Break" (1941) Famous line…"You can't cheat an honest man; never give a sucker an even break, or smarten up a chump."

Marlon Brando in "The Wild One" in (1953), biker film. Line…when asked what he and his gang were rebelling against, he said, "Whaddya got?"

Paul Newman in "Cool Hand Luke" (1967). The chain gang prison warden's saying, and Luke's last words in the film, "What we have here is the failure to communicate."

Clint Eastwood as Dirty Harry in the movie "Dirty Harry." (1971) He says, "Do you feel lucky, well, do you punk?!" And in "Magnum Force." (1973) "A man's gotta know his limitations."

Al Pacino in "Godfather II" (1974) "My father taught me many things here – he taught me in this room; keep your friends close, and your enemies closer."

Television in the 50's and 60's

The very first TV I ever saw was in 1952. Only one man in my neighborhood had one. That was Monsieur Lemay in Waterloo, Québec. He brought it outside so the neighbors could get a look at this newfangled thing. People gathered around it in awe. At 6 years old, I thought it was magical.

Black and white TV

Tube TV

I spoke to a few people who remembered what watching TV was like back in the 50's and 60's. A TV back then was in black and white. It was a real treat in the mid-sixties when color television came in. Although color television was a great improvement, we still had either rabbit ears or an antenna on the roof to bring in the local stations and maybe Hamilton or Toronto. The rabbit ears were part of your TV set, but the antenna was attached to your chimney or anchored somewhere on the roof. Unfortunately, antennas didn't always stay put during some of Buffalo's nasty weather conditions. Quite a few ended up lying down horizontally on the roof. People who were fortunate enough to afford a bit of technology could get a rotary antenna that was connected to a control unit on or near the TV set. This item would actually turn the antenna on the roof to bring in better reception. Non-rotary antenna owners were envious.

Back in the 50s and early 60s in Buffalo, the clearest stations via antennas were channels 2, 4 and 7. Later, we had channel 17, an educational station.

For changing channels and volume control, we had dials on our TV sets; no remote controls. That meant having to get up, walk over to the TV and turn the dial to see - "what else was on TV."

A real challenge for the Baby Boomers and our parents was to tweak the horizontal and the vertical when they decided to act up. That was done by turning little knobs at the back of the TV set. You would be watching television and suddenly, the picture would go sideways. This was a "vertical" problem. You couldn't make out anything at all. It was like the entire picture got squeezed sideways and crunched down. The other interruption in viewing TV was the "horizontal" problem. The picture would become a continuous roll either upward or downward. You could see the program but it sure wasn't fun to watch. If you couldn't make it stop, it meant you needed a TV repairman.

At the TV repair shop, you might only need to have a couple of tubes replaced. That's right, tubes. No hi tech printed circuitry existed back then. If you were technically inclined, you could open up the back of the TV set and look around a bit to find the tube or tubes that looked a bit cooked. Local drug stores would have electronic tube stands and charts to help find the tubes you needed. Hopefully after you put them in it would work. Sometimes it did and if not it was time to trash your TV set.

A lot of the televisions refused to give you good reception. Some folks resorted to putting tin foil (later aluminum) at the tips of each end of the rabbit ear antenna. I don't know if it really helped that much, but a whole lot of folks did this. It became so common to go into other people's houses and see the not-so-good-looking setup. You didn't think much about it. If you had rabbit ears as part of your TV setup, you probably tried the foil tactic in order to get better reception. Sometimes, a dad sent his kid to adjust the rabbit ears to get a better picture and saw that by touching them, the picture got better. He might tell him:

"Alright Jimmy. Stay right there! Don't let go of the antennae. The picture is good. Keep holding! Roger Marris is at bat, and the bases are loaded. I want see if he'll get a grand slam. DON'T YOU MOVE!" - That's the way – that was!

Oh the frustration of bad TV reception. But hope was coming. The great solution to poor TV reception was Cable TV. It started way back in 1948 to allow areas where antenna broadcast signals weren't received or were poorly received. This was primarily in mountainous or geographically distant areas. Televisions hooked up to cable companies really grew in the late 60's and early 70's because it solved the problem of poor reception.

The first three in the Buffalo area were Courier Cable which served the City of Buffalo proper, Amherst Cable serviced the Amherst area and Comax Telcom Cable served several towns outside the City of Buffalo. TV reception was much improved, not to mention the number of stations one could receive. It was a television watcher's dream-come -true; except, it wasn't free. It was the beginning of Pay TV. Not only could you get great reception, more channels, but, you could get movie channels without any commercial interruptions. The means of obtaining more and more television programming was the start of a huge industry that kept growing and growing. Comax became International Cable. They bought out Amherst Cable and incorporated their customers into International's. Subsequently, that company changed hands a few more times. The Pennsylvania-based Rigas family bought International and changed the name to Adelphia Cable. That became Time Warner Cable and as of 2020, it is Spectrum Cable.

Chapter 26 Watching TV

Remembering TV Shows of Days Gone By

Baby Boomers as kids had certain TV shows they just wouldn't miss. Let's see what you remember. Here are some that were around in our good old days of black and white TV, until the mid-sixties when television went to color.

Cartoons

The Looney Tune cartoons were the best! Some cartoon favorites of yours from the past might have been; Mickey Mouse, Felix the Cat, Betty Boop, Bugs Bunny, Daffy Duck, Elmer Fudd, Porky Pig, The Flintstones, The Jetsons, and *Popeye, the spinach-eating tough little sailor.

Today, well…something is missing; like the old style animation, and especially, the incomparable Melvin Jerome (Mel) Blanc that provided so many cartoon character voices. He was born in 1927 and died July 10, 1989 at age 81.

*Popeye the sailor man: Most people don't know that this cartoon character was based on a real person. His name was Frank "Rocky" Fiegel, born in Poland January 27, 1868 and passed away in March 1947. As a retired sailor, he was contracted by Wiebusch's Tavern in the city of Chester, Illinois, to clean and maintain order (bouncer) in the bar. He had a reputation of always being involved in fights. That's how he got a deformed eye; hence the nickname, "Popeye". He always smoked his pipe, which led him to speak with only one side of his mouth. He loved children. That aspect of his character was apparent in scenes when he took care of baby "Swee 'Pea" in the 1980 movie "Popeye" starring Robin Williams and Shelley Duvall as "Olive Oyl."

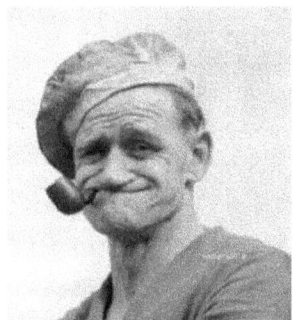
Popeye

Popeye's Tombstone

The creator of the cartoon character of "Popeye" was Elzie Crisler Segar of Chester, Illinois. That's where he met Frank Fiegel. As a young man, Sager would listen to stories about "Rocky," and years later, in January of 1929, he honored him with the comic strip character, "Popeye the Sailor Man."

Segar stated, "There is no accounting of his imaginary adventures which boasted about the exploits of his physical strength, ensuring he never lost a fight. Still, those stories provided me with many interesting scripts." He added, "The man, Frank, and cartoon character, Popeye, carried some inherent features like; courage, chivalry and virility." Segar kept in touch with Frank and had always helped him with money.

Olive Oyl's character was also based on a real person. She was Dora Paskel, owner of a grocery store in Chester. She was described to dress just like Olive Oyl's comic strip and animated cartoon character.

Unforgettable Traits of Cartoon Characters

Which were your very favorite cartoon characters? Mine were; Bugs Bunny with his "What's up doc" line, Elmer Fudd and his inability to pronounce "R's". He'd have a real hard time with my pen name ~ Roger Roberge Rainville. Can't you just hear it? …Woger Woberge Wainville. Sheeesh! Porky Pig was always a blast to listen to with his comical stuttering and unforgettable; "Abbity, abbity, abbity, that's all folks!" when the cartoons ended. And then, there was that rooster, Foghorn Leghorn with his unique southern drawl and delivery, like; "I say, I say boy, you oughtn' be foolin' with that bees' nest! You gonna get stung, boy! Now get on out o' here! I say git, now git!"

Buffalo-based Kids' shows

Howdy Doody, Captain Kangaroo, and the Mickey Mouse Club with Annette Funicello were favorite kid's shows. Locally in Buffalo, on Channel 7, WKBW, we had a morning kid's show called "Rocketship 7" with Dave Thomas and Promo the Robot. In the afternoon, the Commander Tom Show with WKBW-TV's weather man Tom Jolls and sidekick, Bat-Head (director Pete Kolankowitz). The Commander and Bat Head would do skits and in between the skits, KB would show cartoons. One of them was "Roger Ramjet." Do you remember it?

Bathead

True story

It so happened that I worked at KB in '66'and '67 as a mail clerk. I was sorting mail one day, and a troupe of twelve 7 to 10 year old "cub scouts" was being led around the station for a tour. At the very moment they came by me, the station's receptionist called out, "ROGER, could you please come here for a moment?" To which I said, "I'll be there in a minute."

Well, one of the boys looked up at me, made the connection that they were at Channel 7 where the Roger Ramjet cartoons emanated from, stopped, looked and yelled, "ROGER RAMJET!!! You're Roger Ramjet! Can I have your autograph, please?"

I said, "No, no, I'm not Roger Ramjet. I just work here." I couldn't say another word. He cut right in and said, "YES YOU ARE! You're Roger Ramjet! Can I have your autograph……PLEASE! PLEASE!!!"

Roger Ramjet

That set the rest of them off. I got ganged up by all twelve cubs in the troupe. Each one wanted a "Roger Ramjet" autograph. Although I did my best to tell them I wasn't their "cartoon hero," they persisted until I got pieces of paper and signed ..."Roger Ramjet."

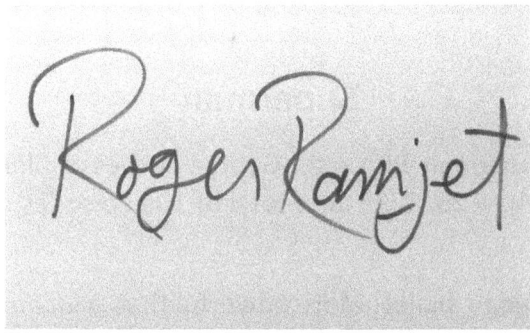

Now then, somewhere, some grown guy(s) has/have an autograph of the famous "Roger Ramjet" who used drugs... you know, the "Proton" energy pill that gave him his super powers to fight criminals. End of story. Not quite! Now and then, a couple of my old neighborhood pals will call me, "Ramjet."

The cartoon first aired in 1965. Ramjet was, as the description goes, "An American patriotic bumbling daredevil squadron leader of do-gooders." He'd pop a Proton Energy Pill (PEP) that gave him the strength of twenty atom bombs for a period of "twenty seconds!"

Sitcoms

The Boomers had an awful lot of sitcoms back in the 50's and 60's. Here are some you might have never missed. Take a look back.

"The Honeymooners" was seen from 1955 to 1956), with main characters Gleason playing Ralph Kramden and his sidekick Art Carney as Ed Norton, "Father Knows Best" with Robert Young (1954-1960), "Make Room Daddy" with Danny Thomas (1953-1965), "Leave It to Beaver" with Jerry Mathers (1957-1963), "My Three Sons" with Fred McMurray (1960-1972), "Hazel" with Shirley Booth (1961-1966), "Mr. Ed" (the talking horse) with Alan Young 1958-1966), "Dennis The Menace" with Jay North (1959-1963), "Donna Reed Show" (1958-1966),

Sitcoms with, Two beds please!

"I Love Lucy" with Lucille Ball and Dezi Arnaz (1951-1957) "The Dick Van Dyke Show" with Dick Van Dyke and Mary Tyler Moore (1961-1966), and "The Adventures of Ozzie and Harriet" (the Nelsons" (1952-1966) were very popular. These notable three sitcoms had one thing in common; in their bedroom scenes, you saw two single beds separated by a night table. Those were the days when Hollywood kept a degree of modesty and moral decorum. Although, Lucy and Ricky Ricardo, Ozzie and Harriet Nelson were actual married couples, the producers figured setting up "two-bed" bedrooms would eliminate any censorship problems. Today's many bedroom scenes are often, way, way too risqué!

I didn't think the Nelson show was a really great show, but as Ricky Nelson got older and began singing songs at the end of the shows, I'd sometimes watch it just to see and hear him sing his hit songs like; "Hello Mary Lou" – "Lonesome Town" –"Fools Rush In" – or "I Got a Woman."

Other Entertaining Shows

The hilarious slapstick comedy of the "The Three Stooges" with Curly Howard, Larry Fine, and Moe Howard was huge – (active from 1922 – 1970). Who remembers the short-lived series called "Man with a Camera." The star was Charles Bronson.

Superman

Another popular series was Superman with actor George Reeves as Clark Kent. It went from September 19, 1953 in black and white until April 28, 1958 for a total of 104 episodes. How many of you can remember how each episode started?

Announcer: Faster than a speeding bullet! More powerful than a locomotive! Able to leap tall buildings in a single bound! Look! Up in the sky! It's a bird. It's a plane. It's Superman!

"Yes, it's Superman – strange visitor from another planet who came to Earth with powers and abilities far beyond those of mortal men. Superman – who can change the course of mighty rivers, bend steel with his bare hands, and who, disguised as Clark Kent, mild mannered reporter for a great metropolitan newspaper, fights the never ending battle for Truth, Justice and the American Way."

Oh, in case you forgot, Superman came from the planet Kripton and the only thing that took is super powers away was "Kritonite"…a material from that planet that somehow made its way to earth.

Tarzan

"Tarzan" with Johnny Weissmuller and actress Maureen O'Sullivan stared in six movies along with Cheeta the chimpanzee. In the last three films, young actor Johnny Sheffield played the part of "Boy." Another five Tarzan films were made with Weissmuller. This time, actress Brenda Joyce played Jane's part. There were a total of twelve Tarzan films made with Weissmuller. Later, back in the jungle, Weissmuller was in 26 TV episodes of the "Jungle Jim" series that began in 1955.

Buffalo connection: As a point of interest to Buffalo people and alums of Canisius High School. When Weissmuller made a visit to Buffalo and wanted to swim somewhere privately, Canisius High School was able to accommodate him by offering him their Olympic size pool. Arrangements were made with the good Fathers there, and Mr. Weissmuller got his workout done.

American Bandstand

With Rock "N Roll being huge with Baby Boomer teens, the list of "got to see" TV programs to watch wouldn't be complete without mentioning "Dick Clark's American Bandstand." Besides the Ed Sullivan show, that's where we got to see the actual artists we listened to on records and radio. Mr. Clark brought on anybody who was a hit-maker in those days.

"Happy Days"

The "Happy Days" series reflecting back to life in the 50's with former kid star, Ron Howard as Richie Cunningham, and the "Fonz" (Henry Winkler) and part of the cast of characters. The Fonz's name in the show was actually "Arthur Herbert Fonzarelli." Happy Days ran from 1974 to 1984.

Soap Operas

How many of you got addicted to watching soap operas back then? Soaps like; Another World, The Doctors, The Guiding Light, The Edge of Night, Days of Our Lives, Guiding Light, All My Children, As The World Turns, Search For Tomorrow, and Peyton Place and General Hospital. The latter was the longest running show. It started on April 1, 1963 on ABC and as of 2020, was on the air 57 years.

Which one was your favorite? And if you were out of the house, how many of you just HAD TO GET BACK home so you could follow up on what happened on the previous show? For some of you, it became a problem, didn't it?

Westerns

The Lone Ranger series ran from 1949 to 1957 with Clayton Moore and Jay Silverheels as Tonto. Tonto's real name was Harold John Smith, a Mohawk Native American from Canada. He actually lived in Buffalo for a while. Those of you who watched the show, I'm sure you remember well the *"William Tell Overture" music that introduced the show. The ranger was known for being masked, firing silver bullets and riding a white horse called, Silver. It was one of ABC TV's top ranked shows at the time. It was said that it was, "ABC's first true hit." (*The William Tell Overture was written by Gioachino Rossini)

Sixties and seventies WKBW disc jockey Dan Neaverth once jokingly said the following on one of his broadcasts, "You can tell if someone is truly sophisticated …if when, they hear the "William Tell Overture," they don't think of the Lone Ranger TV show."

Do you remember the opening for the show when the narrator said: "A fiery horse with the speed of light, a cloud of dust, and a hearty 'Hi-yo……., Silver!'. . . The Lone Ranger!"

Wyatt Earp western series was another popular 60s hit. Everyone couldn't wait for Earp to pull his Colt Buntline Special pistol with its twelve inch long barrel to deal with the bad hombres he encountered. For you gun enthusiast, the pistol shot a .45 Long Colt cartridge.

Zorro: A Walt Disney Production began on October 10, 1957 featuring Guy Williams (Don Diego) as Zorro. It reminded older folks of the art of swordsmanship by illustrious actors such as Tyron Powers in the 1940 "The Mark of Zorro," and Errold Flynn in the "Adventures of Robin Hood in 1938 series.

The 40s, 50s and 60s had a slew of western movies and TV series. Some others that come to mind are, Gene Autry ('50-'55), Hopalong Cassidy with William Boyd, Roy Rogers and Dale Evans ('51-'57), Annie Oakley with Gale Davis ('54-'57), Wild Bill Hickok with Guy Madison, Kit Carson with Bill Williams ('51-'60) Jim Bowie with Scott Forbes ('56-'58), Cheyenne with Clint Walker '55-'63) The Cisco Kid with Duncan Rinaldo ('50-'56), Rawhide ('59-'65) with Clint Eastwood, Bat Masterson with Gene Barry '58-'61, Gunsmoke with James Arness and **Buffalo connection**, Amanda Blake as Miss Kitty (1955-1975), another long running western was "Bonanza" with Lorne Greene, Michael Landon, Big Dan Blocker and Pernell Roberts (1959-1973).

The "Yancey Deringer Series" produced by Desilu Production with actor Jock Mahoney ran only from '58-'59. It was another western that took place in Louisiana, of all places. What intrigued me about the show was that this elegant-looking main character's gun of choice was a concealed four-barrel "Sharps Pepper Box" derringer handgun concealed in his top hat. He also had one up his sleeve and one in his belt buckle. Besides this arsenal, he carried a knife in his belt and had a sword in his walking stick.

His sidekick's name in the series, Pahoo-Ka-Ta-Wah (Pawnee for "wolf who stands in water" was a Pawnee Native American (Real name – *Jay X Brands) He didn't speak, only did sign language. Pahoo wore a colorful blanket that always hid a sawed-off double-barrel shotgun that fired split buckshot. He used that for emergencies. Most of the time, he's used a throwing knife he had in a sheathed on his back.

*Jay X Brands (July 24, 1927 – May 8, 2000) was actually of German ancestry.

Law enforcement and Detective Series

Dragnet with Joe Friday and Lawyer Perry Mason stand out as top runners of law enforcement and trial procedures series for the 60's and 70's. Detective Joe Friday (actor Jack Webb) badge 714 with partner, actor Ben Alexander as Officer Frank Smith. The series began on December 14, 1951 and ended on August 23, 1959. After a crime was committed, Detectives Friday and Smith did their detective work and "always got their man!"

The Perry Mason "legal drama" series with actor Raymond Burr was a weekly CBS TV show that ran from September 21, 1957 to May 22, 1966. He was a "defense attorney." His record for wins and losses, as is quoted in a bio about that, "Mason is known to have lost, in some manner, only three cases during all the shows filmed."

Variety shows

Milton Berle, Jack Benny, Red Skelton, Ted Mack's Original Amateur Hour, Your Hit Parade, People Are Funny, Art Linkletter Show (with segment, "Kids Say The Darndest Things"), George Gobel, Arthur Godfrey.

Ed Sullivan

The Ed Sullivan variety show (1948-1971) was very popular and that's where all of America first saw Elvis in 1956 and the Beatles in 1964, on live TV broadcasts. The crowd went wild. Sullivan couldn't calm the young audience down. Oh, and fans of the show can never forget "Topo Gidio," the little Italian mouse that we first saw in 1963 on Sullivan's show. He made several appearances. And... how many of you remember that when Topo was done performing, in his Italian accent voice, he would say to Mr. Sullivan, "Kiiiss me goodnight Eeedy." Sullivan would do so and Topo would always sigh in a high pitch voice.

Lawrence Welk Show

The long-running Lawrence Welk's and his Champagne Music Show ran from 1951 to1971. People who viewed the program remember Mr. Welk's ~ "N a one, N a two, N a..." as he began conducting the various musical acts.

When I lived in Welland, Ontario in the latter part of the fifties we watched Buffalo Bandstand, a Buffalo, the Philadelphia version of American Bandstand with the "never aging" Dick Clack. Buffalo Bandstand was broadcast from Channel 7, located on Main Street near Utica. Frank Deluisio told me that he and his friends attended Buffalo Bandstand dances when he lived in the Fruit Belt area before moving to South Buffalo. I remember my older brother Jacques, and older sisters Denise and Monique, as well as some of their friends, going to Buffalo to be on the show in 1958.

Late Night Talk Shows

The list of TV watching wouldn't be complete if I left out late night talk shows. These too had a huge following. Probably, the Baby Boomers' favorite was the "Johnny (Wiliam) Carson Show" that ran from 1962 until 1992; that's thirty years! During that span of time, Mr. Carson did 4,531 shows.

Night talk shows go way back to 1954 on the NBC Network with Steve Allen ('54-'57) and Ernie Kovaks doing a stint in '57. Then, Jack Parr took over from '57 to '62. Next in line was the King of Night Talk Shows, Johnny Carson being introduced by his very long-time sidekick and friend, Edward (Leo Peter) McMahon with his famous, "Heeeeeeeeere's Johnny!" The show started off in New York City in 1962 then moved to Burbank, California in 1972.

Other talk shows of the 60's, 70's and into the 80's you might remember were; The Dinah Shore Show ('51' to '57) and Dinah's Place ('74 to '81), The Mike Douglas Show ('61 to '81), The Merv Griffin Show ('62 to '86), The Dick Cavett Show ('68 to '86, The Letterman Show ('83 to 2015.)

Chapter 27 Watching Buffalo Sports on TV

Before Buffalo got professional sports teams like the Braves (basketball), the Bills (football) and the Sabres (hockey), there was another sport seen on Buffalo TV, Pro wrestling. In the 50's and 60's, if you were a sports fan, you watched pro sports teams from other cities, but none from Buffalo. You could watch the Saturday Night Fights, bowling shows, and pro wrestling in the fifties and sixties from other cities.

Wrestling

Wrestling from the Buffalo Memorial Auditorium gave us the only local televised pro sport. We loved seeing *Ilio DiPaolo from Abruzzi Italy take down the Masked Marvel, the Beast or Hans Schmidt, nicknamed "The Teuton Terror." Hans was French Canadian, Guy Larose, from Joliette, Québec Canada.

Ilio Di Paolo

*Ilio actually started his wrestling career in South America after World War II.

Speaking of physical contact sports, the Aud once had Roller Derby matches. Do you remember watching them on TV? They were first seen on November 29, 1948 on CBS TV. WOW! It was way different then from what I've seen lately. Back in the day, both the men and the women were sent flying off the slanted tracks, over railings, and many took very harsh hip checks, elbows and serious falls. If I'm not mistaken, some got into fisticuffs over cheap shots they got.

Basketball – The Braves

Buffalo is a sports town and has a lot to boast about. Our Braves basketball team thrilled Buffalo Baby Boomer basketball fans from 1970 to 1978. Thirty-three year old Paul Snyder sold his Freezer Queen plant on Fuhrman Boulevard and bought the Braves team in 1970. One of the best-known names on the team was Bob McAdoo. Other top players were; Ernie Di Gregorio, Moses Malone, Adrian Dantly, Elmore Smith and John Shunate.

Hockey
Hockey trivia - Hat trick

The term "hat trick" has been used since 1859 in such sports as cricket, soccer, lacrosse and water polo. In hockey, it all started on January 26, 1946 when a clothing store owner in Toronto by the name of Sammy Taft encountered Alex Kaleta of the Chicago Black Hawks who wanted to buy a fedora. Kaleta went into the store, tried on a few hats and when the price was mentioned, he said he couldn't afford it. Back then, hockey players didn't make much money. Upon learning that Katleta was with the Hawks and playing against the Leafs that night, Sammy said to Alex, "If you can score three points against our Toronto team tonight, I'll give you a free hat." Kaleta managed to score four goals in that 6-4 game. The next day, he collected his free hat.

To celebrate this three point feat from hockey players, you've probably seen today's fans toss hundreds of hats onto the ice. It's quite the sight!

The Sabres

Before the Sabres made it to the NHL league, Baby Boomers from the 40's through the 60's remember that there were only six teams then. Up in Canada, they had the Montréal, Canadiens and the Toronto Maple Leafs. South of the border, we had the Boston Buins, the New York Rangers, the Detroit Red Wings and the Chicago Black Hawks. That was it! In 1970, Buffalo got an NHL team – the Sabres. They became part of the Atlantic Division of the Eastern Conference.

The Sabres started off normal enough, but when the line that came to be known as the "French Connection" made big news in the sports world, Buffalo was brimming with pride having such an exciting lineup. It's worth taking the time to highlight the three French Canadians that brought everyone in the Aud to their feet whenever they took the puck down the ice toward opposing teams.

The French Connection

Rick Martin - René Robert - Gilbert Perrault

Gilbert Perrault

No one had ever seen a Buffalo player move like six foot one inch, Gilbert Perrault. It was "poetry in motion" when the Sabres' center wearing number 11 took off and made moves on players that left them bewildered. He was born November 13, 1950 in Victoriaville, Québec, Canada. His career record is 1,191 games played with 512 goals, 814 assists and for a total of 1,326 points. He played 17 seasons for the Sabres from 1970 to 1986.

René Robert

Part of the "French Connection" force, René was the first to score 100 points in one season with 40 goals and 60 assists. He was born December 31, 1948 in Trois Rivières, Québec, Canada. Standing at five foot ten and wearing number 14 on the Sabres' team, this Buffalo right winger ended up with a career record of 744 games, 284 goals, 418 assists, for a total of 702 points. He played 12 years for the Sabres organization.

Richard Martin

Best known as Rick Martin, this left winger Sabre was also from Québec. He was born in Verdun, Québec, Canada July 26, 1951. His career record stands at 685 games, with 384 goals, 317 assists for a total of 701 career points. He was known for his accuracy when firing his wicked wrist and slap shots.

In 1977, he suffered a terrible injury when he got hit hard and his head slammed to the ice. I saw that game on TV and can still see the way he convulsed while down on the ice. He suffered a serious concussion. Rick played eight years with the Sabres, from 1971 to 1982. He left us too soon. He died from a heart attack on March 13, 2011in Clarence, New York at the age of 59.

Terry Pegula was a "super fan" of the French Connection. He and wife Kim had statues especially made to honor the greatest line the Sabres ever had. It stands in "Pegulaville Square," to the left of the southside doors of the arena. Thank you, Mr. and Mrs. Pegula for this magnificent gift to Baby Boomer Buffalo hockey fans. Being that I was a great fan of "The French Connection", and that all three players were born less than a hundred miles from where I was born in – Magog, Québec, I had to have a photo taken next to the monument.

Sabres' "Rip" Simonick – Equipment Manager

Allow me to give kudos to Baby Boomer Robert "Rip" Simonick – a Sabres lifer and Old First Warder. He is a graduate of Timon High and married a Mount Mercy gal named Mary Ann "Maize" McGuire. To date (2020), Rip has been with the Sabres' for over fifty years as the team's "equipment manager." He was inducted into the Greater Buffalo Sports Hall of Fame on October 19, 2019.

For him, it all started in 1964 when the Buffalo hockey team was the Bisons (1940-1970). Rip and his brother Paul were "stick boys, then." When the Sabres became an NHL expansion team, Sabres' coach, Punch Imlach hired him. Rip Simonick has the distinction of having been with the Sabres the longest – from its very start in 1970. He's worked 50 seasons for a total of over 3,500 games. Bravo Rip!

Helmets

These were the days when the guys on the team didn't wear helmets. After Rick Martin's incident, one by one, all the players wore one. Eventually, the NHL and the coaches "highly recommended" that all the players wear one. Among all of the NHL players, there were three individuals who refused to do so right up to their retirement. *Just to mess with you, I'll leave that here for now and give you time to guess, if you can, which players and for which team they played. Keep reading!

*The last player to go without a helmet was Craig MacTavish who played his final game in 1997 for the Saint Louis Blues. In 1979, the NHL required all players to wear a protective helmet but MacTavish was grandfathered in and elected to go "sans" head gear.

Two other diehards also refused to obey the "edict," - Guy LaFleur (aka) "The Flower," (aka), "le Démon Blond" of the Montréal Canadiens. He was one of their greatest assets. He retired in 1991. Another holdout was Rodney Corey Langway who played for the Washington Capitols – retired in 1993.

Football –The Bills

The Bills football team goes back to 1960 with quarterback Jack Kemp, when they played as a charter member of the American Football League. The team joined the National Football League in 1970. Baby Boomers remember the days when the team played at the War Memorial Stadium at 285 Dodge Street and Jefferson Avenue. The stadium was known to the locals as the "Rock Pile," It opened in 1937 and was demolished in 1988.

From 1970 when the Bills made the list of NFL teams with owner Ralph Wilson, the best memories Baby Boomers and others have are the four straight Super Bowl games (1990-1993) they had; all headed by quarterback Jim Kelley - Super Bowl XXV, XXVI XXVII, XXVIII! The one that still stings the most is Scott Norwood's "wide right" kick that would have given Buffalo a win had he made it. I didn't get angry at Scotty for that missed kick. It shouldn't have all been on his shoulders alone. The team as a whole needed to share the blame. They eventually failed three more times in a row. I'll leave it at that. That's the way it was for our Bills. Go Bills!

Honoring Doug Flutie

Doug Flutie

Baby Boomer Doug Flutie was born October 23, 1962 in Manchester, Maryland. Although not a Buffalonian, I need to honor this former Buffalo Bills quarterback. While playing backup quarter back for the New England Patriots under Bill Belichick on January 1, 2006, standing 5 foot 10 inches, this phenomenal 43 year old athlete drop kicked a football between the uprights in a game against the Miami Dolphins. That stunt hadn't been done since November 28, 1948 by Joe Vetrano of the San Francisco 49ers in a game against the Cleveland Browns.

By the way, Flutie's career stat for completed passes, 14,715 yards. That's very good!

Chapter 28 Baby Boomer Influences

of the 50's and 60's

Beatniks

i

"The Beat Generation" was a cultural and literary movement in the 1950's. From that, the term beatnik was coined by Herb Caen in an article in the San Francisco Chronicles on April 2, 1958, six months after the Russian Sputnik I rocket was launched. It was part of the description of the "Beat Generation" -- and, part of that was to portray them as "un-American." The (-nik) suffix was taken from the "Russian Sputnik I rocket that was launched six months before his article.

Beatniks, were into poetry, jazz, art and living a bohemian type lifestyle. They migrated to a place in New York City called Tin Pan Alley. They were portrayed as people who didn't work much, played bongos, rolled their own cigarettes, wore sunglasses, turtleneck sweaters and berets, had mustaches and/or goatees and coined their own slang and use terms like "hey man", "cool", "groovy", "heavy", "hip", "jive", "good and bad karma", "out of site" and so on. The beatnik culture promoted non-materialism and had a "live and let live" approach to life; or a, "do your own thing," mentality.

Back in the sixties, two TV personalities reflected some of the beatnik traits. One was featured in the late fifties and early sixties sitcom The Many Loves of Dobie Gillis (1959-1963). Bob Denver played beatnik, Maynard G. Krebes. He cringed when the word "work" was mentioned. Clean-cut Dobie Gillis was played by actor Dwayne Hickman.

Edd (Kookie) Byrnes played Gerald Lloyd Kookson III in the 77 Sunset Strip detective series seen from 1958 to 1964. On the show, you would hear Kookie used a lot of the beatnik jive-talk and regularly take out his comb to adjust his rock style hairdo. The song, "Kookie, Kookie Lend Me Your Comb" was recorded during that time featuring Kookie and actress Connie Stevens.

Movie Stars

BRANDO

Other influences came from the movies from stars like, Marlon Brando, in a 1953 movie called, "The Wild One" - a motorcycle gang drama with Brando playing the lead role as Johnny Strabler, and Lee Marvin, as Chino, the leader of a rival gang.

Another influential icon was James Dean, seen in the 1955 movie "Rebel without a Cause." Also starring in that film; Natalie Wood, Sal Mineo, and Jim Backus.

Music, TV, magazines and films influenced a lot of what we thought, the way we spoke, the way we dressed and in many ways, shaped much of our personal beliefs and opinions. We were significantly different from our parents which birthed the phrase, "The Generation Gap," in the '60's. Parents and teens were often unable to make good connections when relating the each other. It was a time of rebellion when it seemed that many Baby Boomers worked counter to the ways of their parents. This brings in another term used back in the sixties –"Counter Culture."

Rock Stars

The Baby Boomer generation was hugely influenced by a lot of what came through the fashion industry, music, television and movies. We had a ton of singers and movie stars who we looked up to and noticed how they dressed. In the fifties, a lot of new things appeared on the horizon. The music our folks listened to was way different from what became the pop music teens latched onto known as "Rock and Roll." Bill Haley and the Comets launched this genre and Elvis Presley's music became the biggest thing going in the mid-fifties. Besides the above mentioned, both genders of the young people influenced each other with new dress styles and hairdos.

Presley

Rock Music

Rock and Roll music became an "evil" thing to a lot of the older generation. The term itself was used in black neighborhoods to relate to "having sexual intercourse." It (term rock and roll) was made popular in the 50's by disc jockey Allen Freed who introduced it on his "Moondog Show" and then brought it to New York City and changed the show to "The Rock and Roll show." With Rock and Roll, a whole lot of different dance styles appeared. For sure, there was the "jitter-bug," then things went into novelty dances like the Stroll and the Twist – (1960) made famous by a portly singer by the name of Chubby Checkers who introduced it to the world. Actually, ole Chubby began losing weight as he performed it as part of his act. It became very popular. Along with that dance style, the Peppermint Twist, the Monkey, the Jerk, the Mash Potato, the Swim, the Watusi…

Disco music and disco dancing in the 70's was huge with the Bee Gees being one of the best musical groups putting out some of the biggest hits. A movie with actor John Travolta tied with the Bee Gees was, *"Saturday Night Fever" (1977) - and one of the main songs remembered is *"Staying Alive, recorded that same year. Other songs from the Bee Gees used in the movie were; "How Deep is Your Love" "More Than a Woman" - "Stain' Alive" - "If I Can't Have You" - "Boogie Shoes" – and "Night Fever."

Chapter 29 Changes in the mid 60's and 70's

Young People, the draft, drugs and the Generation Gap

The Sixties' Youths

In the mid-sixties into the seventies, a lot of changes among the younger crowd began to make its way into daily life. We saw it all over South Buffalo and beyond. They dressed differently. They grew their hair long and developed a different way of speaking. For many, their way of thinking was contrary to what moms and dads thought about life and politics. Drug use became a big problem. A large number of them got into an anti-establishment way of thinking and living. Many of their ideas were good, but at the same time, many were way too the "left." A lot of them thought they were really "hip," and that older folks were simply outdated and uninformed.

The changes that came about in the mid-sixties were done by mostly young college age people, but some were younger and some were in their thirties and even forties. It was a movement against some of the norms of society and especially against the government, "the Establishment".

America was in a military conflict in Vietnam and a lot of young Americans believed very strongly that our soldiers had no business being there. Anti-war slogans were seen and heard all over America. Part of the problem was that they didn't know WHY we were fighting in a country so far removed, that it didn't effect our daily lives.

One heard and read slogan such as; "Don't trust the man" (meaning, the government) – "Draft beer, not boys" - "Hell no, we won't go!" - " End the war before it ends you" - "Make love, not war" - "Wage Peace Not War" - "Drop acid, not bombs" - "Give peace a chance" - "Bare feet, not arms" - Burn Pot, Not People."

The Draft

The 60's was a time when many of our young men got drafted to fight the Viet Nam War. Many of us from all over South Buffalo got drafted. As a matter of fact, most of the guys I hung with were drafted. During that time, we heard about guys who were classified as "Conscientious Objectors." Some of them burned their draft cards in protest of the war and resisted going into military service. Others slipped over the border into Canada. If they returned at some point, they were arrested as draft dodgers and faced the possibility of five years in Federal prison and/or a fine up to $250,000. This was not a good time for American Baby Boomers.

Marijuana and Drugs

It was also a time of promiscuous sex and drug use. With that, another slogan became part of the hippie mentality was, "if it feels good do it." All inhibitions and morals went out the window and if you didn't at least smoke pot, you weren't cool. Some names used to refer to marijuana back then were; Pot, Grass, Weed, Acapulco Gold, Panama Red, Columbian, Gold Thai, Blond Lebanese, Sweet Jane, Mary Jane, Devil Weed, Hooch, Hemp, Wacky Weed, Juanita, Texas T, Smoking a Joint and a ton more.

Drinking cough syrup to get high and taking LSD became part of the in things to do. I heard a lot of the drug users back then talk about doing uppers and downers, along with LSD 25, DMT, Purple Haze, and synthetic mescaline. A good number of people graduated to the heavier drug, heroin. Many of them were the guys who came back from Nam addicted.

Generation Gap

The sixties and seventies were some of the wildest and weirdest times the country and our local neighborhoods ever experienced as far as generation division. Little by little, many parents and young people saw a huge gap form between them as the youths adopted the new mind-set of the "hip" people. From that, the "Generation Gap" was born.

Changes in the 60's & 70's'

- Guys growing their hair long

- Guys growing mustaches and/or beards

- Young people's hip vocabulary

- Wild psychedelic music, not even close to what mom and dad ever knew.

- Guys/gals wearing tie-dyed tops and hip-huggers

- Girls going braless, mini and micro skirts, tube-tops and put flowers in their hair

- Bell-bottom pants, sandals worn in the warm and cold weather

- Bare foot young people in public places

- People asked each other "What's your sign?" (Meaning their astrological sign connected to the month they were born). If your astrological sign was not a good match with someone of the opposite sex, it was a negative vibe ~ man!

- Panhandling became a way to scrape up money for basic essentials or drugs

- Smoking marijuana was huge.

- Wanting to buy a VW bus or old school bus and painting it with hip designs

- Possibly head to the Haight-Ashbury area of San Francisco or other parts of California.

- Living in communes or guys and girls living together without the benefit of marriage

- Flashing the Peace Sign

The Peace Sign Origin

The actual "Peace Sign" was the creation of British graphic artist, Gerald Holtom, February 21, 1958. It symbolized the objection of the people against the stockpiling of Nuclear Weapons that occurred after World War II. It was a sort of "Ban the Bomb" icon.

Goya's painting   **peace sign in a circle**   **hand peace sign**

Holtom stated: "I was in despair, deep despair. I drew myself standing with hands palm outstretched outwards and downwards in a manner of painter 'Goya's Peasant' before the firing squad. I formalized the drawing into a line and put a circle around it."

As radio commentator Paul Harvey used to say: "And now, you know the rest of the story."

Hippies "Man!"

Hippies were a group of young people who decided to "chuck" the standard way of life. Much like the Beatniks, they too got into a lifestyle detached from what we'd call "normal living." It had to do with being "free spirits," whatever that meat. They didn't aspire to become successful, many ended in communes where everything was shared and they went into city streets to beg or ask for money ~ we called it, "panhandling."

Their Vocabulary

The use of certain words or phrases became part of daily vocabulary among hippies and young people. "**Man**" was used a lot...like: "Hey man, what's happening?" ~ "Peace, man."

Other phrases were: "Far out" ~ "Out of sight, man." ~ "I'm hip." ~ "That's a bummer, man." ~ "That's cool, man." ~ "Groovy man, groovy." There were many more, but, you get the picture.

This began the decline of the ability to communicate intelligently. The hippie movement threw many of that generation into a dumbing down tailspin where they lost themselves in that lifestyle. Those who indulged in that way of life for a time, but had the good sense to rise above it, came out fine and became productive, proper-speaking members of society.

Unfortunately, the mentality of many from that generation was, "I refuse to grow up." They wanted no mortgage, no career, no future plans, had no goals, no marriage, no kids - no responsibilities. Quite a few ended up living with mom and dad way beyond thirty and even, forty. Sadly, some never left the nest. I personally knew a guy like that. He died in his late 60's while still living with his mom. People like that were branded as "adultescents." It's not a misspelling, it's an actual word. Put it in your adult vocabulary. It might come in handy someday to describe "adult people who still have adolescent or teenage interests and traits." Their bodies grew up but their minds lagged behind.

Chapter 29 Changes in the mid 60's and 70's

Woodstock

Anyone young, into Rock and Roll and in the mood of being in the middle of a huge field with well over half a million people on hot sunny days and there was going to be some of the best bands in the country, you might have said: "Oh yeah! I'm in. Where and when, man?"

August of 1969 will be memorialized in Baby Boomer history as the three day concert called "Woodstock." It didn't actually happen in Woodstock, but on dairy farmer Max Yasgur's land in the town of Bethel, New York. The field was three miles from Yasger's home. Some people say there were well over 500,000 young people in attendance. It was reported that nearly a 1,000,000 had to turn back because of the immense crowds on the roads leading there. Can you imagine that scene? It's mind-boggling.

Woodstock crowd

Those who made it in, did all they could to have a good time and were part of a historical music event. The concert had booked over thirty bands and single performers. They had a good idea of having a rotating stage in order to be able to set up a group on one side while another group performed on the other side. A problem arose when the wheels on the stage got destroyed due to the weight of all the equipment and people. This resulted in huge gaps of time between performers. The show did go on, but much slower than anticipated. Richie Havens opened the show and his performance there catapulted his career. Jimmy Hendrix closed with a memorable rendition of the National Anthem.

My friend, Mike Pasiecznik, asked if I was going. I would have loved to. I didn't have the time or the $24 for a three day ticket. It was a once in a lifetime opportunity but it was probably a good thing I didn't go. I don't do well in huge crowds, and I definitely don't like sleeping on the ground as did thousands of those young people. More power to them. It wasn't my thing.

However, Mike, Skip Reed, Kevin Keane, John Bukowski and Glenn Echum from South Buffalo went, saw it, enjoyed it and returned to their cozy homes.

Mike told me, "We had a stretch of heavy rain, but it didn't last. Most of the time, it was sunny. We had a great time."

On the down side of things, the concert started late, many drug arrests, way too few Johnny-On-The-Spot toilets and an incredible downpour of five inches in three hours that turned the entire place into a mud field with ponds. It was reported that several women suffered miscarriages and, a mother had to be flown by helicopter to a hospital to deliver her baby. The U.S. Army was brought in to assist both concert-goers and performers with food supplies, medical assistance and transportation issues. Two people died during the concert; one from a drug overdose and the second, a guy who was run over by a tractor he didn't hear coming through the field while he was sleeping on the ground.

The promoters were in debt over a million dollars after the concert. It took them years to clear the debt and make a profit through the audio and video recordings sold.

Chapter 30 Baby Boomers and Cars

Cars

Gas Stations

Before any Baby Boomers ever got a car, we got to ride in our parents' car and see firsthand what it was like to drive; starting the car, checking the rear view and side mirrors, putting on the turn signals, putting it in gear, holding on to that huge steering wheel most cars had back then, taking off, stopping and parking. For sure, we got to see what happened when dad pulled into the service station.

When dad went to a gas station, they were full service. There were no snack shops back then. There was air for your tires, oil for you engine or oil changes if the car needed it, gas, and engine repairs. Today it's like going into a mini supermarket. They sell all sorts of things. Back in the day you got service. You'd pull up and an attendant would come out and ask you:

"What'll it be today, sir or ma'am?" You'd answer: "Give me $2.00's worth, please."

Understand that back then $2.00's worth of gas would give you around 8 gallons of gas. Many of the eight cylinder cars held 18 to 20 or more gallons per tank. A lot of those big cars only got about15 miles to the gallon; some even less. If you're tank was low, you might have said to that friendly attendant:

"She's real thirsty. Fill her up, please."

If the tank were near empty, you could fill up for less than $5.00. What does it cost someone today with a Hummer or big old eight cylinder Ford 350 at $2.30 per gallon?

During a full tank fill up, the attendant took time to clean your windows, check the oil level, check your tire pressure and add air to your tires if needed. Some patrons would even tip the attendants for service. In the good old days, no one had to get out of the car, ever. As a matter of fact, you weren't allowed to serve yourself. Today, the gas stations that only sell gas may have an attendant on hand, but all he'll do is pump your gas and nothing else. Cleaning windows, checking the oil and tire pressure is all up to the driver.

A lot of the older cars burned oil and needed to be topped off from time to time. Back in the sixties, I could buy recycled oil for half the price of brand new oil. I got my recycled oil at the cut rate gas station at the corner of Hopkins and Tifft. It came in glass bottles with spouts. For guys with tired old cars that burned a lot of oil, that was the way to go.

Owning a car was a responsibility. You needed to stay on top of things to keep the car rolling. It might have been changing the spark plugs, rotor and rotor cap (when the engine didn't run right). Maybe the timing needed adjusting or the brakes needed brake shoes. There were no disc brakes then. In those days, muffler systems weren't made to last. They corroded faster than you'd like them to, especially with the salt in the streets during Buffalo winters. They were made of regular metal, not stainless steel and there were no catalytic converters or emission control units. Also, there was a time when all cars had rubber tubes in the tires. Tubeless tires were a good invention. As with the recycled oil, I remember buying re-cap tires. For local driving, they were fine. On long highway trips at high speed on hot asphalt, well, that was a crap-shoot. Tires were known to come apart at the seams. Thank God for spare tires, hopefully in good shape.

Now, we get to the business of getting legal and more independent by getting a driver's license and our own car.

Driver's Permit/License

Getting a car for getting around and going downtown or wherever, was definitely one of the things on the minds of most of the guys as they turned sixteen. First, one needed to go through the process of obtaining a driver's permit. How many of you remember the whole process of getting your license? I remember a lot of South Buffalo guys talking about getting legal by getting their driver's license.

We couldn't wait to turn sixteen so we could get our driver's permit at the DMV in the Ellicott Square Building. That was a special time. It was a grown-up thing. The Ellicott Square Building is a classic old building with revolving doors. For those who went there to take the written permit test, can you remember walking in, from either the Main Street entrance or the Washington Street entrance? Once in the building, you'd find yourself walking into the big open space from Main Street and looking up to your left to find that elegant staircase and seeing the sign that read New York State Auto Bureau. Up you went and approached the counter to ask for an application for a driver's permit. You were handed the paperwork along with a little booklet to study for your written test. You took it home and studied until the day finally came when you'd go for it.

You went to the Auto Bureau, walked up those same stairs, approached the counter, and were directed to go sit at a desk where you took the test. Many were scared to death that they would not pass. It was corrected right after you took it, and you were either, elated or demoralized. If you passed, for a fee of either $3.00 or $5.00, you got your permit that would be good for six months. Within that time, if you felt confident enough in your driving ability, you could set up an appointment for the road test at a cost of, I believe, $10.

After obtaining the driver's permit, you would boast to your friends that they might see you behind the wheel of your dad's or big brother's car. In the back of your mind, you would think a lot about the real payoff; actually getting your driver's license. Now, that was really grown-up. I mean, you could go off in dad's car, all by yourself. How much cooler could you be?

In time, you would set up that drivers test. At the time, everyone I knew went to the Williams Street testing site near South Ogden in the East Lovejoy area (The Iron Island). McKinley Parkway, next to the Park Edge Market was another site for testing at one time. When the moment finally came for your road test, you were sweating bullets. It wasn't necessarily because you weren't ready but because you heard about other people who flunked; some once or more times. Your mom, dad, big brother or a friend would drive the car to the site. You waited your turn for the examiner or inspector to approach the car. You would give him your driver's permit and appointment confirmation form. The driver got out, you slid behind the wheel and the inspector got in the passenger side. You waited for directions and prayed you wouldn't screw up... Think back folks. As the man gave you multiple directions for your little trip, did you not get a little pale? The directions might have gone something like this:

"You will be going straight until you come to the first street, make a left, go two blocks, make a right and then another left. Then, go two blocks and pull over to the curb."

In those days, you could fail the test before you actually drove if you failed to put on your left turn signal and signal with your left arm as you pulled away. You had to do both.

If you could actually manage to remember the initial directions until you pulled over to the curb, then you worried about the next two maneuvers. You knew those were the most feared maneuvers of the test: the three-point turn and the parallel park; especially, the parallel park. With either one of these, if you hit the curb, you would fail on the spot. If you really botched up your test, the inspector might cut the test short and tell you to go back to the starting point, that you weren't ready. Plenty of guys and girls came away teary-eyed, only to try again, and for some, try, try again another day. I'm proud to say I pass on the first try.

Dreaming of Getting a Car

As high school students, possessing a driver's license and getting a car was another whole process. It meant getting a job and saving up for one. Probably 99% of us came from "blue-collar" families and getting junior his own car wasn't in mom and dad's budget. It was up to us young hopefuls to work at getting that first car. All the guys looked forward to the day they'd get one. I mean '55 Ford, or '55, '56 '57, 58 Chevy, and so on. Hey, even Eddy Ish's 50's station wagon was cool. For a lot of us it didn't matter what we had to drive. When we finally got a car, as long as it got us around, we were happy, very happy to have "wheels."

Not many of us had our own car during our High School years. Eddy Funeziani, with whom I worked at the Bocce Club on Clinton, had one. I believe it was a 1961 Chevy convertible. Oh yeah, we were a bit envious of Eddy, seeing him drive home after classes while the rest of us did our usual mile or two walk home in all kinds of weather.

Most of the guys I hung out with didn't get a car until they got real jobs. One of the problems with the jobs was that not many paid really good money; so, paying for everyday expenses, and saving up for a used or new car, was really hard. Most of us could only hope to buy something used. My first car was a raggedy eight cylinder '55 Ford I bought from Jimmy McCrory from Mariemont Street in 1964. It had a lot of rust, no heat, no radio, and people in the back seat could see the asphalt through the floorboards as I drove. Hey, what do you want for $85? The cool thing about the car was that it was a three speed on the column model or "three on the tree," as they used to say. I could lay rubber in all three gears. Of course, I never sped. Yeah right. About a year or so later, I upgraded to that classic "59 Chevy Impala, the one with the really big wings.

As you may have noticed, I mentioned only guys going for their driver's license and getting their own cars. I didn't know any young lady age 16 to 18 who talked about getting her license, let alone, buying her own car. It wasn't the norm back then. Most young ladies more or less depended on their boyfriends to get one. More than once, young men would ask their girlfriends for money for gas or repairs. In some respects, they both shared the car. A lot of the guys had car payments and other maintenance expenses or mechanical repairs that only garage mechanics could do. As the ladies got jobs in the mid to late sixties, they got their license and eventually got cars. I remember my own sisters taking busses to go to work downtown, and after saving a few bucks, they bought used cars. Having a car back then was something people appreciated a lot. For many, it was a luxury.

Baby Boomers, dare I even go into modern cars? The mechanisms in new cars have come such a long way and the prices, well, in some cases are extreme. I can remember in 1956, a Volkswagen bug was between $1,300 and $1,500. Today, the price for the same basic car is $20,000 plus. Midsize cars went from $2,500 to $3,500. A brand new 1966 Mustang 2 door hardtop went for $2,370.

Need a Mechanic?

There were a ton of guys who were very good mechanics. Some could take an engine apart in the morning and put it back together so they could drive it at night. Today, tinkering with what's under the hood of your new car could result in a whole lot of grief. In some cars, you're lucky you can get a wrench in to try to fix or adjust anything.

In the good old days, I can remember some of the local guys like Mike Pasiecznik, Billy West, Butch Wilson or Joe Masullo, beefing up their cars and hearing terms like high-performance carburetors, four barrel AFB, fuel-injection, 411 rear-ends, Jack's Custom Traction Master, Muncie Four Speed, synchromesh transmissions, something called posi-traction, three on the column, four-on-floor Hurst Shifters, tachometers to keep an eye on the RPM's, dice on the mirrors, hand-rubbed lacquer paint jobs with maybe twenty coats or so of candy-apple red or metal flaked blue paint, or how about no color at all, just '55 Chevy black primer? How about hood-scoops and skirts, Hollywood mufflers, glass-packs, Continental Kits, chromed-reverse wheels? And, those classy white wall tires and curb-feelers some guys would put on to help prevent them from scuffing those white-walls.

If you were really cool, your steering wheel had what they called, a "suicide knob," on it. I had one on my '55 Ford. Not many of our cars back then had power steering. The suicide knob made it much easier to make those turns, especially when a guy had his girlfriend close to him on the "bench seat" with his arm around her shoulders. Do you remember that guys? Oh, how we loved those bench seats.

Cars back then could easily fit six passengers, maybe seven. That would be three in front and four crammed in the back seat. While I'm speaking of what cars had, let's not forget what the interiors were made of. A lot of us remember real well, the metal or leather dashboards and door panels. Cars back then also had the high/low beam foot-switches on the left side of the floor. Today, they're on the steering wheel column cluster of electronics. They were easy to activate; one click for high beams and another click to go to low beams. Another great thing we had was a "regular size spare tire" in the trunk, not one of those ridiculous doughnut tires they put in there today. If you got a flat back then, you'd put on the spare, and it matched all the other tires. No need to take it easy on the spare. With a doughnut tire, you need to be careful not to drive on it too fast or too hard for any length of time.

In the 40s, 50s, 60s and 70s, when you saw a car, you could tell right away what it was. There was no mistaking the '58 Ford Fairlane from the '58 Chevy, the '58 Rambler, from the '58 Plymouth, the '65 Mustang from the '65 Chevy Nova or '70 Lincoln from the '70 Cadillac. Those were the days when we had cars with great distinctive looks, real chrome bumpers and little vent windows. I loved those vent windows. Speaking of bumpers, back then, you could actually hook up a rope or a chain to them to tow a car. If you try to do that with today's bumpers, you will cause a lot of damage if you can even find a place to hook up. Today's bumpers are not practical. They're there strictly for show. Another great thing they've taken away from our cars, the gutter strips on the edge of the roof. With today's cars, if you open your window when it's raining, you get a stream of water rolling off the roof and pouring inside the car. That's one great idea they threw away. They were also useful for tying down roof racks. Detroit and ALL other car makers should really think about bringing back vent windows and rain gutters. What the heck were they thinking when they decided to do away with them?!!!

Local Motor Men

A few of the mechanically-abled guys took regular cars and suped them up to give them more horse power. Not only was power important, but looks and sound as well. By the way, that term "suped up," it goes way back to 1911. It was a reference to a "narcotic drug" injected into horses to make them faster. In doing this, the horse owners were said to be, "souping up" their race horses (enhancing horse power.) The modern term is actually, "supercharging" factory engines for higher performance, or give them more "horse power," Engine guys shorten supercharged engines to "suped up" engines.

I wondered what Baby Boomer from the old neighborhood might know who had what car back then. I remembered Butch Wilson was one of those car guys. He gave me a lot of information on who owned what car back in the day. I was completely amazed that he knew the owner, the year, make and even the engine size of the machines. He started with:

Sam Fassari's '62 Chevy 409. Then, he kept giving me names and cars; Jim Morgan's '57 Ford, Doug Alessandra's '57 Chevy and '62 Chevy Nova II, Joe Avolio's '65 Chevelle, Steve Moscato's '61 Dodge CONY 383 engine and four speed (on the floor of course) Dick Woolgar's '63 Chevy 409, Gary Schintzius' '63 Tunnel Ram Chevy Nova and '64, 409 Chevy Impala, Ron Wentland's '66 Chevy Nova, Billy West's '56 Chevy called the "Vengance." West did take his machine to local racetracks to compete. Butch himself had a '59 Chevy (big fins), with a 348 W/block, and a 4 speed Hurst shifter.

Those were from the general area where I lived. There were several other machines from Seneca and Abbott that were around and would often test their horse power against any takers from South Buffalo at the Tifft-Ohio Street Drag Strips.

At that time, you had to have four on the floor equipped with a Hurst speed shift or you weren't cool. Speaking of shifters, all of those old boys can relate real well to the three-speed on the column.

According to Bob Regan, the Lasker brothers, Tommy and Jimmy had a white '53 Olds with a Cadillac engine in it. Carmen Nappo from Sheffield Ave remembers the '59 Chevy, the '53 Olds and the '53 Ford he had. And Frank Daluisio, also from Sheffield Ave, had a few classics; '58 Chevy, '61 Chevy Impala, '64 GTO 389, '66 Chevy Biscayne and a few others.

Today, you can only see those magnificent classic cars at various locations on Cruise Nights during the summer months. They are things of beauty. What was your favorite back then?

Sam Fassari's Crew and Cars

Sam Fassari told me that he and his friends hung out on Lockwood and South Park at Parson's and Judd Pharmacy during his early to mid-teens. Jim Morgan was one of his close friends. From his mid-teens to early twenties he hung at Deco 22 and Sperduti's Tavern. His crew was into cars and they even had a car club called the Gear Grinders. It later, became the Torid Torquers. They would cruise together to car shows and drag strips in the early 60s. He mentioned the Dunkirk and Erie, PA drag strips, Cayuga Drag Strip in Canada and finally, the Niagara Drag Strip that opened in the mid-60s. The latter, became their main drag strip.

He also mentioned the illegal drags that were held at the foot of Tifft and Ohio streets. Some of the guys he remembers were, Butch Wilson, Paul "Butch" Tara, Marty Hockey, Larry Courtney, Roger "Butch" Bohn, Dick Woolgar, Steve Muscato, *Jim Anthony, Ray Zielinski, Doug Allesandra, Paul Toms, Bobby Ulrich, Bill Cook, Doug Kroll, John Messore from Whitfield, Bob McDonald from Choate, Ray Berst from Eaglewood and Dick Grangle from Alsace.

*Jim Anthony worked for the Buffalo Fire Department. He retired around 2001 and relocated in Paducah, Kentucky with his wife Mary, to be near family.

Here's what he had to say about a part of his time in South Buffalo and the car scene.

"The 50's and 60's were magical; possibly the best time of my life. We were running souped-up Ford V-8 engines and could outrun the 6 cylinder Plymouths the cops had at Precinct 15, at the time."

The Drag Strips

Now then, these fine law abiding Baby Boomer car owners with their beefed up engines, as mentioned before, tested their horse power against each other from time to time. Butch Wilson talked about testing these machines at night on Tift Street near Fuhrman Blvd. This was pre-Ohio Street drag races. So as to not accuse anyone of speeding, we'll say they revved up their engines as close to the red line as they could. A few guys pushed beyond the red line and blew their engine. I don't know how all those tire marks got on that stretch of Tifft Street.

There was a little game some of the fast car owners liked to play. They'd have a guy sit back in the passenger side of the car. The owner (driver) would put a ten dollar bill on the wide dashboard near the windshield and bet the passenger that he couldn't snatch the bill when he (the driver) said "Go." Once he said "Go" he'd hit the gas and the passenger, try as he may, if the timing was right, could not grab the bill. That was most of the time. The acceleration force was so great in some of those cars that it would pin the passenger to the seat and not allow him to get the prize. Too bad!

A Parting Note...

After several years of hanging around with friends, dating, playing around with cars, racing, hopping bars, checking out different bands in numerous night clubs, the majority of the guys settled down and began to live the kind of life their parents lived. They got real steady jobs, got married, had kids, and a mortgage. It's the cycle of life. What goes around comes around. It's not only what a lot of hip people would call karma, it's the way life is. The Baby Boomers had their youth and did all the things young people do; many had a blast doing it. Now, they've become like their parents. That's not a bad thing, by the way.

So ends our trip down memory lane. Ride on down the road in your '49 Ford, '53 Corvette with the split back window, '55 Buick Electra, '66 Chevy Nova, '68 Mustang 380 GT Fastback, or '70's Dodge Charger. Happy trails!

Closing Remarks

I hope the contents of this book brought you great memories of the way it was during the hay days of the Baby Boomers of the 40's, 50's, 60's and 70's. There's a good amount of information that a lot of folks may have never known about our great area called South Buffalo. I'm sure most of you who are South Buffalonians were able to make connections with a lot of the people, places and events mentioned in the book.

May this work be a source of reference to remember what Baby Boomers experienced in their younger days. So many grand-parents and parents have never taken the time to share with their children what it was like living during their youth. By the time they leave this earth, and have not passed on much information or any at all, it's too late. It's all gone. Many children will ask about their parents' and grandparents' past as they get older.

You who are parents and grand-parents are a wealth of information. Do take the time to pass on stories and experiences of your life and your family's past. In doing that, you'll find that your children and grandchildren will feel better connected to you and have an appreciation of both the good and bad times you lived through. You may not realize it, but most of you have so much you could talk about with the next generation.

The Baby Boomer Generation's children will leave behind some kind of legacy. We had the "Great Generation" who brought the "Greatest Generation" into the world, who brought the "Baby Boomer Generation" into the world. What shall we call the children of the Boomers' generation? Can we hope to maybe call them; the "Enlightened Generation, the "Intelligent Generation," the "Great Achievers Generation" or the "Peaceful Generation?" The last two would be very nice. What will their legacy be all about? What will they leave behind for their own children and grandchildren?

For a lot of the folks from the South Side of Buffalo who lived through the years covered in this book, perhaps, the following fits what they felt about the life there.

"It was great living in South Buffalo. A lot of the memories of the people, places and events have not faded with time. Many have become more solidified in the hearts and minds of those who experienced them."

I sincerely hope I've done a good job bringing many of you back to a time when life was; simpler, friendlier, safer, exciting, and perhaps, more fulfilling. God bless.

The Author

Roger

Roger was born Magog Québec, Canada in 1946; fifth of ten children to parents, Léo Paul and Lucette (Roberge) Rainville. His first language was French. Their family moved to Welland Ontario in 1955 where siblings; Gilles, Jacques, Denise, Monique, Lise, Suzanne, François, Carole and Louie, and he, learned to speak English. They immigrated to the US on April 15, 1959 and lived at 180 East Abbott Grove, Orchard Park. His dad worked at the Ford Plant and mom worked as a waitress at Colonial Kitchen in Blasdell. In April of 1960, the family moved to 72 Altruria Street, South Buffalo. The house number was later changed to 172 Altruria.

Although not originally from South Buffalo, he is proud to tell people, "I am a South Buffalonian." When asked what nationality he is, he always answers, "I'm not a Canadian, I am a French Canadian," with the emphasis on "French". As with people who are proud of being South Buffalo Irish, Italian, Jewish, Polish, Hungarian, German, Puerto Rican, or representing any other nationality, he's also proud of his roots and still maintain ties with his relatives in Québec. He tells folks that South Buffalo is where he spent some of his best years from age thirteen to adulthood. He came to have a great fondness and appreciation for the people and places in the South Park area, as well as, Hopkins, McKinley Parkway, Abbott Road and Seneca Street.

He attended school #29, Holy Family and South Park High School. He was not a good student and came to realize later in life that he had learning difficulties. Still, he went to college at age 38 which was very difficult, but… succeeded. He studied at Buffalo State College to earn his bachelor's degree in secondary education French and Spanish, graduating with a 3.2 average. He attended UB for his master's degree and graduated with a 4.0 average (sigma cum laude.) After college, He worked as a French and Spanish teacher for the next twenty-three years at Canisius High School, and also taught part time at Medaille College for twenty-one years.

He's married to Donna Aures and has two children; Linette and Christian, four grandchildren, Saralin, TJ, Isaac and Evan as well as two great grandchildren Emma and Ethan. He sings and plays rhythm guitar. He's also written many secular and gospel songs, one of which was recorded by gospel singer Jackie Davis.

Besides having written "SOUTH BUFFALO - THE WAY IT WAS," he's written a 152 page autobiography for his family, and two other books. One is based on the story found in Luke 15 in the Bible entitled, "The Prodigal Son" (subtitled) "The Love of a Father," The other book is called - "FIFTY-FIFTY SPLIT." It is a very interesting novel that has connections to the Buffalo area.

He's practiced and taught Isshin-Ryu Karate since 1969 and has achieve the master rank of 7th degree black belt. He's also been an avid motorcycle rider since 1972 and presently rides a Heritage Softail Harley Davidson. Starting in 1981, he was involved in biker and prison ministries in such facilities as: Attica, Wendy, Collins I and II as well as Gowanda Correctional.

Acknowledgements

Adams, Bart,
Adams, Karen
Adamy, John
Anthony Jim
Accordino, Sam
Angie at Mazurek's Bakery
Aures, Kathy (Byrnes)
Avery, Frank
Avolio, Joe
Batchelor, Ralph
Bohen, Timothy
Banko III, Steve
Best, Tom
Benjamin, Art, Nick Kobseff and Lou Sabella
Brooks, Larry
Brucz, Mary (Gugliuzza)
Burke, Matty "Burkey"
Byrnes, Kathy
Caffery, Kevin
Dan Callahan
Caruso, Dave
Castillo, Kevin
Catalino, Ross
Cichon, Steve
Concheiro, Dan and Bernadette
Coghlin Jr., Pat
Colpoys, Ray
Cowan, Tommy
Cudney, Ed and Lori
Czechowski, John
Daluisio, Frank
Daluisio, Annette
Dargavel, Dennis
Dellwalt, Dave Kozak
Denecke, Martin
Denecke, Joe
Di Sarno, Linda Holtz
Dickman, Tim
Dingledey, Lou
Dolan, Chris
Domzalski, Bob
Donnelly, John (Jackie)
Dunlop, Rich
Fitzgerald, Tim
Fassari, Sam
Fitzgerald, Ann (Kenefick)
Fitzgerald, Marie-Ventura
Gannon Paul F.
Gannon, Tom
Erin Gannon
Guadagno, Dolores Antonelli
Guido, Anthony "Chuck"
Gugliuzza, Pete
Gilmour, Patty
Greene, Bob
Golden, Rich
Head, Joe
Heneghan, Mary
Linda Hontz
Bill Holihan
Held, Bill Sr.
Hermann, Pete
Heitzhaus, Jack
Hyde, Bert (Guise)
Jordan, Danny and Joanne
Kane, Paul
Kelley, Tom
Kennefick, Ann
Kennedy, Jim "Digger"
Klass, Billy
Koepnick, Joe and Mark
Kolhbacker, Karen Adams
Kraengle, Maryjean
Kunz, Audrey
Lafko, Marilyn (Sue)
Leahy, Eileen
Leahy Clan…Tom, Peg, Eileen, Pat, Bill, Dan, Susan and Kim
Leonard, Richard
Liberti, Joe
Lovern, Pat (Greene)
Lowman, Hanna
Lucenti, Joe
Mazur, Mike
Mahoney, Jim and Diane
Malley, Michael
Mattingly, Ray
McDonnell, Tom
McEwen, Billy 100
McLaughlin, Art
Miller, Dave (Edson)
Miller, Chris (Edson)
Miller, Ron (Hopkins)
Miller, George (Hopkins)
Miller, Jimmy (Crystal Ave)
Miller, Jim (Pries Street)
Miller, Edward, Iva (wife) and Iva (daughter) (Seneca Street)
Morganti, Joe
Morrissey, Jim
Mulvaney, Chris
Murtha, Larry
Nappo, Carmen
Neaverth, Dan
Nicholson, Bill
Nightengale, Pat
Nolan, Kevin
Orsini, Tony,
Orsini, Pat (Luke)
Overdorf, Peg
Overdorf, Gene
Palmieri, Ralph
Parisi, Joe
Pasquarella , Roger
Pasiecznik, Mike
Petrili, Adele
Pierro, Lorraine
Pugh, Jack   130
Pugh, Kathy
Ralston, Jimmy
Redmond, Mr.
Redmond, Dan
Regan, Bob
Gerry Regan
Richards, Margaret (Nash)
Rodriguez, José
Alan Rohloff
Rohloff, Rose Mary (DiTondo)
Salomon, Lynn
Sanly, Robin
Scahill, Joan Graham
Scaccia, Tony
Scaccia, Maria (Gawronski)
Schuta, Terri
Schneider, Frank
Schintzius, Gary
Seifert, Ken
Shanahan, Terry and Joan
Shea, Dan (Hamburg cop)
Shea, Jerry
Shea, Jim (Buffalo cop)
Shine, Jim
Shine (Witczak) Donna
Sitarski, Carrie
Sibley, Tammy
Slattery, Jim
Spinelli, Dennis and Clara
Starr, Dennis
Starzynski, Marge
Starzynski, Tony
Szczygiel, Peggy May
Szuder, Carolanne
Szymkowiak, Tony
Standish, Eddy
Talty, Dennis
Tutuska, George
Vaughn, Greg
Wagner, Jack
Weber, Marge
Wetland, Ronnie
Wiles, Tim
Wilson, James "Butch"
Williams, Bob and Jeannette
Wojciechowski, (Smokey) Dennis
Zawadzki, Randy
Zoldos, Nacy

www.ingramcontent.com/pod-product-compliance
Lightning Source LLC
Chambersburg PA
CBHW081126170426
43197CB00017B/2764